To my '4.0' friend —
Your second in command —

Gregory V. _____ Cmdr. USN
09-19-1971

Second in Command

Second in Command

The Uncensored Account of the Capture
of the Spy Ship *Pueblo*

BY ITS EXECUTIVE OFFICER
FORMER LIEUTENANT
Edward R. Murphy, Jr.

With CURT GENTRY

Holt, Rinehart and Winston
New York   Chicago   San Francisco

Grateful acknowledgment is made for permission to quote from
Bucher: My Story, by Lloyd M. Bucher with Mark Rascovich. Copy-
right © 1970 by Lloyd M. Bucher. Reprinted by permission of
Doubleday & Company, Inc.

Unless specifically noted, all photographs are U.S. Navy Official
Photographs, courtesy of the U.S. Navy.

To my loving wife, Carol,
to our children, Eddie and Vicky,
and in memory
of
a fine ship
and a great crew

Prologue

The mock trial began in March, 1968, shortly after we moved to our second detention site in North Korea. It would continue up to the very day of our repatriation, and beyond.

It was not an ordinary trial, in any sense of the word. The North Koreans had no part in it. Only the officers of the USS *Pueblo* participated. Of them, one man served as judge, jury, prosecutor, and defense attorney. His name— Commander Lloyd M. Bucher. His objective—to prove that he had no choice but to surrender his ship. The loss of a U.S. Navy vessel automatically necessitates an official investigation. Commander Bucher was acutely conscious of this. Knowing full well that if we survived our imprisonment, a naval court of inquiry would follow, Bucher wanted a single, consistent account of the events of January 23, 1968, one which would absolve him of all blame. To get it he cajoled, threatened, cried, charmed, blackmailed, and attempted to turn one officer against another.

A man obsessed, he needed above all a scapegoat to assume his guilt. As executive officer, second in command of the *Pueblo*, I was a logical choice. Another was Lieutenant Stephen Harris, the officer in charge of the ship's intelligence detachment. Throughout captivity Bucher alternated between us, trying to decide which man would "hang" in his place.

Whether the *Pueblo* had the power to resist, who was at fault for failure to destroy the classified materials, which officer had actually surrendered the ship—these were some of the arguments that raged on, hour after hour, day after day.

Initially, nearly all of the officers objected to these star-chamber proceedings. Then, one by one, they gave in to Bucher's persuasion, at first on the small points, then on the large, less because they agreed with him than because they wanted an end to the harassment that dominated our meals, exercise, and recreational periods, the few occasions we were together. Drilled repeatedly in *Bucher's* version of the capture, many began to wonder about their own recollections. It was, in its own way, a brainwashing as insidious as any devised by the North Koreans.

At the time, I believed that once we were freed, the real story would come out. What I didn't foresee was that the U.S. Navy would be just as anxious as Commander Bucher that a "sanitized" version be accepted. The alternative raised too many bothersome questions, each with far-reaching ramifications. Only occasionally did the truth surface in the *Pueblo* probe, then, in the rush of events, submerge again, as quickly as a submarine that leaves only a few oil slicks as lingering clues to its presence.

This, then, is the "uncensored" account of the *Pueblo* disaster—the version that both Lloyd M. Bucher and the United States Navy had hoped would never be made public. In contrast to the carefully cultivated myth of "Bucher's Bastards"—a crew united under a dynamic leader—it is the story of a ship divided from the moment it was commissioned, then doomed by a tragedy of errors, most of them human, nearly all of them avoidable. It is told now with the knowledge that the *Pueblo* disaster need never have happened and in the belief that the American public is entitled to the facts.

Second in Command

1

"There's a set of rush, top-priority message orders here for you, Ed. They just came in over the wire."

Orders? This was still April. I wasn't due for a change of assignment until June.

"What do they say?"

"I'd better send them over with a messenger," the oceanographic watch officer replied. "They're classified, and this isn't a secure line."

The telephone call caught me totally off guard. I had been given my current assignment, at the Naval Facility, Centerville Beach, Ferndale, California, as humanitarian shore duty. For some years my father had operated a grocery store in nearby McKinleyville. Following his death, the burden of running the store had fallen on my mother, who was in ill health. I had requested temporary duty at Centerville in order to arrange the sale of the store. As yet I hadn't succeeded. I'd counted on the next couple of months to complete the job. Now I wouldn't be able to do that.

Yet receiving new orders always carries an undercurrent of excitement. I tried to guess what my next billet would be. I knew it would probably be sea duty, as the Navy usually alternates ship and shore assignments. And I knew that since the orders had come in over the teletype, rather than by mail, someone was in a hurry. But beyond that, I hadn't a hint of a clue.

"Here you go, Lieutenant," the messenger said, handing me the yellow tear sheet.

```
BUPERS ORDER NR 043927. FOR DLVR TO LT
EDWARD R MURPHY JR 645923/1100 . . .
PROPORICH USS PUEBLO AKL ARREPCOVE XO . . .
```

One of the first things you learn on entering the Navy is to read abbreviations. After nearly seven years of duty, they had become almost a second language to me. BUPERS meant Bureau of Personnel; AKL was an auxiliary light-cargo ship; XO meant that I would be executive officer, second in command. In plain text, the message read:

```
BUREAU OF PERSONNEL ORDER NUMBER 043927. FOR
DELIVERY TO LT EDWARD R MURPHY JR SERIAL
NUMBER 645923/1100 . . .
PROCEED TO PORT IN WHICH USS PUEBLO AKL 44
MAY BE AND UPON ARRIVAL REPORT TO COMMANDING
OFFICER OF THAT VESSEL FOR DUTY AS EXECUTIVE
OFFICER . . .
```

I had served aboard an AKL once before, but I had never heard of the USS *Pueblo*.

Another thing you learn, in any branch of service, is that sometimes mistakes are made. I placed a call to my detailer at the Bureau of Personnel in Washington.

No, there had been no mistake. The *Pueblo* was now in the Puget Sound Naval Shipyard, Bremerton, Washington, awaiting commissioning. An executive officer had previously been assigned to the *Pueblo,* but had failed to pass the security screening. The detailer gave me the phone number of the ship; the CO could answer any other questions I had.

But I couldn't resist asking him a few. Who was the CO?

"Lieutenant Commander Lloyd M. Bucher, an ex-sub-man. This will be his first surface command."

And what's the *Pueblo* like?

"All I can tell you," he replied, "is that she's an AKL. But," he added, "unlike any AKL you've ever seen."

While I pondered that, he remarked, "By the way, Lieutenant, I sent you some papers in the mail today, the application forms for a new security clearance. I'd appreciate

2

it if you would fill them out, get yourself fingerprinted again, and rush them back to me."

I reminded him that I already had a security clearance, Top Secret, then asked, "There isn't anything higher than that, is there?"

His reply was succinct, he didn't elaborate. "There is."

The following day I placed a call to the *Pueblo*. The CO wasn't available, but another one of the officers, a Lieutenant Stephen Harris, was. Harris seemed immensely relieved to hear from me. In addition to his own duties, as officer in charge of a detachment of communications technicians, he had been filling in as exec until my arrival, and was swamped with work.

The phrase "communications technicians" was new to me. Exactly what kind of work would the *Pueblo* be doing? "Oceanographic and electronic research, among other things," Harris answered, "but I can brief you on that when your clearance comes through."

I couldn't help wondering what those "other things" might be.

Harris suggested I call back in a couple of hours and try to reach Lieutenant Commander Bucher then. This time I succeeded. Bucher snapped off his first question like a shot: "How soon can you report aboard?"

I told him that I hadn't had leave in some time and would have to move my family to Bremerton.

"The leave will have to wait," he said. "The ship's due to be commissioned on May 13, and I need you to take charge of the preparations." As for missing the leave, he promised to make up for that later. Talking it over, we agreed that I would report aboard on May 5.

Bucher was hardly more informative than Harris. So far, every time I inquired about the *Pueblo* I ended up with more questions than answers. Enough to convince me that the USS *Pueblo* was no ordinary ship.

Upon my arrival at Bremerton on May 4, I drove directly

to the shipyard. Although I wasn't due to report until the following morning, I had to satisfy my curiosity. It was dark, and there were few lights on the piers. I drove past number five, where the *Pueblo* was supposed to be berthed, three times before determining I was in the right place.

For the man who's going to be ship's navigator, you're off to a fine start, I told myself—lost before you've even found the ship!

Then I saw her: "Boy, she's a long one," I thought. Not until I was closer did I discover that what I had seen was not one ship but two—the USS *Pueblo* and her sister ship, the USS *Palm Beach,* both of which were to be commissioned at the same time.

The *Pueblo* was not only smaller than I had anticipated; I could see, even in the dim light, that she was far from new. And, unlike most Navy ships, it was necessary to climb down from the pier, rather than up, to get on board.

My detailer had been right, at least insofar as the general configuration was concerned. This certainly didn't look like any AKL I had ever seen. For one thing, there was a very large enclosure, whose purpose I couldn't even guess, built over the number-two hatch. For another, she seemed to sprout antenna platforms; I could count at least eight.

Seeing her only added to my questions.

Early the following morning I reported to the Petty Officer of the Watch and was taken in search of the CO. He was just coming out of the port-side mechanical room when I caught sight of him. I had served under my share of commanding officers—a baker's dozen, to be exact—but one look and I knew this one was going to be different.

Lieutenant Commander Lloyd M. Bucher appeared to be in his late thirties. He wore a battered straw hat; sticking out from underneath it was a head of unruly hair that might have belonged to one of the Marx brothers. Obviously overweight, he bulged out of his khaki dungarees.

The dungarees themselves were as wrinkled as if he had slept in them for days. This, I decided, was probably just his working garb. I was soon to learn that such informality was typical of him, whatever the occasion.

"I'm Pete Bucher," he said, returning my salute with a handshake. "And this is the USS *Pueblo*." He seemed to say it half in pride, half in anguish.

A tour followed.

The large built-up section I had noticed the previous night was the research space. Because of its appearance, the men had nicknamed it the "sod hut." "More about that later," Bucher observed, "when your security clearance comes through." Meantime there was lots more to see.

The size of the ship: 176 feet, 6 inches overall length, with a draft of 10 feet and a beam of 32 feet, 9 inches; its propulsion: twin screws with twin diesel engines; its maximum speed: 12.2 knots; its history: built in Kewaunee, Wisconsin, it had been launched in 1944 as *FS-344*, a general-purpose Army supply vessel, was used for ferrying cargo in the South Pacific theater, then taken out of service for a time, after that lent to the South Koreans, and mothballed in 1954. It was transferred to the U.S. Navy in April, 1966, to be renamed the USS *Pueblo* and classified as an auxiliary light-cargo ship (AKL-44). All these things I would learn later.

Bucher's tour revealed a floating hull top-heavy with problems. Lack of watertight integrity was one. Inadequate berthing space—the crew would number 80-plus—was another. Stowage space was less than minimal. There was a steering malfunction. As yet the ship had no guns, and as far as the State Department was concerned, it might never have any. The *Pueblo* was being converted from an AKL to an AGER, an Auxiliary General Environmental Research Ship, and this carried with it a host of additional problems, few of which were anywhere near solution. Commissioning was just eight days away. Usually by the time a ship is commissioned she is ready to be outfitted. With

5

the *Pueblo,* the process would have to be modified, because she wasn't even completely built yet.

My work was laid out for me.

That work was complicated by the fact that I was still in the dark as to her mission. Until I received my "ticket," or security clearance, until I became a member of the intelligence "club"—new terms, first heard from Steve Harris—I would have to stumble along, trying to prepare for an eventuality that remained a mystery.

My first job, however, readying the ship for commissioning, was a fairly standard procedure. In this Steve Harris, who was to share a compartment with me, was a big help. I usually reported aboard ship at 7 A.M. and rarely left until after 11 P.M. Carol understood, being a Navy wife. But little Eddie, who was just one and a half, didn't. In the days that followed, the few times I saw him were usually when he was asleep.

Still I found the job an exciting challenge. And from the start I developed a special fondness for the *Pueblo,* which I found to be a far better ship than I had suspected.

Having to scrounge for needed equipment brought me into contact with a number of men in the shipyard. One day an officer asked Steve Harris and me how we liked serving under Bucher. Noticing a set of dolphins (the insignia of submarine service) on his uniform, I answered cautiously, "He's quite a skipper."

"A word of warning," he said. "I knew Pete Bucher when he was in subs. Watch out for him. He has a positive affinity for disengaging himself from responsibility."

"What do you mean by that?" I asked.

"I mean," he replied, "if anything goes wrong, it will be your ass that will hang, not Bucher's. He'll see to that."

Whatever an officer may personally think of his CO, he tends to be fiercely protective of him when he is criticized by outsiders. This is doubly true of the exec, who as second in command has the responsibility of backing up his commanding officer's every decision. Possibly it was sour grapes. Maybe Bucher had given the man a bad time, or perhaps had received an assignment the other officer wanted. Still, it bothered me.

What bothered me even more was Steve's reaction. He showed not the least flicker of surprise. From his calm acceptance of the remark, I guessed that he had already had his own problems with Bucher.

It wasn't until later that I discovered how major their differences were, or that I realized that as exec I was to be the man caught in the middle.

I sensed enough, however, to wonder: What have I gotten myself into?

2

There are moments when, looking backward, one can see his whole life as a giant puzzle, each piece fitting into place—tiny incidents, seemingly insignificant at the time they occurred, suddenly becoming important to the whole design.

Rarely, however, does one get such glimpses while undergoing the experiences. Time passes slowly; perspective comes hard. Up to a point my life seemed to be fairly disorganized, with no clear goal in sight.

I was born on August 9, 1937, in Berkeley, California. My mother was a schoolteacher and my father operated a retail grocery store. I grew up largely under the care of my two older sisters, Mary and Anne. In 1945 the family moved to Arcata, in the northwesternmost part of the state. This is big-tree country, redwood and Douglas fir, where lumbering is a way of life. Commercial fishing is the second major industry, and I grew up close to boats, the roar and smell of the sea.

My father, who worked stoically hard all seven days of the week, was engaged in a number of businesses. During the late forties three mills to which he had been supplying equipment burned. Large contracts remained unpaid, with his insurance covering only some of the losses. Though deeply in debt, he managed to pull himself out by consolidating his companies into a single general-merchandise store. In 1953, when the store was threatened by a new state highway, he moved the entire business in just twenty-eight days to nearby McKinleyville.

Despite his difficulties, he made sure that all of his children received a good education: Anne went to Stanford and the University of Indiana, Mary to Humboldt State College; in my junior year in high school I transferred to Principia Upper School in St. Louis, Missouri. Principia enrolls young Christian Scientists, which is my religion; it is not a parochial school, and only academic subjects are taught in the classroom, but Principians are supposed to be guided in their daily activities by the moral principles underlying the teachings of Mary Baker Eddy.

"Supposed to" is used advisedly, at least in my case. I was an active teen-ager, out from under parental supervision for the first time. I was also curious. Adam wasn't the only one who found forbidden fruit tantalizing. Smoking and drinking were taboo at Principia; I investigated both, got caught at the latter, and ended up on probation.

In the fall of 1955 I entered Principia College, a small liberal-arts college in Elsah, Illinois, built on a promontory overlooking the Mississippi. The school offers an excellent academic curriculum, but I was far more interested in extracurricular activities. I lasted through two years of academic struggle before dropping out and returning to California. I simply wasn't ready for college and all it entailed.

Back home I helped my father manage the McKinleyville store. Bit by bit he kept giving me more responsibility. First I was in charge of the inventory, then the ordering, and finally I designed an entirely new physical layout for the business. Some time passed before I realized what he was doing. He was presenting me with challenges, initially small ones, then gradually larger ones. And as I met them, my self-confidence grew. I went back to school part-time, fitting in summer sessions at the University of California at Berkeley and at Humboldt State College.

When I returned to Principia in 1958 it was with a whole new attitude. College too was a challenge, which I was anxious to master. Also my understanding of my religion had deepened. It was a gradual change, an inner

9

maturing. I began living the tenets of my own faith, not because this was what was expected of me, but because it seemed the natural thing to do. I've never been a proselyte, anxious to convert or condemn others. I've found it difficult enough to live according to the dictates of my own conscience, without attempting to impose them on others. It was, and remains, very much an inner thing.

This time I not only studied seriously but found I could handle also the extracurricular activities that had derailed me the year before. Chosen to join a seminar group, I spent a quarter-term south of the border at La Universidad Autónoma de Mexico, in Mexico City, studying Spanish. Then, with college by the tail, I began to think of new challenges.

The Navy had always held an appeal for me. An unadmitted one, since on my mother's side of the family there was a long line of career Army officers. During my senior year I decided to try for Navy OCS in Newport, Rhode Island.

This too was a challenge, one I was not sure I could meet. The recruiter told me that eyesight limitations might keep me out of the Navy. I was determined, however, and I succeeded in obtaining a waiver on the eyesight requirements. I was graduated from Principia in June, 1960, with a B.A. in sociology. That fall I headed east for Newport, the following spring emerging a brand-spanking-new ensign in the U.S. Naval Reserve. Despite the fact that I wore corrective lenses for myopia, I had no trouble whatsoever with the intricate navigational charts and logs.

My first billet at sea was on the USS *Guadalupe,* a fleet oiler. As communications officer I was responsible, among other things, for the teletype equipment. These machines, vital to the ship's operation, were continually breaking down. At one point it became necessary to change the printing speed from 60 to 100 words per minute. The new rate increased the breakdown of parts.

Complicating the problem was the fact that there was no one aboard qualified to make needed adjustments and repairs. A request for a radioman with this skill had been refused. Coming down off deck watch one night, I learned that all the teletypes had stopped working. We were far out at sea and didn't have the communications necessary to operate the ship. I knew nothing about repairing teletypes. But we had instruction manuals. Reading them carefully, proceeding step by step, I succeeded in returning the machines to operating order, just as dawn filled the horizon.

I was aboard the *Guadalupe* from March, 1961, to August, 1962, serving under three skippers, two of whom are now admirals. Twice during our tour to the South China Sea off the coast of Vietnam, the *Guadalupe* was awarded the Battle Efficiency "E" as the best oiler in the entire Pacific fleet, and I was particularly commended for my initiative and ingenuity in solving the teletype problem.

It wasn't all work. When in port I got a good sampling of Navy social life, which can be quite heady for a young ensign. Parties were frequent. Though a nondrinker since my Principia days, I enjoyed them as much as my fellow officers, and, just possibly, a little more in that I didn't have to look forward to a hangover the next morning.

Shortly after reporting to my next billet, shore duty at the U.S. Naval Station, Subic Bay, Republic of the Philippines, I was promoted to Lieutenant, Junior Grade. By this time I was determined to make the Navy my career. However, in requesting transfer from the Reserve to the Regular Navy, I again encountered the vision problem. Fortunately, after a thorough examination, Navy medics decided that my eyesight would be no deterrent to my performance as an officer, and my acceptance quickly came through.

It was helped greatly by a strong fitness report from my commanding officer, Captain E. H. Mayer: "Lt. (JG) Murphy approaches his duties with energy and enthusiasm," the captain wrote in my service record. "He is poised, calm, mature, and competent. [There is] evidence of strong leadership qualities."

While at Subic, where I served as assistant personnel and information and education officer, my father died. He

11

had been ill for some time, and my mother had been running the McKinleyville store by herself. This placed a tremendous burden on her, and it bothered me that there was almost nothing I could do to help alleviate it.

During the summer of 1963 I served briefly as second officer of an AKL, the *Mark,* sailing from Subic Bay to Hong Kong and returning.

My final fitness report at Subic was highly complimentary. "Lt. (JG) Murphy," my CO wrote, "is an energetic, determined, and effective officer. His outstanding trait is his success in leadership of men. Quiet and dignified, his personal behavior and military bearing serve as examples to all."

I now raised my sights even further. I wanted to be more than a run-of-the-mill officer. Although I knew the competition was fierce, I applied to the U.S. Naval Destroyer School at Newport, Rhode Island.

Because of my lack of actual destroyer experience, I was turned down. But the selection board, reporting they were impressed with my reasons for wanting to go to destroyer school, left a door open. I was assigned to the USS *Twining,* a destroyer, to gain necessary experience.

My skipper on the *Twining,* Captain Albert T. Sprague, III, was more than sympathetic to my desires. He personally assisted me in drafting another application for the school, and bolstered it with a fitness report referring to me as "one of the most capable junior officer administrators I have seen." This time I was accepted without reservation.

During my six-month tour on the *Twining,* I served as assistant navigator. Navigation fascinated me, and I wanted to get as much experience in it as possible. I also qualified as officer of the deck (fleet). To qualify as an officer of the deck it is necessary to pass a special test, but there are even stricter requirements for a fleet officer, since handling a ship while steaming in a fleet presents the ever-present danger of collision with other ships in the formation.

12

I attended destroyer school from April to November, 1964. Again there were new challenges. Electrical, mechanical, and ordnance engineering were brand-new subjects to me. Mastering them, I felt all the more confident in my choice of career, enough so to make a major personal step.

While the *Twining* was home-ported in San Diego, I had attended a church youth function at San Diego State College, meeting a very pretty and immensely likable girl named Carol Louise Danks. Carol lived in the San Diego area with her parents. She had attended the Principia Upper School while I was in college, but we hadn't known each other at the time.

Although I liked her from the moment I met her, it was two months before I mustered the courage to ask her for a date. She was open and honest, easy to be with. We laughed a lot, but there was in her a vein of seriousness I liked. She understood that I intended to make the Navy my career and that this would involve frequent separations. When I finally got up enough nerve to propose, she accepted, promising to do her best to be a good Navy wife.

At the time, neither of us had the faintest glimmer of all the anguish this would entail.

We were married on November 21, 1964, a week after my graduation from destroyer school. Following a short honeymoon, I settled my new wife in an apartment in El Cajon, a suburb of San Diego, and left for my next assignment, as navigator of the USS *Robison,* a guided-missile destroyer.

I joined the ship just two days after Christmas, while it was at Yankee Station, just off Vietnam waters, relieving the navigator shortly after reporting aboard. The *Robison* was one of several ships involved in the Gulf of Tonkin incident. During my tour, the ship was awarded the Battle Efficiency "E," and I received special commendation as head of the navigation department. On March 3, 1965, I was promoted to Lieutenant.

About the same time, I received discouraging news. The

business my father had cared so much about when he was alive was nearing bankruptcy. My sisters and I had sent money to cover some of the most pressing bills, but the major problem remained: my mother, in declining health, couldn't handle the McKinleyville store by herself. My sisters, absorbed in their families, were in no position to help. I knew I had to make a difficult decision, one which could adversely affect my career.

I decided to ask for "humanitarian shore duty," in order to return to the States and dispose of the family business. However, my mother, fearful that to do so would jeopardize my future, refused to write a letter to the Navy stating the circumstances that prompted my request. The request was eventually granted, nevertheless.

Two billets were available, one in San Francisco, requiring the next grade senior to my rank; the other, calling for a lesser-grade officer, at the Naval Facility at Centerville Beach. However, San Francisco was nearly three hundred miles from McKinleyville, while Centerville was located at Ferndale, one-tenth that distance. I chose the latter. In August, 1965, following a five-week course in oceanography at Key West, Florida, I reported for duty.

The assignment had its compensations. The most important was that I could be with Carol, who was expecting our first child. On December 4, 1965, Edward Renz Murphy, III, "Eddie," joined the family.

At Centerville I held multiple billets, as base maintenance officer, electronics maintenance officer, and assistant operations officer. Early one morning in March, 1966, one of the men spotted what appeared to be a small abandoned boat breaking up in the surf. Lieutenant (JG) Shirley "Lee" Elliott and I volunteered to drive down to the beach to investigate the wreck. After parking the car, there followed a long walk in the soft sand. Along the way we tossed buoys and other equipment from the derelict above the surf line. We were in no particular hurry, because we didn't think anyone was aboard. I'd looked at the craft through binoculars in the exec's office and seen no sign of activity. Not until nearing the ship did Lee and I recognize it as a crab boat, about fifty feet long.

What we didn't know was that the boat had been in serious trouble since early the previous morning, when a fire hose washed off the deck and was caught in the propeller. The radio had been damaged a week earlier in a squall and removed for repairs. The three fishermen aboard had hoisted distress signals, but they had gone unnoticed. At nightfall the craft was anchored in thirty fathoms. By midnight it had dragged its anchor to a five-fathom depth, and at 3 A.M. it was in breakers. One of the fishermen, Arthur Figueiredo, had tried to swim ashore, but due to the heavy surf was thrown back against the boat and swept around the bow. He was almost lost to the sea, when his two partners, George McMurrick and Roger Marshall, managed to pull him back onto the deck.

Only on getting closer did we discover that the crew was still aboard, one man barely hanging on.

Among the materials washed ashore were two coils of nylon rope, used for crab pots. Stripping to my shorts, I tied one end of the longest piece around my waist, handed the other end to Lee, and carrying the other coil, ran into the surf. There was a powerful undertow and, being March, the water was numbing cold. It was a long swim, thirty to forty yards. On reaching the craft I made several unsuccessful attempts to board, but was hurled back. Finally I managed to grasp a cabin window. As the ship righted itself, I was literally thrown aboard.

While climbing up the seaward side of the boat, now wallowing in the surf, I handed the short rope to McMurrick. A moment later the boat rolled into the sea again, throwing me off. I was caught underneath the hull, one foot fouled in the rigging, my head down in the water, when McMurrick threw back one end of the line. I caught it. He pulled me up.

Figueiredo was in a state of shock. Although we kept wallowing back and forth, McMurrick and I managed to get both the long and the short piece of line tied around

15

him and Marshall. After we had eased them into the water, Lee, still holding the long line, pulled them toward shore. As a safety precaution, I held on to the short line until it was completely played out. Once the two men were on the beach, Lee swam out with the long rope tied around his waist, Marshall holding the other end. As Lee was making his approach to the stricken craft, he made a sudden lunge for one of the swinging booms. Catching it just as the boat rocked again, he went sailing across the fantail. He was being swept out to sea when McMurrick caught him. It was then that I realized the line wasn't tied to him anymore. Spotting it floating by the bow, I jumped from the flying bridge into the water, swam out, and got it. However, since I was already washed too far away from the boat to return, I headed for the shore. On reaching it, I rested for a minute or two, then, with the line tied securely around my waist, swam back to the wreck, this time managing to bring both Lee and McMurrick back.

By the time we had gotten all the men to shore, I was covered with cuts and bruises, from being battered against the careening hull. The ship, which continued to break up in the surf, was a total loss. A little while longer and the crew would have been too.

None of us was in shape to make the two-mile hike to the car. Luck was with us, however, in the form of a four-wheel vehicle from the Sheriff's Marine Posse. When we reached our car, Lee drove me back to the facility to receive emergency attention, while the three fishermen were rushed to a hospital. All survived the ordeal.

As a result of the rescue, the Ferndale Chamber of Commerce, the Humboldt County Board of Supervisors, and the State Legislature issued laudatory citations to Lee Elliott and me; California's governor, Edmund G. "Pat" Brown, sent us a congratulatory letter; and, at the request of the three fishermen that the Navy officially commend us, on August 8 the Navy and Marine Corps Medal for Heroism was presented to us at a full-dress public ceremony at the Humboldt County Fairgrounds.

16

Aside from the crab-boat incident, my duty at Centerville was relatively quiet. Although I still hadn't succeeded in selling the store (a deal on which we had counted for months fell through at the last minute), I was growing restless, anxious for a job that would provide some excitement and challenge.

The *Pueblo* would provide that. In a measure far greater than I had dreamed possible.

3

"The Public's Right to Know. The large amount of tax money expended in building and equipping any particular ship necessitates the American public's right to know the purpose and advantage of the new ship and how it is to complement sea power. Commissioning time is the ideal time to inform the public of the ship's assigned role."

So read the first paragraph of the *Guide for U.S. Navy Ship Commissioning and Recommissioning.*

The irony, in the case of the *Pueblo,* was not only that the public wouldn't be permitted to know the ship's real function but that at the time of commissioning neither the executive officer nor most of the rest of the crew knew the ship's real function either.

Saturday, May 13, 1967, was commissioning day for both the USS *Pueblo* and the USS *Palm Beach.* But we were one up on our sister ship. The city of Palm Beach, Florida, sent a lone representative to witness the ceremony; Pueblo, Colorado, had flown in a twenty-one-man delegation. Already we were developing a fierce pride in our little craft.

Greeting and finding accommodations for the numerous visitors was just one of my extra duties. Others included arranging the program, helping set up the speaker's platform, finding seating space for the four hundred expected guests (solved by putting both the speaker's platform and the guest seating on a pier between the two ships), seeing to the problems of the crew and their dependents, and planning the official reception to follow at the officers' club.

18

The commissioning was scheduled to begin promptly at 11 A.M. But when time arrived to move the ship to the pier where the ceremony was to take place, there was no sign of the captain. We waited, until time began to run out. Acting on my own, I finally took charge and moved the ship to her new berth. Bucher didn't arrive until well after the lines were in place.

Just before the commissioning started, I spotted my wife, Carol, happily snapping pictures. I whispered hastily to one of the enlisted men to confiscate the camera and film, before someone placed her under arrest. Picture-taking was expressly forbidden. I couldn't help grinning at her contrite, what-have-I-done-now countenance.

It was an impressive ceremony, the officers and men in full dress blues standing proudly between their freshly painted sister ships. All went well until midway through the proceedings, when the microphone in front of the *Palm Beach*'s executive officer went dead. But that was a minor crisis, easily resolved. Since my microphone was still functioning, I took over the commissioning of both ships until the other microphone was repaired.

Then came the point at which the *Pueblo*'s skipper was to introduce the commandant of the Thirteenth Naval District. But Bucher remained in place, shaking like Jell-O in a paint mixer. Stepping forward in his stead, I made the introduction. But named the wrong admiral! Fortunately he seemed more amused than irritated.

Following the admiral's remarks, the city manager of Pueblo, Colorado, delivered a short speech. It was now Bucher's turn. Although he was extremely nervous, both shaking and stammering, he did well until the closing part of his speech, when, the emotion of the occasion apparently overcoming him, he began to cry. After an embarrassed silence, the ceremony proceeded to its conclusion, as both the USS *Pueblo* and the USS *Palm Beach* were officially declared in service of the United States Navy.

Little things. Failing to show up when needed. Leaving

19

his duties for others. Breaking down under emotional stress. All understandable, considering this was an important day for him, assuming his first command. Little things. At the time I had no way of knowing they were warnings, omens of much greater problems that lay ahead.

For public consumption, the official orders for the *Pueblo* and the *Palm Beach* read as follows: "Technical-research operations to support oceanographic, electromagnetic, and related projects are the assignments given the crews of the two ships. This research is aimed at helping the Navy and mankind toward the complete understanding of the oceans and the improvements of the naval communications system."

But as the outfitting of the *Pueblo* continued, there were abundant clues that this was not the whole story.

As early as the commissioning ceremony we knew that the *Pueblo* would be home-ported and operating out of Yokosuka, Japan. I also learned from going over personnel records in my work in the ship's office that Steve Harris and several of his communications technicians spoke Russian. A picture began to emerge as I watched the equipment for the "sod hut" arrive in sealed crates, to be opened only below decks and out of sight. I realized that only a small portion of it had any relation to environmental research, that most of it consisted of very complicated electronic gear, tape decks, teleprinters, radios, and recording devices. Then there was a triple locking system installed on the door of the sod hut, which could be opened only if you knew the combination; and the antennae were installed on their platforms.

Some of our conversations in the wardroom brought that emerging picture into much clearer focus. Although at this point the skipper and Steve Harris were the only officers who knew the ship's real function, it was essential that I have at least a partial awareness of what we were in for, and although my clearance was still being processed, they made no attempt to exclude me from their conversations.

Three were especially revealing. One discussion concerned the problems our predecessor, the USS *Banner*, had encountered. The second involved the dispute over the ship's guns, or lack of them. And the third involved emergency destruct devices.

The *Banner*, first of the AGERs, had left Bremerton in October, 1965, long before the *Pueblo*'s crew arrived. But Bucher, who had been in Japan when his *Pueblo* orders came through, had visited her in Yokosuka and had talked to her skipper. On several occasions, while operating off Soviet waters, the *Banner* had been harassed by Russian ships. No attempt had been made to fire upon her or to board her, but the cat-and-mouse games had included one near collision with a destroyer. Presumably we could expect similar harassment.

When it came to guns, we were caught in the jaws of a military-political controversy.

Arguing that the AGERs were not warships, the State Department had vetoed their carrying heavy armament. The rationale was that since we were ostensibly engaged in peaceful oceanographic research, and would be operating on the open seas, well outside territorial waters, any show of machine guns or cannon would not only "blow our cover," it might also appear provocative. Every effort should be made to avoid provoking, even inadvertently, an "incident."

The State Department apparently had no objection to our carrying small arms, for antimine maneuvers or resisting boarders. So the *Pueblo* was first loaded with only one .30-caliber carbine, nine Thompson submachine guns, and seven .45-caliber sidearms.

But the Navy wasn't satisfied with only small arms. Commander Service Forces, U.S. Pacific Fleet (COMSERVPAC), responsible for the *Pueblo*'s shakedown training, showed particular concern over our lack of heavy armament.

Actually the *Pueblo* would be the first AGER to experience a shakedown cruise. The *Banner* had sailed directly to Japan after commissioning, her crew given no Stateside training.

COMSERVPAC's representatives in Southern California were interested in learning more about the *Pueblo* before we left Bremerton. To aid them, I flew down to Long Beach, showed them pictures of the ship and its general plans, and gave them a rundown on her conversion.

Despite the State Department mandate, the Navy still felt it a good idea to train our crew, and that of the *Palm Beach,* in the use of .50-caliber machine guns. The *Palm Beach* was scheduled to receive her shakedown training at Guantánamo, so no effort was made to equip her with the 50's before she left Bremerton, but a Navy flagship, steaming up to Seattle for the Sea Fair, dropped off two machine guns for us. We brought them aboard and immediately put them in stowage.

So at this point we had guns which, because of a State Department ruling, weren't to be tested or even mounted.

Thus the situation might have remained, had it not been for the events of June 8, 1967. On that day, for reasons still officially unexplained, Israeli torpedo boats and planes launched an unprovoked attack on the USS *Liberty,* which was in international waters fifteen miles north of the Sinai Peninsula, killing thirty-four U.S. seamen and wounding seventy-five others. The *Liberty* was on an intelligence-gathering mission, it was confessed after some initial denials. Although she was more than three times larger than the *Pueblo,* and carried a much bigger crew, certain parallels were obvious. At the time I wasn't anxious to think about them, knowing that the executive officer of the *Liberty* had been killed on the bridge.

But the Navy considered those parallels carefully and decided to act. Admiral Horacio Rivero, Jr., Vice Chief of Naval Operations, said that henceforth all Navy ships, regardless of mission, would be required to carry armament. He considered 50's minimal. The Chief of Naval Operations also ordered a detailed study of the three AGERs to determine what type guns would be appropriate. The study,

22

begun while we were at Bremerton, considered several recommendations. One was that we should carry 50-mm cannons. These were fair-sized, multipurpose weapons which would be effective against aircraft and most surface targets. However, the 50's were quite heavy, and it was thought that if they were mounted topside they might affect the stability of the ship. The *Pueblo* had been originally designed to carry considerable weight down inside her holds. But in her new role most of her weight was topside, in the research spaces. Just a few pounds in a rough sea could make the difference between whether we did or did not return to port.

Another suggestion, to install 20-mm guns in tubs around the foremast, presented the same problem. Additionally, there was also the consideration of finding adequate stowage on the tightly crammed *Pueblo* for the ammunition required for any size gun chosen. The gun controversy was still unresolved when we left Bremerton that fall.

Another one of the many unsolved problems involved destruct devices. The emergency destruct system was the subject of a special letter Bucher had me send the Chief of Naval Operations about a month after I reported aboard. Within the limitations of security, we tried to lay out the facts of the case. We had the expectation of going on a dangerous mission which would bring us in close proximity to unfriendly nations. Due to the nature of that mission, it would be necessary for us to carry sensitive materials that could have a great impact on national security, should they be seized by an enemy. Yet, with the exception of two slow paper-shredders and one hand-fed incinerator, we were without any means to destroy classified documents or the bulky electronic equipment, should an emergency arise.

Frankly, capture was the furthest thing from our minds. What concerned us was watertight integrity. What if we were inadvertently rammed during a harassment situation such as the *Banner* had experienced? Did we have the

23

ability to remain afloat? And if we were so badly damaged that the ship couldn't be saved, what could we do to destroy our classified paper so as not to leave it floating on the sea for anyone to pick up?

According to Navy directives we didn't qualify for complete damage control or maximum watertight integrity, which, very simply, means the ability of a ship's compartments to independently withstand the normal pressures of the sea. Because of her conversion from an AKL to an AGER, the *Pueblo* had special difficulties in this area. For example, before redesign the forward berthing space had been a large cargo hold. And originally it had a watertight hatch over it. But in conversion a new deck house had to be installed over this compartment, to accommodate the electronics package. With this a watertight hatch was no longer practical.

Eventually we did manage to obtain substantial damage control. But we were much less fortunate when it came to effective emergency destruct equipment.

At first we were told that automatic demolition devices had not been perfected for ships such as ours. Later the excuse changed somewhat. This time we were informed that since the original design of the *Pueblo* had not allowed for any type of built-in destruct system, it would be very costly to embark on such a design modification at this late date. Also—and this was a very important consideration— it would slow up delivery of the ship.

At one point we seriously discussed Thermit as a solution. A chemical incendiary, Thermit can eat right through metals. On inquiring about its availability, we were told that the Naval Ships Systems Command considered Thermit too dangerous to carry. There was always the possibility that, accidentally ignited, it could burn right through the skin of the ship.

As a result, when we left Bremerton we had only hand tools for hacking up cryptographic plates and machinery. As for the classified documents, we would have to resort to shredding, burning, or jettisoning to destroy them.

Bucher swore, however, that he would find some solution to the problem before we set out on our first mission.

With such "clues," it did not take a genius to conclude that, whatever our ostensible cover, our essential function would be intelligence-gathering, that the *Pueblo* was, in short, to be a spy ship.

I didn't lose any sleep over the realization. In fact, the prospect rather excited me, as a chance to participate in an assignment both larger and more important than anything I had ever done.

Too, I had little time for such worries. Although it didn't seem possible, my schedule after commissioning was even busier than before.

Since the AGERs were an entirely new naval concept, we had no pattern for conversion. The *Banner* was no longer around to serve as a guide. Nor was it possible for the *Pueblo* and the *Palm Beach* to reach a joint solution to their problems, one copying the other.

There was a rumor, possibly apocryphal, that the man who ordered the *Pueblo* and *Palm Beach* out of mothballs thought the ships were identical and didn't learn otherwise until they were brought to Bremerton and placed side by side.

Being different in size—the *Pueblo* was both smaller and lighter—equipment that might fit easily into one couldn't be squeezed into the other. This was one aspect of the problem. There was another.

Differences in size aside, it would have been extremely helpful to everyone concerned if our skipper and the *Palm Beach*'s CO, then Lieutenant Commander Douglas A. Raper, had gotten together and standardized the organization of the two ships. But Bucher was a loner; he wanted to do things his own way. And as will be noted in due course, that approach was not only highly individualistic, but not one that anyone else would have wanted to copy.

Actually, according to naval procedure, our group commander, Commander Service Group 1 (COMSERVGRU-ONE) in San Diego, should have required our officers and crew to attend precommissioning school. Had we done so we would have learned the essential elements of organizing this type of ship, accounting methods, supply procedures, etc. But COMSERVGRU-ONE had little liaison with our ship. And for good reason. There was only one man in the entire service force who knew what AGERs were supposed to do. And that was Rear Admiral Edwin B. Hooper, Commander, Service Forces, U.S. Pacific Fleet, who was based in Pearl Harbor.

Essentially we had a staff above us who had little or no appreciation for the kind of ship they were supporting. In fact, later, before our shakedown cruise, there was a major hassle between a group commander and a squadron commander over who actually had control of the *Pueblo*. Nobody knew for sure where we should report. When we reported to one place, we were sent elsewhere. For a while it appeared that we were an unwanted child, that no naval commander was willing to accept us.

This apparently was due, at least in part, to the need for security, but that security was carried to such a degree that no one seemed to know what was going on.

With such confusion in the upper echelons, it is not surprising that the shipyard personnel at Bremerton charged with our outfitting were in the dark as to what our mission would be and how to prepare us for it.

They were not the only ones, of course. Although I had by this time caught glimpses of what was ahead, I couldn't share such knowledge with Carol. The wives, in this case, were the last to know. And when such knowledge did come, in late January 1968, in most cases it came as an incredible shock.

Yet there was a challenge in ferreting out solutions to our problems. Knowing that we were a new ship, the forerunner of a whole new naval concept of a floating intelligence platform, was in itself thrilling. For with it came the realization that many of the snarls I untangled would help execs who came after me.

And there were many such challenges. As an AKL the *Pueblo* needed to provide for only twenty-seven men. As an AGER, we had to carry more than eighty.

Stowage was also a recurring test of abilities. The *Pueblo* simply wasn't designed to hold the amount of equipment that was being placed on board. Nor could the shipyard personnel be of much help in this area, since they had no idea of what most of our secret equipment would be.

The oceanographic equipment was a good example. The outfitters evidently were not forewarned about all the bathy-thermographic gear our two civilian oceanographers would require. As it turned out, provisions for only one oceanographer had been designed into the conversion plans.

After we had jammed all the consumables and spare parts into every nook and cranny, we discovered we had eight more pallets of buckets, bottles, and related equipment, and no place to put them.

In attempting to find a solution, I informed the oceanographic office in Washington, D.C., which, fortunately, sent two men to Bremerton to help bring the stuff on board, test it out, and find ways to stow it. Meanwhile, I did some concerned searching on my own and found small open areas underneath walkways and in overhead compartments. With the assistance of a shipyard design man, we were able to convert these cubbyholes into storage spaces. In addition, we made a convenient stowage space overhead in the passageway in front of the ship's office and used the air-conditioning-equipment spaces for similar purposes.

Often the problem was simply bureaucracy, complicated by the fact that since nobody claimed us, everyone could pass the buck even more easily.

For example, initially we were short of both men and bunks. I put in for additional men and additional berths. But neither was immediately forthcoming. It seemed the Ships Systems Command wasn't going to give us the bunks

27

until we had the men, and the Bureau of Naval Personnel stubbornly refused to authorize the men until we had the bunks.

The additional personnel were finally released to us, during the last week of shakedown. But we still lacked bunks for part of the crew; the only saving grace was that enough men were on leave for us to get by.

I learned, however, that berthed nearby was a soon-to-be-scrapped reserve ship. Gathering some volunteers, we surreptitiously stripped its bunks, actually ending up with three surplus sleeping areas complete with locker spaces.

"Cumshawing," more politely defined as "appropriating" and less politely as "stealing," was also essential in providing seating in the research spaces.

Tremendous expense had been incurred in providing the most up-to-date, new-state-of-the-art electronic equipment for use by Steve Harris' communications technicians, whose work was, after all, the primary task of the *Pueblo*. But through some oversight no one had thought to provide them with chairs on which to sit while they were working.

When I first learned this, I went to NAVSHIPS and Naval Electronic Systems Command (NAVELECSYSCOM) to try to correct the situation. But it turned out to be another game of pass-the-buck. NAVELECSYSCOM said it wasn't their bailiwick, since the seats were not to be electronic. And NAVSHIPS showed little concern because NAVELECSYSCOM hadn't specified what kind of "secret" seats were required. It wasn't until I cumshawed some chairs on my own that the operators even had a place to sit.

Nor were these the only stumbling blocks. For a long time we were short of personnel, particularly lacking mess cooks and enough men to stand watch. Sick-call facilities were inadequate. As exec, one of my collateral duties was being medical officer, in its own way ironic, since I'm a Christian Scientist.

We also had great concern over the compressed-air supply aboard ship. During sea trials, the *Palm Beach* had encountered a strange situation. She ran into a fog bank, forcing her to sound her foghorn—using compressed air. At the same time, she was supposed to maneuver rapidly in various directions. To do so she had to use the air clutch in the main propulsion drive system. But after sounding her foghorn, she discovered she no longer had enough compressed air to change directions.

Since the *Pueblo* had essentially the same equipment, and could anticipate similar difficulties, we requested an additional compressed-air system. But by the time we left Bremerton it still hadn't arrived.

And there were a host of problems involving our internal communications. We badly needed, and repeatedly requested, a general announcing and alarm system, an intercom between the pilothouse and the signal bridge, and a remote unit for a radio telephone on the signal bridge. All of them were denied, mainly for budgetary reasons. To cite only one example of what this meant, should we encounter an emergency situation there was no way for personnel on the bridge to quickly warn those in the research spaces, as there was no 1MC speaker in the sod hut.

Fifteen million dollars had been requested for overhaul and conversion of the *Pueblo* and *Palm Beach,* but budget cuts had reduced the appropriation to less than nine million. Later I learned that these were not the only budget cuts. Originally the Assistant Secretary of Defense had asked for thirty ships to start the AGER program, and got three.

I did manage to obtain a telephone system in Bremerton. This would have provided a telephone in each of the officers' staterooms. Therefore, if a call were placed to the ship, the officer wouldn't have to go to the quarterdeck to take it, as is normal practice on smaller Navy ships. We were the first ship of our size to have such a system. It was my "baby," and we worked hard on its installation. We had managed to get stuffing tubes run through the ship and were just starting to lay the wire when time ran out. There just wasn't enough time to complete all the essential projects, and the telephones joined the long list of things to be done during our next in-port period.

A confused chain of command. An inadequate budget. Not enough time. These were among the *Pueblo*'s greatest difficulties.

But they weren't the only ones.

An additional, and very large complication, was that by this time Steve Harris wasn't the only officer having major differences with Bucher. And some of these were of such a serious nature that they almost precharted the *Pueblo* on a collision course with disaster.

4

The skipper of the USS *Pueblo*, Lieutenant Commander Lloyd Mark "Pete" Bucher, was a hard-drinking, rough-talking submarine sailor who suddenly found himself at the helm of a surface ship.

Orphaned at an early age, he had attended high school at Father Flanagan's Boys Town in Nebraska, dropping out in his senior year to enlist in the Navy. He stayed in two years, from 1945 to 1947, rising to quartermaster second class and through equivalency tests obtaining his high-school diploma. Upon discharge, he worked at various odd jobs, including construction worker and bartender, until 1949, when he enrolled at the University of Nebraska on a football scholarship. While attending the university he signed up for the Naval Reserve Officers Training Program; upon graduation in 1953, with a bachelor-of-science degree, he was commissioned an ensign in the U.S. Naval Reserve. Called to active duty in January, 1954, he served as division and education officer on board the USS *Mount McKinley*, his first and only surface billet as an officer until reporting aboard the *Pueblo* thirteen years later.

In mid-1955 Bucher gained admittance to submarine school, at New London, Connecticut. Upon graduation that December he served as torpedo and gunnery officer of the submarine USS *Besugo*. Finding he liked life on subs, he decided to stay in the Navy, and he augmented in 1958. About this same time Rear Admiral Hyman G. Rickover was interviewing men for nuclear-power submarines, then, as now, a very select program. Following a personal interview

31

and a study of Bucher's record, Rickover turned him down.

Bucher next served briefly as operations officer of the submarine USS *Caiman*, then as assistant plans officer for logistics on the staff of Commander Mine Force, Pacific Fleet. From 1961 to 1964 he served on the submarine USS *Ronquil*, rising from third officer to exec, after which he became an assistant operations officer on the staff of Commander Submarine Flotilla Seven, in Yokosuka, Japan.

Pete Bucher was a maverick, and defensively proud of it. He had come up the hard way, overcoming great obstacles. He was proudest of all of the dolphins he wore. Subs were Pete Bucher's life; his greatest desire was to have a submarine command.

Instead, in January, 1967, at the age of thirty-nine, he was ordered to command the USS *Pueblo*.

The intelligence officer of the USS *Pueblo*, Lieutenant Stephen Robert Harris, was Massachusetts-born, Harvard-educated. The Harris side of his family had arrived at Jamestown in 1614; his mother's side, on which there was a tradition of Yankee sailing-ship captains, stretched back to John Alden of the *Mayflower*. While at Harvard, Steve Harris had majored in English and participated in Naval ROTC, and upon graduation, in June, 1960, he had entered the Navy as an ensign. He had served aboard only two ships prior to the *Pueblo*—the destroyer tender USS *Grand Canyon* and the destroyer USS *Forest Sherman*. He was communications officer of both. In 1963 he attended the Defense Language Institute in Washington, D.C., adding a fluency in Russian to the several languages he already knew. Shortly afterward he entered Naval Intelligence.

Harris was neither CIA nor NSA, as some accounts would have him. He was strictly Naval Intelligence, which, incidentally, dates back further than the two aforementioned agencies. His specialty was electronic intelligence (ELINT). Until the time he joined the *Pueblo*, he had not qualified as an officer of the deck. He reported to Bremerton in March, 1967, a few days before his twenty-ninth birthday.

It would be difficult to imagine two more different backgrounds than those of Bucher and Harris. This was also true of their personalities.

In giving an order, Bucher never asked; he said "I want." Harris always said "Let's do it this way." Bucher had a loud, raucous sense of humor, and a great fund of stories, embellished with each retelling. Entering a crowded bar in which he knew no one, he would in minutes emerge the life of the party. Harris' sense of humor was no less real; it was just more subtle. With a grin, he liked to refer to himself as an "improper Bostonian." Harris liked classical music, especially Rachmaninoff. Bucher liked hillbilly music and his purchase of stereo tapes of that and nothing else for the ship's music system almost caused a small mutiny among the crew, who were finally and reluctantly granted more varied musical fare. Off duty, Bucher drank heavily; except for rare occasions, Harris kept himself under tight control. Harris was not shy; it just took a while to get to know him. Possibly due to Bucher's childhood, when he had been shunted from one orphanage to another, he had an almost insatiable desire to be liked, especially by his crew. On the town, he'd buy them drinks, lend them money, stick up for them in skirmishes with the shore patrol. This made for a most worshipful following, and played hell with shipboard discipline. Harris went by the rules and regulations. Living his maverick role to the hilt, Bucher went out of his way to flout them, except when in his best interests to do otherwise. Harris was moderate in most things; Bucher was inclined to extremes. You were either totally with him or totally against him; he knew no in-betweens. In politics he was far right of center. He had never joined the John Birch Society, though he had attended their meetings and admitted to almost wholehearted agreement with their views. He admired John Wayne, and in his own blustery way tried to emulate him. He was Bucher's "kind of man."

33

Steve Harris and Pete Bucher differed in almost every way but one: when either thought he was pursuing the correct course of action, he stuck to it, regardless of the arguments marshaled against him.

Although I had not yet reported aboard the *Pueblo* at the time, it's a safe bet that the two clashed almost as soon as they met. The differences between them were not only of background and personality; they went straight to the heart of the question of who was running the *Pueblo.*

The issue was authority.

There were twenty-seven communications technicians (CTs) in Lieutenant Harris' intelligence detachment. He firmly maintained that this unit was at least semi-independent of the *Pueblo*'s chain of command. In support of his position, he cited the fact that his detachment was under the direct operational control of Commander in Chief, U.S. Pacific Fleet (CINCPACFLT). Furthermore, he made it very clear that he considered himself the officer in charge of the twenty-seven men.

Lieutenant Commander Bucher did not see it that way. He "read" Lieutenat Harris' status as that of a department head only, not an officer in charge, and insisted that as such he was subordinate to both the commanding officer and the executive officer. *He,* Bucher, was captain of the ship. *He* gave the orders. *He* had authority over everyone aboard. Period. No question mark. And as exec—his emissary—I was responsible for passing those orders along to Harris and seeing that they were carried out. He also insisted that the CTs bear their fair share of shipboard duties, just like the rest of the crew.

Harris refused to buy this. His research department was his elite corps, and a very elite corps at that, many of the men being specialists in their various electronic fields. A fortune had been spent training them for this mission; he had no intention of letting them be used as swab jockeys.

Unknowingly, I was the man in the middle even before reporting aboard. Once on ship, I learned it quickly enough. At this time we were short on personnel, especially mess cooks and compartment cleaners. On instructions of the captain, I used the CTs whenever it was necessary to do so, much to the displeasure of Steve.

Yet the situation went far beyond whether a man was going to wield a mop. It left open many questions. For instance, who was to evaluate the performance of these men, the commanding officer or the detachment chief? In administrative matters, when a CT had a request to make, did he go to Lieutenant Commander Bucher (through me) or to Lieutenant Harris? In a disciplinary situation, who handled it, the ship's captain or the unit leader?

Partly due to this confusion, the CTs became almost a separate ship within the ship.

This had a positive side: it spurred an *esprit de corps* among the CTs, motivated and gave them special pride in their work. But the negative features, the division among the crew and the detrimental effect on morale, were far larger.

Being bright boys, it didn't take the CTs long to sense the schism, and to use it to their advantage, bypassing regulations whenever possible. They did not consider themselves *Pueblo* crewmen. After all, they weren't even allowed to wear *Pueblo* shoulder patches.

I liked Steve, but I couldn't agree with him on this. My own feeling on the chain-of-command controversy was that in all cases the commanding officer of the ship must have ultimate military authority over his entire crew. This is not in conflict with the concept of a separate detachment doing intelligence or other specialized work and reporting directly to a higher command only in regard to their specialty. It's not uncommon to have a medical or dental unit aboard larger ships whose detachment officers outrank both the exec and CO. But in these circumstances, the ship's captain has final authority over the operation and discipline of all personnel.

Actually, at first the *Banner* had had an even more confusing situation. When deployed on her first mission, her commanding officer was a lieutenant, whereas the officer in charge of the intelligence detachment was a lieutenant commander. This created an untenable situation that eventually had to be corrected. The intelligence officer was replaced by a lieutenant, and the CO by a lieutenant commander.

But on the *Pueblo* the problem of divided authority was never to be resolved. With a result that was to prove very costly to the United States.

Some myths have grown up around the Bucher-Harris schism. One has it that Bucher had a lower security clearance than Harris, that he was uninformed as to many of the intelligence detachment's special functions. This was at most only partially true. The two men had the same security clearance; Bucher, however, did not have the same "need-to-know" classifications as Harris, which is not uncommon between officers of differing duties in any branch of the service. Much of the work that Harris did in his research spaces was highly technical, some of it beyond the grasp of a person not similarly trained, as I was to discover on obtaining my own clearance.

Another myth, this one later fostered by Bucher himself, was that often he wasn't allowed access to the sod hut and had not even been provided with the combination to the lock. This was completely false. Steve gave the captain the combination each time it was changed for security reasons. The problem was that Bucher rarely took the trouble to memorize it. He apparently preferred pounding on the door when he wanted in. It was, after all, one way of showing his displeasure with the status quo.

This did not mean Harris wouldn't have liked to have forbidden Bucher access to the intelligence spaces.

One of my former instructors at destroyer school, and a good friend, Commander Earl Chinn, was at the Puget Sound Naval Shipyard while we were there. He was now exec of a brand-new destroyer tender, the *Samuel Gompers*. Bucher met Earl for the first time at the officers' club, and, both men being on new ships, invited Earl aboard to inspect the *Pueblo*. Including Steve's spaces.

The sod hut was supposed to be secure, very secure. Not yet having my clearance, even I wasn't allowed to know everything that went on there, although I did have access. But Earl was given the grand tour. Shown the equipment already installed, lectured on its capabilities. In Bucher's defense, it can be said that he was very proud of the research spaces; they were very new, and extremely impressive. They were also extremely secret.

But there was more to it than simple pride. Bucher had to prove himself boss. If he wanted to bring his friends on board and show them the ship—*all* of the ship—that was his damned business, no one else's, and certainly not some detachment head's. After all, he was the captain.

In defense of Harris, he was security officer aboard the *Pueblo*, as well as intelligence officer. And Bucher did have an extremely lax attitude toward security, occasionally leaving classified-message boards in the wardroom, where anyone who cleaned up could read them. Harris had a double responsibility to see that such things did not happen. His reaction to the Chinn incident was predictable. He blew his top. But then, Bucher must have known he would.

The schism not only remained; it grew wider.

My own differences with Bucher were now coming to the fore.

The exec is go-between for the skipper and the men. He is obliged to carry out the captain's orders, be they a major matter of ship's policy or a minor matter of individual discipline. Not only second in command, he is also the conduit through which the ship's business passes, up or down. Among his many functions is the task of taking pressure off the CO, even though it means taking blame for his policies. In short, the exec is often an SOB—if he is doing his job properly. Whatever his personal feelings, he must stand up for the commanding officer before the rest of the crew.

In return, the CO must back his exec. He may overrule him on a particular decision, but in such a way that it does not undermine the exec's authority. This command structure was basic to every ship on which I had previously served. Not so on the *Pueblo*.

Bucher would countermand orders, without telling me he had done so. He would skip the chain of command entirely. Often the only way I could find out what was going on was from a junior officer. Bucher would reverse himself unexpectedly, jumping from one extreme to the other, leaving me hanging there defending his previous stand.

The result was often chaos and confusion.

Part of the difficulty was, as noted, that Bucher was a maverick. This isn't necessarily bad, even in the service, which can often use a fresh approach, particularly when it comes to things such as cutting through red tape. But when you go against the rules, you have to offer something in their place.

My attitude was frankly that of a "rule-book" sailor, with qualifications. I felt that the rules and regulations usually existed for a purpose. Occasionally they were wrong, in which case they should be challenged. Even more often, they were simply not applicable. This was especially true on the *Pueblo*, which, after all, wasn't like other ships. But when placed in a given situation that I felt was appropriately covered by the rules, I stuck with them, because this was what all my background, experience, and naval training told me to do.

One good reason for following the rules is that they give the shipboard organization a consistent standard. A man, whether crewman or officer, knows what his duties are, what is expected of him, what is or is not permitted. Without some such standard, there is pandemonium. If you do something and are praised for it one day, then blamed the next, you don't know where you stand. And this was the way it was on the *Pueblo*. There was no such thing as prescribed practice. The only rules were those which suited Bucher's whims of the moment.

For example, a prohibition against gambling is a standard inclusion in every ship's organization manual. But not on the *Pueblo*. Bucher had specifically excluded it from ship's rules. Bucher was himself an ardent gamesman; while at Bremerton, he was arrested in a gambling-prostitution raid on a local hotel, his name appeared in the papers, and he was called before and read out by the admiral in command of the shipyard. Charged with gambling, he forfeited his $300 bail. Bucher's only rule regarding games of chance was that they not go on during duty hours. But should he catch crewmen breaking this rule, he wouldn't punish them; he would only put them off the ship for the day, figuring that if they had spare time they could spend it someplace where the game wouldn't interfere with the work at hand. This made sense. However, without arguing the pros and cons of gambling, there are a couple of very practical reasons why it is usually prohibited on ships. One, a heavy loser means a morale problem. Two, when dice and card games go on all night, they make it difficult for men who have early-morning duty to sleep. In both cases it has an adverse effect on shipboard routine.

But Bucher personally didn't like the rule; therefore he ignored it. There were many such departures aboard the *Pueblo*.

Maintaining discipline presented a special problem, due in large part to Bucher's extreme need to be liked by the crew.

As one of only a number of examples, while we were at Bremerton one of the men went UA, unauthorized absence, known in other branches of the service as AWOL. Called to Captain's Mast, Bucher gave him a nonjudicial punishment: restriction to ship. This was duly noted on the man's record. But thinking it over later, Bucher felt he had been too harsh, and decided to reverse himself. This could have been done fairly easily. There is nothing derogatory about going up for a Captain's Mast. The verdict is what counts. Had he come to me, as he should have, since I was in charge of the ship's office and records, I would have suggested that he simply change the verdict.

Instead he went directly to the yeoman who worked for me in the ship's office and had him rip out of the man's service record the page on which the notation of the Captain's Mast appeared. The trouble with this was that such cases are entered several places in the ship's records, and he had obliterated only one of them. The next time we had a records inspection, the discrepancy was caught.

At first Bucher appeared to me to be totally inconsistent, his actions erratic, unpredictable. Then I learned that this was not wholly true. There was a very simple reason for why he did at least some of the things the way he did. It just took time to discover it. Once understood, it provided an explanation for many of his actions and attitudes.

Bucher considered the *Pueblo* his submarine.

To Bucher the signal bridge was the "conning tower," the mess decks still the "afterbattery." In writing the ship's organization manual, he had even once forgotten and said that such-and-such "will not be permitted aboard this submarine." Spotting the mistake, the CTs delighted in saying "You can't do *that* on this submarine!"

Had it just been a matter of terminology, it would have been humorous, nothing more. But it underlay Bucher's entire attitude toward the operation of the ship, and would have a most definite effect on how the *Pueblo* was handled under fire.

Some of the sub traditions which he carried over to the *Pueblo* were most welcome. For instance, about three each afternoon when under way we would have "soup-down," during which a substantial soup course, separate from the evening meal, was served. It was a nice break in routine, and if a man was going on watch, it put something in his stomach before he started.

But other sub traditions adapted less well. One that caused numerous problems was the absence of reveille. On a surface ship, excepting only those crewmen who have had night duty, everyone has to "roll out" at a set time. One may not like it—and who likes to get up?—but at that time work crews are formed and spaces below deck and topside are cleaned. Also, on a surface ship, reveille is the way the crew is mustered, to make sure all are present and accounted for and that no one has fallen overboard during the night. This is, of course, not a problem aboard subs, nor is there a need to clean the topside decks.

The absence of reveille contributed to the crew's affection for Bucher. But it also greatly impeded shipboard routine. Because we had no reveille, many hands were still sleeping when there was work to be done.

Whether it was a sub practice, or just another personal peculiarity, there was also no restriction against lying on bunks while clothed. Aside from general disorderliness, this, plus the absence of reveille, resulted in considerable confusion as to which men were on or off duty.

Another of our newly adopted sub practices admittedly bothered me more than anyone else. This concerned training. In submarine style, the skipper charged me, as executive officer, with training the entire crew.

This type of centralized organization, where the exec is thoroughly familiar with all departments and can easily act in the stead of department heads, is used only on submarines. The standard surface-ship procedure is for the exec to coordinate the various units of the ship, assembling all of the department heads and consulting with them as to the training requirements of their own crewmen. On subs, the exec runs the whole show. He evidently doesn't even consult with department heads. But surface ships, by directive, have a training board made up of department heads and a training officer. This training officer may or may not be the executive officer. Often it is the operations officer.

This sharing of responsibility seemed to me particularly important in our case. None of the officers aboard the *Pueblo* had any experience with an AGER; they couldn't have. The ship was an all-new naval concept. It was essential that we work together as a team to develop procedures that would best fit our kind of ship.

But although it was required for surface ships in official Navy regulations, the captain flatly refused to let me set up a training board. And our training program was very much handicapped. To cite only one example of the need: of the twenty-seven CT's, only four had ever been to sea.

Admittedly, my gripe—and gripe I did, until receiving a flat no—was in this case personal. As exec, Bucher expected me to do everything. Yet, inconsistently, he was constantly undermining my authority, refusing to back me up, skipping links in the chain of command. However, in the sense that such disorder had a direct bearing on the way the ship itself was run, it was more than a personal matter.

Another and far more serious contention between us, again derived from the difference between sub and surface-ship procedures, concerned the placement of the guns, if we were given permission to mount them.

I held, from when we first discussed carrying the 50's, that they should be mounted in or about the pilothouse area, specifically on the bulwarks on the port and starboard sides of the bridge wings. In this position, I reasoned, whoever was conning the ship would have close voice command of the guns. He wouldn't need to rely on a sound-powered phone gun-control circuit, something else the *Pueblo* didn't yet have. Mounted in the pilothouse area, the 50's could also be easily manned. They would be readily accessible from the inside of the ship. They would be close to where our topside ammunition locker would most likely be placed. And, of great importance, the bulwarks would provide at least some protection for the personnel operating the guns.

The skipper wouldn't buy this rationale, even after I had the Puget Sound Naval Shipyard find the general plans of the original hull, which showed that this was approximately where the Army had placed its guns in the earlier days when it had operated the ship. At first Bucher wanted the guns in the eyes of the ship; later he changed this to one midship aft on the boat deck and the other on the starboard bow. If you've ever watched World War II movies on the late-late show, you've often seen them mounted both ways. On submarines.

Championing his preferred position, Bucher said that "the noise was less" and "the arc of shooting greater."

While we were still without permission to mount the guns, the argument was in a sense moot. But there was always the chance it wouldn't remain so.

The placement of the 50's was actually only part of a larger controversy that divided Bucher and me—where to conn the ship in event of an attack.

Again it was a disagreement that accentuated the divergent philosophies of a submarine-oriented commander and a surface-trained officer.

The question was: from what point do you fight the ship in a general-quarters situation?

On submarines, the skipper reasoned, you conn your ship from the highest point. The highest point on the *Pueblo* was the signal bridge. Here was where the arc of vision was greatest, Bucher said.

I disagreed vehemently. Fighting the *Pueblo* from the signal bridge would be an act of pure folly. Anyone up there would be completely in the open, with no physical protection, exposed to gunfire and all the elements.

The place from which to direct battle was the pilothouse, I argued. Here we had easy access to radar and ship's controls. All the channels of voice communication were available. None of them were on the signal bridge; at this time we didn't even have a sound-powered telephone up there. Additionally, there was some protection from bullets and shrapnel in the pilothouse area. On the signal bridge we would be sitting ducks.

Even presuming we never encountered a battle situation, the officers of the deck would "freeze their tails off" standing watch up there in bad weather. An OOD usually stands a four-hour watch. On all Navy ships I had ever served on, he is usually down on the bridge level, near the bulwarks, which afford some relief from wind, rain, and spray.

And, again, in the pilothouse the OOD had all the facilities he needed. He had a sound-powered telephone. He had direct access to the navigational personnel and charts. He couldn't ask for better radar access. He need only walk over and look at it. In the event of an emergency, the radio phone was right at hand.

If, in relating our two sides of the disagreement, I appear to be presenting an overly strong case for mine and almost none for Bucher's, it is for the simple reason that Bucher offered no defense of his position.

For he already had the strongest possible argument on his side. He was the captain, and this was the way it was going to be done.

On Bucher's Magic Submarine.

5

The *Pueblo* was first scheduled to leave Bremerton in April, 1967. That month had long since come and gone. Each week our departure was further postponed because necessary work was still uncompleted. This made it difficult for dependents of the crew, who had to constantly revise their plans and rearrange their housing commitments, and it also added to the already existing confusion over when and where various repairs were to be made. Knowing that a needed part wouldn't be available for two months, did we order it shipped to Bremerton; or San Diego, where we would have our shakedown training; or Hawaii, where we would pause briefly in crossing the Pacific; or Yokosuka, our home port in Japan?

It was June before we had the first of our sea trials. As an omen, it was less than auspicious. We proudly steamed out of Puget Sound, only to have the steering cable part. Ignominiously, we had to be towed back to port.

Steering failures seemed to be almost congenital with AGERs. Our sister ship, the *Palm Beach*, was reporting the same type of malfunction, and the *Banner* had also experienced similar difficulties. In a harassment situation, a steering failure could spell instant disaster. We already knew, from the experiences of the *Banner*, that unfriendly ships might decide to play porpoise close to our bow. If they did, only skillful seamanship could prevent a collision.

Our particular difficulty concerned the electromagnetic steering system, which broke down with almost predictable

45

regularity. When this happened, we were forced to steer the ship mechanically, using the helm, a tricky maneuver under the best of conditions. And there was no guarantee that the best of conditions would always prevail.

Some journalists who have never seen the *Pueblo*—and, alas, probably never will—have delighted in portraying her as a close cousin to the floating tub in *Mr. Roberts.* Both were originally AKLs; and that's about where the comparison ends. Despite a multitude of problems, the *Pueblo* was basically a small but good ship, one in which a man could take a great deal of pride. She was old, but she had received excellent mechanical repair before mothballing. With one exception. Because of rusting, a great deal of work had to be done on the hull. When she first arrived at Bremerton, I was told you could stand in the aft spaces and see daylight through the deck. All that decking had been replaced, however. And while not brand new, the *Pueblo* was in solidly dependable condition. The shipyard in Bremerton had done an excellent job with available funds. Most of her problems were the result of her conversion from an AKL to an AGER. Or a result of the attitudes of those who would sail aboard her.

In my *Pueblo* orders I had also been ordered to attend several schools in San Diego, relating to my assignment as exec. One was a five-day course in personnel administration. I arrived on a Sunday and reported in. That same night there was an urgent call from Bucher. The school would have to wait; I was needed back aboard immediately. Packing hurriedly, I rushed to Bremerton, to find that Ling-Temco-Vought, the company responsible for the installation of the electronics package, had invited the skippers of the *Pueblo* and the *Palm Beach* to visit their headquarters in Texas. It appeared to be a boondoggle. Had it concerned the actual operations of the electronic gear, the intelligence officers would have been sent instead. Ling-Temco-Vought had promised the two skippers a good time, and apparently that was what they had, for Bucher returned with a monumental hangover and a whole new fund of motel stories.

Another of my school assignments was to a three-day course in emergency ship handling. Just before I was to leave, Bucher decided he wanted a few days in San Diego; so he took my place. Except he checked in and out of the school the same day, later explaining that his "room was too hot." On Friday, when he was due back, I received a long-distance call. He couldn't get a plane until the following week. I was to "handle things" in his absence.

In addition to handling my duties *and* Bucher's, I often had yet another job: lying to the admiral of the shipyard. Since Bucher's leaves had to be authorized by him, and on a number of occasions Bucher hadn't bothered to go through that formality, I had to provide cover. Thinking up plausible excuses took a certain amount of imagination. Obviously I couldn't use the one Bucher usually gave me: not being able to get a plane. Considering he was a lieutenant commander, Bucher had remarkably bad luck when it came to being bumped from airplanes. And, curiously enough, he was always stranded in a city where he had a good sub buddy—Denver, Los Angeles, or San Diego.

Each week the admiral held a meeting with the captains of all ships in the yard, during which he was brought up to date on their progress and apprised of any problems. I attended so frequently in Bucher's stead that one of the other skippers once asked me, "What does this character Bucher look like? I don't think I've ever seen him."

Had there been some advance warning, Bucher's absences wouldn't have been a major problem. Unfortunately for the *Pueblo*, they were almost always spur-of-the-moment whims, frequently occurring when he was most needed aboard. As Bucher's fund of wild stories grew, the *Pueblo*'s unsolved problems continued to mount. Finally I gave up any thought of taking the long-overdue leave Bucher had promised me. There was too much to be done.

Unpredictability also characterized Bucher's approach

to any given problem. At times he displayed an astonishing perseverance. Told "No" at every level of the chain of command, he would persist until he had ramrodded through what he wanted. Dozens of needed repairs were made solely because of Bucher's refusal to accept a negative answer. You had to marvel at some of the things he accomplished by sheer staying power. But these times alternated with others when he would give up without the slightest semblance of a fight. Nor was it a matter of priorities; it simply depended on his mood. One day he felt like making the effort. Another day he didn't, and tossed in the towel even before he had started. You never knew which way he was going.

Perhaps, as some of the crewmen were to maintain, the *Pueblo* was jinxed. It did seem that no sooner had we solved one problem than a half-dozen others surfaced. One of my biggest headaches, and the cause of innumerable clashes with Bucher, concerned the operation of the ship's office. The yeomen in charge was very personable, but as a secretary and administrative assistant he was totally inept. Ordered to complete certain paperwork, then questioned about it later, he would, in all sincerity, assure me it had been done. Later I would find it hadn't. The pile-up of uncompleted work was monumental. Some reports were overdue long before I reported aboard. It was a very serious problem, and as exec I was responsible.

At first I tried to train the yeoman in his assigned duties, but it wasn't long before I discovered that this meant I had to do them myself. Finally realizing that he was incapable of even learning, I was forced to find a replacement for him. Although Bucher concurred, it wasn't to be that easy. EPDOPAC, the Enlisted Personnel Distribution Office Pacific, first denied my requests, then finally gave in. We could have a new yeoman. But not until we reached Japan.

The *Pueblo*'s problems were compounded by the fact that we still lacked our full wardroom complement of six officers. The supply officer hadn't yet reported aboard, while the operations officer, Lieutenant (JG) Dave Behr, was staying on only until his replacement arrived. Perhaps because Behr knew he was leaving the Navy soon, he exhibited an I-don't-give-a-damn-what-you-say streak rarely seen in a junior officer this side of mutiny charges. Behr and Bucher clashed continuously. Added to my own differences with Bucher, plus those of Steve Harris, the *Pueblo* at times seemed less a ship than a boxing ring.

Steve's disagreements with Bucher had in no way diminished. A new difference had arisen over the use of the "spy money." The intelligence detachment was separately funded, and not subject to budget cuts inflicted on the ship itself. Bucher had partial authority over these funds and used a portion of them to buy a music system for the ship. Harris objected strongly to Bucher's using the money as if it were his own.

During our next attempt at sea trials we spotted a little runabout in distress. Her motor had stopped, and she was caught in the outgoing tide, right in the center of the ferry route. A family of three was aboard. We had thrown down a ladder, and the wife was just stepping onto it, when, inexplicably, Bucher gave an engine order, nearly swamping the boat and dumping the woman overboard. The incident confirmed what I had already begun to suspect—that the *Pueblo*'s CO was a lousy ship handler. Much as I would have liked to, in the months ahead I could find no reason to revise that judgment.

The incident did have a humorous side. In naming the tiny craft, her owners had ironically decided to call her the *Kittyhawk*, after one of the biggest ships in the Navy. Later we could write in the ship's log: "*Pueblo* towed *Kittyhawk* into port."

In late August the Board of Inspection and Survey tests were held. Suddenly Bucher cracked down: everything had to be in perfect order. The crew had to have clean uniforms, haircuts, and a daily shave. Bucher himself even got a haircut, although it made no noticeable difference, as he apparently had told the barber to spare the shears. Once someone in the wardroom asked why he so rarely frequented tonsorial parlors. "I can't stand to be touched," he said, shivering with revulsion.

We didn't bring up the subject again.

By the time the inspection crew arrived, there wasn't a speck of dust to be found on the *Pueblo*. But our greatest problems were not the sort to be cured by spit and polish. The INSURV tests, which lasted three days, resulted in a thick report listing 462 separate deficiencies.

Despite the months of hard work, the *Pueblo* was still far from RFS—ready for sea. But on the eleventh of September we steamed out of Puget Sound and headed south for San Diego. If to the casual observer we seemed to list noticeably, it was probably from the weight of unfulfilled promises we had to carry.

The steering malfunction would be corrected. In our next port. The additional compressed-air system would be waiting for us. In San Diego. Our wardroom complement would be completed. Soon. We would get a new yeoman for the ship's office. In Japan. The gun controversy would be resolved. Sometime. Destruct devices would be provided. Eventually.

The list threatened to scuttle us before we set out on our first mission.

At sea my evaluation of Bucher rose considerably, with the discovery that he was an excellent navigator.

By now I was trying desperately to find points of agreement, if only for the sake of the ship. The various schisms aboard the *Pueblo* were now apparent to the whole crew, due in large part to Bucher's habit of not confining his gripes to the wardroom but airing them—"chewing ass"—before anybody who happened to be around.

We had, I decided, one big thing in common. We both wanted the *Pueblo* to be a good ship. Although we differed considerably on how to accomplish that, at least it was a start.

On September 15 we reached San Francisco, lying over

50

for a three-day liberty call. While there Bucher received good news: he was to be promoted. On several earlier occasions he had expressed doubt as to whether he would ever rise above lieutenant commander. He didn't say why he felt this. However, from a couple of veiled references we surmised that some of his earlier fitness reports had been less than satisfactory. Apparently the Navy had decided that the AGERs were to be skippered by full commanders, since Doug Raper was to be promoted at the same time.

Not too surprisingly, Bucher's good news occasioned a celebration. The next morning at 3 A.M. Bucher woke all the officers to inform them that since the bars had closed he had decided to bring the party aboard.

Most shipboard rules prohibit the female presence aboard ship after taps. There was no such rule on the *Pueblo*.

Bleary-eyed, we peered out from under the covers as he introduced his newly met friends. No, we couldn't stay in bed. To hell with early-morning duty. The mess steward was ordered to prepare breakfast for everyone.

Since promotions do not occur that often, we joined the crowd, unaware that this was going to be probably the most celebrated promotion in Navy annals.

Back at sea, the steering system again broke down, once or twice a day. Excessive rolling resulted in a very real concern for the stability of the ship. Several times we computed that the roll exceeded 35 degrees. Many problems missed earlier now chose to manifest themselves; for example, when the ship rolled, the chairs in the research spaces slid all over the place. Even without that, Steve was having a time of it, and his biggest problem had nothing to do with security. Most of his CTs, at sea for the first time, spent most of their time leaning over the side.

Shortly after our arrival in San Diego, I became a member of the "club." With my SI (Special Intelligence) clearance, Steve took me on a tour of his research spaces, this time explaining to me exactly what the various equipment did. Prior to this, I had gleaned, from bits and pieces of information, a general picture of our operations. I knew we were to be a flexible intelligence-collecting platform, that we would be steaming on the open seas, just outside the territorial waters of various foreign countries, the sensitive equipment monitoring and recording ship-to-ship, ship-to-shore, and land-based communications; intercepting radar emissions; and surveying foreign fleet activities. What I didn't realize was how sensitive that equipment was, and how much broader its capabilities, extending into areas at which I hadn't even guessed.

For example, there were receivers that could pick up and pinpoint the origins of walkie-talkie messages between commanders and their troops in the field, thereby enabling intelligence to follow troop movements even when they occurred far inland.

I could see now why Bucher enjoyed giving tours of these spaces; the equipment was the very latest state-of-the-art, and even to the layman, fantastically impressive.

Some of Steve's explanations were simplicity personified, and I could have kicked myself for not figuring them out earlier. I had wondered, for example, why Steve needed twenty-seven communications technicians, when the research spaces could accommodate only a much smaller number. The obvious answer—three shifts, nine men each.

But only a few of the answers were that simple. While I listened to him, my mood alternated between amazement and bewilderment. One thing was apparent throughout, however: Steve was proud of his work and convinced of its value.

Steve did not confine himself to present capabilities. He also indicated several directions in which the program would eventually go. For example, we had no way of gathering intelligence on submarines when they were at depth. But in the foreseeable future we would have that capability.

Up until this time I had presumed that our two civilian oceanographers, whom we would pick up in Japan, would function solely as cover for our spying activities. I now learned that they were to play a vital part in our intelligence-gathering. To cite only one example: there is an underwater layer known as the thermal cline, which deflects sonar signals. Thus a submarine can safely operate underneath this layer, without detection from above. Some of the tests conducted by the oceanographers would be for the purpose of pinpointing and mapping these layers, essential data in case of a future invasion.

From Steve I also learned something of the background of the AGER program. Also that our missions had multiple tasking: part would be conducted solely for the Navy, part for the National Security Agency (NSA), and the remainder for both groups.

While we were in port, Steve flew east for ten days of briefings at NSA. He brought back a list of places we might be sent on our first mission. The actual destination hadn't been picked, but we did know the mission would be for the Navy. Steve made it clear, however, that this first mission would be primarily for training purposes. Many of his CTs were green, fresh out of school. Whatever the chosen objective of our surveillance, the basic objective of our first mission would be to give the CTs experience and to teach them to work as a team. Just as the whole crew would undergo shakedown training in San Diego, our initial mission would be a shakedown for the communication technicians.

This point is stressed because, at a much later date, Commander Bucher would publicly express his amazement at how inexperienced Harris' CTs were, how unprepared for their duties. Bucher knew this long before we were on station. The basic objective of the mission was to train Harris' men. Any intelligence collected would be a bonus —frosting on the cake.

After being briefed by Steve, I no longer harbored any doubts as to the importance of our task. Nor my own part in it. As navigator, I would have to see that the *Pueblo* went as close to shore as possible, yet at the same time never crossed that invisible line separating the open sea from claimed territorial waters.

Not long after our arrival in San Diego, the *Palm Beach* stopped briefly to refuel and pick up provisions. When she sailed out of the harbor for her shakedown training at Guantánamo, we knew we would probably be working different waters and that some time might elapse before the two sister ships were reunited. What we couldn't know was that they would never again be berthed in tandem.

By this time the *Pueblo*'s wardroom cast was complete. Gene H. Lacy, our chief warrant officer, was "haze gray" —all Navy. Having worked his way up through the engineman ranks, he brought to his job as engineering officer a wholly professional background, plus a considerable amount of sea experience on surface ships. The first officer to report aboard the *Pueblo,* he had played a major role in the outfitting of the ship, not only overseeing needed repairs and modifications in the engineering plant, in itself a monumental task, but also filling in as supply officer until one came aboard. He was quietly self-assured, easy to work with, and respected by the whole crew. He didn't court that respect; it came naturally, from knowing his job and doing it well.

Gene's differences with Bucher were not as pronounced as Steve's and mine, but they existed. When Bucher announced some far-out scheme that might have worked on a sub but couldn't on a surface ship, Gene might grimace, but usually he said nothing. After nineteen years in the Navy he had seen a goodly number of commanding officers come and go; his attitude was a resigned "this too shall pass." But if the scheme touched on his bailiwick, the engine room, he spoke up. And when he did, even Bucher listened.

Our supply officer, Ensign Timothy H. Harris, no relation to Steve Harris, had reported just before we left Bremerton, green as they come. Although a Navy junior— he was the son of a chief petty officer—he seemed to know almost nothing about shipboard procedures. After graduating from college in Florida, he had been accepted for flight school at Pensacola, then washed out. He was still smarting from that failure when he came aboard. The *Pueblo* was not only his first ship, it was his first assignment of any kind. He had come to Bremerton directly from Pensacola, with only a brief trip to San Diego to attend supply school. Tim had just turned twenty, and looked and acted much younger, which made it difficult for him to keep discipline in his department, since most of the men who worked for him were his seniors in both age and experience. Young, naïve, impressionable, he thought Bucher the epitome of what a commanding officer should be.

Lieutenant (JG) Frederick C. "Skip" Schumacher, who had replaced Dave Behr as operations officer after we reached San Diego, was twenty-four and had known only one previous billet, as communications officer aboard the supply ship USS *Vega*. On graduating from Trinity College in Connecticut, Skip had been forced to make a difficult decision: whether to enter the ministry or join the Navy. Though he had chosen the Navy, the church remained in the back of his mind as his probable career on completion of his current tour. One would never have guessed this on first meeting Skip. For if a prototype for the swinging bachelor existed, Skip was it. Fun-loving, with a silver-gray Porsche complete with an attractive girl in the seat beside him, he seemed determined to live life to the fullest now, knowing that the ministry lay ahead.

When it came to his job, Skip was uncommonly conscientious. Unlike Bucher, when Skip partied all night, he was on deck ready for duty bright and early the next morning. In sharp contrast to Tim Harris, it was not necessary to explain anything twice to Skip. He caught on and dug in immediately, despite the fact that he had inherited my earlier problem of not knowing what the *Pueblo*'s actual

55

mission was to be. Of course, he couldn't be told that until he received his security clearance. This handicap, plus having to clean up the mess left by Dave Behr, plus having to improvise procedures to fit a wholly new kind of ship, made his job more demanding than would ordinarily be the case. With his minimum surface-ship experience, he was inclined to go along with Bucher's sub ideas, backing the captain all the way. Like Tim Harris, Skip Schumacher became a Bucher protégé.

By the time we reached San Diego I could see Bucher in somewhat better perspective. In retrospect, it was apparent he had been a lonely man at Bremerton. His wife and two sons were with him only for a short period. Of his four officers, three had their families with them, and therefore usually weren't available for the nightly bar-hopping he so enjoyed. Moreover, one officer was a Christian Scientist who didn't drink; he couldn't talk to the second without getting into an argument; and he was engaged in a power struggle with the third. The remaining officer, Gene Lacy, was closest to Bucher in age, but although he occasionally accompanied Bucher on his nocturnal rounds, he was inclined to be a "couple-of-beers" man. Also, his wife and three children were just across the bay in Seattle.

With the arrival of Schumacher and young Harris, Bucher found the companionship he wanted. Which, in itself, would have been fine. Except it had other, more far-reaching effects—some subtle, some decidedly not—on the operations of the USS *Pueblo*.

If you are looking for an example of democracy in action, it is best to bypass the ship's wardroom. It has never been, and was never intended to be, a democratic institution. No matter what personal friendships may exist among the officers, seniority remains in force. And the captain is always, under all circumstances, boss.

But sometimes the sheer weight of numbers can be influential. Even the most opinionated skipper is apt to think twice when he finds that all his officers disagree with him. This may not change his mind. As captain, he has to make the ultimate decisions and be held accountable for them, but it can be an aid in putting his views into perspective. While at Bremerton, Steve, Gene, and I could sometimes talk Bucher out of what appeared to be a less than wise innovation. With the support of the two newest and youngest members of the wardroom, the balance shifted. And as time passed, Bucher became less and less inclined to consider the views of anyone else. For whatever he decided, he knew he had two loyal followers. This was one of the more subtle changes.

The major problem of the new wardroom alignment shouldn't have been a problem in the first place, as it concerned after-hours activities and seemingly not shipboard routine. But, unfortunately in this case, the two overlapped.

The captain sets the schedule of his ship. And starting with our arrival in San Diego, Bucher's personal schedule was often to party late into the night, then sleep until after lunch. This meant he was unavailable when needed in the morning. Starting to work late in the day, he would then continue until well into the evening, expecting everyone else to do likewise. This was fine for the bachelors or those who, like Bucher, didn't have their families with them. But it was damned inconvenient for those of us who did have families and wanted to have at least one meal with them. Still, had it been simply a matter of personal inconvenience, we could have adjusted. But it went a step further. From work, Bucher, Schumacher, and Tim Harris would then go out on the town. And it was often here, in the bars, that much of the ship's business took place and many of the captain's more important decisions were made.

One result was that I often learned the captain's decisions from junior officers or enlisted men. I might give Tim Harris an order, only to be told, "The captain said we weren't going to do that," or, "You'd better talk to the captain about that, Murphy. He told me to do something else today." The exec, to repeat an important point, is a conduit. He is supposed to transmit the skipper's orders to the rest of the crew. This is not simply a matter of maintaining the exec's authority; it has an even more essential informational purpose: it enables the exec to know exactly what is going on aboard ship.

And often, aboard the *Pueblo,* I didn't. Unless one of the junior officers chose to tell me.

At best this resulted in an unnecessary duplication of effort. At worst it meant that some things were left undone. For, to complicate the problem, the captain often *thought* he had told me something when he hadn't, but had intended to. To cite one example, which occurred somewhat later, Bucher obtained a number of canvas bags for emergency disposal of classified documents. He also decided that to make them sink faster we should carry a stock of scrap iron. Only the scrap-iron decision occurred during one of his barroom conferences, and was never passed on to me. Net result, the scrap iron was never brought aboard, and wasn't available when needed.

Even at that, under ordinary circumstances the basic problem needn't have been insurmountable. Had the captain abided by standard surface-ship procedures, I, as exec, could often have anticipated him. But Bucher's actions were so erratic that second-guessing became impossible. When you did, and guessed wrong, you were chewed out for it; when you didn't, you were chewed out just the same.

This continual bypassing of the chain of command raised havoc with shipboard routine. And it definitely impeded preparations for our first mission.

There were other ramifications, less important but bothersome. Because he was close to both Skip Schumacher and Tim Harris, and because he could rarely bring himself to exert discipline, when either of the two had to be called on the carpet for something, the captain would give me the job of doing it.

Schumacher usually took it in stride, although he developed a bad habit of questioning commands, asking "why," when often the reasons behind a given decision were nobody's business but the captain's. Tim Harris took it less well. Younger than Schumacher in more ways than age, he saw the situation in simplistic terms: his buddy, the captain, was the "good guy"; the exec, always criticizing him, was the "bad guy"; and in such a classic confrontation, you did everything you could to help the one and frustrate the other. He also quickly learned, as did even some of the enlisted men, that the easiest way to get around the exec was to catch Bucher late at night, when he was off the ship and in a mellow mood, and then present his grievances directly to the CO. Unfortunately for shipboard discipline, orders were constantly being countermanded, usually without my knowledge.

As far as command structure went, the *Pueblo* was in trouble, deep trouble. Almost lost in the clash of personalities was the fact that we were supposed to be a team, working together toward a common purpose.

While the replacement of Behr by Skip Schumacher had ended a great deal of petty bickering in the wardroom, it also inadvertently occasioned a still further split between Bucher and Steve Harris.

Skip was to relieve Dave as communications officer, as well as operations officer. But since Skip hadn't received his security clearance, he couldn't do so. In the interim, someone had to hold down the job. The man most eminently qualified, as Bucher saw it, was Steve Harris, a specialist in communications. But Steve felt otherwise. His other duties were too important and too time-consuming, he argued, flatly refusing the assignment. Bucher could have ordered him to fill the slot. But if he did, and Steve carried his complaint on up the chain of command, there was always the possibility that he, Bucher, might be overruled, thus still further undermining his authority. Instead he chose to avoid the confrontation, and appointed me instead. I filled in as communications officer until our ar-

59

rival in Japan, at which time Skip's "ticket" came through.

Result: more bad blood between Steve Harris and the captain.

Bucher's reason for avoiding this battle was that he had just lost another. Since Steve's arrival aboard, Bucher had been trying to get his communications technicians declared a "department." That way, they, and Steve, would be wholly under Bucher's authority. Late in September Bucher received the word: the CTs were, as Steve had always maintained, a "detachment," not a department, with Steve reporting directly to the director of the Naval Security Group in Hawaii.

Frustrated and angered by his failure, Bucher got back at Steve in the only way he knew how. By this time the 3 A.M. breakfast parties were frequent enough to be considered almost a part of shipboard routine. And every chance he got, Bucher would take his barroom companions on early-morning tours of the secret spaces.

6

Perhaps needless to say, the compressed-air supply had not been waiting when we steamed into San Diego. Nor would we receive it before we left. But we were assured it would be waiting for us in Hawaii upon our arrival. In the interim, we would have to go through shakedown without it. To a large extent, the other promises also went unredeemed. The steering continued to break down, no matter how many hours were spent on its repair. Except for the installation of an extension phone on the signal bridge (to get the parts, not too surprisingly, we had to raid a sub), we had made almost no headway in improving our internal communications. As for securing the seats in the research spaces, we had no luck whatsoever. Steve was having unforeseen difficulties with his secret gear, which wasn't working as it should. Nor was the gun controversy yet resolved. On the contrary, due to a recent State Department ruling, we had to turn in the two .50-caliber machine guns we had!

To all this were now added the special problems of shakedown training.

Sea trials are a process of readying the ship. Shakedown provides the same function for the crew, simulating conditions which they might expect to encounter under way.

Or that, at least, is what it is supposed to do. In the case of the *Pueblo*, we hit a snag.

The basic difficulty was that the training group in charge of our shakedown exercises had no idea what the *Pueblo* was supposed to do. And because of security, we couldn't tell them.

Included in the exercises were standard drills that might prove helpful—such as damage control, general quarters, repel boarders, and abandon ship.

There were also drills that could not, in any foreseeable circumstances, be applicable to the *Pueblo*—such as towing other ships and steaming in a fleet. The *Pueblo* was going to be a loner, operating very much by herself. But unfortunately, we couldn't tell anyone that.

Absent were the drills we most needed—what to do in a harassment situation.

The fault was by no means Schumacher's, who, though in charge of coordinating our training exercises, still wasn't privy to the secrets of the "club." Nor was it Bucher's, who had tried his best, without giving the whole show away, to suggest exercises that might be useful. The closest he was able to come was a battle problem including elements of simulated harassment. But because of heavy fog, we didn't go out that day.

There was another complication. Bucher had started shakedown by conning the ship from the signal bridge, in sub fashion. But, midway through, the training command had called him to task for this.

He lacked full control from the signal bridge, they said. He was without easy access to radar and the facilities of communication. There was only one logical position from which to command the ship, and that was the pilothouse.

It was a familiar argument. But this time Bucher acquiesced.

Although the news secretly pleased everyone who had to stand OOD, I didn't feel I'd scored any kind of victory; it was awfully late in the game for that. Besides, Bucher had given in much too easily. I suspected the last word had yet to be heard.

Because of the switch, shakedown was in many respects a neither-nor operation. The crew was partly trained in being conned from the signal bridge, partly from the pilothouse, but not completely familiar with either. From what point did the captain intend to fight the ship? Where was each man to go in a general-quarters situation? The answers were unclear.

And in due course, that confusion would have its effect on the USS *Pueblo*.

Meantime, a legend was building.

One night Bucher diverted the bartender in the Ballast Tank, the submariners' officers' club, while Tim Harris stole a painting of a nude woman from behind the bar. It took Naval Intelligence to track down the culprits, and to the dismay of the crew, return the attractive booty.

Another night the shore patrol arrested three of the *Pueblo*'s crewmen for being out of uniform. On this point, as on others, I had found it extremely difficult to enforce discipline. All a chastised crewman need do was point to the CO and say, "You think *I'm* sloppily dressed?" These three were by no means in bad shape, however. Two needed haircuts, and the third was wearing blue jeans, the last permitted attire on ship, but not in town. The shore patrol returned them to the ship about 3 A.M., a few minutes before Bucher and Tim Harris came on board. Bucher, according to Tim and the three men, was quite high. He saw nothing wrong with their appearance; moreover, he wasn't about to let anybody give his boys a rough time. He suggested they all pay another call on shore-patrol headquarters. And this time he would do all the talking. That he did, calling the officer in charge a fascist, among other things.

It would be difficult to gauge the importance of the latter incident. The three men were CTs, members of Steve Harris' elite corps. The skipper had stood up for *them*. They too were "Bucher's boys." Probably for the first time since reporting aboard the *Pueblo*, they felt themselves part of the crew. In this sense, Bucher had made a positive contribution to morale and shipboard unity.

Nor did Bucher's stock go down when word got out that

he had been called before the chief of staff of COMSERV-GRU-ONE and censured for his conduct in the incident.

A legend was building. Yet there was something odd about it from the start. It seemed very curious how first in Bremerton, now in San Diego, Bucher seemed almost determined to burn his bridges, and his fitness reports, behind him.

Two other *Pueblo* crewmen had their day with the San Diego authorities. But fortunately in this instance the circumstances were reversed.

Damage Controlman Duane Hodges and Fireman Richard Arnold were walking down the street when they spotted a purse-snatcher. Chasing him, they got the purse back and held the man until the police could be summoned.

Shortly afterward, the San Diego Police Department sent, through regular Navy channels, a citation honoring the two men for their quick action. I took it to Bucher and asked when we could present it.

"Damn it, hold off on that," he told me. "To present it now, we'd have to have a full-dress ceremony, and you know how I hate that."

I did know. Still, the award had been made; it was up to us to see the men got it. Sometime later I brought up the subject again. Bucher's attitude still hadn't changed. The award would have to wait. Meantime, I wasn't to say anything about it to Arnold or Hodges.

While the ship was in San Diego, Carol, Eddie and I managed a quick trip to San Francisco to visit my mother who was still ill. Also, we managed, on one of my rare days off, to take Eddie to Sea World. Steve Harris' wife was away so Carol and I invited him to go along. Later we took him to Carol's parent's home for dinner.

By this time I had gotten to know Steve fairly well and I could sense that something was worrying him. Finally I asked him what it was. Reluctantly he admitted that he was concerned about the skipper's drinking. It seemed to be growing progressively heavier.

I said nothing. As exec, I was in a ticklish position. And as a nondrinker, any opinion I might have was highly suspect.

I had given a great deal of private thought to the matter, but for entirely different reasons. Other officers had told me that Bucher was positively obsessed with the fact that I didn't drink, that he brought up the subject repeatedly in his barroom conversations, that he was sure every time I spoke to him I was looking down on him with the smug attitude of moral superiority.

Was Bucher right? Was I—albeit unconsciously—doing this? I didn't think so. But Bucher obviously believed it true. Why?

Maybe there was a very simple answer, his use of that phrase "looking down." I was 6'1½", Bucher about 5'10". I, of course, did look down on him. Possibly he had some sort of inferiority complex about his height.

But it seemed to me to go deeper than that. Working with him over a period of five months, I had noticed something curious. The things that seemed most to bother him in others were almost always mirror images of his own shortcomings. He was bothered because some of the men seemed to be spending too much time with their families. Another man bothered him because of his devotion to detail. Another because he insisted on following the rules and regulations. And I bothered him because I didn't drink.

But that begged the question. Was Bucher's drinking a problem? I was hardly an expert on the subject. How do you determine such a thing? Certainly not capacity. There were men, I knew, who could drink a fifth a day and still do their work properly. There were others whom a couple of drinks left befuddled for hours. Was it how often he was drunk? Up to this point I could honestly say that I had never, to my knowledge, seen him incapacitated on ship during duty hours. What gauge did you use? I decided, in Bucher's case, that there could be only one standard of measurement. It had nothing to do with how many drinks he had, where he chose to spend his off-duty time, or my personal preferences in regard to the subject. The only valid question could be: was Bucher's drinking such that it had an adverse effect on his job, the preparation of the *Pueblo* for her mission?

Although I didn't admit it to Steve, considering the many times Bucher wasn't available when needed, the number of days he didn't make it to work until afternoon, his confusion over whether he had or hadn't given an order, his inability to follow through on needed projects, I had to come to the conclusion that if Bucher was to be measured against this scale, he would fail to get a passing grade.

A biased, totally unfair judgment? Perhaps.

It was interesting, however, that Steve was concerned also.

I couldn't do anything about what Bucher might read into my expression. But I could go out of my way to avoid conflicts with him.

I had already started doing this, to a certain extent. For example, almost immediately after Tim Harris reported aboard, Bucher had qualified him as officer of the deck. In my opinion, he wasn't ready. He needed considerably more training and experience—more basic exposure to surface Navy—before being made OOD. It really wasn't fair to Tim, I felt, because sooner or later his inexperience would catch up with him, whether on board the *Pueblo* or another ship. But on this subject, as on others, I said nothing, knowing all too well what Bucher's reaction would be.

It was a hell of a way to run a ship, the exec having to go out of his way to avoid encounters with the CO.

And, of course, on a ship as small as the *Pueblo*, there was no avoiding them.

Take the case of the missing binoculars. After colors one night a pair of binoculars disappeared from the pilothouse. When missed the next morning, Bucher asked me to conduct an investigation. I did, quizzing everyone who had

had access to them, even searching the car of a crewman Bucher suspected, but with no success. They might have been stolen. They might simply have been accidentally knocked overboard.

But Bucher wouldn't accept this. At first he charged that the only reason I hadn't found them was that I hadn't looked hard enough. Still later, in the way his memory often altered the facts, he would maintain that I hadn't even conducted an investigation.

Although I kept such thoughts to myself, I couldn't help recalling Captain Queeg and the missing strawberries.

There were times when I had either to disagree with Bucher or fail to do my job as exec. And a part of that job—which brought us into conflict on several occasions—was handling the affairs of the dependents of the crew.

Bucher had a friend in the Long Beach area to whom he wanted to show the ship. The logical solution, of course, would be to have the friend come to San Diego. But, for various reasons, Bucher didn't want to do this. Instead he decided to take the *Pueblo* to Long Beach. Since the Navy would never permit anyone just to borrow a ship for a weekend pleasure jaunt, Bucher decided he would move the *Pueblo* to Long Beach and make our departure to Japan from there. To do this, however, we would have to leave the United States earlier than planned.

But, I reminded him, the wives and families of many of the crewmen were already in San Diego, or on their way there to see us off. Everything had already been arranged. To change the schedule at this late date would upset the plans of at least a hundred or more people.

No, that was the way he wanted it. And that damn well was the way it was going to be.

How he managed it, I still don't know, but he convinced Commander Service Group Three that it would be better if we left from Long Beach.

But then Bucher had a falling-out with his friend. The party was off. Too, his own wife had now decided to come

67

to San Diego for the departure. We would leave from San Diego, after all.

I first heard of the switch one morning while aboard the SERVGRU-THREE flagship, checking scheduling information with her operations officer. Learning I was aboard, the Chief of Staff of SERVGRU-THREE summoned me to his cabin. "What the devil's going on over there on the *Pueblo*?" he asked. "First Bucher wants to leave from Long Beach. Now he says he has to leave from San Diego. Would you please explain to me why he keeps changing his mind?"

All I could do was assure him, more convincingly than I really felt, that Bucher must have a good reason.

So, shortly after dawn on November 6, 1967, the USS *Pueblo* left the continental United States from the port of San Diego.

As soon as we had cleared the harbor and were outside the jurisdiction of the training command, Bucher resumed conning the ship from the signal bridge.

7

All the way to Hawaii, Bucher regaled us with tales about his good buddy, entertainer Don Ho. It was therefore with more than a little anticipation that on the evening of our arrival the whole wardroom complement went to Duke Kahanamoku's in Honolulu for dinner.

Bucher did succeed in getting us a very good table, close to the stage. But when, shortly after Ho came on, Bucher began waving frantically to get his attention, Ho gave him a withering look, making clear that he didn't know him from Adam and was glad of it.

Embarrassed, we pretended not to have noticed.

It was neither the first nor the last occasion on which we would see evidence that Bucher actually believed his own tall tales. Once, when we were having a discussion in the wardroom, the conversation touched on the colleges we had attended. Bucher insisted, with unusual vehemence, that he had a master's degree in petroleum geology from the University of Nebraska. His insistence, however, raised suspicions. Later I looked up his entry in the Officers' Register and found no mention of an advanced degree. There remains some confusion on this point. According to one account of the *Pueblo* case, which relied heavily on Bucher as a source and which he supposedly checked in manuscript form, "He left Nebraska in June, 1953, with a degree in secondary education, an associate degree in geology, and a number of credits toward a master's degree in micropaleontology."

In *Newsweek*'s "Where Are They Now" column, June 8,

1970, Bucher is quoted as saying, "My college degree is in geology. . . ."

According to the biographical fact sheet issued by the U.S. Navy during the Court of Inquiry into the *Pueblo* case, "He received the degree of bachelor of science in education in July 1953. . . ."

Everyone prevaricates sometimes, builds himself up to impress others, embellishes his favorite story for better effect. It is a small and very human failing. I presumed, in the case of Bucher, it was that and nothing more.

I was as yet unaware how real, in Bucher's mind, his fictions could become.

Upon our arrival in Pearl Harbor, one of the first things I had done was to check to see if the auxiliary compressed-air supply had arrived as promised. Part of it had, being airlifted over. But the rest of the shipment, we discovered, had been misdirected to Japan.

We fared little better on our other projects. Considerable time was spent on the steering—we laid over an extra two days for this—but by now we knew that we could only cross our fingers and wait. We still lacked machine guns, and being without them, couldn't hold drills in their use.

By this time it had become apparent to Bucher—from the frozen screams of the OODs—that his idea of conning the ship from the signal bridge wasn't going to work unless he made some modifications. He came up with a drawing of a plexiglass windshield, which he wanted installed in front of the signal bridge, thereby providing at least some protection against the elements. He submitted it to COM-SERVPAC as an urgent, top-priority item.

COMSERVPAC flatly denied the request.

But Bucher had that determined look on his face.

While calling upon the officers of Commander in Chief, U.S. Pacific Fleet (CINCPACFLT), Bucher learned that the target of the *Pueblo*'s first surveillance mission would probably be North Korea.

Recalling the harassment experiences of the *Banner*,

70

Bucher asked what would happen if we encountered a ramming or shooting situation—if the other side suddenly decided to play for keeps?

As Bucher related the conversation to us, shortly after it took place, CINCPACFLT's Assistant Chief of Staff for Operations, Captain George Cassell, replied that "plans for that eventuality exist," and that while there was probably little that could be done for the ship in the way of immediate relief, "there would be retaliation, in force, within twenty-four to forty-eight hours." (Whether Cassell was referring to North Korea or the USSR is unclear. It was Russian ships that most severely harassed the *Banner*. Later, during the Court of Inquiry, Cassell was to deny discussing either contingency plans or retaliation with Bucher.)

Bucher's report of his conversation with Cassell was hardly encouraging. But it was tempered by another statement Cassell allegedly made, that the risk was evaluated as "very low."

The news that we might be deployed off the coast of North Korea surprised me. For some reason I had automatically assumed our target would be the Soviet Union.

My immediate reaction was that the voyage would be much less adventuresome than anticipated.

It would be difficult to decide who was most wrong: Edward R. Murphy, Jr., or CINCPACFLT.

What intelligence information was available on North Korea? I asked Steve.

Very little, he replied. He had picked up some briefs in Hawaii, and would get others in Japan, but in many respects we would be operating in the dark. However, there was one bright light. The *Banner* had operated in those waters in the past, and her schedule called for her to be in Japan while we were there.

Visiting her as soon as possible to pick up all available information on North Korea was top priority, I decided.

Although the staffs of CINCPAC and CINCPACFLT were very much involved in the operations of the AGER program, they had never seen the *Pueblo*. Bucher scheduled an indoctrination tour of the ship. Invited were upper-echelon personnel—commanders, captains, civilians, most of them senior to Bucher in rank. The morning of the scheduled visit, however, we couldn't get Bucher up. Steve Harris and I had to guide the visitors through the ship, carefully steering them past the CO's cabin.

The *Pueblo* stayed in Hawaii only four days. While there, we off-loaded one of the CTs, who was suffering from chronic seasickness. Larry Taylor would not sail with the USS *Pueblo* on her first mission. However, Michael Alexander, his replacement, would.

We steamed out of Pearl about 4 P.M. on November 18. And the steering worked fine, until the next day. By this time I had someone keeping a log of the breakdowns. Between Bremerton, Washington, and Sasebo, Japan, the steering would fail us more than sixty times.

All the old problems remained with us, and in some cases became more acute. Stability worried us more than ever. Once the inclinometer in the pilothouse registered a roll of 47 degrees. We had no reason to believe it was in error.

There were also some unforeseen problems. One day when we stopped to let the men go swimming, a crewman jumped off the side of the ship and landed on the back of Radioman First Class John Mullen. The injury appeared serious, and there was little that Herman "Doc" Baldridge, our hospital corpsman, or I, as medical officer, could do. Fortunately the USS *Samuel Gompers* was in the vicinity and had a doctor on board. Despite an extremely rough sea, we managed to transfer Mullen to the other ship. John Mullen also would not be with us on our first mission.

And there were some familiar problems, in new guise.

I had been aware for some time that the cooks, on Bucher's orders, were using wine and bourbon in the preparation of some of our meals. Suspecting that Bucher was less interested in spicing the food than trying to bait me into a reaction, I said nothing.

72

One of my first assignments on reporting aboard the *Pueblo* had been to triple the ship's alcohol allowance, on Bucher's instructions. I did not question the order, but as a matter of fact argued persuasively for it when the medicinal-alcohol custodian questioned the need for such a large supply for such a small ship. Nor did I say anything about the frequency with which those stocks were broken out for "nonmedicinal" purposes. Bucher was CO, and if that was the way he wanted things done, so be it. Ever since Steve's remark in San Diego, I had given considerable thought to my attitude about Bucher's drinking and had decided that, whatever Bucher might think, there was nothing blue-nosed about it. I was perfectly willing to let Bucher go his way; in return, I expected him to let me go mine.

Unfortunately, Bucher wasn't about to leave it at that. And with what would be known as the "Thanksgiving pies incident," I stepped right into the trap.

One evening, shortly before the holiday, the officers were sitting in the wardroom talking, when, as if on cue, Tim Harris suggested we lace the mincemeat pies with brandy.

When I didn't rise to the bait, Schumacher asked what I thought about it. I replied that maybe we could reach a compromise: spike all the pies but one, leaving that one for those who preferred their mincemeat plain.

"Hell no!" Bucher roared. "We'll put brandy in all the pies, and that's that!"

Thanksgiving Day, Ed Murphy passed up the pie. Which I hated to do, since, spiked or unspiked, I like mincemeat pie. But Bucher had made it a matter of principle.

I'm still not sure what Bucher had expected to accomplish. Perhaps he thought that I would take one bite of pie, get rip-roaring drunk, find I loved the stuff, and thereafter be a constant companion at all his revels. In which case, I suspect he would have been greatly disappointed.

It was, viewed from any angle, a silly way for grown men to behave. Unfortunately, some of my other differences

73

with Bucher during this period, though equally petty, had broader ramifications.

Before my arrival as exec, Bucher had ordered Dave Behr to apply for secret clearances for all the crewmen who didn't have them. Behr not only neglected to do this, he neglected to tell me about Bucher's instructions. While we were under way Bucher asked me about the clearances. I had no idea what he was talking about. He was positive, he said, that he had ordered me to obtain them at Bremerton. Well, he said, since I had goofed again, I was now to stay up all night if necessary issuing a secret clearance to each man who lacked one. I couldn't issue a clearance, I told him, without first applying to Naval Intelligence for a background investigation and then waiting to see what the result of that investigation was. I not only could issue them but I would, he told me, and, per his orders, I did. It was not only contrary to Navy regulations, it was also ludicrous from the standpoint of security to automatically issue clearances to everyone.

Another of our disagreements again concerned the dependents. Eleven families were to join us in Japan. As exec, I had to coordinate their travel plans, arrange flight schedules, and see that everyone had a passport, the proper health injections, and travel allotment. All this had been completed before leaving Hawaii. As is traditional in the Navy, the families were to be flown over shortly after our arrival in our home port, Yokosuka.

Bucher decided that since we were running late, he wanted to delay the arrival of the families three or four weeks. It was almost a replay of our argument over whether the ship should depart from San Diego or Long Beach (and I suspected that more bachelor parties were the real reason behind this change also), but this time the resulting inconvenience was much greater. Most of the families were already packed and had given up their housing, expecting to leave on a certain date.

Bucher's family wasn't coming to Japan. His request for moving expenses had been disapproved, since the Navy

74

had already paid to send his family there on an earlier occasion. This admittedly galled him. My family was coming. Since Carol and Eddie were staying with Carol's parents in San Diego, they wouldn't be badly inconvenienced. But most of the other families, lacking stand-by quarters, would.

Eventually a compromise was reached, with a lesser delay than Bucher wanted, two weeks instead of three or four, but involving a shuffling of eleven schedules nonetheless.

Later, Bucher would make the remarkable admission that he had delayed the arrival of the families in order to "get even with Murphy."

It was the same kind of logic he exhibited when he took his companions on tours of the secret spaces to get even with Steve Harris.

Bucher had a habit of writing "nastygrams," reminders of incidents that he wanted to recall when he made his next fitness reports. Now, with increasing frequency, I was to find, in places I couldn't avoid, little penciled notes with the name "Murphy" featured prominently on all of them.

By the time we reached Japan on December 1, relations between us had deteriorated so badly that each went out of his way to avoid the other.

By this time, however, I had decided to do something about it.

8

Behind the impressive title Task Force 96, was one man, its commander, Rear Admiral Frank L. Johnson, and a small, token staff.

Prior to our arrival in Japan, Task Force 96's "navy" had consisted of one ship, the *Banner*. With the addition of the *Pueblo,* it had, by contrast, what amounted to a "little fleet."

Fortunately for the *Pueblo,* Rear Admiral Johnson wore two hats. He was also Commander, U.S. Naval Forces, Japan (COMNAVFORJAPAN), with a far larger organization. And from the moment of our arrival in Yokosuka, COMNAVFORJAPAN couldn't do enough for us. If anything, Johnson seemed to show a partiality to his mini-fleet.

After the months of buck-passing, it was a most welcome change. Although an old destroyer man, twice winner of the Navy Cross for heroism in World War II, and well aware of the difficulties of trying to conn a surface ship from the signal bridge, Johnson even approved Bucher's request for a plexiglass windshield when Bucher claimed he couldn't put to sea without it.

With the assistance of COMNAVFORJAPAN, one by one the long list of essential repairs diminished. We obtained the rest of the auxiliary compressed-air supply and had it installed. The engines were given a complete overhaul. Again an attempt was made to correct our steering difficulties. Long-sought parts were cumshawed from surface ships, subs, offices, wherever we could find what we needed and could get away with stealing it. Bit by bit, piece by piece, the *Pueblo* was beginning to shape up.

It was here that Bucher and I found common ground. Whenever an obstacle was overcome, we experienced a mutual sense of accomplishment. At these times the officers of the *Pueblo* felt like a team. But it wasn't enough. Those moments occurred too rarely to remedy what had, from both Bucher's and my own point of view, become an untenable situation. Each of us, unknown to the other, was trying to find a way out.

Despite the new-found help, several of our major problems resisted solution. The yeoman we had been promised on arriving in Japan took one look at the *Pueblo* and decided he wanted no part of it. Ordinarily, once ordered to report aboard, he would have had to do so or show good cause why not. But he was an old-timer and threatened not to reenlist. This left us in a difficult position. Our present yeoman was a first-class. EPDOPAC could not authorize another first-class so long as one was already aboard. There remained only one solution. It pleased no one, but it was the only alternative we had: to bust our present yeoman to second-class for failing to do his job properly. But Bucher couldn't bring himself to do this. So the mess in the ship's office continued to accumulate. Whenever I could find time, I did what I could to correct it, but to really succeed I would have had to devote my full energies to that job alone, and, as exec, this was only one of the many necessary duties.

In one area, COMNAVFORJAPAN's extreme helpfulness proved to be a liability in disguise. The *Pueblo* was brand new to the job of intelligence-collecting. No one was quite sure what intelligence publications we would need, once on station. We were aware that many of the standard intelligence pubs we were carrying, while required by regulation, were useless to an AGER, and eventually, after numerous requests, we were able to off-load some of these, including those sent to us by someone in the chain of command who thought we were still an AKL, as we kept receiving an AKL's allotment of intelligence pubs. But with a great many others we couldn't be sure. And whenever we talked to anyone, say an officer in the intelligence section of COMNAVFORJAPAN, he would hand us a few more reports "which might prove helpful." Too, the *Pueblo* was carrying a shipload of specialists. Each had his own needs, whether he was a CT who had to be able to repair a sensitive electronic device, or a cryptographer with code books. Because we were short on stowage space already, the amount of classified material was becoming a major problem.

It was further compounded by the rift between Bucher and Steve Harris. As security officer, Steve was responsible for all the classified publications we carried. But because of their differences over the issue of authority, neither he nor Bucher was inclined to consult with the other any more often than absolutely necessary. Soon we had classified documents literally stacked in the aisles. This was just one of the reasons we were so anxiously awaiting the arrival of the *Banner*. We hoped her officers could give us some guidance on what we would actually require.

The quantity of classified material that was accumulating made it even more imperative that we find additional means of emergency destruction. Weighted canvas bags were not a really satisfactory answer, for inside the hundred-fathom curve, in which we would most often be operating, the water would usually be too shallow for jettisoning, divers being able to recover anything we threw overboard. And the bags would be of no help in destroying the bulky machines in the sod hut.

Bucher really pushed himself on this; this was his "baby," and he was determined that before we left port he would solve this if nothing else. But up and down the chain of command the answer was negative. No one had explosives we could use. Bucher was able to locate a demolition expert, a young lieutenant, who came aboard and inspected the *Pueblo*'s spaces. But he recommended carrying Thermit, and the Navy remained opposed to its use. Ordinarily this wouldn't have stopped Bucher, but the safety factor did concern him. For some reason he was less worried that the Thermit might accidentally ignite than that some crewman might go berserk and trigger it accidentally. Bucher finally said he would be satisfied if he could lay his hands on just a few dynamite kegs with primer fuses, which could be carefully controlled, reducing the danger of scuttling the ship. But despite our continued searching, there seemed to be none available.

By this time the gun controversy, though still by no means resolved, had entered a new phase. In a message that reached us at Yokosuka, Chief of Naval Operations (CNO) in Washington ordered the immediate installation of .50-caliber machine guns on all the AGERs. They were not to go to sea without them.

The score now read: State Department 2, Navy 3.

But it was not yet the last inning.

CNO had suggested that each ship carry three guns, and the ship-repair facility at Yokosuka was charged with designing mounts and finding the weapons. They accomplished the first, installing three mounts on the *Pueblo;* but when it came to the guns, they encountered problems. We had turned in our two guns in San Diego. And the best they were able to forage on such short notice were four guns—two for the *Banner,* two for the *Pueblo.* None was in especially good shape. All were old and subject to misalignments.

Their placement? Despite all arguments to the contrary, Bucher had one mounted midships aft on the boat deck, the other on the forecastle, in the eyes of the ship. Not only did the latter have a restricted firing arc; but also, to reach it you had to go through the door from the passageway in front of the sod hut, zigzag across the deck to the forecastle ladder, go up the ladder, then cross the forecastle to the gun—openly exposed every inch of the way.

Nor was placement the only problem. Polling the crewmen, we discovered that the majority, including our gunner's mate, had never fired a .50-caliber machine gun before. To help prepare them, Schumacher, as weapons officer, conducted a crash familiarization program on a local Marine Corps range. However, because the decision came so late, there was no opportunity to exercise the guns in a general-quarters drill before getting under way.

Rear Admiral Johnson was not pleased with the CNO order. On completion of its current patrol, the *Banner* would have made sixteen missions, all unarmed, all without serious incident. Although she had been involved in a number of touchy situations, she had never been fired on. Her lack of arms, he felt, was her best defense; it bore out her cover of peaceful oceanographic research. Changing the rules might well change the way the game was played. With guns, she could appear provocative. Too, as Johnson would later testify, he did not think that .50-caliber armament provided "a significant defensive capability." On this last point I don't think there was anyone outside Washington who would have disagreed. So two .50-caliber machine guns were installed, an impotent garnish on Bucher's Magic Submarine.

Problems the *Pueblo* had, in abundance. But our navigational team was not among them. From Bremerton on, we had worked closely together, and I was extremely proud of their capability. In addition to myself, as ship's navigator, our team included: Quartermaster Charles Law with whom I had served earlier aboard the USS *Guadalupe,* and the only enlisted man aboard ship to qualify as OOD; Alvin Plucker, also a quartermaster; Signalman Wendell Leach; Clifford Nolte, an electronics technician; and Photographer's Mate Lawrence Mack.

As for our navigational equipment, it was the best available, and while in Japan we spent considerable time checking and rechecking it to see that it was working properly.

Our radar was a commercial model, purchased on the open market; so in the unlikely event the ship fell into enemy hands, nothing secret would be compromised. Calibrated during our conversion at Puget Sound, it needed little maintenance. I did have Nolte make a range check before we left on our mission, however, and once under way he would be charged with making continuous checks of the radar display.

While radar is a device for determining the presence and location of an object (say, another ship, or a shoreline) by (1) measuring the time it takes for the echo of a radio wave to return from it, and (2) determining the direction from which it returns; loran (an acronym for LOng RAnge Aid to Navigation) is a device by which a navigator can locate his position by calculating the time displacement between radio signals from two known stations. On board the *Pueblo* we carried two types of loran, A and C. The difference between them was largely one of frequencies; also, C, being a newer system, had more precision. Under way we would use both, but rely on C more than A. Both models were calibrated in Yokosuka. Although our loran receivers were accurate enough, loran signals are often difficult to identify, due to atmospheric and weather conditions. This can, and frequently does, result in inaccurate loran readings. However, such inaccuracies are obvious to an experienced navigator, and when they occur, they can easily be checked out by other navigational means, such as celestial observations, visual bearings, or—with the captain's permission—fathometer readings or a radar sweep. Permission for the last two was required, because to use either would mean breaking EMCON (emission control) or radio-radar silence. (Radar is an active emitter, loran a passive receiver.) We were under instructions to maintain EMCON until such time as we believed we had been spotted.

We had the azimuth circle calibrated aboard the USS *Samuel Gompers*, while she was in Yokosuka. As for the sextants, we would calibrate them while the ship was at sea. The fathometer, used as a backup navigational aid, checked out fine. The master gyro compass, a Mark 18

Sperry model, exhibited a 1–1.5-degree easterly error. This was not serious, so long as we were aware of it, as we were, and so long as the error remained consistent. Twice daily, in the morning and in the afternoon, we took azimuths to determine the exact degree of error.

Once under way, the steering compass would be checked with the gyro compass every half-hour as well as every time we made a major steering change, while every four hours the master compass would be checked with all the repeaters and the magnetic compass.

Only one aspect of the navigation had given us concern. The pitching of the ship can affect the horizon, throwing off the navigation. Before our departure from Bremerton, I had been afraid that the *Pueblo,* an unstable platform at best, might do this, for pitch she did. But since we had steamed from California to Japan without this happening, it seemed unlikely it would do so later.

All in all, the navigational department of the *Pueblo* was in excellent shape.

Would that had been the case with all departments aboard ship.

The families arrived on December 17. Since there was no base housing available, I had found a house at Ishiki Hyama, near the Emperor's summer palace, but most of the "settling in" I was forced to leave to Carol, even though she was pregnant, expecting our second child the following March, and had to care for young Eddie, two years old now, and a handful. There was little time for reunions. Too much remained to be done aboard ship. I had often heard that Japan was a spectacularly beautiful country; I had little opportunity to verify this. One Sunday Carol and I did manage a quick train trip to Tokyo, but that was it. Nor did it look like there would be much sightseeing in the future. We would be at sea and on station about thirty days, in port seven to ten days, then out again for another thirty. By the time we caught up on the events of the preceding month, we'd be gone again. I did arrange to buy a car, a Japanese-made Tovopet, so Carol would have her own transportation. Since Rose Bucher wasn't coming to Japan, Carol would be senior wife and would have to handle any crises that came up among the dependents.

For Pete Bucher our arrival in Japan was like old home week, except it stretched out more than thirty days. He had left Yokosuka—where he had been on the staff of Submarine Flotilla Seven (SUBFLOTSEVEN)—just one year before. Many of his old sub buddies were still around. If an excuse for a party was needed, and one rarely was, there was always his promotion. When not on the ship, he was usually to be found in the Sanctuary, a submariners' club.

After an initial spurt of activity, Bucher had slipped back into his old habits. Only this time his absences from the ship, the lost mornings, the "incidents," the squabbles often occurring through the haze of a hangover and probably more often than not motivated by it, were much more frequent.

We had little more than a month in Japan before leaving on our first mission. And that time was running out fast. Essential work—work vital to our mission—wasn't getting done. Over and over again I would go to COMNAVFOR-JAPAN headquarters on ship's business and be asked "Where's Bucher? We set up a briefing for him and he didn't show." Or "We're here to help you. That's our job. Admiral Johnson is very unhappy that Commander Bucher doesn't take advantage of us more." The intelligence section was particularly concerned with Bucher's failure to utilize their resources.

The officers took it upon themselves to pick up whatever information they could. Steve located a set of slides showing Russian, Chinese, and North Korean ships we might be expected to encounter, and the officers and a number of the senior enlisted men—those like Law and Leach, whose

83

security clearances made them privy to the target of our possible surveillance—would conduct recognition tests. All this helped, but we were still counting heavily on the assistance of the *Banner*.

She arrived on December 20 and nested abeam with the *Pueblo*. Admiral Johnson arranged several meetings between Bucher and her skipper, Commander Charles Clark, and ordered the other officers of the two ships to work together as closely as possible. Whenever I had a few minutes free, I would spend them on the *Banner*, talking to either Clark or his exec, Dick Fredlund.

The tales they told were more than educational; they were a little hair-raising.

Clark had been CO of the *Banner* for the last seven of her sixteen missions. En route to Vladivostok, the primary objective of his first mission as captain, they had entered the Sea of Japan and followed the Korean coastline northward, passing through the area where the *Pueblo* was tentatively scheduled to operate. But except for one North Korean radar that had briefly tried to lock on them, and several patrol boats and fishing boats that showed no interest, it had been a quiet, uneventful mission. Until they reached their operating area, and then the harassment began. A Soviet nuclear sub kept submerging off one side of the ship, reappearing on the other. Three guided-missile destroyers had taken turns pretending to ram her. One destroyer made a nightly habit of running straight at the *Banner*, then, at the last possible minute, swerving so as to miss her—by less than fifty yards.

This harassment was to be the pattern of most of the *Banner*'s missions. Several times the Soviets had pointed their guns at the ship. A destroyer once signaled, "Heave-to, or I will open fire." After checking his navigation and determining that he was still well outside territorial waters, Clark had decided to call their bluff, proceeding on course at one-third speed. The destroyer did nothing. On another occasion a Soviet ship was so intent on playing games that, after passing within twenty yards of the *Banner*'s stern, she collided with her own relief.

Clark's predecessor on the *Banner*, Lieutenant Robert Bishop, had encountered similar harassment, including one very tense situation, when the ship was surrounded by nearly a dozen Chinese trawlers off Shanghai.

Clark considered himself fortunate that most of the Russian skippers had been excellent ship handlers. Had they not been, he doubted that the *Banner* would still be around.

Fredlund demurred: most of the credit, he felt, belonged to Clark, whose ability at the helm he considered second to none.

I wondered to myself how Bucher would fare in a like situation.

Predicting what the Soviets would do was an impossibility, Clark had decided. Occasionally a Soviet ship would sail by, the crewmen waving in friendly recognition, then turn around and commence some of the most frightening harassment he had ever seen. In the evenings the *Banner* would show movies on the fantail. On more than one occasion the Russians would pull up behind the *Banner* and watch the American films.

With the Russians, Clark believed, we had reached something of a "Mexican standoff." We had spy ships; they had spy ships (their "fishing trawlers," seen so often off U.S. coasts and in the vicinity of U.S. Navy maneuvers, had actually given the United States the idea for the AGER program). If they sank one of ours, they knew we could sink one of theirs.

I did not think to ask Clark what would happen if the same situation occurred with North Korea or China, neither of whom maintained spy ships against which we could retaliate.

I would later give a great deal of thought to the question.

Clark was far from complacent about the situation. He had often thought that if a war was going to start, he would probably be the first to learn of it. Nor did he nurse any illusions about what would happen to the *Banner* if one did start. Although an aircraft-strip alert had been called as standby protection for the *Banner* on one previous occasion, he felt that by the time either planes or ships could reach him his fate would already have been decided.

Like Admiral Johnson, Commander Clark was not happy about the installation of the .50-caliber machine guns. His unarmed status, he believed, had been his one ace in the hole.

The *Banner* had made one other mission off North Korea, this one also uneventful. But Clark admitted that he worried about the North Koreans. Eleven months had passed since the *Banner* had made her last patrol in those waters; a lot could have happened in that time. Also, the *Banner* had spent only a small amount of time in the area, the longest being when they lingered a day and a half off Wonsan. The *Pueblo,* because she could carry more fuel, could remain on station a week or so longer than the *Banner*.

Both Clark and Fredlund warned me about other difficulties they had encountered in the Sea of Japan. Loran was considered only marginally effective from about 11 P.M. to 3 A.M. During daytime loran produced better results, but still presented problems, chief among them reflected signals which were strong enough, and lasted long enough, to be mistaken for the bona-fide thing. As for communications, a delay of up to twelve hours in reaching Japan by radio was not uncommon. I made notes on all this and later passed the information along to Bucher and those most concerned.

Our hopes that the *Banner* could suggest solutions to our more pressing problems were ill-founded. She also was top-heavy, and didn't know what to do about it. She also had steering problems, though not so frequent as ours. And when it came to classified materials, the *Banner* not only carried far more than Clark felt necessary, she also lacked adequate means of emergency destruction.

86

A few days before Christmas, Bucher announced that we would celebrate the holiday by holding a party for a group of orphans.

None of us wanted to deny the orphans a party. But by this late date most of the crew had already made other plans (many had found girl friends within a day after we landed), while those of us who had our families in Japan had been hoping to spend the day with them.

The real reason came out rather quickly. Bucher had been talking to the skipper of "another sub," as he put it, and since his sub was doing it, Bucher didn't want to be outdone.

We had the party, and it was a great success. Charles Law played Santa Claus. There was cake, ice cream, candy, and film cartoons. The orphans enjoyed it, as did the rest of us sharing in their delight. But by now Bucher's sudden whims were beginning to get under the skins of even such ardent followers as Tim Harris.

As the date of our departure grew closer, the work piled up. One night Bucher returned from the Sanctuary and told me that before we left Yokosuka he wanted every egg individually dipped in paraffin and every head of lettuce separately wrapped in waxed paper.

I was so surprised that I asked him to repeat the order to make sure I had heard him correctly. I had.

Having worked in a grocery store, as well as having worked closely with the supply officers on several ships, I knew that lettuce would stay fresh if properly refrigerated; and there was no need to coat the eggs, since all eggs for overseas shipment are automatically treated with preservatives. But telling Bucher anything, once he had made up his mind, was an impossibility.

For example, on our arrival in Japan, Bucher had wanted to make a big impression on his friends who were to be waiting for us on the pier at Yokosuka. And he had. By missing the pier entirely, steaming right by it. When we tried to steer him right, he got angry. He had been in

Yokosuka before; we hadn't. A tug had to come out and guide us back.

Egg-dipping and lettuce-wrapping, although clearly unusual, definitely fell into the province of the supply officer. I passed on Bucher's orders to Tim Harris, and waited for his anguished scream. It came immediately.

I felt sorry for Tim. Like everyone else, he already had his work laid out for him. This idiotic whim of Bucher's would mean taking men badly needed elsewhere away from their duties for several days. By this time, however, I had found a way around Bucher. Admittedly it was sneaky, but the important thing was, it worked.

One of Bucher's closest buddies was Lieutenant Angelo "Flip" Di Filippo, who was on the staff of SUBFLOTSEVEN. Using just the right amount of sarcasm, Flip could talk Bucher out of anything. I cornered Flip and told him our problem. Flip thought Bucher's new scheme hilarious, but promised to see what he could do. The following day Bucher rescinded the order.

By now even some of the crewmen were surreptitiously referring to the *Pueblo* as the USS *Caine*.

There were two parties Christmas week. Bucher's promotion—already celebrated in San Francisco, San Diego, Honolulu, and Yokosuka—culminated in a "wetting-down" party that Bucher gave in a balloon-strewn room of the officers' club on the night of December 28.

After the traditional toasts, the six *Pueblo* officers stood next to the piano, arms around shoulders, grinning, and sang together in disordered harmony. Pictures were taken, and a print given to each of us. But I needn't look at it; the scene remains frozen in memory. At the time, I had reason to believe this would probably be the last time the six officers of the USS *Pueblo* would be photographed together.

About that, I was wrong. Less than a month and a half later we would assemble for another group portrait. Only this time there would be no singing, nor smiles on any of the faces.

That scene, too, is impossible to forget.

Of late, Steve Harris had seemed very concerned about something, a worried look rarely leaving his face. But on the night of Bucher's wetting-down party, he had a delightful time applying a lighted cigar to Bucher's balloons.

I was unaware that behind the façade of seeming joviality, and perhaps contributing more than a little to his air of overfrantic merriment, Steve was seriously considering bursting still another balloon, one which could finish Commander Lloyd M. Bucher's career in the United States Navy.

Although I had guessed that Steve's concern was in some way related to our conversation in San Diego, I was still almost totally unprepared for the bombshell when it came.

"I've got a tough decision to make," he confided to me one night. "I've got to decide whether to pull Bucher's ticket."

"*His security clearance?*" I asked, knowing full well what he meant and realizing the ramifications. If Steve did this, and he had the authority to do so, Bucher would be finished in the Navy. Not only would he be removed from command of the *Pueblo*, he would never again be promoted or given any kind of responsible assignment.

Steve enumerated his reasons. I knew most of them. Bucher's contemptuous disregard for security. The early-morning tours of the secret spaces. The way he left classified material lying around for anyone to see. The wholesale issuing of secret clearances without background investigations. His habit of discussing ship's business in whatever bar he happened to be in. Just a start. The big problem, as Steve saw it, was that Bucher's drinking had reached the stage where it not only had an adverse effect on the readiness of the *Pueblo*, it also constituted a grave danger to the security of the whole intelligence-collection program.

When Steve had first broached this subject in San Diego, I could honestly say that I had never seen Bucher drunk aboard ship during duty hours. I could no longer say that. Since our arrival in Japan, he had been drunk often, on occasion being even too drunk to move the ship. But, unfortunately, this didn't keep him from driving an automobile when he was in no condition to do so. One night he had smashed a borrowed car into the back of a Japanese vehicle. Although no one was seriously hurt—Tim Harris had been riding with Bucher—only the services of an attorney and an out-of-court settlement had kept the affair from coming to the attention of COMNAVFORJAPAN.

Shortly before this, Steve had been forced to pull the clearance of one of his CTs, the last man to be transferred off the *Pueblo*. Although quite young, he had a serious drinking problem. And when he drank, he talked too much.

There wasn't a single thing that the CT had done, Steve said, that Bucher hadn't done also. If anything, his tendency to brag about all he knew was greater. But there was one big difference. Bucher had access to far more sensitive information.

That Steve would even consider such a move indicated how serious he felt the situation had become. Steve was due to report to San Francisco on March 1; this would probably be his last, or next to last, mission. And Bucher would be gone no later than May; his replacement had already been ordered in. The easy way out would be for Steve to ignore the problem, letting the next man handle it if he chose to do so. But if he did, and something happened, he would have to live with the knowledge the rest of his life, Steve said. He admitted he didn't know what to do, that he lay awake nights fearful Bucher might compromise the entire AGER program.

I suspected that Steve had confided in me because he knew I was also agonizing over a not unrelated decision. I was proud of what we had managed to accomplish in outfitting the *Pueblo*, despite all the obstacles we had faced. I believed in the potential of the ship. I felt the whole AGER concept offered tremendously exciting challenges. But I could no longer take Bucher. Not even for just five months. Since our arrival in Japan, I had been trying to find a way to get off the ship. I had approached several people, including Dick Fredlund, the exec of the *Banner,* to see if they would consider a switch. None would.

Not until much later did I learn that at the same time I was trying to find another exec for the *Pueblo,* Bucher was doing the same thing, even asking some of the same people I had approached, although, diplomatically, none of them had told either of us about the other's inquiries. Obviously the word was out: there's bad trouble on the *Pueblo;* don't get involved.

This left me only one choice. It was a difficult one, and, like Steve, I too needed more time to think about it.

Although our sailing order was delayed pending final approval from Washington, by the last week of December we were aware that we would be leaving Yokosuka on January 5, and that, barring a last-minute change, the objective of our surveillance remained North Korea. For a time Bucher considered taking the northern route, but on learning that there was heavy ice in that area, he decided we would go south around the end of the island of Kyushu, then north to the port of Sasebo, and from there deploy for the Sea of Japan to carry out our assigned mission.

This left precious little time for everything we had to do to get ready. Not even all our personnel had yet reported aboard.

During the last days of 1967 our two civilian oceanographers joined us. Harry Iredale, III, was twenty-four and in common with most of the rest of us, this would be his first mission aboard an AGER. The second oceanographer, Dunnie "Friar" Tuck, thirty-six, had sailed aboard the *Banner* in 1967 on patrol off China and the USSR. So we would have at least—or rather, *exactly*—one experienced man aboard.

On one of my last visits to the *Banner* Commander Clark frankly told me how disappointed he was that Bucher

91

hadn't availed himself of more information about the *Banner* and her missions. After all, we were both AGERs, and his experiences, he felt, could prove valuable.

I was still hearing similar complaints from the staff at COMNAVFORJAPAN. One lieutenant commander in the intelligence section was especially unhappy with Bucher's apparent lack of interest in the information they had so carefully compiled.

A former subman, Commander Clark had known Bucher since submarine school. Although we had never exchanged so much as a word on the subject, I was sure that he was well aware of Bucher's habits. Going to his safe, Clark took out a stack of classified documents. "Here, give these to Pete," he said, "and try to get him to read them."

Included were the highly secret trip reports on every one of the USS *Banner*'s previous missions.

They too would sail aboard the *Pueblo* when she left for North Korea.

She looked to be in her mid-teens, and was dressed in typically flashy bargirl attire. The only thing unusual about her was where we spotted her. Not on the street or framed in a lighted doorway, but coming up out of the starboard passageway. She paused a moment to accustom her eyes to the bright morning sunlight, then, with a saucy smile and a friendly wiggle of the hips, stepped from the *Pueblo* onto the bow of the *Banner*, and then onto the pier—to the cheers of appreciative sailors on both ships.

Checking with the watch, I learned that she had come aboard about 3 A.M. with one of the officers.

I made a mental note to check all the compartments before we left on our first mission, to make sure that none of her friends were still aboard.

Our last days in Japan were busy ones. Just a few days before our scheduled departure, the last four CTs reported in. James Kell was replacement for a chief petty officer due for reassignment. Kell volunteered to take just one mission. Ralph McClintock replaced a man still hospitalized following an appendectomy. McClintock was due to be discharged in less than four months. David Ritter replaced the CT whose clearance Steve Harris had lifted. And Don Bailey had come along to help with our communications with Japan.

We were still short a radioman, however, to replace Mullen, the man hurt in the swimming accident.

On January 3 we learned our mission had been approved, and two Marines joined the crew of the *Pueblo:* Sergeant Robert Chicca and Sergeant Robert Hammond. And neither wanted to be aboard. Both their wives were pregnant, Chicca's in her eighth month. But they had still another reason for questioning their assignment. They had been ordered aboard the *Pueblo* as Korean-language experts, to translate monitored North Korean radio broadcasts. Both had studied Korean in language school. But that had been in 1965, and neither had used it since. Chicca thought he might be able to catch a few words, if spoken slowly enough, but that was it. Though Steve Harris was obviously disappointed, there was nothing he could do about it. They were the only men available.

With the arrival of the two "Korean-speaking" Marines, there wasn't a man aboard the *Pueblo* who didn't have a fairly good idea of our destination.

Many were frankly disappointed. The consensus seemed to be: what possible interest could that dinky little country be? It was difficult to get enthusiastic about such an unimportant mission.

It's quite possible Commander Bucher shared the same view.

That same day Admiral Johnson personally inspected the second member of his "little fleet." Although some problems remained—we still lacked adequate means of emergency destruction, and we still had serious doubts about the steering—the admiral was generally satisfied with what he saw. By this time Bucher's plexiglass windshield

93

had been installed. Pausing in his inspection of the pilot-house, Admiral Johnson peered out the port side, then walked over and did the same on the starboard side. "My, you certainly do have excellent vision from here," he said, aiming the remark directly at the skipper. Bucher swallowed hard. It was our first indication that Johnson must have seriously questioned the need for Bucher's fancy sundeck and his plan to conn the ship from the signal bridge.

Bucher had ordered me to make sure that all the pay records were aboard ship before we sailed. There was a good reason for this: if, on our return, we stopped first in Sasebo or some other port, the men could be paid there.

However, after I complied with Bucher's orders, several of the men—Photographer's Mate Lawrence Mack, Radioman Second Class Charles Crandall, and others who had their families in Japan—had approached me asking that their records be left in Yokosuka, so their wives could draw on their pay during their absence.

This seemed a reasonable request, and I had these particular records taken ashore.

The morning of January 4, the day before our departure, the *Pueblo*'s officers were supposed to appear in Admiral Johnson's office at 9 A.M. for a briefing. This was not the hour at which Bucher was accustomed to arise, and he was in a foul humor. While waiting on the pier for a ride up the hill, Bucher asked me if all the pay records were aboard. I told him they were, except for . . . Bucher blew up; I had willfully disobeyed a direct order! The crew's pay records were going to be on board whether they liked it or not, he bellowed, chewing me out with a long series of colorful expletives.

A junior officer learns to suppress his anger. Yet, long after that anger had diminished and I had asked Lieutenant Flip Di Filippo of SUBFLOTSEVEN to talk his old friend Bucher into leaving behind the pay records of those crewmen, I couldn't get Bucher's final statement out of my mind: *"How do you know we'll come back here, Murphy?"* he had shouted. *"How do you know we'll ever return to Yokosuka?"*

Since Yokosuka was our home port, it seemed a very odd thing to say, and all the officers looked at Bucher curiously. Later I asked Steve if there were plans afoot to shift the *Pueblo*'s base of operations elsewhere. Steve was sure no such change was contemplated. I decided Bucher had simply gotten carried away in his argument. That had to be it. I could think of no good reason why the *Pueblo* wouldn't return to Yokosuka.

"What help can we expect if we get into trouble?" Bucher asked the briefing officers.

There was an "on-call" support arrangement with Fifth Air Force and the Seventh Fleet, they assured him. However, much less reassuringly, they added that due to the Status of Forces agreement with Japan, no aircraft could be launched from there. There were jets in South Korea and on Okinawa, but since this particular mission's risk was evaluated as minimal, they wouldn't be placed on strip alert. Nor would there be any large U.S. ships in the immediate vicinity. In short, if we got into serious trouble and needed help, it would be sent, but could take time.

But other than the usual harassment, nobody expected any trouble.

The two briefing officers also stressed that in order to appear as unprovocative as possible, the canvas covers were to be left over the machine guns unless it became necessary to use them. And they were to be used only if we had exhausted all other options.

This point was stressed not only during the briefing but also later in a conversation between Bucher and Admiral Johnson, which Bucher related to us. According to Bucher, Johnson had repeated this several times.

I privately wondered if Admiral Johnson, in reiterating this point so strongly, had sensed that Bucher was inclined to think of himself as the U.S. Navy's version of John

Wayne, and was afraid that he might get gung-ho and decide to start his own war.

That evening, the last night before our departure, I worked late, then took Carol and Eddie to the officers' club for dinner. As we were coming through the lobby, a young lieutenant walked up to me and said, "I've been looking for you." It was a minute before I recognized him as the demolitions expert who had inspected the *Pueblo*. "I found what you wanted," he added with a pleased grin.

Taking him off to the side, I learned that he had located as much TNT as we could use. All we need do was drop by and pick it up the following morning, along with the instructions for its use.

The *Pueblo* wasn't scheduled to leave until 9 A.M. There would be plenty of time to bring it aboard.

Bucher, Schumacher, and several other officers were seated at a table across the room. Unable to contain my excitement, I went straight to them and told Bucher the good news. He was like a little child learning that Santa had brought him what he wanted after all. This was his special project. Now, at the last possible moment, we'd licked this problem, just as we had licked the dozens of others before it! Should the need arise, the *Pueblo* finally had a way to destroy all her classified cargo.

While Bucher was still exulting over the news, I told Schumacher where he could find the TNT and told him to bring it aboard first thing in the morning. As weapons officer, this was one of his responsibilities.

I returned to Carol with a big smile on my face. But I couldn't tell her why I was so happy, and she must have thought me a little strange. Here I was leaving my family for a whole month, and I was beaming with pleasure. But I couldn't help it. We'd solved our greatest problem.

The hours before our departure were frantic. Since the date and time of our sailing were supposed to be secret, the families couldn't come down, although I'm sure all of

96

them knew exactly when we'd shove off. Probably a goodly number of the bargirls in Saki Town did as well. I'd said my good-bye to Eddie before dawn, while he was still asleep. Just maybe, after this mission, he wouldn't have to have an absentee father anymore. I had kissed Carol good-bye at the same time, not expecting to see her again until February 4, when we were scheduled to return.

Several days before, on an odd impulse which I still can't explain, I'd bought Carol a Valentine and left it where she would find it, writing on the envelope, "Not to be opened until February 14." Though we were due back ten days before that, I couldn't shake the feeling that for some reason we might be delayed.

But I did see Carol again, just before the ship left. For some time she had been looking for a hand-warmer for me, one that would fit inside a glove. Clark and Fredlund had warned me what the weather could be like this time of year in the Sea of Japan. That last morning, Carol had located one, and a pair of gloves, and rushed down to the ship to give them to me.

There was only time for a quick good-bye. Everything seemed to have been delayed until the last minute. Our sailing order still hadn't arrived; we'd have to depart without it. We were so rushed that I had to abandon my intention of checking to see if there were any women aboard; just making sure all the crew was there was job enough. No one likes to end a last night in port. There is a tradition, sanctified not by regulation but by practice, of seeing how close you can shave the time and still make the ship. Some finished with just minutes to spare.

Adding to the confusion was the fact that we were still short a radioman. There was only one service-force ship at Yokosuka, the USS *Mars*. After some frantic telephoning, I convinced her exec—a full commander—that our needs had priority over theirs. I had to run over to the ship, however, and pick up the man. Less than a quarter-hour before our scheduled departure time, Radioman Second Class Lee Roy Hayes came aboard, griping every step of

97

the way. And I couldn't really blame him. He had been yanked off the *Mars* so fast that he hadn't even had time to call his girl and tell her he couldn't see her that night.

Hayes was the last man to board the USS *Pueblo*. Now, for the first time, we had a full crew of eighty-three—seventy-five enlisted men, six officers, and two civilians.

Bucher had brought a number of friends aboard for an eggnog party. With perhaps just a trace of sarcasm, I asked him if he would like to take command.

After the last guest had gone ashore, he climbed up onto the signal bridge; and while the loudspeaker was playing the ship's theme song, the Herb Alpert—Tijuana Brass rendition of "The Lonely Bull," the USS *Pueblo* steamed out of Yokosuka channel and headed south.

It was not until we were well under way that I got an opportunity to ask Schumacher if he had had any trouble bringing the TNT aboard.

Sheepishly he admitted, "I didn't get around to it."

For a moment I was so stunned I couldn't speak. Then I became so incensed that I couldn't trust myself to. Searching out the captain, I told him what I had just learned.

Bucher expressed not the least bit of surprise; he was already aware that Skip had goofed. Nor did he really appear concerned. Maybe we could find some in Sasebo when we stopped there. If not, we'd have another chance to pick it up before leaving on our next mission.

But for the USS *Pueblo* there would be no second chance.

9

Within hours after leaving Yokosuka, the *Pueblo* was caught in the rebellious waves of a young sea. To a sailor, a young sea means a newborn storm, with swells and troughs alternating in rapid succession. To keep the ship on course, two men were needed at the helm. Even without steering problems—and despite all the work that had been done in Yokosuka, we still had them—considerable dexterity was required just to keep her headed fair.

In crew's berthing, shoes floated through drenched compartments; men, cracking heads and shins, swore loudly, then with the next roll cracked them again; and even the thought of food brought an instantaneous reaction. Earlier, the "old salts" had ridiculed the CTs for their seasickness; now, as they leaned over the side, hoping the wind wouldn't change, you couldn't tell one from another.

Inside the sod hut the still-unsecured chairs raced across the deck from bulkhead to bulkhead, often tossing their occupants out before they crashed.

Below, in the auxiliary engine room, the two generators which supplied power to the research spaces broke down. Although Lacy's personnel succeeded in fixing one by using parts from the other, to make both operative we would have to get replacement parts in Sasebo, if they were available at all.

As the pitches and rolls grew worse, the men began seeing in the storm an omen: something's wrong with the *Pueblo*, has been from the start; never trusted her from the moment I saw her; I had a feeling about this mission.

You can squelch such talk. But not for long. Once it starts, it spreads.

Then, on the following day, the storm subsided. And the men remembered that this was the second such blow the *Pueblo* had survived, her second baptism of the elements. Some of the rolls measured 57 degrees, but she had made it, remaining upright despite her topside weight. The old girl was all right, after all. Again one began to feel affection for the little ship.

The sail order finally came in over the teletype, while we were still en route to Sasebo. Decoded, it read:

DEPART SASEBO JAPAN WHEN RFS ABOUT 8 JAN 68. CHECK OUT OF MOVREP SYSTEM AND PROCEED VIA TSUSHIMA STRAITS TO ARRIVE OPAREA MARS ABOUT 10 JAN. (The sail order made the common error in referring to Tsushima Strait in the plural.)

Not only wouldn't we be ready for sea by January 8; it looked as if we wouldn't even be arriving in Sasebo by then.

MOVREP SYSTEM meant movement-reporting system. After going through Tsushima Strait, between South Korea and Japan, we were to proceed to the first of our three operating areas. These had been code-named Mars, Venus, and Pluto. The northernmost boundary of Pluto was below Vladivostok, USSR. Venus and Mars were farther south. All three paralleled the rugged North Korean coastline.

ATTEMPT TO AVOID DETECTION BY SOVIET NAVAL UNITS WHILE PROCEEDING OPAREA MARS.

Intelligence had alerted us to the presence of two Soviet ships in the vicinity of Tsushima Strait. The pair—a Rigel-class destroyer and a tanker—were apparently moving back and forth between Sasebo, Japan, and Pusan, South Korea, monitoring shipping in both ports. Although we would try to avoid them at this early stage of our mission, later we were to watch the watchers, in an attempt to learn exactly what they were up to.

100

OPERATE OPAREAS MARS, VENUS, AND PLUTO,
CONCENTRATING EFFORTS AREA(S) WHICH APPEAR
MOST LUCRATIVE.

The length of time we remained in an area was left to our discretion. If Steve felt his "electronic fishing" was especially good in any one spot, we would concentrate on it.

DEPART OPAREAS 27 JAN AND IF NOT UNDER
SURVEILLANCE, MAINTAIN STRICT EMCON CONDITION.
PROCEED SOUTH ALONG KOREAN COAST TO VICINITY
TSUSHIMA STRAITS.

INTERCEPT AND CONDUCT SURVEILLANCE OF SOVIET
NASIMA STRAITS.

This would be phase two of our mission—observing those two Soviet ships. Had the crew known of these instructions, they might have been able to generate more excitement about our assignment.

TERMINATE SURVEILLANCE TO ARRIVE SASEBO 4 FEB
68. EARLIER DEPARTURE AUTHORIZED TO ENSURE TEN
PERCENT ONBOARD FUEL UPON ARRIVAL SASEBO.

This would put us back in Yokosuka about February 6 or 7, if all went well. Maybe a few days later, since it looked as if our departure from Sasebo wouldn't be on schedule. But still, home plenty of time before Valentine's Day.

There followed a number of SPECIAL INSTRUCTIONS:

CPA TO KORCOM/SOVIET LANDMASS/OFFSHORE ISLANDS
WILL BE THIRTEEN NM.

The *Pueblo*'s closest point of approach to the Korean Communist coastline, the Soviet landmass, and the offshore islands of either, would be thirteen nautical miles.

International law, as accepted by the Convention of the High Seas, adopted by the United Nations Conference on the Law of the Sea in Geneva in 1958, prescribes as territorial waters a distance of three miles offshore. The United States was a party to this agreement. Some of the Communist countries, however, including North Korea, claim their territorial waters extend out twelve miles. While we

101

might differ with them over this point, our instructions were explicit. We were to observe the twelve-mile claim, plus a one-mile buffer zone, for safety's sake.

UPON ESTABLISHING FIRM CONTACT WITH SOVIET
NAVAL UNITS, BREAK EMCON AND TRANSMIT DAILY
SITREP.

Emission control would be broken, and a daily situation report sent out only when we had been spotted.

OPERATE AT LEAST FIVE HUNDRED YDS AS NECESSARY
FOR VISUAL/PHOTO COVERAGE . . . [THIS] APPLIES
REGARDING CONDUCT IN EVENT OF HARASSMENT OR
INTIMIDATION BY FOREIGN UNITS.
DO NOT INTERFERE WITH SOVIET EXERCISES BUT
MAINTAIN A POSITION ON THE PERIPHERY FOR
OBSERVATION PURPOSES.
IF UNABLE TO ESTABLISH OR GAIN CONTACT WITH
SOVIET UNITS WITHIN TWENTY-FOUR HOURS ARRIVAL
TSUSHIMA STRAITS, ADVISE ORIG. IMMEDIATE
PRECEDENCE.

They saved the kicker for last:

INSTALLED DEFENSE ARMAMENT SHOULD BE STOWED OR
COVERED IN SUCH A MANNER AS TO NOT ELICIT
UNUSUAL INTEREST FROM SURVEYING/SURVEYED
UNIT(S). EMPLOY ONLY IN CASES WHERE THREAT TO
SURVIVAL IS OBVIOUS.

With the exception of a few biblical passages, it is doubtful if so few words have been so oft interpreted. Yet the meaning is crystal clear. The .50-caliber machine guns were to be uncovered and used only if there was an obvious threat to the ship's survival. This did not, as some would contend, prohibit the *Pueblo*'s skipper from uncovering and using the guns. On the contrary, the orders admitted there might be occasions which called for such use. That determination it left solely to the CO, or, if he was incapacitated, the exec. EMPLOY ONLY IN CASES WHERE THREAT TO SURVIVAL IS OBVIOUS: those ten words would long haunt not only the crew of the USS *Pueblo* but also the entire U.S. Navy.

102

On the way to Sasebo, Bucher did try out the guns, firing a few short bursts himself, then turning them over to the gunner's mate to do likewise. But no attempt was made to run drills in their use.

Because of the storm, it was January 9 before we reached Sasebo. That same day, Rear Admiral Norvell Ward, Commander, Service Group Three, talked to Bucher, then inspected the *Pueblo*. Ward would later state that when he asked Bucher about the *Pueblo*'s problems, Bucher mentioned nothing to him about the need for additional destruct devices. In Bucher's defense it could be said that Ward, although a rear admiral, was not cleared for information about the *Pueblo*'s actual intelligence operations. However, this did not keep Bucher from discussing the need for destruct devices with the demolitions expert and others in Yokosuka; and Ward, who had administrative control over the ship, was, after all, in charge of seeing that she had all the equipment she needed.

Following the inspection, and before giving permission to go ashore, Bucher assembled the crew on the mess decks for a short speech. Since the contents of the sail order were restricted to a few persons, most of the crew considered the rumor that North Korea was our objective was scuttlebutt. Bucher wanted to bring an end to the speculation.

Occupied with ship's business, I didn't attend the meeting. However, I did hear about it in detail from several of those present, and this account is reconstructed from their recollections.

"I know you've all been wondering where we're going and how long we're going to be gone," he began. "Well, it's none of your business. This is classified information. So stop surmising.

"What I can tell you," he went on, "is that our mission is necessary, and it is perfectly legal. And that is all you need to know."

Despite his boyish I-know-something-I-can't-tell-you approach, Bucher's talk made sense, at least from the standpoint of security. If told our schedule, it was inevitable that at least a few of the crew would succumb to the temptation to make future dates with some of the comelier bargirls.

But, in typical Bucher fashion, he couldn't leave it at that. "Some of you are already making plans for when we return," he said. "All I can say about that is, don't. We may not be back for a whole year."

If by his remarks Bucher had intended to decrease speculation, he failed miserably. With this he not only doubled the talk, he left the crew nervous and ill at ease.

The officers knew what Bucher meant. But few others did. If on completion of our mission there remained enough fuel, Bucher was thinking of returning to Yokosuka via Shimonoseki, the strait which separates the Japanese islands of Honshu and Kyushu, in this way bypassing Sasebo entirely. But Bucher didn't specify Sasebo in his remarks; he gave the impression that he might be talking about Japan.

Just more Bucher histrionics? Perhaps. Yet Bucher seemed determined to give the impression that he was en route to some kind of rendezvous with destiny.

One had the feeling he was acting out the role of a sub commander from some favorite World War II movie.

And maybe he was. If so, one needed only a single guess as to its star.

As events transpired, he was to be in error only about the time. For the crew of the *Pueblo* there would be no return to Japan.

We remained in Sasebo longer than planned, waiting for the replacement of a key piece of Steve's electronic test equipment to be flown in by special courier. During this time we solved one big problem, made a very small and all too temporary dent in another, and failed at all the rest.

Chief among the failures was the inability to locate either TNT or Thermit. So the *Pueblo* would sail without sufficient destruct devices. From my own personal knowledge, I can't say whether there was even an attempt to locate either while we were in Sasebo. Following the incident in Yokosuka, Bucher left this to Schumacher. If either he or Bucher made inquiries in Sasebo, they didn't mention it during the months ahead.

Next in importance were the parts needed to repair the generator. They were unavailable and we would have to leave with it inoperative. Then there was the fact that our internal communications still left much to be desired. Also, we were still top-heavy. And we had failed to find a way to secure the chairs in the sod hut. So it went on down the list of unsolved problems.

The successes: *Finally* the ship's steering was repaired, after nearly seventy breakdowns since Bremerton. And, obtaining a "hazardous-duty allowance," Steve was able to off-load some of the classified intelligence pubs. Not enough, however.

The question is often asked: were all the classified documents the *Pueblo* carried really necessary?

To that there is a simple, emphatic answer: no. But with an important qualification: since no one either aboard or ashore appeared to know for sure which ones were necessary and which ones weren't, we had to sail with them all.

For Bucher, Sasebo was the last chance to party. He made the most of it. When Captain Forrest A. Pease, the chief of staff for COMNAVFORJAPAN, called asking for Bucher, I had to cover. In a way it was fortunate that we hadn't finished laying the lines that would permit us to route outside calls directly into the individual officers' cabins. For though it was still early in the evening, Bucher was too far gone to answer.

COMNAVFORJAPAN was anxious to do anything possible to hasten our departure. Had Lieutenant Harris' equipment arrived, and would we be able to depart the morning of the eleventh? I assured the chief of staff that both answers were affirmative.

105

If COMNAVFORJAPAN had any last-minute questions or instructions they wished personally to direct to Bucher, they had missed their chance.

Carol and I had been separated only a few days, yet it suddenly became the most important thing in the world that I talk to her, feel the warmth in her voice, let her know how much I loved her. If there is anything truly inscrutable in the Far East, it is the Japanese telephone system. The likelihood of even reaching Hyama seemed remote, yet, miraculously, after searching the base for an open line, I succeeded in contacting her on the very first try.

Although unaware of the nature of our assignment, Carol knew all too well that I was unhappy about the situation aboard the *Pueblo*. More often than I liked to remember, I had come home late at night thoroughly frustrated over my failure to obtain some necessary repair or to interest the CO in material I felt important to our mission. Carol listened, understood, and tried in a multitude of little ways to relieve the pressure I was under. Being a service wife is rarely easy. Yet through the hectic years of our marriage Carol's only complaints had been humorous ones. She was aware that I was agonizing over an important decision. Although it was one that would affect us both, she had not tried to influence me one way or the other, realizing that this was a choice I had to make myself. I now told her I had made up my mind. Starting with my return, our life would be different. No more long separations. Eddie would finally have a full-time father. As would "Shoop Shoop," who was expected in March. (I suspect that most parents have interim nicknames for their children before they are born. When Carol was pregnant with Eddie, she had yawned all the time. Jokingly we had called him "Hum Hum." Although we were hoping our second child would be a girl, and had tentatively decided on the name Victoria Lynn, the nickname had been derived from a catchy little child's rhyme "Shoop shoop hula hoop.")

106

And I would have the time to sell the family business. I knew that still disturbed my mother.

I could tell that Carol was relieved, not so much because of the choice I had made as the fact that the worrying was over. When I finally hung up, the sound of her voice remained with me. I would savor it often in the days ahead.

We had scheduled our departure from Sasebo for 6 A.M., before dawn, so as to slip out of port unnoticed if the Soviet ships happened to be in the vicinity.

At 5 A.M. a courier arrived with a new shipment of classified documents that someone up the chain of command had thought "the *Pueblo* just might need."

This single delivery, which went to Steve, more than compensated for all the pubs he had been able to unload.

Not all the paper we carried was classified.

Bucher, and Bucher alone, had forced me to the decision I had made. His peculiarities—many of which had seriously contributed to the unreadiness of the *Pueblo*—had left me dispirited. When we had made progress in one area, Bucher had counteracted it by failing to carry through in another. His unavailability when there was vital work to be done, his habit of playing hopscotch with the chain of command, his lax discipline policies, his flouting of regulations, his general tendency to pass the buck, his shortcomings as a CO—all these things led me to consider what, after more than seven years in the Navy, was a major step. The failure to bring aboard the TNT—which I felt, and still feel, Bucher was as responsible for as Schumacher—provided the final tipping of the scales.

Had I been able to assess the situation coolly, rationally, and from a distance, I would have realized that Bucher was a misfit, an oddball, the mistake that turns up in any system. But by now his antics had so embittered me that I lacked that perspective. I had served under a number of excellent COs in the past; the irresponsible actions of one bad one made me forget all the rest. In my profound dis-

107

gust, I blamed not Bucher but the U.S. Navy. All I could think was: if the Navy can entrust such a man with a command, and an important one at that, then this isn't the place for me.

I wasn't even going to wait to learn Steve's decision about whether he would pull Bucher's clearance.

When the USS *Pueblo* sailed from Sasebo, Japan, on the blustery winter morning of January 11, 1968, locked in my safe was a rough draft of my resignation from "Bucher's Navy."

I'd have to put up with the guy for just this one mission. Knowing that, I felt freer than in a very long time. That feeling, however, was to be short-lived.

10

Tsushima Strait is some sixty miles long and forty miles wide. With luck, we felt we could steam through without being spotted by the Soviet ships. And luck was with us: we didn't even catch a glimpse of our Russian counterparts. But something else was waiting for us at the end of the strait as we entered the Sea of Japan—a winter storm, the kind about which Clark and Fredlund of the *Banner* had warned us.

On Bucher's instructions, I charted a course that would keep us close to the Japanese coast the first day, hoping the weather would be better here, hoping too that among the fishing boats and other ships we would be less conspicuous.

The latter was wishful thinking at best. With all her rounded domes, multiple antennae, direction finders, and other protuberances, the *Pueblo* was about as inconspicuous as a billowy maternity dress. From even a good distance you could see that she was pregnant with electronic gear.

The first day out, we lost another generator, one of the two that supplied the ship's power. If another broke down, we'd have to switch to the small auxiliary and abort the mission. The steering malfunction was in the past, however. That, fortunately, was one of the few problems we had been able to off-load in Japan.

The second day, January 12, we made a run for it across the Sea of Japan toward Korea. But there was no outrunning the storm. As we headed northward, parallel to the

Korean coastline, its icy blasts remained a constant companion.

Most of my time now was spent in the pilothouse or abaft it in the charthouse. Although as navigator I didn't have to stand set watches, I did have to take morning and evening star fixes and had to be available whenever there were any questions about the navigation. Since on EMCON we couldn't light off the radar except when absolutely necessary, this was fairly often. Earlier, as mentioned, I had been concerned that the ship's lack of stability might affect the navigation. I needn't have worried. The majority of the fixes I personally took were close to classic textbook problems. The sextant, the star shots—almost all were pinpoint fixes. But I knew better than to get overconfident. The erroneous loran readings were frequent enough to be called commonplace. Too, although we had several seasoned navigators—Bucher and Law the best of the lot—not everyone was as reliable. Coming around the southern tip of Kyushu, en route to Sasebo, we had nearly plowed into a reef. Tim Harris had been OOD. I had given him the course, but, due to his lack of navigational experience, he had neglected to make the necessary corrections. Fortunately someone had spotted a light dead ahead. But Tim was catching on. At first he was seasick much of the time, but he was now beginning to get his sea legs.

As we moved north, the weather grew colder, and shipboard activities settled into a routine—watches, meals, afternoon and evening movies on the mess decks or in the officers' wardroom. It could have been any routine voyage. But it wasn't, and though not everyone knew our sail order, there was a different feeling aboard ship—not apprehension exactly, rather a kind of waiting.

In the crew's quarters the poker game rarely stopped, one man dropping out to be replaced by another.

Boredom began to set in.

But before it had time to catch hold, the weather worsened. A freezing-cold wind descended from Siberia. There was snow now. And ice. With all our topside weight, danger was acute. Just four inches of ice high up on the ship, and over we would go. It would be that simple, and that quick. A special de-icing team was organized under the direction of First Class Bosun Mate Norbert Klepac. Steam hoses were turned on the decks; the water refroze before it had a chance to roll off. Wooden mallets and salt were broken out, and the men put to work chipping ice off decks, handrails, and equipment. It had to be done carefully, otherwise you could chip away paint, wires, or a fixture.

The snow and ice were so bad now that Bucher gave up trying to conn the ship from the signal bridge and moved back down to the pilothouse. But only temporarily. He wasn't about to admit his idea impractical. When weather improved, back up he went. So up and down the conn shifted.

My own relations with Bucher matched the weather. One day he went into the ship's office looking for some papers. He found them, finally. And much else. Now, when it was far too late to obtain a replacement, he called the yeoman up for a Captain's Mast and busted him to second class. Most of his rage, however, he reserved for me. I took it. Knowing I had only to bide my time, it should have been a little easier. It wasn't.

By January 14 we were about parallel to Wonsan, North Korea's major seaport, but well out to sea, rarely coming in closer than thirty miles. Still, we now caught occasional glimpses of land.

Speculation increased. The *Pueblo* had a pretty savvy crew. Many of the men had already figured out that we were off the Korean coastline. However, it wasn't necessary to guess. One man always claimed to have "the straight poop": Communications Technican Michael T. Barrett. Barrett, who had been nicknamed "Barnyard," was the *Pueblo*'s official scuttlebutt expert. He could tell the most outrageous falsehood in such a convincing manner that even if you knew better you walked away half-believing him. Had he said we were approaching Hawaii, one would have begun making plans for a luau—despite the snow and ice.

Of the eighty-three men aboard, less than a dozen, excluding the CTs, actually knew the ship's mission. Of that number, probably only two were really enthusiastic about it: Tuck and Iredale, our civilian oceanographers. The U.S. Naval Oceanographic Office's charts of North Korea's eastern coastline were Japanese-made, and dated back to the 1930's. The information they hoped to gather would be extremely helpful in updating not only maps but also all other hydrographic studies. Now periodically we would stop the ship so they could make a Nansen cast. Although time-consuming, taking the better part of an hour, this was a fascinating operation. A steel cable was lowered into the water. Attached to it at measured intervals were bottles, upside down. Once the cable was played out, a lead weight was slid down it, upending the bottles, which then filled with water from the various depths. Returned to the surface, the temperature and salinity of the water were then measured and recorded.

We were getting close now. On January 15 we headed farther out to sea, and with no other ships in sight, practiced removing the tarpaulins, loading and firing the machine guns. While setting no new speed records, we did prove that, should the necessity arise, the guns could be fired even under conditions of heavy icing. But neither Bucher nor Schumacher felt it necessary to run through the general-quarters drill.

The guns were recovered. We hoped to test them again at a later date. What we couldn't know was that we had uncovered them for the last time.

On January 16, a bone-chilling day that made me doubly grateful for the hand-warmer Carol had bought, the *Pueblo* reached the northernmost limits of her operating area, the 42nd parallel, just below Vladivostok, even with the boundary separating North Korea and the Union of Soviet Socialistic Republics.

We were finally on station.

112

The change in the CTs was immediately obvious. For a full year many of them had been assigned to the *Pueblo*, and, with the exception of a short period when Steve tested some of the equipment by monitoring the message traffic and locating the whereabouts of other U.S. Navy ships, they had been working outside their specialties, quite often at what they considered menial chores. You could actually see the difference, as they straightened up and set to. This was what they had been trained for. They were now in their element.

Since they were no longer available for other duties, these jobs automatically transferred to the other crewmen, and resentments arose. Nor was this the only cause of friction. In the months they had been together, many of the CTs and the regular crewmen of the *Pueblo* had become close friends. Now the regular crewmen wanted to know what was going on, but the CTs, under strict orders from their detachment head, couldn't tell them. Not being "in the know" grated on some of the men. Not too surprisingly, some of the CTs also made the most of the situation, on occasion even slamming the door of the sod hut in an inquisitive face. The old division, for a time almost nonexistent, was back.

The change in Steve Harris was pronounced too. He had a job to do; he wanted to do it, without interruptions. From here on in, his manner made clear, he wasn't about to take any of Bucher's gaff. He couldn't care less about the details of shipboard routine. Bucher was placed in a position somewhat analogous to that of a taxi driver, his passengers telling him where they wanted to stop and how long they wanted to stay at each place.

The wounds, never healed, were rubbed even rawer in the salt air of the open seas.

Our schedule called for us to head south, parallel to the North Korean coastline. Four areas were of special interest to U.S. intelligence—the ports of Chongjin, Songjin, Mayang Do, and Wonsan. That same day we cruised south to a point off Chongjin, dipping in closer to shore than we had been at any previous time, fifteen miles. With the "Big Eyes," our 22-inch binoculars, you could see the smoke from the factory chimneys.

We lay to there for the rest of that day and all the next, hoping to sneak a look at shipping and military installations. From this point on, the need for precise navigation was critical, the getting of it extremely difficult. Still in EMCON, we were in an environment almost wholly absent of the usual navigational aids. Such visual helps as lighthouses, installations, and other landmarks were uncharted or did not exist. With the exception of a few mountains, this was unfamiliar coastline. While Steve and his men were sleuthing, and the *Pueblo* was laid to and wallowing, we spent a good bit of our time trying to pick up and correlate navigational information that could be used in updating our maps. It wouldn't help us, but it could be of great aid to the next ship that came along. Fredlund had warned me about the difficulty of obtaining fixes; it's catch as catch can, he said. If anything, he understated. Although ideally I wanted to take fixes every twenty minutes, when inexperienced men were on the bridge it often took at least that long to take just one. Whenever there was any serious question about our position, I would get the CO's permission to break EMCON just long enough to get a few pings on the fathometer or to make a quick sweep of the radar.

Twice a day Tuck and Iredale took Nansen casts. Each morning Kenneth Wadley, the gunner's mate, checked to make sure the canvas covering the machine guns wasn't frozen over.

Our first stop was a disappointment. We spotted very little shipping, freighters and fishing boats mostly. As for Steve's equipment, it worked well enough, but he just wasn't getting the raw data he expected.

One thing he did learn, however. The North Koreans had picked us up on their radar. We discussed this at some length, in the pilothouse, then later in the wardroom. The consensus was that the North Koreans had just picked us up on a sweep and had no idea what they had.

Steve wanted to move on. On the night of the seventeenth, under cover of darkness, we deployed farther south, arriving off Songjin the next day.

By this time we had established our mission pattern: out twenty to twenty-five miles at night, so there was no possible chance of accidentally drifting into territorial waters; in sixteen to thirteen miles from shore during the day. As a further precautionary measure, Bucher had Law cross-hatch on our maps, in red pencil, an area thirteen miles from shore or any island. This area was to be off limits at all times—with no exceptions. A blue line was then made a mile farther out, fourteen miles from shore or any island. The *Pueblo* was not to cross this line, Bucher instructed the OODs, unless he personally was on the bridge.

The pickings at Songjin were only a little better. Several types of defensive radar were spotted, and some message traffic was monitored and recorded. On the positive side, Steve's CTs were learning to work as a team—after all, the primary purpose of the mission. If nothing else, Tuck and Iredale were accumulating an impressive amount of oceanographic data. But we had hoped for more.

After two days off Songjin, Steve decided to move farther south. American intelligence had reason to believe that North Korea had her submarine fleet, consisting of four obsolete Russian boats, based at Mayang Do. We arrived there on the night of the nineteenth. The next morning we looked for the subs, but saw nothing of them. Possibly they were at Wonsan, which was also used as a sub base, and which was still ahead on our agenda. We did see two large merchantmen leaving the port, but leafing through our identification pubs, we were unable to find corresponding silhouettes. We guessed from certain similarities that they might be from one of the Balkan countries. But identification was by no means positive.

Had they spotted us also? We were inclined to doubt it.

115

I wasn't on the bridge during the afternoon of the twentieth when Steve reported one of his antennae had stopped functioning. As related to me later, two men were sent aloft to replace the inoperative equipment. Bucher had the conn at the time. To minimize the roll, he headed into an off shore sea. In turning, however, he passed the thirteen-mile line, going in to about 12.8 miles from shore—violating not only his own instructions but also our sail order.

But still, however, well outside the claimed twelve-mile limit.

Perhaps anticipating my reaction, Bucher instructed Law, "Don't tell Murphy about this." He didn't, until much later.

Which was perhaps best, for I had other things on my mind. Shortly before this, Steve had confided to me, "They've got fire-control radar locked on us now."

We had anticipated this might happen, at some point. And since we were well out to sea, this did not mean we were in any danger, nor did it even mean we had been identified. We may well have been just another blip on their scope, possibly one of a number. Yet, realizing that they were watching us was disconcerting.

For just a moment I was able to put myself in the place of the North Koreans.

It was just at dusk, on January 21, that we spotted the ship, steaming southward at about twice our speed. Calling Photographer's Mate Mack to the bridge, we had him take pictures of her. It was too dark, however, to get clear shots. But as she passed, about five hundred yards off our port bow, we could see a single man on deck, and Steve was able to make a positive identification of the ship. She was North Korean, a modified SO-1 subchaser. After passing us, she proceeded south toward Wonsan.

This was the first military craft we had encountered since arriving on station. Again there was a discussion on the bridge. Had we been spotted? She had passed close. Still, it was almost dark, and she had shown no apparent interest. Lacy was sure she had seen us. Schumacher, Steve Harris, and I were unsure, but were inclined toward agreement with Bucher, who was positive she had not.

Our orders were clear. We were to break EMCON and send out a situation report only when firm contact had been made.

Bucher decided it hadn't. The radio remained silent. That night we moved farther south, to take up station off Wonsan.

That same night a team of over thirty North Korean shock troops, having successfully crossed the demilitarized zone several days earlier, made a raid on the Blue House, the Seoul home of South Korean President Park Chung Hee. Their assassination attempt came within one hundred yards of succeeding.

For weeks prior, North Korea's Radio Pyongyang had been broadcasting propaganda attacks on both the United States and South Korea, charging them with alleged invasions of North Korea's airspace and territorial waters. The broadcasts were heavy with threats of what North Korea would do the next time such incidents occurred.

Along the demilitarized zone, instances of North Korean belligerency increased at a rate unmatched since the cease-fire.

No one thought any of these events important enough to pass on to the USS *Pueblo*.

We missed out on another bit of news. On January 22 the gun controversy between the Navy and the State Department was finally resolved. As a result of the study begun while we were still in Bremerton, CNO decided that henceforth all AGERs would be armed not with the largely ineffectual .50-caliber machine guns but with much more formidable 20-mm cannons. Twin 20's were to be mounted on the *Banner*, *Pueblo*, and *Palm Beach*.

For the *Pueblo*, the decision came just 11 days too late.

117

It was warmer now, and ice no longer a major problem. We were due east of Wonsan when, at 12:25 on the afternoon of January 22, the watch reported what appeared to be two fishing boats approaching.

I was navigating in the charthouse. Going to the Big Eyes, I was able to make out the names on their gray sides. These were later translated as "Rice Paddy 1" and "Rice Paddy 2." Their configuration was familiar. I was sure I had seen it in one of the identification pubs I had been studying. Thumbing through it, I determined they were Soviet-type trawlers, but with slight modifications, indicating they were probably North Korean-built.

An order was sent over the louspeaker for all hands to lay below decks. We didn't want the visitors to count the crewmen, and wonder why so many.

One of the trawlers steamed directly toward us, then swerved aside, passing less than one hundred yards off the starboard bow, close enough for us to see fishing nets and some half-dozen men on the deck. They weren't wearing uniforms, and there was no sign of armament.

Skip, as operations officer, was drafting a SITREP. I carefuly pinpointed our position for him. We were twenty miles from the nearest land. I had no doubts about this. Our dead reckoning (DR) fixes tallied perfectly with the readings I got from the loran, radar, and fathometer.

The two trawlers disappeared to the northwest.

At this time we were flying the international signal for hydrographer, but not the national ensign. Would they accept that as identification? I doubted it.

Curious to see if Steve had been able to intercept any of their radio messages, I went below to the sod hut. He had picked them up, all right, but the North Koreans had spoken too quickly for our two Marine interpreters, Chicca and Hammond, to make out the words.

I was still in the sod hut when the two ships reappeared sometime later. Returning to the bridge, I again confirmed our position: we were well outside any claimed territorial waters. This time when they passed, the number of per-

118

sonnel on deck had increased significantly. Several of the men were pointing cameras at us. Mack snapped his shutter right back at them. Obviously, after our first contact they had been ordered to return and photograph us. But still no sign of guns, and still no attempt at harassment. After passing us, they headed straight for Wonsan.

This time there was no need for debate. We had been spotted. By about 1700 hours (5:00 P.M.) the SITREP was ready. Handing it to Radioman Lee Roy Hayes, Bucher told him to break EMCON and radio Japan we had been detected.

It took our radiomen fourteen hours to make contact with Japan and relay the message.

By this time it was the morning of Tuesday, January 23, 1968.

11

On January 23 I arose before dawn, to shoot morning stars, but there was too much overcast. However, since we were no longer on EMCON, I was able to establish our exact location by using the radar and fathometer. At dusk the previous night we had left our operating area to move farther out to sea. Since I had last taken our position, shortly after midnight, we had drifted slightly, to the southeast, but we were still well outside North Korean territorial waters, twenty-five miles from shore, sixteen miles from the nearest island, Nan Do.

It was quiet, just before the dawn. But I knew that the silence could be a mask. During the night the CTs had logged eighteen contacts, the closest about three thousand yards. At 0145 (1:45 A.M.) someone had sent up an orange flare. It had illuminated the sky for about thirty seconds, but was too far away to reveal either the *Pueblo* or any other ship.

Were the North Koreans looking for us? If so, there was no sign of them now. As day broke, visibility increased, though some haze remained; scanning the lightening horizon, I saw no trace of any other silhouettes, not even a lone fishing boat.

From the OOD I learned that although the radio operators had stayed on the teletype all through the night, they still hadn't succeeded in getting a secure line to Japan.

A little after seven, Commander Bucher came topside. By taking radar cuts on the island of Nan Do, we verified the position I had earlier logged. After being briefed on the night's activities, Bucher asked for a course that would take us fifteen to sixteen miles from the island of Ung Do. This was not too far from where we had been the previous day, and it would place us in a good spot to monitor coastal traffic and to observe ships leaving the port of Wonsan. I recommended a course of 300. As the order was passed below, the *Pueblo*'s engines came to life, their deep-throated hum vibrating through every part of the ship.

Serve on a ship awhile, and its sound becomes a part of you. You can shut your eyes and recognize it anywhere.

Lacy replaced the OOD at 0745 (7:45 A.M.). Gene's wife Mary Ellen and my wife Carol were good friends, and in between our other duties, Gene and I talked about some of the things we planned to do when we returned to Japan. I didn't indicate that the Murphys would probably be staying there only briefly. I hadn't told Gene about my decision to quit the Navy and the *Pueblo*. I had been busy much of the time since our departure from Sasebo, and I hadn't found any spare minutes to polish the rough draft of my resignation. It remained in the safe in my office. When the time came, I wanted to present it to Bucher personally.

"*A secure line to Kamiseya!*" The crypto room jubilantly reported the news a few minutes after nine. The radiomen were now sending out the SITREP of the previous day. Schumacher, on Bucher's orders, began preparing a second SITREP, encompassing the activities of the night. A backlog of other messages was also sent out, while we still had the circuit to Japan.

As we steamed toward our position, the morning passed routinely. Though it was warmer now than it had been since we first headed north, a small amount of ice had accumulated on deck during the night. A crew was put to work clearing it. As he did every morning, Gunner's Mate Wadley checked the tarpaulins covering the two machine guns, to make sure they weren't frozen. He would later testify that they were not.

We reached our operating area about 1000 (10:00 A.M.)

and lay to dead in the water while the CTs got to work. Although some low-lying haze to the west obscured our visual observations, our position was easily verifiable by radar, which showed the distinct outlines of the peninsula of Hado Pando and the two offshore islands, Yo Do and Ung Do, the latter being closest to us, the other farther south. I gave Skip our new position for inclusion in the second SITREP: 39 degrees 25.2 minutes North, 127 degrees 55.0 minutes East, 15.8 miles off Ung Do.

The morning was typical in yet another respect. Although we were not far from Wonsan, North Korea's biggest east-coast seaport, Steve Harris reported no significant ELINT. Thus far, in terms of intelligence collected, the voyage had been a disappointment. Over the last couple hours the CTs had picked up an unusual amount of radio chatter, but it was too fast for our two marine interpreters, Chicca and Hammond, to make out. They recorded it, intending to play it back later with Korean dictionaries in hand.

Steve Harris would later testify that at about 1100 (11:00 A.M.) he posted the ship's destruct bill on the sod-hut door. This listed the order of priority in which classified materials—both documents and machines—were to be destroyed in an emergency, and tasked individual men with specific assignments. The trouble with this, which became apparent only in retrospect, was that it was geared to a general-quarters situation. If GQ wasn't called, the men wouldn't be in their assigned places to carry out the work. But then, Steve undoubtedly presumed, as would anyone else, that in any conceivable emergency we would go to general quarters.

I never saw the destruct bill. Nor, as their testimony would later indicate, did most of the rest of the crew.

At 1145 (11:45 A.M.) Law replaced Lacy as OOD. Law was a good man, blustery, cocksure, but dependable, well-liked by both officers and crew, and already an excellent navigator. We had known each other since serving together on the USS *Guadalupe*. Law's relationship with the captain was at times bombastic. His description of Bucher —"like a mail-order catalog: big, fat, and full of cheap shit"—was probably familiar to everyone aboard the *Pueblo*, except the CO.

About the same time Law arrived, I took our noon position, and after reporting it to the captain, went down to the wardroom to join the other officers for lunch. Passing the message board, I noticed the evening menu: chop suey. For lunch our cook, Harry Lewis, had prepared turkey, with cranberry sauce, peas, and mashed potatoes and gravy. That he managed to serve eighty-three men from our minuscule galley was a miracle of the highest order.

As we ate, we discussed our encounter with the trawlers the previous day. At the time, there had been some disagreement over my identification of the ships. However, after Mack developed his pictures in one of the heads that doubled as a makeshift darkroom, the photos had been compared with those in the identification pubs. Everyone agreed that I had called them right. No one attached any great importance to the incident or to the fact that we had been spotted. If anything, we were all a little bored and perhaps just a trifle disappointed that thus far the voyage had been so uneventful.

It was an odd feeling, though, knowing that while we had been developing our pictures of them, they had probably been developing theirs of us. I wondered how they felt about their American visitor.

We were soon to learn.

At about noon Law called Bucher from the pilothouse on the telephone. A contact had been spotted to the south, coming from the direction of Wonsan. It was more than five miles away and appeared to be heading in our direction.

Spooning another helping of food onto his plate, Bucher told Law to call back if the ship came within three miles. He also ordered him to light off the radar and verify the position I had given him just fifteen minutes earlier.

Law called back less than five minutes later. My position was exact, and the ship was now less than three miles away and closing fast. There was no longer any question of its direction. It was headed straight for us.

I suspect that every man at the table automatically computed the time and distance and came up with a speed in excess of twenty knots. This automatically put it out of the fishing boat, trawler class.

In the crypto room, outboard of the sod hut, Radioman Don E. Bailey interrupted the message he was transmitting to Kamiseya, Japan, to quickly tap: COMPANY OUTSIDE.

Swearing that it was a damned inconvenient time for visitors, Bucher pushed back his plate and hurried from the wardroom to the signal bridge. I was right on his tail.

On reaching his observation platform, Bucher took the Big Eyes from Law, at the same time yelling down the voice tube to the pilothouse that he wanted Steve Harris to report to him immediately with his identification manuals. Because there was no telephone link beween the signal bridge and the sod hut, each order had to be repeated by whoever was manning the phones in the pilothouse, a waste of precious time and potentially a source of confusion.

Bucher followed this with a call for Mack to appear on the double with his camera.

"You should hear things buzzing down there!" Steve exclaimed excitedly on coming up off the ladder. "They must have every fire-control radar in the country locked on us. If they wanted to, they could blast us right out of the water!"

By this time the ship had closed to less than a mile. Taking the glasses, Steve immediately identified her as a Soviet-type SO-1 subchaser, length 130 feet, top speed twenty-five knots. Through the binoculars we could see that she was flying the North Korean ensign. We could also see that she was armed with twin 57-mm cannons, her men on deck at battle stations. She was a warship, primed and ready for action, and she was headed straight for the *Pueblo* at close to flank speed.

Bucher had a choice to make, and it had to be made quickly.

Although referring specifically to the Soviet ships in the Tsushima Strait region, our sail order clearly applied to any unfriendly ship we might encounter:

. . . REGARDING CONDUCT IN EVENT OF HARASSMENT OR INTIMIDATION BY FOREIGN UNITS . . . OPERATE AT LEAST FIVE HUNDRED YDS AS NECESSARY FOR VISUAL/PHOTO COVERAGE . . . DO NOT INTERFERE WITH SOVIET EXERCISES BUT MAINTAIN A POSITION ON THE PERIPHERY FOR OBSERVATION PURPOSES.

But this wasn't our only guide. We had the experience of the *Banner* to draw on. Observe; don't get involved; when threatened, *disengage*—this was the course of action Commander Clark had followed on all his missions. It was also the procedure we had followed thus far on this voyage.

But to disengage in our present position would mean to light off the engines and make a run for the open sea.

Whether because he felt to do so would look as if he were running from a fight, or whether because, a gambler at heart, he was sure he could buck the odds, Bucher decided to bluff. He gave no engine orders. The *Pueblo* remained dead in the water. As with most of his decisions, he did not ask any of his officers for concurrence or advice.

There is some disagreement over whether Bucher or Tuck then suggested that as "cover" the oceanographers should take a Nansen cast. Both, however, agreed it was a good idea, and Tuck hurried toward the well deck to drop the bottles. At the same time, Bucher ordered Signalman Leach to hoist flags identifying us as a hydrographer.

For some reason CT Barrett had followed us to the signal bridge. And as usual, "Barnyard" had the straight poop, which he offered gratuitously: the ship wouldn't dare fire on us, because it would cause an international incident.

As the subchaser drew closer, Bucher shouted a number

of orders down the voice tube: for Schumacher to report with message blanks for a Pinnacle alert to Japan; for Lacy, who had just sat down for lunch in the wardroom, to come up and replace Law as OOD; for all personnel not on official business to stay below decks. The latter order was repeated over the loudspeaker. Already a crowd of curious faces had gathered at the rail, wanting to see what a Communist gunboat looked like.

Knowing that Schumacher would need an exact fix on our position, I ran down the ladder to the charthouse. As I verified our location, I could see the SO-1 on the radar, its shape looming larger and larger. Coming out onto the O-1 level for a firsthand look, I encountered Photographer's Mate Mack.

"My God, Mr. Murphy," he gasped. "She's got her guns pointed right at me!"

The subchaser was now less than a thousand yards away. With his telephoto lens Mack could almost look down the barrels.

I tried to calm him with quiet assurances. But inside I knew exactly how he felt.

Apparently about this same time, while I was still below, Lacy, arriving on the signal bridge to replace Law, asked Bucher if he wanted to sound general quarters. Bucher's reply was negative. Although the SO-1 was obviously at general quarters, her men at battle stations, Bucher felt, he later explained, that if the *Pueblo* were to do likewise, she would appear provocative, thereby violating our written and verbal orders.

Churning up our port side, the SO-1 suddenly reduced speed and began to circle us in a clockwise direction. Her signalman now ran up a message, the first attempt to communicate with us: WHAT NATIONALITY?

In response, Bucher had Leach run up the biggest American ensign we had aboard.

The subchaser was now close enough that we could see the men on deck. All too clearly. There were about a dozen North Koreans, wearing quilted green uniforms. Al-

126

most all carried automatic rifles. They were watching us through binoculars and the gunsights of the twin 57-mm cannons.

By the time they had completed their third circle, they had lowered their original flags and replaced them with another set.

This one read: HEAVE TO OR I WILL FIRE.

"Murphy," Bucher yelled down the voice tube, "what the hell's the precise meaning of 'heave to'?"

I was sure Bucher knew it as well as I, but just in case it had some international meaning with which we were unfamiliar, I called Steve Harris, who by now had returned to the sod hut. I knew he had a dictionary there, because I'd used it.

"There's only one meaning," he said. " 'To bring a vessel to a standstill.' "

Hurriedly scribbling the definition on a piece of paper, I ran up the ladder.

There was at least one advantage to Bucher's asinine decision to conn the ship from the signal bridge, I decided. It was a damned good way to lose weight.

I handed the sheet to Bucher. His puzzled look matched my own. How could we come to a standstill if we were already dead in the water? We could only guess the North Koreans meant for us to stay exactly where we were.

Following me back down to the pilothouse, Bucher rechecked our position. It hadn't changed. We were 15.8 miles from the nearest land, the island of Ung Do. There was not even the remotest possibility that we were inside their claimed territorial waters. Law, Bucher, and I had all clearly established this. The loran readings could conceivably be in error, but not the radar, the fathometer, and all our other navigational aids. And by now I had checked each more than a half-dozen times.

Returning to the signal bridge, Bucher had Leach hoist a new set of flags: I AM IN INTERNATIONAL WATERS.

But he couldn't leave it at that. He had to add the Bucher

touch, a nose-thumbing gesture of defiance: INTEND TO REMAIN IN THE AREA UNTIL TOMORROW.

Bucher probably felt he had good reason to be cocky. Thus far his bluff appeared to have worked. Nearly forty minutes had passed since the subchaser was first sighted. Although the SO-1's circles grew ever tighter—she had by now closed to not more than a hundred yards—there was no indication that this was other than the standard harassment the *Banner* had experienced. Even the "Heave-to or I will fire" threat wasn't novel. But there were two differences. The *Banner* had been moving when the Soviets hoisted their signal; Clark had ignored it and continued to disengage. And we were not dealing with the Russians or the Red Chinese, but with a new and unpredictable adversary.

With five words from Gene Lacy, who was at the Big Eyes, the whole picture changed: "Three more contacts, bearing 160!"

They were closing, and fast, from the general direction of Wonsan. In what seemed an amazingly short time, the white wakes changed to sharp configurations. After thumbing through the pubs, Steve identified them as North Korean P-4 motor torpedo boats, length 63 feet, maximum speed fifty knots, or four times faster than the *Pueblo*.

Bucher apparently questioned Steve's identification, arguing with him several minutes before accepting it.

He then barked several orders: Tim Harris, who was already on the signal bridge, was to keep a running narrative of everything that transpired; Schumacher was to prepare a new Pinnacle, apprising COMNAVFORJAPAN and CINCPACFLT of our worsening situation, this message, on Schumacher's suggestion, to be upgraded from FLASH to CRITIC, a designation reserved for possible international incidents, which would give it priority over other message traffic and route it all the way up to the White House; and I was to set up a team to chart the movements of the four ships.

128

But still no engine order. And no order to man the machine guns.

There were eight to ten men in the pilothouse. Grabbing several, I put them to work mapping positions.

Bailey was keeping the circuit up with small talk:

```
I SURE COULD USE SOME LIBERTY NOW . . . I
DIDN'T THINK I'D MISS THE OLD LADY SO
MUCH . . .
```

This was interrupted when the first Pinnacle was handed him for transmission; it went out at 1254 (12:54 P.M.).

The P-4's approached on our port beam. They were at general quarters, all their guns pointed at the *Pueblo*. The lead ship swerved under our fantail and passed down our starboard side. She then steamed over to the subchaser, now idling some two hundred yards away.

Kamiseya:

```
DO YOU HAVE ANY MORE TRAFFIC? HOW IT FEEL TO
BE THREATENED?
```

Bailey:

```
GOT SOME MORE COMING IN A MINUTE BUT DON'T
HAVE IT IN COMM YET. WE WILL PASS IT AS SOON
AS I GET. IT IS WORSE OUT HERE NOW, GOT
MORE COMPANY AND NOT DOING SO GOOD WITH
THEM . . .
```

The time was 1315 (1:15 P.M.).

The sound was unmistakable. We heard the roar even before they came in sight. But they were not American jets but MIGs. A pair of them. They made a quick pass over the *Pueblo*.

I was too preoccupied to do more than acknowledge their presence. Watching through my binoculars from the pilothouse, I could see that the men on the decks of the SO-1 and the P-4 seemed to be conferring. Then I saw something that sent chills down my spine. Rubber tires and rope mats had been slung over the side of the P-4, and some dozen men, wearing helmets and carrying automatic arms, had moved from the SO-1 onto the P-4's deck.

They were forming a boarding party!

Running back up the ladder to the signal bridge, I told the skipper what I had seen. But Bucher had just spotted it himself. I expected him to call repel-boarders Drill. But he didn't. He just stood there quivering with anger. They had called his bluff! Suddenly all his accumulated failures and frustrations came out in one loud bellow of rage: *"I wish I could dive this damn thing!"* Bucher cried.

12

The P-4 began backing down on the *Pueblo*'s starboard bow, fenders rigged for boarding. Finally, one and a quarter hours after the high-noon maneuvers had begun, Bucher decided to leave the area. I had returned below when he called down for a course recommend that would take us to deep water in the quickest possible time.

"Zero-eight-zero," I advised.

Bucher accepted the recommendation and passed an order to Chief Monroe Goldman in the engine room. There was a big puff of smoke. Although INTEND TO REMAIN IN THE AREA UNTIL TOMORROW was still flapping in the breeze, anyone within miles could see that we were lighting off the engines. Bucher had Leach haul down the flags and replace them with a new message. Again the temptation to get smart proved irresistible. Bucher had to save face, even if it meant the Orientals had to lose theirs. THANK YOU FOR YOUR CONSIDERATION, read the new flags. I AM DEPARTING THE AREA.

To Helmsman Ronald Berens he shouted down through the voice tube: "All ahead full."

Swinging around in a wide circle, the *Pueblo* started for the open sea.

"Stop! For God's sake, stop!" The anguished cry came from "Friar" Tuck. We had forgotten the Nansen cast; the *Pueblo* was still towing her "cover"; the quick start had brought the bottles boiling up to the surface astern of us.

Bucher ordered speed reduced to one-third. As the equipment was brought back aboard, several more precious

131

minutes were wasted. But not wasted by the North Koreans, who used them to take up positions around the *Pueblo*. We were now surrounded by ships. The P-4 began backing down again. She came to within twenty feet. The men at the rail could look right into the unsmiling North Korean faces.

With the bottles up, Bucher ordered speed increased to two-thirds, then full. But we'd lost the element of surprise, if ever we had it. The North Korean ships stayed right with us. While two of the P-4's played porpoise across our bow, weaving back and forth at no more than twenty yards in spumes of spray, the SO-1 began closing on our port quarter, trying to force the *Pueblo* in toward land. Bucher kept ordering course changes—"Come right ten degrees"; "Come right ten more degrees"—in order to present the smallest possible target.

By this time Pinnacle 2 had gone out. Bailey, in the crypto space, couldn't see what was happening. He had to rely on what passing crewmen told him. And someone confused rumor with fact. At 1326 (1:26 P.M.) Bailey tapped:

```
AND THEY PLAN TO OPEN FIRE ON US NOW. THEY
PLAN TO OPEN FIRE ON US NOW. THEY PLAN TO OPEN
FIRE ON US NOW . . .
```

Schumacher asked Bucher if he wanted him to man the machine guns. Bucher's reply: negative. Later he gave three reasons for his decision. One, he still felt that only ordinary harassment was involved, and did not want to appear provocative. Two, because of the exposed positions of the guns, it would mean sure death for whoever he sent to load and fire them. And, three, he was sure the tarpaulins were iced over and therefore would have to be chipped off before the guns could be used. Both the first and the second justifications had validity, especially the second, although one man and one man alone was responsible for that exposed placement. But if Gunner's Mate Wadley's testimony is to be believed, the third reason appears a specious afterthought.

According to both participants, there was no mention in the discussion of using the ten Thompson submachine guns the *Pueblo* also carried. These were stored in the ammo locker, and readily accessible, but apparently neither man thought of them.

In any case, Bucher had made the fateful decision. The *Pueblo* would not fight back. Not a shot would be fired, in anger or defense.

Bucher was trying his best to extricate us, but every time he ordered a course change, the faster SO-1 compensated. Moreover, the positions he gave were gradually turning us back toward land.

We were in a tight spot, and it was getting tighter. On my own I decided to try to reach Japan on the Hi Comm. There was one danger with the encrypting machines. The sending and receiving sets had to be in perfect synchronization. If not, it was necessary to set up a test pattern, then send the message out all over again. At this stage we couldn't risk interruption of our contact with Japan. The Hi Comm would provide a direct, voice-telephone link with our headquarters. It was not "secure," or encoded, but at this stage, as far as I could see, that was no longer of any importance.

Shortly before this, Lacy and Tim Harris had come down to the pilothouse. After giving Tim our current position for inclusion in his narrative—we were now 15.6 miles from Ung Do—I picked up the Hi Comm phone.

The moment I did, the P-4's suddenly, in unison, veered away from the *Pueblo*. If anyone had any hope they were abandoning their harassment, it was short-lived. For almost immediately it became apparent why they were putting distance between themselves and the *Pueblo*.

We had become a target.

With a horrendous roar, the twin cannons of the SO-1 belched fire, the shells whistling high overhead. A warning, or bad aim? As if in answer, the second volley crashed

133

into the radar mast, demolished Bucher's plexiglass windshield, and shattered glass all over the pilothouse.

Automatically everyone hit the deck. As we got back to our feet, Law ran topside to see if anyone had been hurt. But we knew at least Bucher was alive. "The bastards shot me in the ass!" he moaned over the voice tube.

I became aware of another voice, this one speaking directly into my ear. In diving for the deck, I'd held on to the Hi Comm phone. "Stand by to change frequencies," the operator in Japan kept repeating. "Stand by to change frequencies." Talk about bad timing, this was the worst possible! Frequency shifts on the Hi Comm occurred only twice a day. At the very moment we most needed to get through, we'd caught one of them! I couldn't believe our bad luck. "Stand by to change frequencies." I tried repeatedly to break in, but the operator wouldn't stop talking long enough to give me a chance.

Aside from cuts from the glass, no one in the pilothouse appeared to have been wounded. Someone—Bucher or Law—called down to report that although everyone on the signal bridge had sustained injuries, none was serious enough to require a corpsman. I called below to see if there were any casualties, but none was reported. Apparently all the shells had hit the upper part of the ship.

From the tube came a voice that was unmistakably the CO's: "Get on the 1MC and order 'Prepare to commence emergency destruction.'"

"Prepare to commence" when they were firing at us?

We relayed the order, in the excitement forgetting, as obviously had Bucher, that there was no loudspeaker for the 1MC in the sod hut. Since there were also no portholes, Steve Harris and his technicians were completely out of touch with what was going on.

Now the P-4's opened up on us. The machine-gun bullets rattled against the sides of the ship like hail. Bucher suddenly decided the signal bridge was not the best place from which to conn the ship after all. He scampered down the ladder, Law, Leach, and CT Steven Robin, who had been helping identify the ships, almost landing on top of him.

All except Law had been wounded during the earlier salvo: Leach had pieces of shrapnel in his leg; Robin had a lacerated arm; while one metal splinter had creased Bucher's ankle and still another lodged in his rectum. He seemed as much humiliated as hurt. After determining that no one appeared seriously wounded, Hospital Corpsman Herman "Doc" Baldridge, who had been keeping the quartermaster and weather logs, asked permission to lay below to break out first-aid supplies. I granted it.

I was still trying to get through on the Hi Comm. I told Bucher what I was doing and reported my lack of success.

Bucher exploded, cursing me for taking it upon myself to act without his permission. "Do you think I want the whole world to know what's happening?"

I tried to keep my temper in check, but only half-succeeded. "The Communists already know," I replied heatedly. "All I want to do is make sure the Americans know also."

There was a long pause; then Bucher muttered, "Go ahead."

But we were still caught in the change of frequencies. Although trying both the old and new channels, I couldn't get in a word.

I was on the starboard side of the pilothouse, in the navigation section, and Bucher and Lacy were over on the port side, next to the annunciator. Therefore I didn't personally hear the following conversation, but both men later agreed it went about as follows: Lacy, who was still OOD, again asked Bucher if he should call GQ. Not yet, Bucher replied. He then asked Lacy how long it would take to scuttle the ship. Two and a half hours, Lacy answered. But he advised against it. The temperature of the water was such that it was doubtful if the men could survive for more than a few minutes. Too, the water was shallow enough for divers to recover our secrets.

135

Bucher yelled over and asked our present depth. "Thirty-five fathoms," I yelled back. We would have to go out to a hundred before we could safely jettison. But even if we succeeded in reaching that point, scuttling was probably out because of the time element.

Had Schumacher not forgotten to bring the TNT aboard, we could have blown a hole in the side of the ship, scuttling her in minutes.

Another salvo from the 57's ripped into the *Pueblo*, this one knocking out all the remaining windows in the pilothouse, one of the shells missing Tim Harris' head by inches. Dropping to the floor, he resumed furiously scribbling his narrative, while Bucher continued giving Berens course corrections and I kept trying to get Japan on the Hi Comm, unaware that the antenna coupler had just been shot off.

By this time one of the CTs had reached the sod hut and told Steve Harris what was happening. Steve called the pilothouse and asked permission to start emergency destruction. The question was relayed to Bucher, who replied with a flat "No," hesitated for what seemed a full minute, then said, "Yes."

"Commence emergency destruction," I yelled over the phone and the loudspeaker.

I still have no idea what, if anything, Bucher was thinking. He would give a command, then, as quickly, either qualify or countermand it. Probably, like the rest of us, he was still in a state of shock. It seemed inconceivable that the North Koreans would dare fire on us when we were in international waters, but they had, and it seemed to take everyone, myself included, several minutes to adjust to this fact. It was as if one part of the mind was saying, *It couldn't be happening!*, while another part was affirming, *But it is!* Instinctively, from all our training, we looked to the CO for leadership. But it was obvious that he was as confused as the rest of us. Almost every command he gave was first suggested by someone else.

Bailey:

136

SOS SOS SOS SOS SOS SOS SOS SOS. WE ARE HOLDING
EMERGENCY DESTRUCTION.WE NEED SUPPORT. SOS SOS
SOS. PLEASE SEND ASSISTANCE . . .

Gene Lacy again asked Bucher if he should order general quarters. Bucher hesitated, then gave the order, which I relayed over the 1MC. But almost immediately he changed his mind: "Make that a *modified* GQ, all personnel except those already topside to remain below."

If there was any doubt about Bucher's earlier decision, it was now resolved. The guns of the *Pueblo* would not be manned.

It was a strange order. In effect, it meant we weren't going to general quarters at all. What drills we had conducted were for naught. Since the sod hut was topside, it meant those CTs not already there couldn't carry out their destruction assignments. It also meant that the pilothouse, the very nerve center of the ship, would not be properly manned. For example, lacking a phone talker, who ordinarily would have manned the 1JV circuit, we would have to rely on hand-held phone sets. It was the old daisy-chain concept: if one man does not show up to replace another, he can't replace the man he's assigned to replace, and so on down the line. I could visualize the confusion below. For a moment I thought of arguing with Bucher, then decided against it. As I'd learned over and over again, the hard way, he not only discouraged, he resented advice.

We were still steaming at full speed, 12.2 knots. Bucher kept giving Berens course corrections. I finally gave up on the Hi Comm, turning it over to one of the radiomen, in hopes he would have better luck, and joined in the destruction efforts, passing stacks of classified documents to the men who were moving back and forth between the pilothouse and the incinerator on the O1 level. Remembering the secret material in my file cabinet, I gave CT James Shephard the keys and told him to lay below and get rid of it. I then got on the horn and reached the yeoman in the ship's office, ordering him to begin destruction if he hadn't already, starting with the highest classification and work-

137

ing down. Law had emptied the OOD's safe. I told him to destroy everything but our logs, charts, loran books, and other navigational records. By firing on us while we were in international waters the North Koreans had violated every accepted law of the sea; it seemed to me that in some way they would have to justify their actions. Thus it was extremely important that all our navigational records be preserved, as they constituted evidence that at no point had we intruded into claimed territorial waters.

We were still well outside them now, but the SO-1 and the P-4's were gradually forcing us in closer.

More salvos followed. Each time the shelling started we would hit the deck, then carry out our duties from crouched positions until it stopped. Berens was becoming very proficient at steering while squatting down; he could still see what he was doing, but at the same time was presenting the smallest possible target. Alvin Plucker, who was handling the quartermaster's notebook, and Roy Maggard, who was lee helm, had no need to remain standing. Tim Harris had by this time moved into the charthouse. It was now obvious that the SO-1 was concentrating its fire on the pilothouse. It was also obvious that fire was getting increasingly accurate.

It seemed they had us every which way. Four ships to one. We couldn't outmaneuver or outrun them. Because the guns were unmanned, we couldn't even fire back. With one misstep after another we had blundered into a stalemate from which there seemed no way out except to stall for time until help arrived. Bucher's sole contribution as CO at this point was to wander from one side of the pilothouse to the other, muttering strings of curses at the North Koreans.

Gene Lacy, as shaken as everyone else, but still in complete control of himself, asked Bucher, "Are you going to stop this goddamn ship?"

Again Bucher hesitated. Then within sight of anyone who happened to be looking—as were Lacy and I, and as Schumacher, Tim Harris, Law, and Berens probably were

138

also—Bucher nodded his head in assent. Lacy pulled back the annunciator to Full Stop. As the engine room responded, the *Pueblo* gradually decreased speed until she lay dead in the water.

There was a stillness, as both the *Pueblo* and the shelling stopped.

Bailey, 1337 (1:37 P.M.):

WE ARE LAYING TO AT PRESENT POSITION . . .
THIS CIRCUIT ONLY CIRCUIT ACTIVE . . . PLEASE
SEND ASSISTANCE. WE ARE BEING BOARDED . . .

Kamiseya, 1338 (1:38 P.M.):

QSL [ROGER] YOUR LAST AND PASSING ALL INFO.

Again Bailey was wrong about the boarding. The SO-1 had now raised a new set of signal flags: FOLLOW ME. I HAVE A PILOT ABOARD.

This time, on his own initiative, without prompting, Bucher ordered, "Ahead one-third."

The *Pueblo* began following the SO-1.

Bailey, 1345 (1:45 P.M.):

WE ARE BEING ESCORTED INTO PROB WONSAN REPEAT
WONSAN. WE ARE BEING ESCORTED INTO PROB WONSAN
REPEAT WONSAN . . .

After obtaining our current position for transmission by Bailey, I decided to lay below to check the progress of the destruction. Stepping out onto the deck, I saw that, despite a great deal of frantic activity, it was going very slowly. Our two inadequate paper shredders could chew up only an eight-inch stack of paper every quarter hour, and then the shreds had to be burned. The incinerator's limit was three pounds, and only loose sheets at that; each of the bound publications, and there were dozens of them, had to be torn apart, sheet by sheet. Already there were stacks of paper piled up next to the incinerator, and they were growing higher every minute.

Below, a number of small fires were smoldering in the

139

passageways. Because the ship had been sealed when we went to modified GQ—portholes closed, ventilation shut off—the clouds of acrid smoke lingered, scorching eyes, throats, nostrils.

We were making progress, but it was slow and entirely piecemeal. I couldn't help thinking the TNT would have made all the difference. But it was too late for such thoughts, much too late. Lacking a quick means of destruction, we had to make the best of those remaining.

"What's going on, Mr. Murphy?" the men asked. "What's going to happen to us?"

Though obviously nervous and possibly a little frightened (and in this they were not alone), there was no sign of panic. I told them I was sure help was on the way; in the meantime, the important thing was to destroy every scrap of classified material they could find. Whenever I spotted a man not already occupied, I put him to work tearing or burning pages.

Going to my stateroom, I checked to see if Shephard had found all the classified documents. He had. The only papers left in my safe were unstamped. Among them was the draft of my resignation, outlining my differences with Commander Bucher. At the time, I didn't even remember it, much less think to destroy it.

Later I would greatly regret that oversight.

Though I didn't go into the sod hut, the CTs later described a scene straight out of Dante's *Inferno*. Three or four small fires were burning; there was no way for the smoke to escape; it just grew thicker and thicker. One CT swung a sledge hammer against a radio console; the handle broke. Others, wielding sledgehammers and fire axes, found they bounced right off the metal. Sensitive the equipment may have been; delicate it was not. For a time it appeared that their efforts would prove more damaging to each other than to the electronic gear. But with aching arms they kept hacking away until piece after piece was reduced to a mass of twisted steel. The machines, however, weren't the only problem. Adding to the confusion was the still-unresolved question of whether classified documents could or could not be jettisoned. Earlier Steve Harris had told his CTs that nothing should be thrown overboard before the *Pueblo* reached a water depth of 100 fathoms, or 600 feet. Anticipating that moment, two huge laundry bags had been filled with documents. But since Steve's initial order, the situation had changed; we were now heading not for deeper water but shallower, as the SO-1 led us toward land. Still Steve hadn't countermanded his instructions. Although he knew that in doing so he was disobeying a direct order, CT Peter Langenberg took it upon himself to haul one of the bags to the rail and pitch it overboard. He intended to do the same with the second bag, but as events transpired, he never got the chance.

In the tiny crypto room, Bailey asked CT Donald McClarren to relieve him on the teletype so he could destroy his secret communications lists. Turning around to get them, he found Steve Harris kneeling in the middle of the floor. As politely as possible, Bailey asked him if he could do his praying elsewhere, as he was in the way. Harris, according to Bailey, then got up and left the room.

Shortly after I left the bridge, Commander Bucher left it also, going below to his stateroom to make sure it was clean of classified materials and to get a pair of .22-caliber pistols from his locker. He gave them to one of the sailors and told him to toss them overboard. As an officer, he later explained, he did not want his personal sidearms to fall into enemy hands.

It would appear that by this time Bucher had reconciled himself to the probability that the *Pueblo* would be boarded and searched.

I hadn't. I still had hopes that help was on the way, and that it would arrive in time.

Bucher was not the only one addicted to old movies.

It is also possible that by now Bucher had even decided

to surrender the ship. At some point—his later statements are contradictory when it comes to the key point of exactly when this occurred—he told Gene Lacy that he was considering surrender, Lacy agreeing that under the circumstances it might become necessary. By his own admission, Bucher did not mention this to any of his other officers.

On his return to the pilothouse, Bucher, for the first and only time on January 23, asked his executive officer for advice: "What do you think we should do, Ed?"

While below, Bucher had looked into the sod hut. He was enraged over how much classified material was as yet undestroyed, and since his return to the bridge he had called Steve Harris at least twice to ask for a progress report and to chew him out for the delay. Steve had reported some success: most of the machines had been smashed beyond repair, and the most important single item in his care, the encoding disks, had been reduced to powder; but much remained undone.

As far as I could see, there was only one course of action left us, and that was to buy as much time as possible. "Stall," I advised. "We need every minute we can get to complete the destruction." In the back of my mind was also the hope that, given enough time, either the Navy or the Air Force could rush aid to us.

In effect I was only suggesting that we continue what we were already doing. Despite angry signaling from the SO-1 for us to increase speed, we continued to follow at one-third.

Bucher seemed to consider this a moment, then nodded agreement.

The activity in the pilothouse had in no way diminished. Just as soon as we thought we had found all the classified materials, someone would uncover another hoard. Although the burning continued, we were now jettisoning everything we could lay our hands on; despite the shallowness of the water, this way there was at least a chance it wouldn't be seized. Overboard went Mack's cameras, film,

142

and negative files. Tim Harris destroyed his running narrative, Bucher his tape recorder. Looking for something with which to sink a batch of classified pubs, Radioman Lee Roy Hayes spied Radarman Clifford Nolte's toolbox. Over it went, accompanied by Nolte's enraged bellow. Some of this activity must have been seen by the North Koreans. They couldn't miss the clouds of smoke that were coming up out of the passageways.

This time, without asking anyone for advice, Bucher decided to gamble again. Wanting to see what would happen, he later stated, he ordered the *Pueblo* brought to Full Stop.

The answer came quick enough. Dropping back, the SO-1 fired a heavy barrage of shells that smashed into the center part of the *Pueblo* on the starboard side, the area from which most of the smoke was coming.

Bucher seemed stunned by what had happened. It was a full minute or more before he again ordered, "Ahead one-third."

"Damage Control Two reports three casualties, one critical!"

Another call followed moments later, from either Law or Baldridge: "Mr. Murphy, we need morphine!" As medical officer, I had charge of all drugs, which were stored in a safe in my office. Running down the inside ladder, I saw that at least one shell had gone through the passage between the CO's stateroom and the officers' wardroom. Three men, who had been in the passageway burning papers from the cryptographic safe, had been hit. Marine Sergeant Robert Chicca had a hole the size of a silver dollar in his upper thigh. As bad as the wound was, it was the least serious. Fireman Steven Woelk had sustained a terrible wound in his lower abdomen. Worst hit, however, was Fireman Duane Hodges, whom the shell had caught almost squarely in the groin, ripping his intestines open and almost completely severing his right leg. Chicca by this time had been moved to my stateroom, but Woelk was still standing in the doorway. After I broke out the narcotics

143

and gave them to Doc Baldridge, we got him in a prone position. As soon as Doc had finished giving Hodges a shot, he cleaned Woelk's wound and put on a large battle dressing. Hodges was trying to say something. I crouched down by his head so I could hear him. He asked me how bad his wound was and if he would be all right. Although I knew the answer, I glanced at Doc. Unseen by Hodges, he shook his head sadly. I had always liked Hodges. He had helped me build storage cabinets in the ship's office and in my stateroom, and I had been impressed by both his good humor and the way he got things done. Service regulations being what they are, an officer and an enlisted man can rarely become friends, but they can develop a mutual respect. Hodges and I had that, I felt. Since the purse-snatching incident in San Diego, I had badgered the captain to give Hodges and Arnold their award. It was a small thing, I knew, but the realization that now Hodges would probably never learn of it shook me.

While I didn't want to lie to him, I also wanted to make it as easy for him as I could. I told him that Doc was giving him the best care possible, that he was not to worry, he was in good hands, he was going to be fine. Doc added other assurances. Hodges didn't reply, and his blue eyes rolled up and fixed on me. Then they glazed. He had lost consciousness.

Not until then did I notice that the destruction had stopped. The cryptographic safe was only half-emptied. Most of the fires had gone out. The passageway was splattered with blood and gore; the men seemed reluctant to re-enter the area. I ordered them back to work, then went to the adjacent mess decks, and finding a similar scene, got the crewmen there organized and ripping and burning again.

When I returned, Doc was trying to get Hodges' pulse. He couldn't find it. Hodges' breathing was shallow and extremely ragged. "*Oxygen!*" Doc yelled. The equipment was stored with the operating table on the mess decks. I sent a man running to get it.

144

McClarren:

ARE YOU SENDING ASSISTANCE? ARE YOU SENDING
ASSISTANCE? ARE YOU SENDING ASSISTANCE? ARE
YOU SENDING ASSISTANCE?

Kamiseya:

WORD HAS GONE TO ALL AUTHORITIES. WORD HAS
GONE TO ALL AUTHORITIES. COMNAVFORJAPAN IS
REQUESTING ASSIT. WHAT KEY LISTS DO YOU HAVE
LEFT? LAST WE GOT FROM YOU WAS "ARE YOU
SENDING ASSIT." PLEASE ADVISE WHAT KEY LIST
YOU HAVE LEFT AND IF IT APPEARS THAT YOUR COMM
SPACES WILL BE ENTERED?

About this time Bucher entered the crypto room and had
McClarren send out his reply:

HAVE O KEY LIST AND THIS ONLY ONE HAVE. HAVE
BEEN REQUESTED TO FOLLOW INTO WONSAN. HAVE THREE
WOUNDED AND ONE MAN WITH LEG BLOWN OFF. HAVE
NOT USED ANY WEAPONS OR UNCOVERED 50-CAL. MAC.
DESTROYING ALL KEY LISTS AND AS MUCH ELE
EQUIPT AS POSSIBLE. HOW ABOUT SOME HELP. THESE
GUYS MEAN BUSINESS. HAVE SUSTAINED SMALL WOUND
IN RECTUM. DO NOT INTEND TO OFFER ANY
RESISTANCE. INTERROGATIVE QSL. INTERROGATIVE
QSL. DO NOT KNOW HOW LONG WILL BE ABLE TO HOLD
UP CIRCUIT AND DO NOT KNOW IF COMM SPACES WILL
BE ENTERED.

Kamiseya:

ROGER, ROGER. WE DOING ALL WE CAN. CAPT HERE
AND CNFJ [Commander Naval Forces Japan] ON
HOTLINE. LAST I GOT WAS AIR FORCE GOING HELP
YOU WITH SOME AIRCRAFT BUT CAN'T REALLY SAY
AS CNFJ COORDINATING WITH I PRESUME KOREA FOR
SOME F-105. THIS UNOFFICIAL BUT I THINK THAT
WHAT WILL HAPPEN.

Bailey:

ROGER YOUR LAST. ROGER YOUR LAST.

It was now 1409 (2:09 P.M.).

Bucher came down the ladder, and looking at Hodges,

145

who was still unconscious, ordered Baldridge to amputate his leg. Doc shook his head. An amputation would serve no good purpose, he told Bucher; it would only start the bleeding again. His tone was firm, making it clear that he knew what he was doing and Bucher did not.

On seeing the captain had left the bridge, I started back topside. The SO-1 was no longer firing now, but the P-4's were. As I came out onto the 01 level, I could see paper scattered all over the deck on the port side just aft of the pilothouse. I recognized the sheets. They were from ship-identification pubs and were stamped SECRET. I guessed someone had dropped them when the firing resumed. There was a P-4 off our starboard quarter nearly astern of us. It wasn't firing, but I knew it could do so at any moment. Crawling on my hands and knees, but keeping a nervous eye on the P-4, I started picking them up.

Bailey:

SURE COULD USE SOME HELP NOW.

Kamiseya:

ROGER, ROGER. WE STILL WITH YOU AND DOING ALL WE CAN. EVERYONE REALLY TURNING TO AND FIGURE BY NOW AIR FORCE GOT SOME BIRDS WINGING YOUR WAY.

Bailey:

ROGER, ROGER. SURE HOPE SO. WE PRETTY BUSY WITH DESTRUCTION RIGHT NOW. CAN'T SEE FOR THE SMOKE.

Kamiseya:

ROGER, ROGER. WISH I COULD HELP MORE. ALL INFO YOU PASS BEING SENT TO AREA COMMANDER AND THEY IN TURN COORDINATING FOR WHATEVER ACTION GOT TO BE TAKEN. SURE PROCESS ALREADY BEING INITIATED FOR SOME IMMEDIATE RELIEF. COMSEVENTHFLT, CNFJ, AND NSA GROUP PAC ALL GOT INFO RIGHT AWAY.

Bailey 1415 (2:15 P.M.):

ROGER YOUR LAST AND SURE HOPE SOMEONE DOES
SOMETHING. WE ARE HELPLESS AT THIS TIME.
CANNOT DO ANYTHING BUT WAIT.

With a big sigh of relief, I grabbed the last sheet. Then
to my dismay I saw a mass of pages, at least fifty of them,
underneath the boat davit. To reach them I'd have to crawl
toward the P-4. Hoping no one aboard was looking, I
inched forward, then grabbed as fast as I could. With the
last one in hand, I hurried to the side and threw the documents overboard. At least a few of our secrets wouldn't
fall into enemy hands.

One of the P-4's resumed firing. I couldn't see which
one, but guessed it was my nearest neighbor, as I could
hear the splatter of the machine-gun bullets all around me.
I felt no pain and was convinced they had missed. All the
same, I wanted to put as much steel as possible between
me and them. I dashed back across the deck.

It was then I saw the captain. He had come back topside
while I was gathering the classified pages. He was standing
on the port wing, frantically waving his white stocking cap.
"Stop firing, you bastards!" he yelled over and over.

Seeing him waving the white emblem of surrender, I
realized for the first time that Bucher intended to give up
the ship, that he was, in fact, at this very moment doing
exactly that.

147

13

Perhaps because the North Koreans had no way of knowing that Bucher was the *Pueblo*'s captain, the firing didn't stop. Moments after I returned to the pilothouse, the SO-1 let loose another barrage.

"Hit the deck," I yelled. Everyone did. Each previous time this had happened, the firing had let up after a brief interval. But this time it didn't; it was sustained, concentrated, as if the North Koreans were determined to punish us for disobeying their orders, even if it meant smashing us into submission. "Stay down until they stop shooting," I ordered. None of the eight or ten men present questioned that command.

But one late arrival did. *"You sons of bitches,"* Bucher screamed, entering from the port side. *"You cowards! Get up off the deck!"*

Later Bucher would say that the men were all lying in a pile, quivering with terror, that no one was manning the ship. Not true. Some of us were crouched, a few were prone, but each man knew his assigned task and was doing it; we retained control of the ship throughout, albeit from less exposed positions. Bucher would also state that when I didn't get up he helped me to my feet with a well-placed kick astern. This too never happened. And, for Bucher's sake, it is perhaps best it didn't, for I was in no mood to become a scapegoat for his ill-conceived actions.

After a few minutes the firing subsided, then stopped. But Bucher's mood was little improved. And it grew worse when Steve Harris called to report that there was just too

148

much paper and too little time. He asked Bucher to tell Japan that at least some of our classified pubs would probably be compromised.

Bucher favored Steve with an even choicer set of swear words.

I again checked our navigation—we were still a good distance outside the twelve-mile limit—then helped Schumacher start drafting a new message to Japan. One of the men asked if he could destroy the main transmitter. Negative, I replied; that should be the very last thing to go. I did give him permission to destroy the one for the Hi Comm network. By now we had discovered that it was inoperative.

There was no need for both the captain and the exec to remain on the bridge. With Bucher's consent, I decided to go below to see if I could help in the destruction or the care of the wounded.

Bailey:

DESTRUCTION OF PUBS HAVE BEEN INEFFECTIVE.
SUSPECT SEVERAL WILL BE COMPROMISED.

Kamiseya:

CAN YOU GIVE ME A LIST OF WHAT YOU HAVEN'T
DESTROYED? CAN YOU GIVE ME A LIST OF WHAT YOU
HAVEN'T DESTROYED?

As I started below, I happened to look aft through an open door and saw the P-4 with the boarding party come alongside on our starboard quarter. I didn't see the message the SO-1 hoisted about this same time, but later learned they had ordered us to come to all stop. I did feel the change in the engines, as, following Bucher's instructions, Lacy pulled the annunciator back. And I heard, over the 1MC, a message that sent a wave of nausea from my stomach to my throat, Bucher ordering: "Lay aft to the starboard quarter to assist the boarding party."

It wasn't enough that we had to surrender; we had to help the bastards aboard too.

Boatswain's Mate Norbert Klepac, Commissaryman

149

Harry Lewis, and Boatswain's Mate Willie Bussell from the forward repair party went aft to assist the North Koreans.

I think I know how each man felt.

Shortly after this, Lacy came on the 1MC to remind the crew that they were subject to the military Code of Conduct. "You are not required to tell more than your name, rank, and serial number," he explained.

Later I learned that this announcement, like nearly all of the positive suggestions made on the bridge that day, had first come not from Bucher but from someone else, in this instance Gene Lacy. Bucher had forgotten about the Code.

Unfortunately for the crew of the USS *Pueblo*, and the United States, this would not be the last time he would do so.

Baldridge shook his head when I asked him how Hodges was doing. He also informed me that several other men— including Radioman Charles Crandall and CT Peter Langenberg—had been wounded in the earlier salvos. He had given them what help he could.

Chicca was still in my stateroom. Someone had propped his legs up and put a blanket over him. He was worried about the Code-of-Conduct announcement. "What do I do, Mr. Murphy?" he asked. "I'm dressed like a sailor, but I'm a Marine."

I assured him the Code applied to all branches of the service. "Just name, rank, and serial number," I repeated.

Chicca was obviously in pain, but he was holding up well. I realized that, insofar as I knew, all the crew had behaved well. Maybe it wouldn't go down in the history books as one of our finest hours, but at that moment I felt very proud of them, proud to be their exec.

Coming through the passageway, I had spotted several partly burned documents and had picked them up. Going into the head that was located between the captain's cabin and mine, I tore them into tiny pieces, threw the pieces into the toilet, and pulled down the handle to flush.

Nothing happened. I had forgotten that the pump had

150

been cut off when we went to general quarters. Suddenly the futility of it all hit me. There was a chair next to the john. I collapsed into it. I was physically and emotionally drained. Had I tried, I doubt seriously if I could have summoned the strength to get up. I just sat there staring dumbly ahead. There wasn't anything more that could be done. It was all over.

Bailey, 1432 (2:32 P.M.):

HAVE BEEN DIRECTED TO COME TO ALL STOP AND BEING BOARDED AT THIS TIME.

Kamiseya:

ROGER YOUR LAST. IT ON WAY TO CNFJ.

Bailey:

FOUR MEN INJURED AND ONE CRITICALLY AND GOING OFF THE AIR NOW AND DESTROYING THIS GEAR.

Kamiseya, 1435 (2:35 P.M.):

ROGER, GO AHEAD. CAN YOU TRANSMIT IN THE CLEAR?

There was no answer from the USS *Pueblo*.

"There was nothing else I could do, Ed." Commander Bucher had laid below to his stateroom to put on long underwear, an extra pair of socks, his flight jacket, and commander's cap. I just stared at him as he dressed for the formal surrender.

I felt sorry, for all of us, the whole crew of the *Pueblo,* but most of all, oddly enough, for Bucher. His first command, and he'd lost his ship. A number of his men were wounded, one dying. He cared about his "boys." What had happened to Hodges must have deeply shaken him. I could feel nothing for him now but sympathy. Not since reporting aboard the *Pueblo* had I felt as close to him as I did at this moment. It was as if all our differences had been obliterated by the North Korean gunfire. We were no longer adversaries. We were, literally and figuratively, in the same

151

boat. And that boat was now the proud possession of a hostile nation.

Like the other officers, I had dressed that morning— ages and ages ago—in informal cold-weather gear, khakis, leather flight jacket, stocking cap, no emblems of rank. But I couldn't bring myself to get up and change clothes. I just sat there watching Bucher. It didn't seem there was anything more to say, but, incredibly, for several minutes we exchanged small talk. The words have since faded from my mind, but not the impression they made. It seemed inconceivable that we could be talking like this, about such inconsequential things, considering the enormity of what was happening.

When he finished dressing, Bucher went topside. I sat there for a few more seconds, then wearily rose and started to follow him. As I stepped into the passageway I almost collided with a North Korean soldier. His dark Oriental face was the opposite of inscrutable; hatred was written all over it. He pointed his bayonet-rigged automatic rifle straight at my stomach.

Authors' note: All teletype transcriptions to and from the USS *Pueblo* are exact, including stated times, and are from transcriptions monitored in Japan and declassified and made public during the *Pueblo* Court of Inquiry.

14

The fact that I couldn't understand his commands seemed to anger him even more. Prodding with the bayonet, he directed me toward the ladder. When I didn't move fast enough to please him, he gave me a quick, paralyzingly painful kick in the back.

The height of the kick startled me almost as much as the pain itself. I had been unaware that a North Korean soldier is trained to use his feet as adroitly as his hands, that he can stand next to a man and deliver a kick to the head. Unfortunately, I was to become all too familiar with that particular lesson.

From the boat deck I was shoved down the outboard ladder to the fantail. Some dozen crewmen were already there, including Schumacher, Tim Harris, Klepac. We exchanged silent, grim looks. Earlier, on my way up the ladder, I had heard an announcement over the 1MC that all crewmen were to report to the well deck. I presumed the rest were there now. We had only two guards, one who stood above us on the 01 level with a submachine gun, the other on our same level and just a few feet away with an automatic rifle. It would be fairly easy to overpower the one with the automatic rifle, but taking the other would probably cost someone's life. Still, the impulse to try was tremendously strong. So was the desire to dive over the side, although I knew that even if they didn't shoot at us we wouldn't last long in the cold water.

We had been standing, but a sudden burst of gunfire made us all dive for the deck. The firing ended as quickly as it had started. It sounded as if it could have been from the P-4. Why would the North Koreans fire on the ship when their own men were in command? Had some of the crew tried to resist and been gunned down? Was the skipper dead? I didn't know.

Another North Korean arrived carrying strips of torn sheeting from the bunks. With impatient motions, he indicated we were to blindfold each other. Someone behind me put a strip over my eyes. It was tight at the top, but not at the bottom. I tilted my head back and found I could see out.

In moving, however, my leather jacket rubbed against the back of my neck, and I felt a slight irritating sensation. Reaching back, I found my hand was covered with something sticky and warm. It was blood. At some point I had been wounded, but just when, and whether by shrapnel or machine-gun fire, I didn't know. It couldn't be too bad, I decided, or I would have noticed it before this.

I wondered about Hodges, Woelk, and the other wounded. Were they being cared for? Was Hodges still alive?

After about twenty minutes, someone barked a command. When we didn't understand, the North Koreans helped us. Gestures, prodding, slaps, kicks: these would constitute our new language. We were to stand and be marched forward and then below.

The blindfold was just loose enough that I could see where we were going. Down the starboard side, through the bloody passageway, past the gaping hole. To my horror, I also saw that I was walking on a carpet of classified documents.

We were taken into the crew's forward berthing area. Someone shoved me. I sat down, sandwiched between two bunks, my head in my hands, as if exhausted. Actually I was peeking out. Though my view was limited, I could get some idea of our situation. Nearly the whole crew had been jammed into the compartment. Six, maybe eight guards, most of them busy rifling footlockers. Not counting the

154

wounded, there were at least seventy-five of us aboard capable of resistance. Even though they were armed and we were not, those were not bad odds.

Still no sign of Bucher. I was the senior officer in the compartment. If any action were taken, I'd have to initiate it.

Say we overcame them, what then? I was sure the other ships had remained in close proximity. I also felt sure that they would have no hesitation in resuming firing even if it meant killing their own men.

What was needed was a distraction. That and more time.

Later I would learn that similar thoughts had passed through the minds of nearly everyone present. We were all waiting for the same thing, for U.S. planes or ships to appear—for a chance.

My ears almost ached from straining to hear the welcome sound of American jets.

Instead they heard the *Pueblo*'s engines increase from one-third to all ahead full.

Occasionally one of the crewmen would make a remark. Seaman Stuart Russell voiced the hope that the North Koreans enjoyed the "candy" in his locker, because it was his favorite brand, Ex-Lax. Someone else asked if anyone knew any good "numbers" in Wonsan. Senses of humor were intact. But the remarks were quickly followed by sharp slapping sounds, then groans. "This is the exec," I said *sotto voce*. "Cool it for now." I braced myself for the slap or kick, but it never came.

We waited. And waited. How much time had passed since the boarding? One hour, two? Closer to the latter, I guessed. By now we must finally be deep inside North Korean territorial waters. Would that hamper rescue efforts? I didn't know. I hoped not.

Damn but my kidneys ached! Apparently the others had the same problem. "Benjo," somebody yelled. When the

Japanese word for "toilet" brought no reaction, someone else moaned, "Man, I got to take a piss!" Several of the men made gestures, indicating their need. When this didn't work, one simply stood up and began urinating in his helmet. With this the North Koreans got the message. Individually they removed blindfolds and led the men to the head. Finally my turn came. With the blindfold off I tried to take in as much of the scene as I could. All the officers were present, except Bucher. Maybe they were keeping him in the pilothouse to steer the ship. Were our own men in the engine room? If we got that break, if those planes ever came, it could make all the difference. Who had been there when I went below? Goldman, Blansett. I couldn't spot them in the compartment.

The guard cuffed me for taking too long.

This time on my return the blindfold was fastened securely.

We waited. Then the engines again stopped. A few minutes later they started again, all ahead full. More boarders? Probably.

Where were those American planes?

I was nearly knocked off the bunk as the *Pueblo* smashed into the side of a pier. Then the engines died. There was a last creaking and groaning as the ship came to rest, then no more vibration, no more hum, just the lap of water against the hull and the scurrying of footsteps on the deck above.

I had heard the sounds of the USS *Pueblo* for the last time.

There was a sudden flurry of activity, and lots of curses. My blindfold was yanked down, and I was prodded to my feet. The guards were searching the men. Some complained, but only once. The North Koreans were expert at rabbit punches, too. Then came my turn. If they tried to take my wedding ring, I was determined to resist. But they didn't try. They did take a pen-and-pencil set, my wallet and

156

sunglasses, and the hand-warmer Carol had given me. I was surprised they left my watch, because they were taking those of some of the other men. Maybe it was because the band was pretty beat up.

It was a scavenger operation as much as a search for weapons. The bloody bastards were nothing more than pirates, albeit in military dress.

I was ordered to climb to the top of the ladder to the main deck. It was a moment or two before I realized the command had been in English, admittedly broken English, but it meant that at least one of our captors could speak the language. This limited the possibility of exchanging messages with the crew. He could understand what was said.

Above deck, a worse realization hit me. It was dark and cold. The sun had gone down. Our chances of being rescued had now diminished considerably.

Two guards noticed I still had on my watch. They tried to wrench it off my wrist, but the band held.

Another North Korean bound my hands in front of me with what looked like fishing cord. He pulled it so tight that the blood wouldn't flow. Then, after they had refastened my blindfold, which had been hanging loose around my neck, I was yanked by the hands across the well deck and off the port side over a makeshift gangway they had laid between the ship and the quay wall.

My feet hit concrete, then loose dirt. Voices, many of them; they sounded angry. Also the whirr of a running engine. Almost immediately I was shoved up some stairs, onto what I was sure was a bus, then knocked back into a hard wooden seat.

Someone was sitting next to me, but I couldn't tell who. I raised my head. A whack against the back of my skull knocked it down. Startled, I instinctively raised it again, only to have the same thing happen.

I got the point. Heads were to be kept bowed, in the manner of criminals. Thinking back on it later, I realized

157

that our status was made plain in that moment. We were not prisoners of war, not captives of some military action, but criminals, and would be treated accordingly.

"How many guys?" a voice yelled into the bus. Despite the slang, the speaker was obviously North Korean. How many guys what—on the bus, on the ship? There was a chorus of confused answers. I tried to recognize at least a few of the voices, couldn't. However, I was sure that none was the captain's. With so many of us, there had to be at least two buses; maybe he was on the other one.

"Who the dead guy?" the same speaker asked.

So Hodges had died.

The bus jerked forward. It was old, rickety, almost springless, and the road bad. Attempts to speak—"Water," "Benjo"—brought instant retribution. We kept quiet, the silence only periodically broken by the wail of the bus's horn.

After what seemed a full hour, the bus came to a stop. Again the angry voices, as if we were surrounded by a crowd. From the other sounds, I knew we were in a railroad station. Pushed off the bus, then pulled forward by the rope which bound our hands, we were shoved onto what had to be a train. The compartment was musty and icy cold. Again I was pushed into a wooden seat; if possible, this one seemed even harder.

My head stayed down. I was already learning to respond like a prisoner.

With the start of the train, my lingering hopes began to fade. While we were still aboard ship there had seemed a fair chance of rescue; at least the United States knew approximately where we were, and in time could have located us. But now even we had no idea of our location, and no way to communicate such knowledge if we did.

What would the United States do? I thought of several possibilities; almost all were unlikely. None, especially a retaliatory strike against Wonsan or some other North

158

Korean city, offered much hope for us. And then I thought of Carol.

Sometime in the near future the news would be made public, the wives and families notified. Carol was a strong person; she had an inner strength that grew from her deep faith. But she was also a woman, and a very feminine one at that, seven months pregnant, with a two-year-old son to look after. Almost alone in a strange land.

And there was not a thing in the world that I could do to make it any easier for her. Except pray. I did.

I also touched the thin gold band on the third finger of my left hand, knowing that the matching one was on hers. This too was a link.

But even if Carol held up, there was also my mother, still ill in San Francisco. How would the news that her only son was a prisoner of the North Koreans hit her?

I had to stop such thoughts. The important thing now was to plan ahead. What could we expect? Would they shoot us? I didn't know, but I was sure if they did we would be questioned at length before it happened. And here we were in an odd position. Technically the United States was no longer at war with North Korea. Although I was not even sure whether North Korea had signed the Geneva Convention—only later did I learn that they had not—I intended to lean hard on that, insisting that as a military prisoner I need only give name, rank, and serial number. In short, I intend to adhere to the Code of Conduct. My recollections of the Korean conflict were sketchy. I did recall, however, the stories about torture and brainwashing. If we were going to be treated the same way, how would I fare? Frankly, I didn't know. I made no rash promises to myself, only that if such techniques were used, I would do my best to hold out. Only time would tell whether my best would be good enough.

A moan from across the aisle relieved me of such thoughts. Someone was in great pain. From the voice, I could tell it was Woelk. I'd hoped that by now, because of the obvious severity of his wound, he had been rushed to a

159

hospital. But I had credited our captors with more humanity than they possessed. It was not a mistake that I would make again.

He was crying for water. Risking another rap on the head, I yelled, "This man needs water and medical aid! For God's sake, somebody help him!" Perhaps because several other voices took up the chant, no one was hit this time. And a few minutes later Woelk was given water. But there was no indication that they were doing anything for his wound. The moaning continued. I knew Woelk. He was no crybaby. He was hurting, and badly.

There was a shuffling of feet toward the front of the compartment, then the command, "Sit down."

"How many men aboard ship?" someone asked, in English but with an unmistakably Oriental accent.

"Eighty-three," came the reply. "Seventy-five enlisted, six officers, two civilians."

Thank God, I thought, recognizing the voice; *Bucher's alive!*

But my relief was suddenly tempered by the realization of what he was doing.

"What ship mission?"

"To measure the radioactivity of sunspots," Bucher replied.

There was a very empty feeling in the pit of my stomach. What Bucher was saying was of course gibberish; from what I could hear, he was betraying nothing classified. But that he was saying anything—more than name, rank, and serial number—meant that he had abandoned the Code!

The ramifications of this hit me in waves. Every crewman in the compartment could hear him; each now knew that, despite the announcement over the ship's loudspeaker, we were no longer playing by the rules. From here on, each man was on his own. Each would have to improvise, make his own way, but always at the risk of contradicting the others.

160

Damn Bucher's need to entertain! Thanks to the lead of our skipper, the *Pueblo*'s crew had lost its one chance to maintain a semblance of unity.

Only later did I see how the North Koreans had used his weakness to their advantage. As far as I could tell, Bucher had not been in our compartment when the train first started. He had been brought here, and probably to the other compartments as well, to be reinterrogated, so the whole crew could understand that since their captain was talking freely, they had no reason not to do likewise.

The questions, and answers, continued. I tried to make out everything that Bucher was saying, so we could have one consistent story, but I could only catch bits and pieces. ". . . waste propagation theory of sunspot activity . . . peaceful oceanographic research . . . doctor for my wounds . . ." After about fifteen or twenty minutes the interrogation stopped. I presumed Bucher had been removed from the car. But these were not the last questions. "Who executive officer Lieutenant Murphy?"

So someone had identified me, not just by name and rank but with my job. I suspected—perhaps erroneously—that it was Bucher who had done so.

I raised my bound hands. Somehow grabbed them and yanked me up the aisle, pushing me into probably the same seat Bucher had just vacated.

"What ship mission?"

I parroted Bucher's reply.

"You CIA!"

I vehemently denied this.

"Who ordered you to spy on North Korea?"

"I demand that you give our men medical aid. The Geneva Convention—"

A clout to the back of the head.

"Admit you are CIA!"

"My name is Edward R. Murphy, Jr. My rank is lieutenant in the United States Navy. My serial number is—"

Another clout, much harder this time.

161

Fortunately the interrogation was brief, less than ten minutes. And as yet the North Koreans did not really seem to comprehend the importance of their capture. Their questions indicated little interest in the equipment aboard, but undisguised amazement that such a small ship had such a large crew. Someone had told them I was navigator, but nothing was asked, at this stage, about intrusion. Yet in just the few minutes that they questioned me, some of the other dangers inherent in abandoning the Code became apparent. When you answered one question and not another, that second area became suspect, was pinpointed for further investigation. If you lied in answering one question, eventually you would have to do the same with another, and still another, until you ran the risk of being tripped up by your own fictions. If they questioned all eighty-two of us, there were bound to be contradictions, unintentional slips. Putting these together with what they had recovered from the ship, it wouldn't take them long to form a composite picture.

If they knew what they were doing. There remained the possibility that they did not. It was a slim hope.

Even though Bucher had thrown the Code out the window, we did have one other guideline. Those of us with access to classified information knew its importance. If we could only hold that back.

"Eat."

It was not until they brought us food that I realized how hungry I was. I guessed it was about two in the morning, but had no way to determine this, as they did not remove the blindfolds. At least fourteen hours had passed since our interrupted lunch.

Our "meal" consisted of a piece of hard bread and a ladle of warm water. As thirsty as I was, it was difficult to keep the water down. Later I learned that all water in North Korea is boiled before use, to kill germs, then served warm.

When we had finished eating, I tried to sleep, couldn't. From across the aisle came the screams of Woelk.

162

The train slowed, then stopped. A guard moved down the aisle taking off the blindfolds and the rope handcuffs. My hands throbbed with pain as the circulation returned. I was then taken to the restroom. Although the window was steamed over, I could see the sky was lightening. I looked at my watch. It was 5:30 in the morning.

While most of the men were prodded off the train, the guards motioned for several of us to remain behind to carry off Woelk.

CT Francis Ginther, Seaman Dale Rigby, Fireman Norman Spear, and I each took a corner of the stretcher, trying to lift it carefully so as to cause Woelk the least amount of pain. It wasn't easy. The stretcher, specially designed to maneuver a man past the equipment in the tight confines of the engine room, was very limber and had no rigidity. And Woelk was a big man, weighing around two hundred pounds. Even with the four of us, it was an effort to lift him.

Since leaving the ship no attempt had been made to change his dressing. He was still wrapped in a plastic tablecloth from the wardroom, the dried blood binding the plastic to the wound. Infection had apparently set in. The stench was so strong we had to turn our faces away to keep from gagging. Ignoring the North Korean gestures to hurry, we eased him out as gently as possible.

As much as a man might wish to know the future, there are times it is good he cannot. Although I wasn't to learn its ramifications until much later, one such time was occurring right now. While I was helping carry Woelk's stretcher, the other five officers of the USS *Pueblo* were being taken off the train, heads bowed, hands up in the air, while popping flashbulbs and snapping shutters recorded the event. Within days photos would be released to the world press, captioned "Officers of the captured American spy ship *Pueblo*." At the same time the North Koreans would announce that one of the men aboard the ship had been killed resisting capture, But they withheld his name.

163

Carol Murphy, shown the pictures of the *Pueblo*'s officers, would be able to find everyone. Except her husband.

The pre-dawn light revealed a cold, sterile city, its buildings gray and lifeless, its people—there were large numbers of them, being held back by a row of soldiers—almost nondescript in their sameness.

Urban industrial. Block after block of two- and three-story structures, with dirty stone fronts, grimy windows, behind which were rows of unshaded yellow lightbulbs.

I'd seen pictures of places like this before in magazines. For a moment I felt panic. Those pictures had been of cities in Russia! We had been on the train a long time. Could we have traveled that far?

But the Oriental faces relieved this worry, although they replaced it with another. Never before had I seen such undisguised hatred. If it hadn't been for the soldiers, who were roughly shoving them back, I was sure they would have killed us. As it was, they spat, shook fists, hurled curses. Those angry voices I'd heard in Wonsan: the scene must have been the same. Why such anger? Although I didn't then know, in time I would find out.

Later I would also learn that the city was Pyongyang, the capital of North Korea.

More buses were waiting, and the guards motioned us to board. Trying to get Woelk up the steps, I stumbled, and got another kick in the back.

This time, when the bus started, we weren't reblindfolded. Although we still had to keep our heads bowed, I managed to sneak glimpses out the nearest window. At each corner were large numbers of people, queued up in orderly lines. I guessed they were waiting for buses. Earlier I had wondered what so many people would be doing at the train station at such an early hour. Later I would learn that with only the exception of those who work at night, all North Koreans are required to rise at the same hour and go to work at the same time; that around the clock, the life of every man, woman, and child is regimented. Even without

164

this knowledge, the street-corner scenes reminded me of George Orwell's *Animal Farm*.

About a half-hour later the buses left the road, passed through a gate into what appeared to be a military compound, then stopped in the courtyard behind a large building.

Again the North Koreans gestured for us to get out. This time Seaman Ramon Rosales lent an extra pair of hands to ease the burden of the stretcher.

The building—which we christened "The Barn"—was rectangular, brick, four stories high, and at first glance appeared to be a barracks of some kind. From the number of guards awaiting us when we got off, there was no question as to its new use. It was not the Pyongyang Hilton; it was the *Pueblo* prison.

Prodded through the door with kicks and jabs, we were given little time to inspect our surroundings. But we were immediately hit by the strong, almost overpowering smell of disinfectant. The place seemed to have been saturated with it. The stairs were ahead, three flights. I hoped we wouldn't have to carry Woelk up them, but we did, all the way to the top. Poor Woelk remained conscious throughout.

At the head of the stairs was a large lobby, from which branched out two long corridors, with rooms along both sides. Following the shouted commands of the guards, we took Woelk into one of the rooms and as carefully as possible placed the stretcher on the floor. The guards then pointed to three men—Chicca, Crandall, and Rigby—indicating they were to remain with him.

Ginther, Rosales, Spear, and I were assigned the room directly across the hall.

By American standards, our one-room apartment for four should have had a "Condemned" sign nailed to the door. The floor was very greasy, as if it had just been oiled, the filth ground into the wood. The floorboards were warped, with big gaps between them, some about an inch wide.

The room measured about ten by eighteen feet. In each

corner was a crude wooden bed with a single dirty blanket and a sack mattress filled with what appeared to be rice husks. At the foot of each bed was a straight-backed wooden chair. A rickety table, a single unshaded lightbulb hanging from the high ceiling, and a radiator that wasn't working completed the furnishings.

Later I was told that prior to our arrival the building had been used for North Korean officer candidates. I hated to imagine where the enlisted men lived.

As soon as the guard slammed the door, we checked the windows. They were nailed shut. They were also double, consisting of two frames of wrinkled glass. A white sheet sandwiched between them made them entirely opaque. There was no way you could either get air in or see out.

But the guards had no trouble viewing us. The cracks in the door were almost large enough to stick a finger through.

We each picked a bed, then collapsed onto it. No one was in the mood for talk, but one of the men asked me if we had intruded into territorial waters and I assured him and the others that we had come nowhere near doing so.

After a time the building grew quiet, except for the occasional cries of Woelk. I lay there, with all my clothes on, too exhausted to undress, too tired to sleep.

It was then that I remembered something that had occurred just after the start of the Korean war, in June, 1950. I was not yet thirteen at the time. I could recall my sister Anne saying: "Boy, I'm glad you'll never get involved in that."

15

Early on the morning of January 24 a stern-faced guard threw open the door, stomped into the room, and slammed down something on the table.

Our first meal in the Barn consisted of dry bread and four tins of a watery slop that apparently was the North Korean equivalent of soup. We would nickname it *crème de garbage*.

I had hoped the whole crew would mess together, providing a chance to exchange information and to see how the others were doing, but our captors went to elaborate lengths to keep us apart. When the guards escorted us to the head, only two or three men from any one room were taken at the same time, while all the other doors along the hallway remained closed.

The head was past the lobby, toward the end of the hall, but we could smell it most of the way to our room. In addition to three squat toilets, there were four urinals, all cracked. Unless you were careful, you would find yourself with wet feet.

"Bali, bali! Bali, bali!" All the way back the guards screamed the words at us, at the same time prodding us with their guns. "Bali, bali" obviously meant "Hurry, hurry." We'd had our first lesson in Korean.

Shortly before noon our door was thrown open, and one of the interpreters bellowed, "Any officer here?" I stood and followed him out into the hallway. Steve Harris, Schumacher, Tim Harris, and Gene Lacy were already there. Bucher was just emerging from a room two doors down, on

167

the opposite side. All the officers were still alive. For the moment, at least.

Heads bowed, we were marched to a large room at the far end of the hall. It was very dimly lit, lending a feeling of ominousness to the scene. Four or five North Korean officers were seated behind a long table near the windows. At the end of the room was a smaller table, behind which were three men. One was an interpreter, whom we later nicknamed "Max." From their shoulder boards it was apparent that the remaining two were "brass." The one with a big single star, we later learned, was a general. His companion, with four smaller stars, a senior colonel. Directly in front of them and toward the center of the room were six chairs. We were ordered to sit in them.

The atmosphere was unmistakably that of a trial. The accused: the crew of the USS *Pueblo,* as represented by her officers.

The general barked an order. Max translated: "Each stand, give name, rank, job aboard ship."

Starting with Bucher, we did, all of us giving the correct information, except Skip, who stated his job was "First Lieutenant." Another lie we would have to remember. And just what were the duties of a ship's First Lieutenant?

"Why you spy on the Democratic People's Republic of Korea?" the interpreter translated the general's scream. Without waiting for an answer, the general accused us of conspiring with South Korea to start a war, of being CIA, and of intruding into North Korea's territorial waters.

So I'd guessed correctly. "Intrusion" was to be the name of the game. Having to justify their illegal seizure someway, the North Koreans had fastened onto this. But the United States would know better, I felt sure. We had radioed our correct position more than a dozen times.

Bucher stood and forcefully denied the charges. The ship had been in international waters, he protested. There was nothing illegal about its activities. Then he added, "If you will release the ship and crew, I'll remain in North Korea in their place."

It was an incredibly brave act. There was no question about the skipper's sincerity. He meant every word he said.

But the general angrily ordered him to sit down, and ignoring the offer, repeated the charges. At the finish of each, as if on cue, the "jurors" would shake their fists and shout curses.

The general asked why fifty thousand American troops remained in South Korea. Bucher replied that while he had no idea of the exact number, he presumed that they were there because the South Korean government had asked them to stay.

Thus far the colonel had remained silent. But with this he jumped up and began beating his fist on the table, at the same time firing curses at us with such machine-gun rapidity that Max didn't even try to translate. For a moment it looked as if the colonel would leap over the table and try to kill us. But the general, looking frightened, ordered him to sit down, and he complied.

Although the vehemence of the attack startled us, there was something very rehearsed about the whole scene. Still, we now paid the colonel closer attention. He was about 5'7", very thin, wore glasses, had very intense eyes. His shock of jet-black hair was combed straight back, without a part. Had it not been for his buck teeth, he might have been called handsome. As it was, it was not a face you were likely to forget.

We would have no chance to do so. Although after this interrogation we would not see the general again, the colonel was to become our chief inquisitor. We would nickname him, with more than begrudging respect, "Super Colonel," or for short, "Super C."

If we did not confess to intrusion, the general resumed, we would be shot. Each of us was again ordered to stand and make our choice.

One after another, all six of us denied the intrusion charge.

Another long diatribe from the general followed. By this time I was beginning to wonder if North Koreans ever spoke

169

in anything softer than a shout. Max translated only a portion of what he said. But it was enough. "You will be shot before sundown."

Super C and Max smiled with obvious pleasure at the verdict.

The trial was over. Forbidden to speak to each other, we were marched back to our rooms.

On the way I wondered whether I should tell my cellmates—Ginther, Spear, and Rosales—about the threat. I decided against it. I didn't believe it, for one thing. And, whether it was true or not, there was no need to cause them additional anguish.

When they asked what had happened, I described the interrogation in detail, omitting only the final part.

It was winter; the sun would set early. When the guard brought lunch—again the same slop—I felt encouraged. Surely they wouldn't waste food on us, even food this bad, if they were going to kill us in a few hours. But each time I heard the tramp of boots in the hall, I froze, expecting the door to be thrown open. Then, late in the afternoon, two vehicles pulled into the courtyard and remained there, their engines idling. Had they come for us?

Although the windows were opaque, some light filtered in. I watched its colors change. It was the most beautiful sunset I had ever seen.

It had been a bluff after all.

That night, for the first time since our capture, I slept soundly.

Had I looked at our predicament dispassionately, I would have realized that the North Koreans couldn't stop at this. They had to find support for their charges, and there was only one way they could obtain it. Fortunately, my tiredness dulled such thoughts. Fortunately, because it would be the last easy sleep I would have for a very long time.

170

On awakening the next morning my cellmates were amazed that I hadn't heard all the activity during the night —doors slamming, people tramping up and down the halls, curses, crashing sounds. At one point they thought they had heard Commander Bucher's voice, but they couldn't be sure.

That same morning—it was now Thursday, January 25—I was taken to a smaller room on the same floor for my first solitary interrogation. Super C was in charge. Also present, in addition to several guards, were Super C's chief of staff, "Colonel Scar" (so named because of a large three-legged scar on the back of his neck), and an interpreter we later aptly named Wheezy. That afternoon I was taken out a second time and put through the same routine. The questions were identical to those earlier asked: what job aboard ship, why you spy, why you want to start war with Democratic People's Republic of Korea? With a single exception: the focus now was on the intrusion, which they claimed had occurred on the twenty-third, the same day we were captured. We had been "caught in the act," they maintained. We need only admit this, and apologize, and we would be released.

Not having the Code to fall back on, I had to improvise. In these initial sessions I stuck closely to the oceanographic-research story, keeping my answers short and succinct, volunteering nothing, never elaborating. "I don't know" became my favorite phrase. As much as possible, I tried to play the "quiet one," hoping they would think me either stupid or uninformed. Only occasionally would I break the pattern of monosyllabic answers, to deny that we had intruded or to demand medical aid for Woelk and the other wounded men.

They were not happy with this, but except for the pushing and shoving by the guards on my way to and from these sessions, no force was used against me. There were repeated verbal threats, however, and several times during

171

the interrogations I heard heavy crashing sounds, as though a body had been knocked against a wall. Once the sounds were punctuated by a lone cry.

Toward the end of the afternoon session Super C changed his tack. "You might as well tell us everything, because your captain has already confessed."

"I don't believe that," I said, and I didn't.

"It true. Would like to hear recording his confession?"

"I'd like to hear it from the captain himself."

Super C shook his head.

From somewhere down the hall, perhaps another room, I heard what sounded like Bucher's voice, but so muffled by the walls and distance that I couldn't be sure. ". . . espionage activities . . . intruding . . . disguised my ship . . . spied . . . criminal act . . ." I could catch only isolated words and phrases.

There was no doubt it was a recording of someone. But I wouldn't admit, even to myself, the possibility that Bucher had already broken.

On returning to the room, I found Rosales and Ginther very concerned. While I was gone, a squat, burly officer had come in and taken out Spear, handling him roughly.

They, too, had heard the cry.

About an hour later Spear was shoved through the door. He staggered to his bed in the far corner, then collapsed. They had beaten him so badly that it was several minutes before we could get him to tell us what had happened. And then the words came reluctantly, through a haze of pain. Kicks, gun butts, judo chops—all had been used to pummel him into submission.

And he knew nothing of importance. Spear was a fireman. He possessed no classified information. It occurred to me, and confirmation came later, that possibly one man from each room had been singled out for such treatment, as an object lesson for the others.

The burly officer who worked over Spear was given a special nickname: "King Kong."

That evening we were taken to a supply room on the same floor and ordered to strip. The supply personnel, curiously, all wore gauze masks, as if afraid we would contaminate them, a concern with sanitation that would exhibit itself in odd ways throughout our imprisonment.

We were allowed to keep our belts, wristwatches, wedding rings, pen-and-pencil sets, cigarette lighters, and, if we wore them, eyeglasses. They confiscated all our other possessions, including clothing, dog tags, wallets, family pictures. We never saw them again.

We were then issued new uniforms. They were of dark blue, heavily quilted material, and looked very much like those seen on pictures of prisoners taken during the Korean War. In addition, we were each issued a a pair of undershorts, a pair of long johns with draw strings at the ankles, a sweat shirt, a pair of sweat pants, a hat, a pair of shoes, and one pair of socks. The socks were the most colorful item of apparel; some were blue, others green, mine were bright red. The shoes were thickly insulated tennis shoes, and in my case several sizes too small.

We were given no chance to bathe, nor were we given medical treatment for our wounds.

Instead of being returned to the room with the others, I was taken down and across the hall to the room from which I had seen Bucher emerge on the morning of the meeting with all the officers.

I hoped that my request to speak to the captain had finally been granted, but I found the room deserted.

As an officer, the interpreter explained, I was to have the privilege of a separate room. Since Commander Bucher had complained about the room being too cold, they had assigned him to another and given this one to me.

The loneliness hit me the moment the door closed. They might call this privilege; to me the separation from the others was punishment. I hadn't realized how much their companionship meant until it was taken away.

It appeared to be a converted storeroom, to which had been added a bed, a table, and a slat bench. A bare bulb dangling from the ceiling, which remained on night and day, completed the dreary decor. I could see why Bucher had complained; the lower pane on the outside window was missing, the room was on the north side of the building, and the freezing winter wind poured in. I put on all the clothes they had issued me, and was still cold.

There was another interrogation that night, which lasted until 2300 (11 P.M.).

They had two themes now.

Confess and return. This was their favorite. "As soon as you sincerely confess, you will be returned home as quickly as possible." The stress was on the word "sincerely."

Why you hold out? This was their second favorite. "Your captain already talk, why you remain stubborn?" Each time they said it, I would ask to see him. Each time the same answer, "Not possible."

At one point during the questioning I again heard the recording, only this time I could make out more of the words.

I heard it again during the morning and afternoon interrogations on the twenty-sixth, and though I was not about to admit it to my captors, any hopes I had that this was not Bucher's voice began to fade.

That they were playing the recording so often made me suspect that they were using it to coerce the rest of the crew into confessing.

On the twenty-sixth the nature of the interrogations changed. They stopped asking vague, generalized questions and began to zero in on the *Pueblo*'s mission plan. It was obvious from the explicit queries being hurled at me that they were either piecing together classified documents captured with the ship or little by little squeezing substantial bits of information from other members of the crew. They knew that we had departed from Sasebo on January 11; that our operating areas were code-named Pluto, Venus, and Mars; that Lieutenant Stephen Harris was in charge of a special research detachment aboard the USS *Pueblo*.

174

"What do you know about the operations of Lieutenant Harris' detachment?"

"Nothing; my job was to navigate; I was unaware of any of the other activities aboard ship."

For just a moment I thought they had bought my dumb act.

"You attended Principia College," Super C stated. "Is Principia code for CIA?"

They seemed obsessed with making me CIA.

At the same time I was denying this, I was wondering who had told them about my attending Principia. Only then did I see that Super C had my service records spread out on the table in front of him. That shook me. I had hoped the yeoman in the ship's office had destroyed them. This opened entirely new avenues of inquiry, inasmuch as the records listed all our previous assignments. I recalled my tour aboard the USS *Robison*. Were they aware that it was a guided-missile destroyer? If so, how much could they assume I knew about nuclear weapons, about the U.S. Navy's operational plans in event of war? Almost every one of my prior assignments had its touchy security aspects, a few very hush-hush.

Too, with a listing of all the schools I'd attended, my dumb act suddenly became much less convincing.

I looked across the table and met the eyes of Super C. Gradually, bit by bit, we were coming to know each other better. I had underrated him at first, mistaking his bombast, his repetitious tirades, for lack of intelligence. I now realized that he missed very little, that he was storing up answers, both mine and those of others, sifting and comparing them. Thus far he had been patient with my denials of intrusion, my "I don't know" replies. I wondered how long that patience would last.

As navigator of the USS *Pueblo*, my confession of intrusion would be essential to North Korea's case.

Each time an interrogation session ended, I would feel an immense relief. It was short-lived, for immediately I

175

would be returned to my refrigerated room and the monotony that now constituted my days.

The initial shock of our capture was beginning to wear off, to be replaced by a regimented dullness. We were awakened before dawn. Breakfast. Interrogation. Lunch. Another interrogation. Dinner. Another interrogation. Sleep. The only variation, trips to the head. It was already becoming disturbingly routine.

The three meals were identical. As an officer, my fare had improved slightly. There were pieces of turnip and raw fish in the soup, but they did nothing to the taste, which remained flat, totally devoid of any kind of seasoning, as bland as the cup of warm water they also gave me.

There was another change. Instead of the guard, a Korean woman brought in the meals. She was short, dumpy, and well past her prime, but she was the only woman I had seen since our capture. Any expectations of feminine sympathy I might have had quickly vanished. She totally ignored me. The room might as well have been empty.

Even though the meals were bad, and always left me still hungry, they at least meant that for a few minutes I didn't have to sit and stare at the walls. In one respect, and only one, I even looked forward to the interrogation sessions. In one of the interrogation rooms the upper portion of the window wasn't covered. By sliding my chair over, very gradually, I could sit in the sun and for a few minutes be warm. I was beginning to appreciate small things like this.

Sitting or sleeping on bed during day forbidden. When in room prisoners required sit on the straight-backed chair. Looking through window forbidden. Attempting to exchange messages will be dealt with harshly. Speaking loudly forbidden. Speaking in hallway forbidden.

There was nothing to read, nothing to do, except listen. And think.

Since my move into a single cell I hadn't seen another member of the crew. I heard them, however, or at least

176

thought I did. Sitting alone in the room, I became sensitive to sound. The whole building seemed an echo chamber. It was impossible to tell how many of the cries were for effect, how many for real.

I knew that there was probably a single man in each of the rooms on either side of me because whenever I heard two voices, one was always unmistakably Korean. I presumed that, being billeted singly, they were also officers. But I had no clue as to who each was. It was against the rules, we had been told, to raise your voice to a guard. As a result, while the guards shouted, the prisoners spoke softly, making it impossible to recognize either voices or words.

I knew, from my trips down the hall to the head, that some of the rooms held more than four men, perhaps as many as a dozen, since I could hear a number of voices. I guessed that the whole crew was being detained on the same floor. But I had no idea what the other three floors were used for, how many guards there were, where they were stationed.

I did know, from observing where the sun rose and set, that the first room I had been in was on the south side of the building, my current room on the north, while the head was located on the northeast side of the hall, the individual interrogation rooms on the southwest. Maybe it was navigator's habit, but having my directions straight made me feel a little more secure.

The loneliness was bad. But the not knowing was worse. Not knowing whether the footsteps in the hall meant they were coming for you. Not knowing if an interrogation session might be the last. Not knowing if the whole crew was still alive and what they were going through. Not knowing if the voice on the tape was really Bucher's. Not knowing what, if anything, the United States was doing to effect our release.

I thought about that a great deal.

That the idea of rescue now seemed extremely improbable did not mean that I didn't conjure up such fantasies—

I did. But each time, I would have to come back to reality, and it was as bleak and harsh as the walls around us.

Would the United States go to war over this brazen act of piracy? It seemed unlikely. There would be diplomatic protests, speeches in Congress and the UN, but war? I didn't think so, especially since we were already so deeply involved in Vietnam.

Retaliation in force? Had this occurred the same day we were seized, I don't think it would have surprised any of us. But too much time had now elapsed. Yet this possibility obviously worried our captors. During one of the interrogations I had stated that the United States would deal harshly with North Korea if the crew and ship were not released. Super C and the others were instantly alert. There was no question but that they were apprehensive about U.S. reaction. While I was still in the room with the three crewmen, we had heard what sounded like heavy machinery being swiveled around on the roof. We guessed that it was an antiaircraft battery. More than once I found myself listening for the whine of jet planes. Yet my emotions were torn. I wanted the United States to strike back at North Korea with all the force she could muster. Yet I knew if she did it would almost certainly result in the extermination of the entire crew, and perhaps trigger counterretaliation by the Soviet Union or Communist China. If nothing else, I suspected that the fear of an all-out nuclear war would incline the United States toward restraint.

What about retaliation in kind—the United States seizing a North Korean ship and its crew for use as barter? In preparing for our first mission, I had read intelligence reports on North Korea's "Navy." It was almost nonexistent. Some of our carriers had almost as much tonnage as all of North Korea's ships put together. They certainly had nothing to compare with our intelligence ships. The Soviet Union and Red China, yes, but not the Democratic People's Republic of Korea. The whole stalemate philosophy—if they seize one of ours, we can always seize one of theirs—just didn't apply to North Korea. In not realizing this, someone

178

up the chain of command had goofed, and badly. Too, it was apparent from the Korean war that our captors had little regard for human life. If we did seize, say, a fishing boat, they would probably announce that the United States had destroyed the ship and all its crew, and use this as justification for doing likewise.

The more I thought about it, the more I realized that our fate probably depended less on what the United States did than on North Korea's intentions. They literally held us and all the cards.

That this was true—that a two-bit power such as North Korea could attack the world's strongest country with near impunity—struck me as almost unbelievable. It still does.

What, then, of North Korea's intent? I tried to run through some of the possibilities. It could be that if we confessed, they would release us as promised—but I doubted this. Far more likely, to my mind, was a "mock" propaganda trial, followed by imprisonment or—and this was a very real possibility—execution. It was also possible that they might execute us anyway, without going through the formality of a trial, after wringing out of us as much classified information as they could. We could be sure of only one thing: they would keep us just as long as we were useful to them, and no longer.

The more I thought about it, the more hopeless our situation became.

These were not the only possibilities, however. There was one other, the least likely, yet in its own way the most tantalizing: escape.

There were more interrogations on January 27.

Then, on Sunday, the twenty-eighth, five days after our capture, Super C's patience came to an end.

16

"You will confess that you intruded into the territorial waters of the Democratic People's Republic of Korea for the purpose of to spy!"

"No, because we did not intrude."

Super C was not present. A junior colonel, three-star, was acting in his stead. Max interpreted.

I was told to strip to my shorts. A square wooden stick was placed behind my knees, and I was ordered to kneel. At the same time, I was required to keep my torso straight and my hands stretched high above my head.

The discomfort was instant. In this position, my leg muscles forced the stick into the back of my knee joints.

I didn't think I could stand it for more than a few minutes, but I lasted over two hours. When dismissed, I could barely stumble back to my room.

As I lay on the bed, nursing my aching muscles, I could hear a voice. The recording again. It seemed to be coming from way down the hall, yet this time, perhaps because I had heard it repeated so often, I could make out most of the words. Bucher, or somebody who sounded like him, was admitting to intruding to 7.6 miles from some island.

Early the following morning, Monday, January 29, I was taken back to the interrogation room and given another chance to confess. What had happened the previous day was only a little sample, the colonel told me.

Again I was forced into a kneeling position, the stick between my legs, my arms raised. After a time I lost all feeling in both my arms and my legs. Then all the muscles in my body began to quiver.

180

My interrogators asked some questions. I can't remember what they were or what I replied, only that my answers seemed to make them angrier. Two guards began kicking my numb legs, then my back, then my sides and chest. It was a karate-type kick, each separate and distinct, each very painful.

After a time I began to lose consciousness and toppled over onto the deck. My tormentors let me lie until I was fully conscious, then ordered me to assume the same kneeling position. Only this time I was handed a wooden chair and forced to raise it above my head.

I held it as long as I could; then my arms gave in, the chair crashing onto my back as I doubled over in pain. Viciously they began to kick me again, and again, and again.

Suddenly they changed tactics, letting loose a barrage of punches to my face and head. Each felt as if I had been smashed with a mallet. This must have gone on five, perhaps even ten minutes, until, semiconscious, I mumbled that I would write a confession.

I was returned to my room and given pencils and paper and left alone to work on the document. They came and got it late that afternoon.

I waited, knowing what was coming, aware that I had only bought a little time and that it was running out.

That evening I was called before Super C. He was livid. The interpreter parroted his menacing screams: *"You confessed to nothing! Garbage, all garbage! Nothing but lies! You play me for the fool? You confessed to nothing!"*

"Yes, I know," I replied. "There was nothing to confess to."

Super C took out his service revolver and put it down on the table in front of him. Through Max he asked, "Are you ready to die?"

"Yes, sir, I am."

"You know I have the authority to kill you?"

"Yes, I'm sure you do."

He gestured toward the weapon. "I'll give you twenty minutes to write your will."

"I've already written a will," I answered. "I'm ready to die." And I was. I had lost all fear of death. At that moment it seemed the only avenue of escape open to me, the only way to avoid compromising the information I possessed.

Super C was furious. Though not realizing it, I had called his bluff. He let loose a string of Korean curses. But the interpreter put only one phrase into English. "Shooting you is too quick!" he spat out.

Super C barked an order. I was roughly dragged from the room into another across the hall.

The window was wide open, the temperature below freezing. However, I didn't feel the cold for long.

A junior officer, whom we later dubbed "Solutions," ordered me to remove my glasses and strip to my shorts. He and another officer then took a piece of wire and tightly bound my hands behind my back.

A powerful kick sent me sprawling face-first across the floor.

Both officers began kicking me simultaneously. Then the three guards gleefully joined the "game." I felt as if my rib cage was caving in.

Suddenly my drooping body was yanked upright. As before, a stick was jammed between my knees, but this time instead of kneeling I was forced to squat on the balls of my feet. I soon lost my sense of balance and began to fall over backward. One of the guards kicked me to the floor. All five resumed their blows, alternating fists and feet, pummeling my face, head, back, legs, groin. I struggled back upright and resumed the stick squat.

The routine was repeated several dozen times. Each time I was floored, I had to pull myself back up again. One kick smashed into my mouth, filling it with blood; another tore my left ear half off.

I lost consciousness at least six times, but a sharp slap or kick would always revive me.

Several times, while lying there, I heard voices coming

182

from the room across the hall. I recognized one as belonging to Schumacher. He was discussing his confession with someone, apparently an interpreter. Another time I heard Tim Harris. He too had already confessed and was assuring someone that he had been sincere. I tried to hear more, but the kicking resumed. I was numb, completely numb, and yet the pain still got through to me. My muscles were now in spasm with every kick. I wanted to die, yet realized that there was no way I could get them to kill me. They would always stop short, leaving me wishing I were dead.

"All the other officers confess. Why you only stubborn one?"

Later I would learn that this was not true. One officer held out longer than I did, Gene Lacy. Gene, who knew almost nothing of security matters, was badly beaten, then stripped and forced to sit on a hot radiator. Even then it was not until he heard Bucher's confession that he too broke.

The kicking continued. I lost all track of time and place, the only reality was the uninterrupted pain.

I regained consciousness once to find that I was no longer cold but strangely warm. Then I realized that I was warm because I was lying in a pool of my own blood.

I passed out again, then was kicked awake.

"All right, I'll confess," I said. But maybe I only thought I said it, because the kicking didn't stop.

Someone was helping me to my feet, helping me slip the clothes onto my bloody body. I couldn't even put on my glasses. I was taken into the other room, where Super C was waiting. I tried to speak but couldn't. My throat, jaws, and tongue were paralyzed. Minutes passed before I regained feeling in even half my tongue.

It was sometime early on the morning of Tuesday, January 30, a week to the day after our capture. It had taken them seven days, but they had broken me. "I'll tell you what you want to know," I blurted out.

17

Of course, they did not want to know the truth. They only wanted me to parrot their Big Lie: that the USS *Pueblo* had been seized while deep inside the territorial waters of the Democratic People's Republic of Korea.

This time when I returned to my room an officer and an interpreter accompanied me. They stayed with me the rest of the night while, propped up at the table, I labored over the confession.

The words swam before my eyes. Periodically I would slip into unconsciousness, only to be shaken back awake. It was an effort even to hold the pen.

The officer, Major Spot, so named because of a bald patch, "suggested" most of the contents. Depressed as I was, there was some satisfaction in knowing that his stilted Communist phraseology—"peace-loving D.P.R.K.," "U.S. imperialistic aggressor forces"—would be a dead giveaway that the confession had been obtained under duress. Bad grammar, incorrect usage—I put it all down, hoping every word would get through and cast doubt on every bit of "proof" offered by the North Koreans.

Shortly before dawn they left me, with my pain and guilt.

I tried to ease myself onto the bed, but just the movement was torture. Once I managed to lie down, I tried different positions, hoping one would relieve the throbbing agony, but I found only new places that hurt. The pain at the base of my spine was so excruciating that I couldn't bend my back. I wouldn't be able to do so for two months.

Yet, in its own way, the guilt was worse. I could tell myself that I had held out as long as humanly possible, that the body can stand only so much and no more, that Bucher had broken first, that there was no reason for me to be the lone holdout—but these were only words, and there was no balm in them. The guilt remained.

Put to the test, I had failed.

The screams cut through my troubled sleep. The beatings were still going on. There is no way to describe the sound of a boot smashing against flesh and bone. But I felt it. With an incredible sort of transference, every blow seemed to be occurring within my own body. The stick was there again, biting into the muscles at the back of my knees. My arms ached as I tried to keep the chair aloft. Though knowing what would happen, I had to let go. My body tensed, waiting for the kicks. When they came, only an effort of suppression kept me from echoing the cries. With the officers out of the way, they were working over the enlisted men now. I don't know how I knew, but I did. I felt sure I recognized the voice of the man being beaten in the next room. From his initial, stubborn refusal through what seemed hours of torture until he finally caved in and "confessed," CT James Shephard's reactions seemed almost identical to mine. His confession too was a lie. Shephard admitted that he was the man in charge of the research department. He wasn't. Whether he was confessing this because it was what they wanted, or whether because he was trying to take all the responsibility unto himself, thereby sparing the others, I didn't know. All I knew was that whatever he said, I would have to back him up. I listened as intently as I could, trying to make out his every word.

Day and night the beatings continued. Slipping in and out of delirium, I lost track of time. At some point the bleeding from my torn ear and reopened neck wound stopped. After one or two days, or perhaps three or four, I was no longer urinating blood. And somewhere in be-

185

tween were more "conferences" with Super C and his goon squad.

"You must be sincere."

Super C had been lecturing me on "sincerity" for nearly an hour. It was apparent that the North Korean equivalent of the word had far broader meanings than its English counterpart. To Super C sincerity meant complete surrender, total abject conformity with his wishes. You were sincere only when you did everything you were told to do, exactly as told to do it. Sincerity was a synonym for compliance with the party line. Anything else was deviationism, and had to be rooted out and corrected.

I was not sincere because, despite the threat of more beatings, I still refused to include three important admissions in my confession.

"The other officers confess to them, why not you?"

I wondered how often Super C had used that phrase, not just with me but with the others. And to what effect.

I decided to see if two could play the game.

"I am sincere," I said. "These things are not true. If I confessed to them I would be telling lies, and that would be insincere."

I knew Super C probably wouldn't buy that, but the translation took time and would further postpone what I now felt was inevitable—more torture.

Super C wanted me to admit that I knew what went on in the research spaces. I refused to do so—I had, in fact, included a statement in my confession disclaiming such knowledge. I was all too aware what would happen, both literally and figuratively, if I opened the sod-hut door. Only by denying awareness of the activities of the CTs could I convincingly withhold the classified information I possessed. Once that door opened, even a little bit, there would be no closing it. There were, I realized, a couple of ways I could be found out. Someone could be tortured into stating that I had such knowledge. Or they could find the access list. That was my biggest worry, inasmuch as this single sheet of paper gave the names of all those cleared to enter the research spaces. I hoped it had been among the documents that were destroyed. Apparently it was, because I was never confronted with it. But the possibility that I could be, at any moment, left me far from secure in my lie.

The second point Super C wanted included in my confession was that I was CIA. He was most insistent on this, although it wasn't until later I learned why. But I was equally emphatic in my refusal. In admitting this, I would be making myself a civilian, rather than military, and as such could be shot as a spy. It was a tenuous distinction, and one the North Koreans might choose to ignore, but I wasn't about to help them do so.

The third point he demanded was a blanket admission that most of the crew of the *Pueblo* had been trained as espionage agents. My reason for refusing to state this was very simple: I had no intention of putting anyone else in jeopardy.

Surprisingly, Super C seemed to accept my reply, at least for the time being. When I was given my revised confession to copy and sign, these admissions were not included. Any satisfaction I had was temporary. On reading the document, I discovered that someone with a fair command of English had edited it. Nearly all the stilted phraseology was gone. It sounded all too "sincere."

The case against Edward R. Murphy, Jr., CIA agent, was impressive, or so thought Super C. Having carefully collected all the evidence, he now confronted me with it.

One, I had attended Principia College. I started to explain it all again, but he would permit no interruptions.

Two, Centerville, my last assignment before reporting aboard, was another school for spies. Where he got this notion, I have no idea. It certainly would have amazed those assigned to the base.

Next, all the other officers had dress-blue uniforms.

But in searching the *Pueblo,* they had found none for me. Therefore I was not an officer, but a civilian, and must be the CIA man. That puzzled me for a moment, until I remembered that I had left one set of my dress blues in the cleaners at Yokosuka and had spilled something on the other set. I'd stuffed them in my laundry bag, there being no need for them on the rest of the voyage. I was surprised they had gone through the ship with such care. I hoped the classified documents aboard weren't receiving as close scrutiny as our laundry.

Only later did Super C admit that they had been looking for the uniforms because they wanted all the officers in formal attire when they signed their confessions. Unknowingly, my sloppiness with a glass of orange juice had frustrated that.

Super C had saved the clincher for last.

In the Communist military hierarchy the number-two man was always the party man, the political commissar, the real boss. It was the same in all countries, Super C asserted. Therefore, as second in command of the *Pueblo,* I had to be President Johnson's man, the government's representative, CIA.

Try as I did, I couldn't dissuade Super C from this notion. Nor would I be able to do so during the entire time of our captivity.

Having proven that I was CIA to *his* satisfaction, Super C turned somewhat expansive. Did I have any questions? He would be glad to answer them.

What about our wounded, I asked. Were they being cared for? I was especially worried about Woelk, since I had stopped hearing his cries about the same time the North Koreans had decided to play rough with me.

All the wounded were being properly cared for, Super C assured me. Woelk had been operated upon and moved to a modern hospital, where, despite the fact that he was an enemy of the Korean people, he was receiving excellent care. The others had received similar attention.

Knowing that no attempt had been made to treat my own wound, I remained somewhat skeptical, though I wanted very much to believe him.

When would we be released?

When we were sincere in our apologies, he promised. And very soon, he said, we would be given a chance to prove our sincerity.

He dismissed me before I could ask anything more.

The guilt remained, but gradually I was able to place it in perspective. I had broken, once, but that didn't have to mean the end of my resistance. Thus far in the interrogations I had been able to restrict my answers to those things which they already knew or could learn from the materials seized aboard the ship. I had parroted their lie, but I had divulged no classified information. The questions I most expected, and dreaded, hadn't been asked. At least not yet. The North Koreans seemed far more intent on getting us to agree to *their* version of the facts than digging to find the real truth. Propaganda, not intelligence, seemed their main interest.

Too, in his insistence that I was CIA, I had glimpsed a weakness in Super C, or rather in the regimented mentality of our captors. For them there was only one truth, the party line. If what we told them conflicted with what they had been taught—no matter how simple or how rational our explanation might be—they were incapable of accepting it. This could make for some very rough moments. It was also a big blind spot. And maybe, in time, we could use it to our advantage.

But these were only little chinks in the armor. Everything appeared to be on their side. They were the puppet masters, we the puppets. Although I had begun to stop reacting to my guilt, the memory of that night remained vivid. Footsteps in the hall, a single cry—and there were many such—would bring it all back. The hatred of the guards for us was obvious. All that was needed to unleash them was a nod from one of the North Korean officers. Using our fear, they could enforce compliance. That was our biggest weakness.

On our side was the knowledge that the United States knew we hadn't intruded.

Then it hit, hard. *Or did they?*

On January 23 we had radioed our correct position at least six or eight times. But had we ever, at any time since breaking EMCON, informed our headquarters in Japan that we had *not* intruded?

I had seen only a few of the SITREPs, but I was afraid I knew the answer.

It wasn't hard to imagine what had happened in the United States after our capture. One of the first things the Navy would do would be to find out everything they could about the *Pueblo*'s skipper, Commander Lloyd M. "Pete" Bucher. And it wouldn't take them long to discover that he was a maverick, given to doing things his own way, regulations be damned. Realizing that the early portion of our voyage had been largely unsuccessful from an intelligence standpoint, might Bucher have taken it upon himself to go in "just a little closer" to see what he could pick up? Someone was sure to ask that question. And, until the United States had a positive answer, one way or the other, there would remain a nagging doubt as to whether our confessions were true or false.

That scared me. Somehow we had to assure them that at no time had we intruded.

But how?

Early on the evening of February 3 a guard threw open my door and motioned me out into the hall. Expecting another interrogation, I was surprised to see Steve Harris standing there. We were forbidden to speak, and, heads bowed, we couldn't even exchange glances as we were marched down the stairs and out of the building.

Despite the presence of the guards, on reaching the

courtyard I couldn't resist looking up. Although there was deep snow on the ground, the sky was clear. For the first time since our capture I was able to see the stars and moon. The same moon, I realized, was over Japan. Another link with Carol and Eddie.

The guards prodded us onto a rickety bus. We were the only passengers. Although somewhat apprehensive, I tried to put the time to good use, attempting to note as many landmarks as I could. Each day I tried to add to my meager store of information. Unable to resist bragging about their capital, Super C had let slip in one of the interrogations that the train had taken us to Pyongyang. I knew we were no more than thirty minutes away by bus. Guessing at its slow speed, I'd judged the distance at under twenty miles. But I still lacked enough clues to determine the direction. I was hoping that this unexpected trip would furnish them, but after about five minutes we stopped beside what, in the moonlight, looked like an athletic stadium. Before I could make out anything else, we were *bali, bali*ed into a concrete blockhouse, handed soap and towels, and ordered to strip.

After eleven days without a shower, it seemed too good to be true, but there was no mistaking the smell of the hot steam.

There was both a shower and a large *hotsi* bath in the adjoining room, the latter filled almost to the brim with steaming hot water. The icy cold shower stung, reopening my wounds, but that was a small price to pay for the chance to clean them out. Fortunately, neither had infected.

I looked at Steve, and was startled. More than any of the others, I had worried about him, sure that once the North Koreans learned that he headed our complement of "spies," they would give him extra special attention. Until seeing him in the hall, I wasn't even sure he was still alive. Yet, in contrast to my own body, which looked like a black and blue patchwork quilt, there didn't appear to be a mark on him.

You can work over a man with devastating thoroughness, I knew, and if it's done right, never leave a visible trace. Just my luck to get bumbling amateurs.

The moment I eased myself into the hot water, all other considerations vanished. The effect was immediate and near miraculous, and not only on my back. The heat seemed to purge everything we had been through, to cleanse us both inside and out. Had the North Koreans taken its psychological effects into consideration, I'm sure they would never have let us bathe.

But, as we were to learn, their motives were other than hygienic.

All too soon the guards ordered us out of the water. We were returned to the Barn. The bus was so cold my hair froze.

The following day I was given a haircut and shave. They were making us presentable for something. It could be for any number of *other* reasons, I told myself, not wanting to be disappointed if it didn't happen. It didn't necessarily mean we were going to be released.

There was no hint of it in my next confrontation with Super C. After the first few days, when Max had interpreted fairly often, Super C's usual interpreter was a man we dubbed Silver Lips. Wheezy seemed to appear only when we were in trouble; he was a cussing expert. Which interpreter was present provided a clue as to what to expect.

The interpreter was Wheezy.

It began deceptively, with still another lecture on the importance of sincerity. Super C was exceptionally fond of old Korean proverbs. By now I knew many of them by heart. He was also addicted to illustrating each point, using his hands and any convenient object. Often it wasn't necessary to wait for the translation; the gestures told it all. And, as usual, it took him a very long time to get to the point.

But when he did, despite the warning presence of Wheezy, it caught me totally off guard.

"You were not sincere, because you lied to us, Executive Officer Murphy. And we found you out!"

Which lie? I wondered.

"You confessed to only one intrusion," he screamed. "And there were six!"

So they were going for quantity. The lie wasn't big enough. They had to make it even bigger.

As navigator, he continued, I must revise my confession to include these newly admitted facts. Also, I must mark these intrusions on a chart, so the whole world could see what we had done.

An officer was assigned to help me. With his little tin star he reminded me of the comic-strip character Deputy Dawg.

Like all the other officers I had seen so far, Deputy Dawg was army, not navy. Although he made a big pretense of knowing what he was doing, a few simple questions indicated his expertise was self-bestowed, backed by no more than a smattering of navigational training.

A chart of North Korea and the Sea of Japan was spread out on the table in front of me. I recognized it as being from the ship. The first alleged intrusion—7.6 miles from the offshore island of Yo Do—was already indicated by a vague, wiggly circle. If they were really this inexact, there might be a possibility of using the situation to our advantage. What I really wanted was a way to foul up the chart so royally as to cast doubt on all the intrusions. Yet it would have to be something which stood a chance of passing the scrutiny of men with far more navigational savvy than Deputy Dawg. And, as yet, I hadn't an idea how, or even if, I could accomplish it.

Deputy Dawg had a list of coordinates which he claimed had been taken from our navigational records. Recognizing them, I explained to him that these were derived from spurious loran readings which the more inexperienced members of my navigational team had logged. That a line had been drawn through them in the position log, I told him, proved that they were in error. Also, the disparities between these entries and those which came both before and after them clearly established that they were wrong.

He would have none of it. They were intrusions, he insisted, turning ugly. Shrugging my shoulders, I set to work. As he read off the entries, one by one, I was to calculate the positions and mark them on the chart, together with the date and time each of the six "violations" had taken place.

I dawdled, pretending to be careful and methodical, actually studying the chart, at the same time doing some mental calculations.

Then I found it! It was both simple and perfect. The likelihood of it being spotted by the North Koreans was, I felt, negligible. But it would be something else when it came to the attention of U.S. Naval Intelligence. As much as I would love to take credit for it, Deputy Dawg, expert navigator, deserves full honors. He literally gave it to me. My sole contribution consisted of keeping my mouth shut when I spotted it.

When I'd finished charting the last intrusion, Deputy Dawg picked up the chart and looked at it with obvious satisfaction.

It was very impressive evidence. Unless you happened to be Navy.

The *Pueblo*'s top speed was 12.2 knots.

In order to make all six intrusions at the stated times, the *Pueblo* would have had to travel at speeds up to 2,500 knots.

Back in my room, I tried to mentally re-create the chart, especially that portion of the coastline from the fortieth parallel (opposite Pyongyang) south to the demilitarized zone (DMZ).

It would have been much easier if I could have drawn

194

it. I had a pen and paper—the North Koreans most kindly having supplied us with a number of sheets of coarse brown wrapping paper, for toilet purposes—but the risk of detection was too great. I'd have to rely on my memory, adding details each time I was shown the chart.

Unfortunately, this particular chart was strictly navigational. It showed little of the actual country, and lacked the topographical details—rivers, mountains, towns—that would be most helpful in any escape plan.

Several days later, I was taken back down the hall, this time to be shown the ship's navigational records, which, according to our captors, "proved conclusively" that the USS *Pueblo* had intruded.

From his beaming countenance, I gathered that Deputy Dawg had played more than a small part in their creation.

Closer study confirmed this supposition. Not only were the forgeries badly done, they contained errors so obvious that no U.S. Navy ensign—even on his first day out of OCS—would have been deceived by them.

In some cases, as with the position log, they had taken our actual records and, after clumsy erasures, put in their own revised entries. Many of the records, however, had been fabricated in their entirety, by using blank multilith forms found aboard the ship.

A typical example was what they later identified as the *Pueblo*'s visual-contact log, which contained all six alleged violations. To my great pleasure, I found they had bought the timed intrusions, including the one which had us going 2,500 knots per hour, or 500 miles in twelve minutes.

Being unfamiliar with U.S. Navy practice and regulations, they made other subtler, but, to the experienced eye, equally obvious mistakes.

A blank chart from the U.S. Hydrographic Office had been used for our track chart. What the North Koreans did not realize was that a chart covering such a large area would not be used for navigational purposes. Several smaller charts would be used while the patrol was still in progress; then, when it was completed, the data would be copied onto the large charts, which would then represent an overall history of the entire mission. Furthermore, their fabrication contained exact times for each position and each course change. On an authentic chart only representative entries would be time-dated.

But the North Koreans were not looking for my appreciation of their counterfeiting. Having observed that some of the records had been signed by me, they wanted me to sign these also.

This was another of their tricks, which they used in various ways during our captivity. Had they asked me to verify their fraudulent records at the start, I might have refused to do so. Instead, they merely had me chart the six bogus intrusions. Having done this much, however, I could certainly have no objection to also verifying the same information in the records. Or so they argued. To do otherwise, of course, would prove that I was insincere.

Actually, it was two tricks. Once I signed them, they could take them to Commander Bucher and say, "See, your executive officer signed these; there is no reason why you shouldn't do likewise."

I only hoped that Bucher would look at them very carefully. He was an expert navigator, and they should give him some great laughs. And I suspected that, like the rest of us, he was badly in need of some, right about now.

Still I pretended reluctance, not wanting them to know how anxious I was that these particular records be widely publicized. After some additional persuasion—a reminder of the night of January 29—I signed, in the lower-right-hand corner: "Drawn by Edward Renz Murphy, Jr., Executive Officer/Navigator, and confirmed by . . . ," leaving space for Bucher's signature.

Here again I had been able to undermine their efforts. A genuine track would not be signed by the navigator and the captain, but would be prepared by the quartermaster, approved by the navigator, and submitted to the captain for inclusion in the mission report. Only the mission report itself would be signed by the commanding officer. In addition, the real McCoy would not contain the phrase "drawn by," but "plotted by," while "approved by," not "confirmed by," was proper naval usage.

Although I felt I had already done a good day's work, the North Koreans were not content to leave it at that. The pens disappeared. A team of photographers—Bucher later christened their director "Jack Warner"—was brought in to capture for posterity Executive Officer Murphy pointing to the six "untrusions," as I had begun to think of them, as well as indicating the places in the ship's record where they were "authenticated."

I tried to move around in my chair, so they would photograph my best side, *i.e.,* showing my torn right ear. But they had anticipated that. All the profile shots were from the left side, and in the front shots, with my head turned slightly to the right.

"Point to each of the intrusions!" Deputy Dawg ordered.

Bad manners or not, I was only too happy to comply, using the middle finger of my right hand as pointer.

Was it an internationally recognized gesture, or strictly native to the United States? I didn't know.

After they had taken a few hundred feet of footage, and no one had remarked on my "giving them the finger," I felt more self-confident, and, pointing to two intrusions at the same time, extended my index finger and little finger, signifying "B.S."

My only regret was that I couldn't see the faces of the men in U.S. Naval Intelligence when, magnifying glasses in hand, they examined the photographs.

My secret knowledge kept me happy for days.

Something was up. The guards, a surly lot at best, were almost jolly. The evening of February 7, they bustled from room to room, inspecting each, but giving no indication of what was happening.

Of such small things are dreams made. When, shortly

197

after, the *Pueblo*'s officers were summoned to one of the interrogation rooms, the first thing I noticed was that Wheezy wasn't present. Whatever the news, it probably wouldn't be bad. When the guards weren't looking, we exchanged quizzical glances. All six of us must have been wondering the same thing: Could it be that we were going home?

A brief announcement shattered the illusion. Tomorrow, February 8, was the twentieth anniversary of the founding of the Korean People's Army. Although we were admitted criminals, by the grace of Premier Kim Il Sung we would be allowed to participate in the festivities.

But that was not exactly the way they put it. Rather, it was "by the grace of and/under wise leadership of Supreme Commander Marshal Kim Il Sung, Peerless Patriot, National Hero, Iron-willed Genius-General, Ever-victorious Strategist, Beloved and Respected Leader of Forty Million Korean People . . ." Every time, the same long rigmarole. Never simply Premier Kim Il Sung (and when one of us was so disrespectful as to refer to him in the abbreviated form, he was quickly corrected). Later, when given propaganda materials, we would find such incredible lists of titles reprinted every time he was mentioned.

As with the nicknames bestowed upon the North Korean officers and guards, we would formulate our own private names for the premier and his legendary mother, Kang Ban Sok. Too, our captors never used the phrase "North Korea." It was always "Democratic People's Republic of Korea." Whenever I heard the initials "D.P.R.K." I mentally translated them as "Damn Pirates Residing in Korea," while, instead of referring to our jailers as "Koreans," they became "KORCOMs"—the U.S. military designation for Korean Communists.

Small satisfactions, their only value morale. But, because there were few such, they were important.

Following the announcement, we returned to our rooms, disappointed, yet looking forward to any change in the monotonous routine.

Early the next morning one of the guards brought in a checkered plastic tablecloth and draped it over my table. A few minutes later, breakfast arrived. Compared to our usual daily fare, it was a veritable smorgasbord, consisting of turnip soup, hard-boiled eggs, fish, rice cakes, apples, sweet paste, bread and butter, sausage, octopus, dried squid, plus a plate of hard candy and cookies. There had to be a catch to it, I decided.

There was. We could not eat until after we had been photographed with our sumptuous repast. The photographers started working from the opposite end of the hall. By the time they reached my room, I had played a dozen games of ticktacktoe on the tablecloth, and the food was quite cold.

But, cold or not, it was the most food I had seen since our capture, and I left nothing on the plates.

Lunch was nearly identical. When I had finished— leaving only the cookies and candy for later—an officer whom we called "Clean Floors" burst into my room with two glasses and a bottle of wine, complete with submerged ginseng root. Clean Floors spoke no English, and there wasn't an interpreter in sight. Oh, oh, I thought, sensing an international incident in the making, not even sure the North Koreans had a word corresponding to "teetotaler." As tactfully as possible, with gestures and shaking of the head, I tried to convince him that I didn't want the wine, that he should give my share to one of the others. By the time I had gotten my point across, he had already filled both glasses.

Most unhappily, he rebottled the wine, using a dirty piece of paper as a funnel. That anyone could refuse such largess apparently puzzled him. I suspected that he would have to take both shots to get over the experience.

That afternoon, rules were relaxed, and we were allowed on our beds.

As I lay there, it occurred to me that the seizure of the American "spy ship" must have *made* this holiday commemorating the twentieth anniversary of the Korean People's Army. It was only then I began to wonder if the planning of the forthcoming celebration might have been a factor in the capture of the ship.

The holiday mood did not carry over to the following day. Once again we were back to fish soup and dry bread. And the attitude of the guards became even more vicious.

It was fairly easy to discern why. They were of peasant stock, their only education propaganda, large doses of which consisted of hatred for Americans. In a Communist country a man who does not work does not eat. Yet here were eighty-two Americans, enemies of the Korean people, eating regularly, being provided with housing, given cigarettes if they smoked, and even served occasional banquets. As bad as our situation was, in many ways it was undoubtedly better than their own. I could see the puzzlement in their expressions, and suspected their political commissar must be having one tremendous morale problem. We could also feel their resentment, in a variety of quite tangible ways.

Many were petty. Because we were required to stand and snap to attention whenever a guard entered the room, they delighted in going down the hall throwing open doors. They would do this for hours on end, day and night.

Shoving and tripping of the men as they went to the john or to an interrogation was another favorite tactic. And, when they felt they could get away with it, they played rougher.

It wasn't often we got a chance to get back at them, so when one came, we eagerly grabbed it.

Because I had been rationing my cookies, allowing myself only one or two a day, I was aware how many I had. One morning I awoke to find two missing. The next night, pretending to be asleep, I watched as one of the guards slipped into my room and took a couple more from the plate.

I knew exactly what would happen if I made a direct accusation. I'd get the hell beaten out of me again. Then

200

I thought of a way I might be able to carry it off. Super C delighted in planting the seed of an idea, then letting us suggest it as if it were our own. Maybe a little turnabout was in order.

By this time I had ferreted out several hiding places for contraband material. One was the wooden top of my table, where there was a bent nail. Wrapping all but one of the remaining cookies in a piece of paper, I wedged the package in between the nail and the bottom of the table-top.

The duty officer spoke English. The next morning, when he came in, I went into my act.

"I hate to complain," I said, "but I think that maybe one of our men got loose last night and stole my cookies."

"One of *your* men?" he asked incredulously. "That impossible!"

"Well, all I know is that I had nearly a full plate of cookies last night, and now there is only one."

The officer scratched his head, eyed the cookie plate, then left the room.

A few minutes later the sergeant of the guard came in. He didn't speak any English, but that didn't matter. Methodically he searched the room. As was the case in previous searches, not wanting to soil his uniform, he did not get down on his hands and knees, and therefore missed my hiding spot. Finding nothing, he made me empty my pockets.

The one weakness in my plan—the possibility that I might have eaten all the cookies myself in a fit of gluttony—did not seem to occur to him. When he left, it was obvious he was angry.

The next day there was an entirely new set of guards. I imagined that the culprit had been caught and had confessed. At his "sincerest," however, he could only admit to the theft of four cookies. The others had to pay the price for the rest.

Later I learned that several of the crewmen, confronted with a similar problem, had devised their own retribution, which admittedly one-upped mine. The men in CT Charles Sterling's room began missing apples. To get back at the thief—a guard known as the Fly, so named from an old science-fiction flick—Sterling took the most appetizing apple they had and punched small pin holes in it. Then he marinated it in urine. The next time they were all out of the room, the apple disappeared. As did the Fly. When he returned to work several days later, there was a decidedly pale cast to his complexion. They didn't miss any more apples. Nor did I lose any more cookies.

One evening shortly after the holiday I was taken before the first naval officer I had encountered since our capture —a three-star captain from the Navy of the Korean People's Army.

He handed me a typewritten sheet of paper, then, while I was reading it, delivered a long lecture on its contents. On my return to my room, he said, I was to memorize everything on the sheet, then, with rice glue supplied by a guard, paste it on the back of my door as an ever-present reminder.

RULES OF LIFE

During the detention the following will be strictly observed:

The daily schedule will be strictly observed.

You will always display courtesy to the duty personnel when they enter your room to deal with you.

You must not talk loudly or sing in your room.

You must not sit or lie on the floor or bed except on Sundays and during prescribed hours, but should sit on the chair.

You must wear your clothes at all times except while washing your faces and in bed.

You must take care of the building, furniture, and all expendables issued to you.

You will keep your rooms and corridors clean at all times.

You will entertain yourself only with the culture provided.

If you have something to do, ask permission from the guards, who will escort you to the appropriate.

There was more:

You will be punished severely and unconditionally if you commit any of the following:

In case you make false statements or refuse questioning or hint others to do so.

In case you attempt to signal other rooms by this or that means.

In case you make unauthorized writings.

In case you show disrespect to any of the duty personnel.

In case you make any other offense.

The next day I was taken back down the hall, handed an identical sheet of paper, and given exactly the same lecture all over again, as if for the first time.

It was a consoling thought, knowing that the North Korean military was just as subject to bureaucratic snafus as was the U.S.

Yet just the fact that they had seen fit to draw up such a list of rules was depressing. It indicated that, despite our hopes, we wouldn't be going home anytime soon.

===================== **18** =====================

Reporter: "It's some time since you came here. I would like to hear your impressions of your life here."

Captain Bucher: "Yes, sir. My impression, as commanding officer, has been that the Democratic People's Republic of Korea is very progressive and has a gentlemanly and understanding people."

Our first press conference, held on February 15 in the main interrogation room in the Barn, had just begun. Despite the bright lights, microphones, and note-taking reporters, it was less like "Face the Nation" than the first run-through of a high-school play. There was no spontaneity, no give-and-take between reporters and participants; each had his assigned role to play. The questions had been typed in advance, then handed out to individual newsmen. All were North Korean. There was no pretense of journalistic impartiality. Each question was delivered with righteous indignation. As for the actors—the six officers and the senior oceanographer of the *Pueblo*—each had been coached separately for several days previous in his part. At various times I'd worked with Colonel Specs, Major Spot, and Wheezy. Until marched into the room and sat down behind the long table, facing the cameras and audience, none of us had any idea what the others were going to say.

The play analogy went a step further. The North Koreans even had their own "plants" in the audience. Once our eyes adjusted to the bright lights, we could see that every third seat was occupied by one of the KORCOM offi-

cers, in civilian dress. Excluding cameramen, actual newsmen probably didn't number more than six or eight.

But it differed from a play in one important respect.
None of the leading characters had the slightest desire
to be in the spotlight. All were nervous, apprehensive. It
was the first time all the *Pueblo*'s officers had been brought
together since "sentenced to death" the day after our capture. Each had gone through his own private hell since
then, and it showed. All had lost weight, looked tired,
gaunt, Bucher more so than anyone else. His speech, always somewhat sluggish, was now markedly so. When
finished, he sat down listlessly. I tried to catch his eyes,
but couldn't. Each time, he would look away. It was as if
the KORCOMs, or the surrender itself, had destroyed his
will to live.

Reporter: "I have read your confessions. You all admitted the crime of the *Pueblo*. And I would like to hear
about it in detail."

My cue to tell about the intrusions. I had spent a great
deal of time on this answer, wanting to get a single message across.

". . . it was at this point where the charts and records
show our first intrusion into your coastal waters. . . . It
was off Kaltan, where we were shown intrusion approximately 9.8 miles from your coast . . . the charts and
records again showed . . . here again our charts and records show . . . our tracks and navigational records again
show . . ."

Examine the charts and records, I was trying to say:
there's the answer as to whether the intrusions actually
occurred.

An officer we dubbed "Square Head" was serving as
moderator. There were two translators, Wheezy and another junior officer who prided himself on his knowledge
of American slang. Our name for him was derived from
one of his favorite expressions: "Let's Not Bush Around
the Beat."

The lights were hot, and after the chill of our rooms

205

made us sleepy. As the press conference droned on, each man on cue standing and reciting his set piece, it was an effort to stay alert. But one reply snapped us all back to attentiveness.

Reporter: "Research Officer, I have a question to ask you. You said that you had a special detachment under your command, and I want to know how the detachment performed its mission."

Research Officer Stephen Harris: "Yes, I, as research officer, am in charge of a special detachment of thirty people, including myself, whose primary purpose is to assist the commanding officer in his intelligence-collection efforts by providing him any information which has been intercepted through listening to radio signals or intercepting radar waves.

"The second function of the special research department is to intercept, collect, and record all radio or radar signals of interest to us, submit the recordings and copied transmissions for analysis to the National Security Agency near Washington, D.C. It is also to collect radar signals, make recordings of these, and submit them to Pacific Command Electronic Intelligence Center for analysis.

"On technical matters concerning collection of electronic signals, I receive my order directly from the Director of U.S. Navy Security Group Pacific, located in Hawaii. . . ."

This was strong stuff, and all of us looked at Steve Harris in surprised alarm. What had the KORCOMs done to him to get this kind of information?

It began slowly.

Skip Schumacher started the ball rolling, mimicking the North Korean's stilted English. "My job is as operations officer very important one on board the ship. . . . The narrative report contained all of the informations which we collected. . . . The narrative also included each off course and speed change of the ship. . . ."

Next I flubbed one of my cues, intentionally. While still

206

in my room, being prepared for the press conference by Colonel Specs and Wheezy, I had been questioned about our military relationship with the Japanese. Flippantly I replied that we had none, that the Japanese were not in our chain of command. The moment I saw Wheezy's expression, I knew I had goofed. He was delighted with my reply, and wanted me to repeat it verbatim. Now, at the press conference, when the cue came, I pretended to miss it. It was bad enough that the United States was involved, without bringing in the Japanese too.

It spread. Schumacher began coaching his replies in a singsong voice. Lacy stretched his out interminably. Suddenly becoming aware of what was happening, Bucher joined in. Asked about a statement of Japanese Prime Minister Sato and Foreign Minister Miki that the *Pueblo* had not been in territorial waters but on the high seas when captured, Bucher replied in mock seriousness: "That's nonsense! I am sure Japanese Prime Minister Sato and Foreign Minister Miki were not on board our ship. That's incomprehensible! If they were on board, they would have been captured together with us, and detained in the Democratic People's Republic of Korea, wouldn't they?"

It was building. Captain Bucher: "We have committed a grave crime against the Democratic People's Republic of Korea, for which we are deeply shy. . . ." Executive Officer Murphy: "I would like to say I think our feeling since we have been here has changed thoroughly. I like to say I have been particularly deeply impressed by the gentlemanliness of the officers that we have met." To illustrate how deeply their gentlemanly impressions went, I moved as stiffly as possible, to show I couldn't bend my back. Operations Officer Schumacher: "When I return home I will tell my parents as well as my girl friend and my colleagues what a serious and inhuman crime we have committed." Leave it to Skip to get a female in there.

From just a tiny spark, the spirit of our resistance was beginning to smolder into flame. As if sensing it, Square Head quickly snuffed it out, bringing the press conference

207

to an end with a hurried denunciation of U.S. imperialistic aggression.

It was a humiliating experience, both for us and for the nation we represented. There was no doubt the North Koreans would get propaganda mileage out of it. Yet, petty though our tricks were, for us they marked a new beginning. We were still alive, still capable of a united effort to thwart our captors. If nothing else, that alone was tremendously encouraging.

For a few minutes it brought Bucher out of his lethargy. Then, as we rose to leave the room, he slipped back into it again, depression settling over him as visibly as the coming of night.

Although I had not been able to examine them myself, I had noticed that the newsmen had been handed photographs of the counterfeit navigational records. These, together with my repetitive statement that "the charts and records show," meant there was probably a fair chance the message would reach the United States. Although I suspected the North Koreans would edit the movie footage before releasing it to the world press—shots of my still badly swollen ear probably being scissored out—my statement about the intrusions was too important to their case to be deleted.

Yet I couldn't be sure of this. There had to be some other way to get the word to the United States that the intrusion charge was bogus.

One chance came about shortly after the press conference. And, for a while, I thought it just might provide the solution.

As the next stage in their propaganda offensive, the North Koreans decided the whole crew should write a joint letter of apology to the D.P.R.K. government. The officers were divided into two teams, Bucher heading one, I the other, each to draft a separate version, the best parts of each then to be merged in the final draft.

Each team tried to outdo the other in the use of stilted phraseology. And we came up with some superb verbiage. It was a hilarious document—until the KORCOMs put their editors to work on it. When they had finished, it reeked of sincerity.

They were on to our little tricks.

Actually, there was evidence that they had been for some time. One day we were given our first serving of "culture," North Korean style. It consisted of a copy of *Our Nation Today and Tomorrow*, the collected speeches of Kim Il Sung; a pictorial magazine, *Korea Today;* a stack of propaganda tracts; and back issues of the *Pyongyang Times*.

An English-language version of this remarkable newspaper was published once a week for foreign distribution.

Reading it, I learned for the first time the North Korean version of the *Pueblo*'s capture. The patrol boats, I discovered, had "returned the fire of the piratic gang who put up an arrogant resistance." They were talking about us! It appeared that even the KORCOMs were ashamed to admit that we had surrendered without the least semblance of a fight.

I was also surprised to learn that the *Pueblo* carried "antiaircraft machine guns" and "scores of shooting weapons, tens of thousands of rounds of ammunition, and hand grenades and quantities of arms and equipment for espionage activities." It was a wonder those peaceful little patrol boats ever captured us.

The article, which appeared in the February 1 issue of the paper, ended with the most remarkable threat I had ever read: "If the U.S. imperialists and the traitorous Pak Jung Hi puppets persist in their reckless acts of provocation, the heroic Korean People's Army, which is prepared as ever-victorious revolutionary armed forces, each of whose men is a match for one hundred foes, will in cooperation with the entire Korean people wipe out the aggressors at one blow at any time."

209

Far less amusing were the confessions of the other *Pueblo* officers, which I now read for the first time.

Bucher had written two. In his first, apparently the same one we had heard in the recording, Bucher had stated: "The U.S. Central Intelligence Agency promised me that if this task would be done successfully, a lot of dollars would be offered to the whole crew members of my ship, and particularly I myself would be honored." In their haste to justify the seizure, the KORCOMs had obviously released Bucher's initial confession without giving it very close scrutiny, for this and several other examples of unconventional usage had slipped through. Following the publication of Bucher's statement, however, someone must have noticed and alerted our captors, for such wording was absent both from Bucher's second confession and from those of all the other officers, including mine.

(On January 24 a Pentagon press release was given to reporters which stated: "The style and wording of the document provided unmistakable evidence that this was not written or prepared by any American. Typical of the propaganda sham is the suggestion that the CIA had promised Commander Bucher and his crew 'a lot of dollars.'" Although we only learned of it much later, that blew the ball game.)

The confessions made depressing reading. A lot of little hard-earned victories crumbled before my eyes. When one of us had adamantly refused to insert a statement, someone else had unknowingly proved obliging. For example, Bucher stated that most of the crew members had been trained in espionage techniques, Schumacher that all of them had. Moreover, Schumacher's confession contained a statement which, it seemed to me, went far beyond any of the others: "The intelligence material collected by me was to be used for the attack against the Democratic People's Republic of Korea."

This was damn close to a declaration of war. Yet I had no idea what Skip had gone through, what he had been told to include in the statement and hadn't. This was true

210

of all the confessions. It was unfair to judge them without knowing the circumstances of their creation. The same applied to Steve Harris' admissions during the press conference, which reappeared in even more fulsome detail in his printed confession. Steve was probably the only man aboard the *Pueblo* who knew what classified documents had been captured, what information compromised. He alone knew what could be safely mentioned, what couldn't. And only he knew what he was still holding back.

It was unfair to judge someone when you didn't know all the facts. Yet, unconsciously, one did so. I kept recalling what Steve had said, together with what I had learned when we were taken to our bath. And if *we*, knowing what we did, judged each other, what of those in the United States and elsewhere in the world?

As starved as I was for reading material, their cultural garbage was wholly unpalatable. The repetitious praises of Kim Il Sung not only literally put me to sleep, they also provided me with a means to do it without being punished. When the guards peeked in the cracks in the door, they saw me sitting on the bench, back to the door, book open on my knees, seemingly engrossed in rapt concentration. All I had to worry about was dropping the book or snoring. I also found that if I stacked up the magazines, papers, and books and sat on them, my back was raised just enough on the bench to relieve much of the pain. I was far more comfortable in this position than on the bed itself. As an added bonus, after I had sat on the material for a couple of hours, it was as crumpled and dog-eared as if it had been avidly read—graphic evidence of my sincerity.

Again all the officers plus oceanographer Tuck were assembled in one of the interrogation rooms.

"Here is the crew of the *Pueblo*," Super C said, indicating a package of cigarettes on the table, "and here is the President of the United States," he said, pointing to his lighter at the opposite end. "The question—how does the first communicate with the second?"

It was Super C's favorite game, planting an idea. He obviously wanted us to write another letter, this one to the President, but the suggestion had to be ours.

We pretended deep concentration, then puzzlement. Baiting Super C was an extra-special pleasure.

"If crew want to send message to President," Super C hinted, "what to do?"

Friar Tuck couldn't resist the temptation. He suggested helpfully, "How about placing a long-distance, person-to-person call to him at the White House?"

Suppressing our grins was next to impossible. But we managed. Super C was very old-school Oriental when it came to losing face. We could get away with a certain amount of obstinacy, but if he thought we were ridiculing him, he reacted violently.

Eventually someone suggested the obvious—another crew letter, this one to the President of the United States. An excellent idea! exclaimed Super C. He would be only too happy to comply with our request.

We didn't share his enthusiasm. And our resistance to the idea became even stronger when Super C indicated that what he wanted was nothing less than a demand that the President of the United States apologize to the North Korean government for our aggressive acts.

Not bloody likely, I thought.

The letter to President Johnson marked a new stage in the propaganda efforts. First we had been forced to admit the bogus crimes. After admission came apology, but our apology to the North Korean government wasn't sufficient. It was the "Johnson warmongers," as Super C often referred to them, who had to repent now; only when they did so, humbling themselves before the whole world, would we be freed.

If our release depended on this, I thought, we might as well give up all hope.

Although several of us tried to temper the language of

212

the petition, Super C knew both what he wanted and how to get it. By this time the beatings of the enlisted men had stopped. They could resume any minute, Super C threatened.

As it was, a number of the crewmen refused to sign the finished petition until brought before Bucher and given a direct order by him to do so.

Marine Sergeants Robert Chicca and Robert Hammond had been badly beaten when it was discovered they had lied about speaking Korean. Policarpo Garcia, our leading supply petty officer, and Rogelio Abelon and Rizalino Aluague, our two steward's mates, had received especially vicious punishment because the KORCOMs thought they were South Koreans. They were Filipinos. Baldridge also had it very rough, when our captors learned from his service record that he was married to a Japanese girl. But, except for Hodges, all the members of the crew were still alive.

The messages were passed furtively, during our petition-writing sessions. Whispered asides, with no movement of the lips. Little pieces of paper, rolled into small balls, dropped where another crewman could quickly pocket them.

Schumacher, having been on Bucher's letter-writing team, had seen more of the captain than I had. "The CO's in pretty bad shape," Skip whispered to me just before the close of one of our sessions. "I'm afraid he's going to try to do something stupid, like cash in his chips."

"Tell him to hold in there," I whispered back.

"I did," Skip replied, *sotto voce*. "I also told him that I'd tried to kill myself twice, and that wasn't the answer."

Later I was able to round out the picture. During one of the meetings, Bucher had slipped Schumacher a note in which he said he doubted if he would ever get out of this alive. He also passed Gene Lacy his black sapphire ring, asking him to give it to his wife and sons if anything happened to him. Lacy had passed it back, with a note saying

213

that he was sure all eighty-two of us would go back at the same time.

There was no question that Bucher was suffering acute depression, and had been for some time. Although I didn't learn this until later, not long after our arrival in the Barn Seaman Edward Russell had been assigned to act as Bucher's orderly. One day, while Russell was cleaning Bucher's room, the guard stepped outside long enough for Russell and Bucher to talk. Russell asked what was going to happen to them. "They'll get what they can out of us, then get rid of us," Bucher ominously replied. Russell carried the message back to his cellmates. Bucher, apparently, had second thoughts about the effect of his remarks on morale, for the next day he passed Russell a note telling him to ignore what he had said, that he was sure the United States would come to our rescue.

But just looking at Bucher you could see that he was falling apart. The frustrating thing was that, isolated as we were, there was almost nothing we could do to help him, except to pass on encouraging remarks on the rare occasions we were brought together.

I was concerned about him, but I was even more concerned about some of the other members of the crew. As exec, a good part of my time had been spent handling the problems of the enlisted men. I knew the personal situations of most. Some—with pregnant wives, sick children, shaky marriages, financial indebtedness—must be having a very rough time of it. One thing was in their favor, though; they had cellmates who could work at cheering them up.

With habitual regularity I asked Super C if I could see the whole crew. Request denied. Could we send and receive mail? Same reply as last time you ask.

As much as possible, I tried not to think about my own situation at home. Carol was due to have our baby March 30. I managed to avoid worrying about this, at least for the time being, by telling myself that if all went well I might be with her when the baby arrived. Concern about my mother, however, wasn't as easily banished from mind.

Bucher and Schumacher were not the only ones to contemplate suicide.

From early in our detention I had worried that someday one of the guards would carry his harassment just a little bit too far, and I'd swing at him, with predictable results. In order to partially cover myself, should this happen, I began to act a trifle demented. For long periods I would pace my room, mumbling to myself. Then I would stop and stare vacantly into space, as if seeing something no one else could. At the appearance of certain guards, I'd begin shaking violently. It spooked the guards, I could tell that. Concerned, the duty officer took me to the doctor.

Until this time I had been unaware that we had a doctor and a nurse assigned to us. Their temporary office was on the same floor in an interrogation room. The doctor had me close my eyes and extend my hands. Immediately I started shaking from head to foot. Deciding I was nervous from lack of sleep, he gave me a package of sleeping powder.

Periodically I'd again go into my act, each time being given another prescription.

I'd taken none of them. All were stashed away—at first under the table, then behind the radiator—in case things got too rough and other secrets than the *Pueblo*'s captured their interest.

My major worry was that I might be trapped into a position where the disclosure of classified material would become unavoidable. If this happened, I had to have a way out.

Thus far, however, it hadn't happened. Teams of translators were obviously working their way through the captured documents, as indicated by the questions that were being asked in the interrogation sessions. Yet, to my delight, I discovered they had encountered an immense stumbling block: the U.S. military's habit of abbreviating everything. That this might simply be a means to speed

215

up communications did not occur to them. They were sure it was code, and that being true, the encrypted messages had to be very secret indeed. Even the most innocuous orders—thirty days' leave, reduction in rank one grade— took on sinister undertones. The temptation to foul them up, using this blind spot, was much too great to resist.

By this time I had discovered that if an answer sounded either military or nautical, chances are they would buy it. At least for the time being. And we were living day by day. For example, COMBATCAMGRUPAC actually stands for Combat Camera Group Pacific, but I told them it was Commander Basic Air Training Command Group Pacific. This sounded very important. And, unless someone told them otherwise, there was no way they could learn that this particular command was nonexistent.

By the same token, when confronted with someone else's lies, no matter how farfetched, you confirmed them.

No one ever spelled out the rules of the game. We just tumbled to them naturally. Often this became almost a secondary means of communication—knowing that others were also at work fouling them up did wonders for the spirit. Of course, there was always the chance of being caught, but to a certain extent the very volume of military paperwork worked to our advantage. Our captors seemed much more concerned with getting through what they had than in giving a particular subject concentrated attention.

Oddly enough, what they did concentrate on was relatively unimportant from an intelligence standpoint. They were obsessed with supply and logistical support. They couldn't get enough of it. Tim Harris, I later learned, had to make a list of all the supplies he had ordered for the *Pueblo*. Days were spent itemizing such things as rolls of toilet paper.

Often as not, the answers to their "big" questions weren't even classified. How many men in U.S. Navy? How many in U.S. National Guard? Where is Treasure Island located? I made them work hard for such answers, giving them up only with seeming reluctance, under threat of force, not telling them, of course, that they could have the answers for the price of a *World Almanac.*

That they so often overlooked the "hard-core" intelligence information, or seemed unaware of its importance, later led some to conjecture that they had a separate team of specialists working on these documents and did not want us to know that they realized their value.

If this was the case, they missed a rare opportunity to confirm their findings, or to use this information to pry open doors to knowledge even more important.

For a while I did fear that they might bring in intelligence experts from other Communist countries to help decipher the data. That they were not asking the right questions now, I warned myself, did not mean they couldn't start asking them tomorrow, or the day after.

This uncertainty nipped any complacency in the bud.

One could never be sure, with Super C, who was baiting whom.

Several times I had the feeling that he was telling me something only to test his security, to see if the message reached anyone else.

For example, one day he informed me that the capture of the *Pueblo* had been accidental, that the North Korean patrol boats had actually been lying in wait for the *Banner.*

I didn't know whether to believe him or not, and still don't. However, I did give some thought to the question of whether our capture was premeditated. The readiness of our prison—the bunks and bedding, the nailed-shut windows, the sheets between the panes—seemed to indicate they had been expecting us. Yet if the building was already in use as a barracks, it would have taken only a few hours to prepare it for our occupancy, and we had been nearly twenty-four hours in transit between Wonsan and the Barn. Too, there were no locks on the doors, no bars on the windows. Also, during the first couple of weeks, everything—from the random nature of the initial questioning,

217

to the confusion over which men were or weren't officers, to the interrogations and beatings—had seemed hastily improvised to fit the occasion. We were not issued regular prison garb until we had been there several days. The "Rules of Life" had appeared only after several weeks of detention. In none of this could I find evidence of foresight or planning.

I gave far more thought, however, to a "disclosure" Major Spot made about this same time, which was that U.S. and D.P.R.K. negotiators were meeting at the truce site in Panmunjom to discuss our crimes. That steps were being taken to effect our release was tremendously encouraging news. If it was news. Yet I could see no reason for Major Spot to lie to me about this.

Or maybe, sensing all sorts of possible reasons, I wanted far too much to believe him to acknowledge them.

There was good news: "You will be allowed to write a letter to your wife."

And bad: "You must include the following things." After which followed a list of propaganda demands which the North Koreans obviously hoped would pressure President Johnson into apologizing.

"I can't write that," I told them. "My wife is eight months pregnant and this would only upset her."

To my surprise, they seemed to accept my answer. I was allowed to leave out most of their garbage, whether because they actually felt sympathy, or for other reasons, I don't know.

I stayed up all one night working on the first draft in the dim, flickering light in my room.

It was unacceptable, of course, as were the half-dozen that followed. Even when they had accepted the final version, they delayed sending it for some time. Although written in late February, it went out with a March 11 dateline.

Again I wanted to get a single message through: that the intrusion charges were phony and that the evidence of this was in the records and charts.

218

I addressed the letter to "Mrs. Carol Danks Murphy." "Danks" was my wife's maiden name, but she never used it in signing, preferring "Carol Louise Murphy." Just seeing the envelope should give her a clue that the letter was not what it seemed.

"Dear Carol and Eddie," I began. "I have prayed continuously and know that God has been your direction and strength during this experience. He certainly has been mine."

My captors were not happy with that first paragraph, because of the reference to God, but they let me include it, probably because they wanted the letter to appear authentic.

Following the propaganda inclusions, which I kept to a minimum and put in as odd English as possible ("our return is waiting upon the United States government to admit our crime, intrusions, offer guarantees not to happen in future, and sincerely apologize"), I was able to get in something I also felt vital that the United States know, in case they had not understood our last SITREP: "To tell the truth, at the time of our capture we couldn't destroy all our equipment or material in time, so these became insurmountable evidence against us."

The key message was worked into several paragraphs: "I hope that you might have some contact with the Navy by now so that your needs are being cared for. . . . We can't explain our action, but I hope that by now you and our government have seen photographs of all the evidence. I never had any idea that we had all that material. . . . Perhaps showing this letter to the Navy may help them understand the real facts at the time of capture. Especially if they were to know that the charts, logs, and records clearly show our numerous intrusions into their territorial waters. I wish I could personally show this evidence, because I'm positive it would erase any doubt as to our guilt of the crime of espionage for which we were detained. . . ."

I ended the letter with the only "sincere" statement in it,

other than the opening, my heartfelt love for my wife and son.

Carol was bright. I could picture her reading the letter and saying to herself: This isn't Ed. He's trying to tell us something.

I was sure that a casualty assistance calls officer had been assigned to her and all the other *Pueblo* wives and families, and that when she showed him the letter he would rush it to the Pentagon.

Explaining that my mother was seriously ill, I asked Colonel Specs, their letter-writing expert, if I could write to her also. He gave me an odd look, then shook his head.

With not a clue as to what was going to happen, the crew of the USS *Pueblo* was lined up in ranks in the main hallway. It was the first time we had been reunited since our capture, only Woelk being absent.

Something was up, something important.

"Gentlemen, I have great news!" Captain Bucher announced, a big grin on his face, the first we had seen since our capture.

Instant silence.

"Something you've all been waiting to hear!"

You could feel the excitement mounting.

"We have received a telegram from the United States!" Again he paused, as the hopes of every man in the room rose.

"Electrician's Mate Gerald Hagenson's wife has had a baby. It's a boy. Both mother and son are doing fine."

Even Hagenson looked crestfallen. For the first time, the whole crew got a clue as to how sick Bucher really was. Even Skip and Tim Harris were too embarrassed to look at him.

We filed back to our rooms.

"*Bali, bali! Bali, bali!*" Down the stairs, out into the snow and bitter cold.

It was late, after 2200 hours (10:00 P.M.), on the night of February 24. And the whole crew was present.

"Exercise," one of the English-speaking KORCOM officers commanded.

We were too surprised to move.

"Captain, you must lead your men," the officer shouted. "Exercise, it's time."

Bucher just stood there. It was impossible to tell whether he was being stubborn or was unable to pull himself together. "Captain, we *want* to exercise," one of the men pleaded. Obviously exasperated, Bucher barked, "Someone get out there and lead this fucking crew in calisthenics."

I stepped out and took command, leading the men through a series of exercises. Rather halfhearted ones, I must admit, because I still couldn't bend my back. But the important thing was that we were all together again. I was sure that in the dark ranks, messages were being passed.

One or two days later, one of the KORCOM officers came to my room and asked me to pick an enlisted man to lead the exercises. Without hesitation, I recommended Quartermaster Law. Bucher, I later learned, made an identical recommendation. So Law became leader of the enlisted men. If the KORCOMs had any idea how exceptional a leader he would be, and not only in calling cadences, they would never have appointed him.

During one of the interrogations, I asked Super C why we were allowed to exercise only at night. He explained that this was for our own protection, that if any of the local populace saw us, they would surely kill us.

Maybe. But I suspected our captors were not anxious for us to study our immediate surroundings in daylight.

Not long after this, an early-morning exercise period was added, but indoors. Only at night would they take us outside.

That our muscles ached, that we nearly froze in the cold that roared down from Siberia, bothered us not at all. For a few minutes we had a chance to escape from our holes. And despite the watchfulness of the guards, a crude communications network was set up. Crew problems or questions requiring wardroom-type decisions were passed up the line to a senior enlisted man, who awaited his chance to pass them along to an officer. In turn, word was passed down the line that the chain of command still remained in force, that any plans for escape had to be coordinated with the captain, who, together with the other officers, would evaluate their chances of success.

It was a beginning, and it was almost immediately followed by other opportunities.

A Ping-Pong table was set up, first in a large room, then in the lobby on the third floor. For a half-hour each day we were allowed to play. Then, on two successive Sundays, the officers were permitted to play cards. That interpreters were usually present, and that we were forbidden to discuss anything other than the game, only meant that we had to be especially devious. After our long isolation, we were starved for news, and exchanged it avidly, even if only bits and pieces at a time:

Woelk had been operated on while still in the Barn, crudely, with no anesthetic, two guards holding him down. When his condition worsened, he had been moved to a hospital somewhere outside the compound.

The wounds of the others seemed to have healed, although many of the men had diarrhea or were beginning to feel the effects of malnutrition.

There was disagreement over whether the talks at Panmunjom would accomplish anything. Bucher, for one, felt the United States had goofed badly by not bombing North Korea immediately after our capture. Yet we had read in their propaganda pamphlets about the exchange of two helicopter pilots after similar negotiations. The big stumbling block, everyone agreed, would be the D.P.R.K.'s insistence that the United States apologize.

Both Bucher and Schumacher had tried to kill themselves shortly after capture by sticking their heads in the water buckets in their rooms. It didn't work.

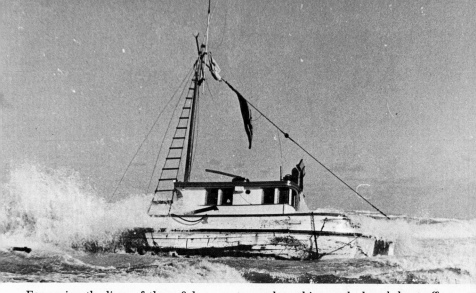

For saving the lives of three fishermen trapped on this wrecked crab boat off the coast of northern California in 1966, Lieutenant Edward R. Murphy, Jr., was awarded the Navy and Marine Corps Medal for Heroism. Less than three years later, when the crew of the USS *Pueblo* was repatriated from their North Korean prison, Murphy's commanding officer, Commander Lloyd M. ("Pete") Bucher, would accuse him of cowardice.

Following her capture, the U.S. Navy released this official photograph of the USS *Pueblo*. It was some time before an alert observer noticed that the ship was going backward. Although the press created the myth of a ship united under a dynamic leader, the truth was that the *Pueblo* was strifetorn from the moment she was commissioned, then doomed by a series of human blunders.

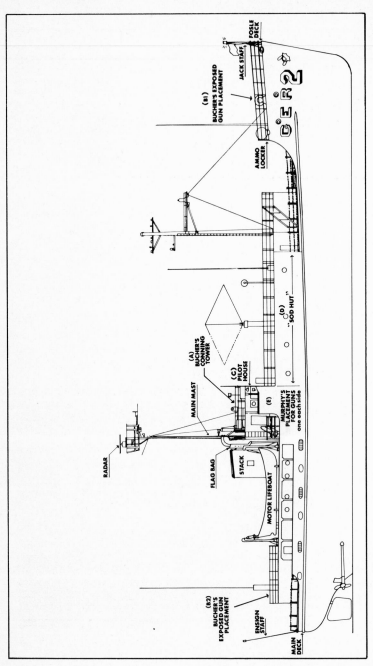

The *Pueblo*, showing (A) the tower Commander Bucher conned the ship from in submarine fashion; (B1) and (B2) the gun emplacements, also set up as on submarines; (C) the pilot house; (D) the "sod hut," the most secret section of the ship, yet its security was repeatedly violated by Commander Bucher; and (E) the area, on each side of the ship, where Lieutenant Murphy had hoped to place the guns, protected by the bulwark, in approved surface craft fashion.

Shortly after noon, on January 23, 1968, the *Pueblo*'s watch reported a "contact, closing fast." Pictured here is a North Korean modified SO1 subchaser similar to the one spotted by the *Pueblo*. Murphy, Executive Officer and second in command of the *Pueblo*, believes that had Commander Bucher followed U.S. Navy orders to disengage when threatened, the *"Pueblo* incident" need never have happened.

A Soviet built, P-4 class torpedo boat, of the type that surrounded and fired upon the *Pueblo*. In contrast to the *Pueblo*'s top speed of 12.2 knots, these North Korean ships had a maximum speed of about 50 knots and were armed with machine guns, torpedoes, and mines.

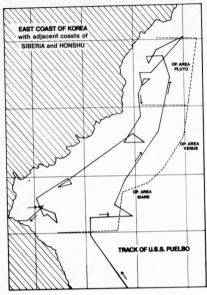

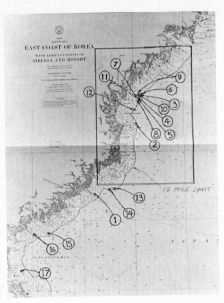

Left: A chart showing the actual journey of the *Pueblo*. Right: A chart of the North Korean coastline, showing the 17 alleged intrusions. What Murphy, navigator of the *Pueblo*, never told his captors was that 3 of the intrusions put the *Pueblo* on land, while another had her traveling at a speed of 2500 knots. Through this and other tricks, Murphy was able to get the message to U.S. Naval Intelligence that the intrusion charges were false.

U.P.I. Radiophoto

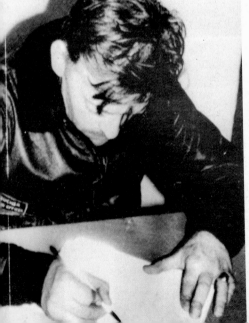

Commander Lloyd M. Bucher signing a "confession" admitting the *Pueblo* had violated North Korea's territorial waters. Only after Bucher broke and abandoned the Code of Conduct did the other crew members sign similar bogus admissions.

Photographs released by the North Koreans showing the "humane" treatment of the crew as they presumably enjoyed the intricacies of tea ceremonies and letter writing. The reality was far more grim. In the top photo, Research Officer Lieutenant Stephen Harris is on Murphy's right, while Fireman Steven Woelk, badly injured in the attack on the ship is on his left. Note the middle finger of Murphy's hand in this photo.

Left: The only known photograph of the crew's second detention site in North Korea. Sarcastically dubbed the "Country Club," it was here Hell Week took place. Right: An official North Korean photograph of the officers of the USS *Pueblo*. Left to right: Ensign Timothy Harris, Supply Officer; Lieutenant (JG) Carl Schumacher, Operations Officer; Commander Lloyd Bucher, Captain; Lieutenant Edward Murphy, Jr., Executive Officer and navigator; Lieutenant Stephen Harris, Research Officer; and CWO Eugene Lacy, Engineering Officer. Note the extended forefinger and little finger of Lieutenant Murphy's left hand.

Wide World Photos

Pueblo crewmen told the North Koreans that the extended middle finger was a good luck sign. But when *Time* published this photograph and explained the real meaning of the gesture, the North Koreans realized they had "lost face" before the rest of the world. This was one of the causes of Hell Week. Seated left to right: Fireman Howard Bland; CT Donald Peppard; CT James Layton; Chief Engineer Monroe Goldman. Standing left to right: Boatswain's Mate Ronald Berens; civilian oceanographer Harry Iredale; Engineman William Scarborough; and Quartermaster Charles Law.

The September
press conference,
one of several
propaganda spectacles
staged by North
Korea to "puncture
the arrogance of
the Yankee devils."
Despite all their
precautions, the
Pueblo's officers
used these
occasions to get
messages through
to the U.S.

Above: For 11 months the families of the *Pueblo* crewmen waited, hoped, and prayed. Lieutenant Murphy's wife Carol is pictured here with their son Eddie and their daughter Vicky, born 2 months after the capture of the *Pueblo*. Below: This mimeographed form letter, with names typed in, was the U.S. Navy's way of informing the families of the *Pueblo* crew of the capture.

In late December of 1968, the long negotiations between North Korea and the United States at Panmunjom resulted in a remarkable compromise. In return for the release of the crew, the U.S. would "admit" the bogus intrusions, at the same time publicly repudiating their own statement as a lie.

Above: North Korean guards on the "Bridge of No Return." Below: The repatriation of Petty Officer Duane Hodges, killed in the attack on the *Pueblo*.

On December 23, 1968, exactly 11 months after their capture, Commander
Lloyd Bucher led the 82 *Pueblo* crewmen across the bridge from North

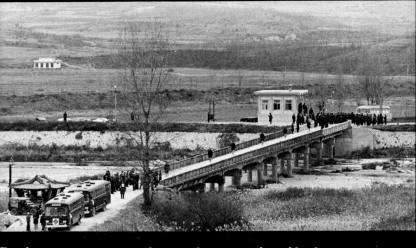

For those waiting to cross, the procedure was unbearably slow.

The 82nd and last man across the bridge, Lieutentant Edward R. Murphy, Jr. The worried frown quickly turned into a broad grin as Murphy realized he was a free man once more.

Grateful and happy *Pueblo* crewmen on their way to their first American meal in 11 months. In addition to the injuries received while undergoing torture, all suffered from malnutrition, some of the men losing as much as 70 pounds.

"We—I—surrendered because it was nothing but a slaughter out there. . . ." Commander Bucher addressing an impromptu press conference in South Korea. Bucher's version of the ship's surrender would undergo numerous changes following his release.

The crew of the USS *Pueblo* arrive at Miramar Naval Air Station, San Diego. Petty Officer Hodges returns home.

Admiral Allen M. Shinn welcomes home the crew of the *Pueblo*. A tense Commander Bucher is on the left. With him is his wife Rose who, along with the other wives of the *Pueblo*'s officers, actively campaigned for the release of the crew.

Thousands line the route as the *Pueblo* crewmen are taken to Balboa Naval Hospital in San Diego. Girls in hair curlers and sweaters convinced the crewmen that they were indeed back in the U.S.A. Christmas morning the Navy Exchange in the hospital was opened so the men of the *Pueblo* could buy gifts for their families. Executive Officer Murphy is shown with civilian oceanographer Dunnie ("Friar") Tuck.

Executive Officer Murphy answering questions at a press conference held shortly after the crew's return to the U.S. Realizing that Commander Bucher was in no shape to deal with the press, Navy officials placed him in isolation and put Murphy in charge of the crew. Relief at being home was overshadowed by the realization that the ordeal was not yet over. The Court of Inquiry lay ahead.

Commander Lloyd M. Bucher and Lieutenant Edward R. Murphy, Jr., receiving Purple Hearts for wounds suffered during the attack on the *Pueblo*. The conflict between the two officers was only hinted at during the Court of Inquiry.

A scene from the U.S. Navy's Court of Inquiry into the surrender of the USS *Pueblo*. Due to backstage agreements, many extremely damning pieces of evidence were never mentioned during the proceedings, such as why Bucher neglected to bring aboard the TNT that could have been used to destroy the *Pueblo*'s classified cargo or to scuttle the ship.

Left: Commander Bucher testifying at a "secret" session of the court. His attorneys are sitting at the table on his left. Right: Counsels of the court. For two months the court, composed of five admirals, listened to the testimony. Then, on May 6, 1969, their verdict was made public.

The first, and only, group photograph of the 82 *Pueblo* crewmen and 2 civilian oceanographers, taken a month after their return to the United States. For them, the case of the USS *Pueblo* will never be closed.

Favorite nicknames for officers and guards were exchanged. The doctor's nurse was dubbed Flo, for Florence Nightingale. It was agreed that, unlike all the other North Korean women we had seen, she had possibilities. Which indicated we had already been in prison much too long.

Tim Harris argued that his room was colder than mine. I told him to stuff toilet paper in the cracks around the window, as I had.

The one thing we most wanted to discuss, we couldn't, because of the risk of being overheard. What questions had been asked each man in the interrogations? It was essential that we compare notes and learn this, in order to determine exactly what classified material had been compromised. That, unfortunately, would have to wait for future opportunities.

Bucher seemed to perk up somewhat during these sessions, but he remained tired, pessimistic, depressed. The rest of us did what we could to lift his spirits. We were not altogether successful.

Still, it looked as if our situation was changing for the better.

Then one day the guards goofed, leaving both Photographer's Mate Mack and me in the hall alone at the same time.

"They're asking me about carriers, Mr. Murphy! What should I do?"

Mack had been assigned to an aircraft carrier prior to receiving his *Pueblo* orders.

"Don't tell them anything classified," I advised him. "If they touch on something sensitive, lie."

It was the rule of thumb I had been using myself. That we had departed from the letter of the Code of Conduct didn't mean that we couldn't adhere to its spirit.

Yet Mack's question disturbed me. Did it mean they were now going after the hard-core stuff? That same day I again went into my loony act, adding still another packet to my hoard of sleeping powder.

223

On the afternoon of March 5 there was an unusual amount of noise in the compound—vehicles arriving, shouted commands. I knew something was up even before Solutions barged in and ordered me to clean my room. But I anticipated nothing more than a high-level inspection, until receiving a second order: all personal belongings were to be placed in the bed sheets and wrapped in a tight bundle.

Dinner was early. Shortly after this, they took away not only the bundle but also the bed.

There was no mistaking the meaning. We were going someplace. Panmunjom?

I wanted it to be true, yet had to admit the possibility that it was not.

When I was sure no one was peeking through the cracks in the door, I reached behind the radiator, took out the sleeping powder, and slipped it inside my hat band.

It was night by the time we received the order to fall out, then were herded down the stairs and out of the building onto buses. I slipped into the seat beside Bucher. We managed to exchange one quick glance before lowering our heads. The hope was written on his face, too.

The buses moved slowly out of the compound. All the windows were covered, but even had they not been, I'm sure none of us would have looked back. The Barn was not a place we'd want to remember. We had been there forty days and forty nights.

19

"Keep hands in coat pockets!" The shouted order came from Chipmunk, one of the junior officers. It was a ridiculous command, as whenever the bus careened around a corner some of the men would slide off their seats.

Bucher complained.

Laughing sarcastically, Chipmunk chided, "You must overcome!"

From then on, anytime we had a complaint, this would be the standard reply.

A bridge, a culvert, a check point, a second check point, another bridge—I tried to memorize the route. I was sure, from the turns, that we were going south, toward the DMZ. But the buses stopped after no more than a half-hour, and we were ordered off.

We were still somewhere on the outskirts of Pyongyang.

The building in front of us was far more impressive than the Barn, so much so that we would dub it the "Country Club." It was three stories, of prefabricated construction, and almost new. Two large columns flanked the front entrance. On entering, we were ordered to remove our shoes. The floors were marble. There was even marble paneling on some of the walls. Plus a number of paintings, nearly all, of course, of Comrade Kim Il Sung.

Obviously this was a showplace of the sort the North Koreans were fond of using in their pictorial propaganda, with the implication that it was typical. Later, on discovering that there was an obstacle course and a number of firing ranges on the grounds, we surmised that the building had previously been used as a model military training camp.

During a short indoctrination there was no hint of immediate release. On the contrary, it was stated that this would be our home until the United States apologized. We were all assigned rooms, on the second and third floors. Again each officer was given his own room. Bucher and I, Steve Harris, and Tim Harris were on the second floor; Lacy and Schumacher on the third. All the others were billeted in groups of four and eight.

My room was larger than its counterpart in the Barn. It was also clean, well lighted, and well ventilated. The walls had almost new plaster. The wood on the floor was shiny, with only a few cracks. There was a radiator which actually gave off heat. The door was solid, with no peepholes. If a guard wanted to look in, he had to either open the door or bend down and look through the keyhole. The windows were not covered. As I would learn the next morning, I even had southern exposure, the warm sunshine I had been yearning for.

My bed and bedding from the Barn had been moved into the room prior to our arrival, but all the other furniture was new. Included was a table, a chair, a nightstand with a drawer and shelf compartment, and a wash pan. And, in one corner, there was even a rubber-tree plant!

Shortly after our arrival, Super C conducted an inspection. Before leaving my room, he warned me that if anything happened to the plant, he not only would hold me responsible, he would send me to North Vietnam to find a replacement.

He said this in Korean, but the interpreter caught his whimsical tone.

Super C was not without a sense of humor, but underneath was a cold, calculating KORCOM officer. I never let his occasional touches of whimsy, or his oft-expressed "concern" for my welfare, blind me to the fact that we were enemies playing a deadly game.

While still marveling at our new surroundings, we were

226

ordered out of our rooms and marched up the stairs to the third floor into a large room, where, to our surprise, we were shown a movie.

It was entitled *The Tractor Driver,* and, under any other circumstances, I probably would have roared with laughter, it was so bad.

The hero, who looked like Cantinflas, was a city dweller. Good Communist that he was, he gave up his one day off to help the farmers meet their production quota. Faced with the dilemma of maneuvering his tractor through the muddy rice paddies, he hit upon a novel solution—he installed a rowboat under its front wheels. Of course, the scheme didn't work, he still got mired in the mud, but that wasn't the point of the movie. The point, as nearly as we could fathom it, was that he had the "chollima" spirit; he would try anything to increase his productivity.

I'd come across the word "chollima" frequently in the propaganda tracts. The chollima was a mythical super-stallion who could cover 4,000 leagues in a single stride. This legendary creature had become the national symbol of North Korea, which—or so went the propaganda—had leaped from the past into the future under the dynamic leadership of Kim Il Sung. Every peasant was constantly urged to emulate this accomplishment: to work at chollima speed, with chollima energy, to accomplish chollima results.

That tiny North Korea could flaunt the greatest power on earth by seizing one of her ships showed chollima. It also showed "juche."

As frequently used, and also nationalistic in character, "juche" meant self-determination, self-sufficiency, independence. The tractor driver had juche, because he did not ask for the help of someone else. North Korea had it, we were told, because she did not need the assistance of any other country. (Later we would observe some hilarious exceptions which would poke holes in this myth.) Gradually we came to realize that there was a "Juche Curtain" between North Korea and the rest of the world, which

227

separated her from even her Communist allies, Red China and the U.S.S.R.

This, we were to discover, had a special relevancy to the *Pueblo.*

Since our arrival at the Country Club I had yet to see a familiar face among the guards; not only had the entire guard force been changed, but so had the attitude of our new custodians. Thus far, at least, they appeared far less antagonistic. It was sometime before we discovered the reason for this: the party line had changed. Once we had admitted and apologized for our crimes, the onus for these acts was lifted from our shoulders and placed squarely on those of the government of the United States. Almost over-night the criminals had been transformed into victims of U.S. aggressive imperialism. The attitude of the new guards reflected the change.

However, the KORCOM officers—Super C, Colonel Specs, King Kong, Chipmunk, Major Spot, etc.—remained the same. And they reminded us, while we were assembled for the movie, that our status was still something less than that of pampered tourists.

We did not appreciate our humanitarian treatment! We were insincere! Already one of the crewmen had tried to burn down the building!

Single file, we were marched through one of the rooms past the evidence, a large cigarette burn in a mattress cover. Since the mattress belonged to CT Michael Alexander, our captors judged him guilty. As he stood there, eyes downcast, we filed past him muttering "Bad boy" and "Shame." No beating would be necessary, the North Koreans decided, for he had already suffered a much worse punishment: he had "lost face" among his comrades.

It was a good lesson to know.

The surprises were not yet over. There would be Ping-Pong, volleyball, and card playing. Meals would be served in a common dining hall. And that night, for the first time since our capture, the lights in the rooms were turned out.

Semilivable rooms, new guards who as yet had shown little overt animosity, recreation, the chance to associate with other members of the crew—these were all positive changes.

But there was one minus that more than outbalanced them.

Our new residence looked too damn permanent.

Yet, no matter how bleak the situation, the mind can conjure up some hope. Mine came from the sudden change in our treatment. I could understand this if they were getting ready to let us go. But if they were only going to prolong our detention, what was the purpose of moving us out of the Barn?

There was a simple answer. But my hopes so blinded me that for a time I couldn't see it.

Bells on all three floors announced reveille. There was only time to slosh our faces with cold water before we were hustled out into the predawn chill for exercises.

While we were thus occupied, the guards were not inactive. Looking up at the lighted windows, we could see their silhouettes as they moved from room to room conducting searches.

They missed the cache in my hat band.

With typical North Korean inconsistency, we were made to strip down to sweat suits before being taken outside in the snow to exercise; then, returned to the warmth of the building, we were again made to don our heavy coats. We perspired. And with no change of clothing, the perspiration accumulated. Before long every man had a rash, fungus, or one or more running sores. I developed a bad case of athlete's foot, plus a series of warts on the sole of one foot.

Room cleaning followed the exercises, then a trip to the head. It was just as filthy as the one in the Barn, but, on our own initiative, we worked hard to keep it clean.

Meals were served in two shifts, in a large room on the

third floor. Except for an occasional plate of cookies or apples, the food was the same, inadequate. We continued to lose weight. As nauseating as our fare was, one new change made it even more so. Before each meal we had to wash our hands in disinfectant. Its smell permeated everything we ate. As for its hygienic effect, there was none, for after dipping our hands in the smelly mixture, we all dried them on the same filthy towel.

Twenty minutes was allowed for each meal. Military-school style, we sat and rose on command. At first our captors let us sit wherever we chose. This ended when they discovered that some of their prize plastic tablecloths had slits in them. They had only themselves to blame. Shortly after the move, they issued all of us small pocket-knives and nail clippers. That some of the men may not have been able to resist the temptation to destroy something North Korean was not too surprising. After that, however, we were assigned seats.

The issuance of the knives was like a slap in the face, and undoubtedly was intended as such. It indicated how unconcerned they were about their security.

Talking during meals was forbidden. But, despite the tight security, messages were passed.

After the first nine days, our captors decided to reward the officers with their own wardroom. Like most of their rewards, we found the change a punishment. However, there were still opportunities to mingle with the crew in the recreation periods, and after a time the officers' meals were served by—though neither cooked nor prepared by—*Pueblo* crewmen. The lines of communication remained, and, through use, grew stronger.

For an hour after lunch, usually from 1300 to 1400 hours (1:00–2:00 P.M.), we were allowed to participate in sports. Volleyball and basketball were permitted, baseball was not. The ban was purely nationalistic. When Korea was occupied by Japan, the Koreans had been forced to adopt this pastime. As with most other things Japanese, it was discredited when the occupation ended.

230

That anything Japanese was anathema to our captors was borne out in various not always unhumorous ways. While the rest of the world referred to "Asiatic sleeping sickness," it was "Japanese sleeping sickness" to the North Koreans.

It was while we were on the playing field one day that I learned that some of the crewmen were secretly assembling parts for a radio.

Both mornings and afternoons, when not used for interrogations, were usually devoted to individual study of the "cultural" materials, and, on occasion, lectures. The KORCOMs called these sessions "reeducation."

The first step in reeducation was an attempt to wipe the slate clean of all our previous "misconceptions." Such as everything we had been taught about American government, politics, and history.

Socialism was better than capitalism, they argued, because their system provided greater equality for all individuals. By contrast, they pointed to the treatment of minority groups in the United States.

There were two blacks on board the *Pueblo,* Boatswain's Mate Willie Bussell and Commissaryman Harry Lewis. That they appeared to be as well liked as any of the other crewmen bothered the North Koreans exceedingly and they spent many hours attempting to convince the two men how bad their lot was. Their refusal to echo the KORCOM propaganda infuriated the North Koreans.

That Policarpo Garcia, a Filipino, was one of the leading petty officers aboard the ship was equally incomprehensible to them. It contradicted everything they had been taught.

I seriously doubt if there was even one of us who felt our system of government perfect in all respects, who felt proud of the way the Indians, blacks, Mexican-Americans, and others had been treated at various times in our history. But we were not about to admit this to the North Koreans. Completely united on this, we felt that these were our personal problems as Americans, to be worked out among

231

ourselves, not to be exploited for someone else's propaganda gains.

When it came to American history, the North Koreans literally rewrote such events as the signing of the Declaration of Independence, the Louisiana Purchase, and the fall of the Alamo, all the heroes becoming capitalist villains. As one of the crewmen later put it, "It was like watching westerns in which the Indians won every time."

Two of our young CTs, Wayne Anderson and Peter Langenberg, were particularly good at rebutting these historical fictions. Both had the ability to bout with our captors on a scholarly basis. Unable to win them over, the KORCOMs feigned great sorrow that these two intelligent crewmen had been duped by the lies of the Yankee imperialists.

Not all of the crewmen had as solid educational backgrounds. A few, though not converted by the North Korean arguments, were at least confused by them. I felt then—and still feel—that in these days of psychological warfare, U.S. military personnel need more exposure to the history of American institutions and the comparative values of the democratic way of life. Our best defense against Communist propaganda, I believe, is a strong confidence in our form of government, based not on blind faith but enlightened understanding.

That the Communists seemed to be making some inroads with their "reeducation" efforts was due less to the logic of their arguments—often nonexistent—than to a feeling that the government of the United States was doing little, if anything, to effect our release. Whenever we learned through the grapevine that a particular crewman was "down," we would make a special effort to talk to him on the playing field. Mostly, however, we relied heavily on the senior crewman in each room to bolster morale. The job they did was incredible.

Though the fear of more torture never entirely left us, morale was generally much higher after the move to the Country Club. Yet as days became weeks, then months,

232

it was understandable that some felt abandoned. We could try to reassure them that the United States government was doing everything in its power to free us. But the truth was, we had no proof of this. What passed for news was first filtered through a propaganda screen, then sifted, sorted, and carefully parceled out. We knew only what the KORCOMs wanted us to know. And we could never be sure it was true.

This was one reason we had such great hopes for the radio. Just knowing what was going on outside the Juche Curtain could set many fears to rest.

After the evening meal, the officers were allowed to play cards in the wardroom, provided the duty officers gave permission, and if Super C didn't decide to deliver a three- or four-hour lecture instead. One of his favorite tricks was to start these just before dinner, so by the time we did eat, the food was cold. Super C, of course, would have eaten earlier.

Lacy taught pinochle to those of us who didn't know how to play it; Bucher and Schumacher did the same with bridge.

Concentrating on the game was difficult, since for the first time since our capture we could talk with relative freedom. It seemed there were a million things each of us wanted to know.

The fact the guards were never far away, and the possibility of the room being bugged, limited what we could say, but we were able to put together a fairly accurate picture of what questions had been asked in the interrogations and what documents compromised. It was apparent that each of the officers had managed to withhold the information which he deemed most important. It was also apparent that there were whole areas—especially sensitive ones, too—which our captors never inquired about. That continued to puzzle us.

Details of the seizure, the death of Hodges, the brutality of certain KORCOM officers and guards, the tricks of Super C—all were discussed. Little pieces began falling

233

into place. And, occasionally, there were new mysteries. For example, after the crew had been removed from the ship at Wonsan, Steve Harris had been brought back aboard to open the sod-hut door. That meant that someone had been talking, had abandoned the Code and identified Steve as the research officer, even before we got on the train.

Eventually the talk moved to our torture.

The trick with the gun had been tried on nearly all of us. With Bucher and Schumacher, the KORCOMs had actually pointed the pistol at their heads, then snapped the trigger—on an empty chamber. Although he had held up through a very severe beating, Bucher had finally broken, he told us, when the North Koreans had threatened to shoot the crew, one by one, starting with the youngest member. Only then had he signed the confession.

That he had broken first, less than forty-eight hours after the surrender, apparently bothered Bucher. I don't think this concerned anyone else, at least not in the same way. We were all too well aware that the KORCOMs could pack a hell of a lot of concentrated torture into a few hours.

Exchanging recollections, we became aware that, among the officers, Bucher, Lacy, and I had received the most severe punishment. What Tim Harris and Schumacher had gone through, though bad enough, was just the preliminary to what we had undergone.

While we had been talking, Steve Harris had remained silent. Someone asked what sort of punishment he had received. Had they beaten him badly?

No, they hadn't beaten him at all, he admitted. In fact, they hadn't laid a hand on him.

There was a long, uncomfortable silence while this sank in. Then someone changed the subject.

We all must have thought about it. I know I did. And later it would become an obsession with Bucher.

I felt I knew Steve a little better than the others did, having shared a stateroom with him. At first I think we all reacted to his admission in the same way: with both amazement and resentment. But as I thought about it over a longer period of time, I came to realize that each of us had his own Waterloo. For most of us it had been physical torture; for Steve, it was psychological. Given the complex inner makeup of that creature known as man, who could say whether what Steve had undergone was any less intense or devastating than what we had? Just as no two men react to anything identically, so must the breaking point of each differ.

To some of the questions, I realized, there could never be answers.

As happy as we were to be reunited, the old divisions had already started reappearing.

The reason behind the move to the Country Club was quite simple: the surroundings better suited North Korea's humanitarian-treatment claim. One of the first things our captors did after the move was refilm our first press conference, in the most impressive room in the new building.

With only a few additions, the questions and answers we were given to memorize were unchanged. In a sense, they were stuck with the "script," because an edited transcript of the first press conference had already been printed in the *Pyongyang Times*.

Did this mean the first film had never been released? We were afraid it did. (Not until much later did we learn that the final film contained portions of both press conferences. Left on the cutting-room floor were most of our little tricks, plus all the shots of my battered ear. My often repeated "the charts and records show . . ." remained, however.)

Not long after this, we were again ordered to write letters home. My request to be allowed to write my mother was again denied, but I was given permission to write another letter to Carol and Eddie, plus one to my sister Anne and her husband Bill Drebohl.

As with our first letters, once a final draft was approved, we had to copy each letter three or four times, then the individual copies were mailed from different countries. Our captors were sure that unless this was done, "Johnson's spies" would seize and destroy them.

Emphasis was again on pressuring the U.S. government to apologize. However, these letters had a special urgency, since both Super C and Major Spot had reiterated that if an apology were not immediately forthcoming from President Johnson, we might be brought to trial as war criminals. Major Spot also warned that they would not be as lenient with us as the Russians had been with Francis Gary Powers. Powers, I recalled, had been sentenced to ten years' imprisonment, then released after a year and nine months, in exchange for Soviet spy Rudolf Abel. I didn't consider twenty-one months "lenient." But Major Spot meant something else, I was sure. Powers could have received the death sentence.

As for the possibility of a trade, I seriously doubted if the United States had a single prisoner of interest to the North Koreans.

The KORCOMs were not as careful with these letters as with the first we wrote. In writing to Carol I was able to hint at the location of our prison compound: "My room has a southern exposure, which allows me warm sunshine during our days.

"As I gaze out my window, I imagine that somewhere there must be a border station through which I so want to pass. It is perhaps only a day or so away, but it may as well be on another planet if our case is not settled immediately." Though forced to include their propaganda, I was able to cast doubt on my sincerity by phrasing it in quaint English: "Quite distasteful are the fruits of our imagination when pondering our plight, should immediate affirmative response not be proffered by the United States government." That we could get away with such tricks on some occasions, and not on others, seemed to indicate different translators at work.

Both Anne and Bill had fine senses of humor. I began

236

my letter to them, "Please don't be offended that I am now a criminal. I am sorry for any disgrace I may have caused you all. . . ."

Yet I was also anxious to utilize any opportunity to get a message through. Having seen how few changes had been made in my letter to Carol, I decided to risk using a simple code.

One section began: "Bill, imagine that you, instead of being an airman stationed in Hawaii as you were, imagine if you were one of the enginemen or cooks on our ship and are now declared a criminal and detained in the Democratic People's Republic of Korea for conducting espionage in their territorial waters. . . ."

Later I began another paragraph: "What I would give to have been in your shoes in Hawaii!"

Bill had been in neither the Air Force nor Hawaii. I used this means to tip off him—and Naval Intelligence—that the rest of the statements in those paragraphs, which detailed the intrusions, were "B.S." In the other paragraphs, however, which were not prefaced by a lie, I stated that much of our electronic data and many of our other records had been captured intact. "I saw a huge table stacked with highly classified material which had been taken from the ship. . . ."

Though written earlier, both letters went out with a March 24 dateline.

While working on the final draft of my second letter to Carol, I included a sentence which read: "Please give my love to Mom and all."

Reading this, one of the interpreters asked, "Don't you know your mother is dead?"

My stunned expression startled him. It was as if he suddenly realized he had said too much. When I tried to question him further, he refused to reply. Nor could I get answers from Super C.

Were they just taunting me, trying to break down my morale? The interpreter's confusion seemed all too real. I was afraid that I had accidentally learned the truth. And

237

I couldn't shake the feeling that perhaps my capture had been a factor in her death.

On March 17 Woelk was reunited with the crew. All the officers assembled on the stairs to greet him as he was returned from the hospital. He had lost considerable weight and was very pale, but he had retained his boyish grin and was able to walk, though with difficulty.

"Jack Warner" and his camera crew recorded the event for the world press. Later a statement was released over Woelk's signature describing the humanitarian treatment he had received, and praising the skill of the surgeons. What he told us privately was another story altogether. The North Koreans had no conception of modern medicine. Their treatment was straight out of the dark ages. Weeks passed between changes of his bandages. That he was still alive, we were sure, was due entirely to his will to live and not to their barbarous butchery.

As the end of March drew closer, I had to accept the probability that I would not be with Carol when she had the baby.

Her first birth had been without complications. By now I was sure that she and Eddie would have returned to the United States and would be living with her parents. She would receive the best possible care. Knowing that helped.

Yet it was not an easy time.

"You hate the captain, that is so?" Super C asked through the interpreter.

"No, of course not," I replied, puzzled at the sudden turn in the interrogation. I had been brought before Super C to be persuaded to write another letter. Bucher again had to write to the President. As second in command, I had been assigned the Secretary of State, while all the other crewmen were made to write their governors, senators, or congressmen.

"Captain Bucher is a bad man, yes?"

238

"No, he's a good man." What the hell was Super C getting at?

"Why you lie? You play me for the fool? You owe captain no loyalty." Then, to my amazement, he listed some of my past differences with Bucher.

Then I understood. They had found the rough draft of my resignation!

But it didn't stop there.

"The captain hates you, Executive Officer Murphy." With this he enumerated some of Bucher's criticisms of me. The accusations—the pay-records dispute in Yokosuka, for example—were too explicit to be guesswork. Someone, either Bucher or one of the others, had been talking, I decided.

Then I caught myself. This was exactly what Super C wanted us to do, turn against each other. Divide and conquer: one of the oldest tricks in the world. And still one of the most effective. He had used my letter of resignation as the opening wedge. He probably hadn't even told Bucher there was such a letter, just quoted my criticisms verbatim, as if I had confided them to him. And Bucher, in turn, had probably reacted angrily, making his own charges.

Or—I suddenly realized—maybe Bucher hadn't even said a word. Maybe the KORCOMs had simply found a few of the "nastygrams" the skipper wrote about his officers.

If true, Super C had accomplished all this with just a couple of sheets of paper! And he had almost succeeded!

Super C might call the rules, but that didn't mean we had to play the game. "Commander Bucher is a fine man and a good officer," I said, with a conviction that startled even me.

Super C's trick brought to the fore something that had been worrying me since our move to the Country Club.

That the United States might believe the intrusion charges greatly disturbed Bucher. Obviously, when the

239

navigational records had been taken to him for signing, he had been too distraught to spot the discrepancies.

I wanted to put his fears to rest. I wanted to assure him that through the inconsistencies in the timed intrusions, my finger gestures in the navigational photographs, the reiterated phrase "the charts and records show," and the tricks I'd used in the letters home, the message *must* have gotten through. Yet each time I started to say something to him, I hesitated. In part it was because of the fear of being overheard. But that was only part.

I knew what the KORCOMs could accomplish with torture.

I knew too that if Bucher had broken once, he could do so again. And his mental state was still far from stable.

If the KORCOMs ever discovered that they had been made to "play the fool," had lost face before the whole world, particularly through their own propaganda devices, someone would pay for it. And I didn't want it to be the crew of the *Pueblo*.

It was an unpleasant realization. But I had to face it. I couldn't trust Bucher with this information.

20

An earthwork wall, twelve to fifteen feet high, enclosed the prison compound. Guards with submachine guns patrolled the top.

There was a single gate to the compound. It was heavily guarded.

Presuming that we could make it over the top, or out through the gate, our difficulties would be far from over, for the compound was surrounded by villages and rice paddies: even if we managed to avoid the houses, progress through the fields would be impossibly slow. And farther beyond was nothing but flat land. We were in the midst of the Ryongdae, one of the great plains of Korea. If a group of men tried to make their way across the open plain to the sea, aerial surveillance would quickly spot them.

Unless, that is, they traveled at night.

I began to visualize a few possibilities. Thus far, however, I still lacked enough information to formulate a workable plan. Where were ammunition, foodstuffs, extra clothing, keys to the vehicles, gasoline stored? How often did the guards change, and how many of them were there? What vehicles regularly left and reentered the compound, and at what times? How far was it to the mountains, or the sea, and exactly what lay in between?

Inadvertently, the KORCOMs would literally hand me the most important answers.

Someone—recollections differ—decided it would break the monotony if we had another holiday to celebrate. Easter was suggested. To be frank, no one was sure what day Easter fell upon this year—the date we finally picked, April 7, we later discovered was Palm Sunday. An even bigger problem was that the North Koreans had said we couldn't celebrate either official U.S. or religious holidays. Easter, we told them in all innocence, was a worker's holiday. Approval was granted.

Since Sunday was already a day of rest, the holiday meant no change, with one exception. Obviously someone did a little homework, because that Sunday we were each presented one hard-boiled egg, apparently the gift of a KORCOM Easter bunny.

An officer, whom we called the Imperialist, informed us that he knew all about the holiday. "This is the day Easter died," he told us smugly. We marveled at his remarkable fund of knowledge.

The North Koreans had an ambivalent attitude toward religion. They never missed an opportunity to ridicule it. ("Don't you know that God is dead?" they told some of the crewmen; "He was shot down by a Russian rocket.") Yet ostensibly one of their three political parties was a religious party.

In their "reeducation" efforts they often scoffed at religion. The villain in one of the movies we saw was a Korean clergyman. This pockmarked, weasel-faced man of the cloth, upon catching a hungry young boy stealing apples, had branded his hand with a hot iron.

This was a true story, Captain Queer and Captain Nice, the two interpreters of our Friday-night movies, told us.

The KORCOMs denied they were antireligious, yet in early April they ransacked the rooms, seizing contraband, particularly crosses and other religious objects the men had made. We concluded that there was a freedom from religion, not of religion. We were free to pray, just as long as we weren't caught at it.

In reality, in their cult of personalities, Kim Il Sung was venerated like a god, while North Korean women made sobbing pilgrimages to the shrine of his late and much lamented mother, the legendary Kang Ban Sok.

Such inconsistencies didn't bother a people who often called Kim Il Sung "the father of forty million Koreans," while reliable estimates put North Korea's population at no more than fifteen million. As for juche, North Korea's oft-repeated claim to total self-sufficiency ("We import *nothing*," Super C proudly boasted), even with our very limited view we saw ample evidence to dispute this. One of the movies showed a North Korean truck, piled high with sacks plainly labeled "Portland Cement." All our confessions were written with Bic ball-point pens. (At first I thought the KORCOMs might have found them in ship's stores, but on checking with supply personnel learned this was not the case.) While their favorite claim, that North Korea made all its own automobiles and hadn't imported a foreign-made vehicle in sixteen years, was belied as we spotted from our windows: Japanese-made Toyopet trucks; a Willys Jeep station wagon; and a 1957 Plymouth convertible. On hearing of the latter, "Barnyard" Barrett circulated the rumor that it was to be awarded to the man who refused repatriation.

It must be said in favor of North Korea that it is very likely the only country in the world that makes brand-new used trucks. These cumbersome vehicles—made from long-obsolete Soviet blueprints—would bounce down the roads at night with headlights flickering, alternately growing bright and fading dim, in common with all the electrical lighting we had seen in North Korea.

The Willys pulled into the compound one day loaded with speakers, electrical wiring, and other sound equipment. To date our music had consisted of what we could hear from the loudspeakers in the adjoining villages. We almost came to pity the poor Korean peasant. From the time he arose in the morning until he collapsed onto his rice-husk mat at night, he was barraged with martial music and propaganda. He couldn't even escape into the rice paddies, for the amplifiers were turned up so high the sound followed him there too. And the music—traditional peasant fare, consisting of the discordant cacophony of reeds, woodwinds, and drums—was bad even to those of us who appreciated Japanese music. I once told one of the interpreters, Captain Nice (a misnomer if ever there was one), of my dislike for North Korea's modern jazz. He quietly admitted that it didn't turn him on either.

"The men would like some different music," Super C told us a week or so after I spotted the truck. "You officers must make the decision whether they may hear other records or not."

Having seen the equipment, I knew the question was already decided, but we went through the formality anyway, so Super C, dispenser of all blessings, could grant our humble wish. From then on we heard Russian-plagiarized North Korean classical music, which, though still bad, was at least better than their juche product.

I was never deceived by the fact that so many of Super C's tricks were transparent. I hated Super C—if "hate" is a strong enough word—but I never questioned his dedication or skill. No one else in the prison put in as many hours; for him there was no day of rest. That he had been assigned to us meant that he was probably one of North Korea's top officers. The respect that the other KORCOM officers and guards showed him also seemed to support this. We might laugh inwardly at his ridiculous poses (once, describing how American soldiers allegedly treated Korean women and children, he pretended, with howls of anguish, to pound nails into his head), but the inescapable fact was that he had broken eighty-two men, some of them trained in resisting such efforts. He was skillful enough to crack their leader first, then, using this as a club, pick off the others. And he was shrewd enough to know that for some, like Steve Harris, the threat of torture would be more frightening than the reality.

Bucher never understood Super C. Perhaps he never even tried. With his simplistic way of looking at things, Super C was just a dumb Commie. Underrating an enemy can be a costly error, and it was one Bucher made time and again.

On the opposite side, to the discomfort of all the other *Pueblo* officers, Super C seemed to understand Bucher all too well. He treated him with the condescending contempt a master chess player might accord an overtouted amateur. It was obvious he felt him an unworthy adversary. Early in our detention he apparently ferreted out most of Bucher's weaknesses, for now he played on them. Bucher hated regulations. Super C made sure he lived a totally regulated life. No one else was harassed so continuously by the guards. Let him leave a wash pan on his bed, or forget to fasten a button, and they would nail him. Often they framed him into provocations. There were times when the rest of us could relax. There were no such moments for Bucher. It was just one of the ways Super C wore him down, and it worked.

Super C never laid a hand on anyone. He was never present when the beatings occurred. Yet he let it be known that any treatment we received, good or bad, came from him alone. When one of the guards slapped Schumacher for some minor infraction following one of our card games, Bucher complained to Super C, and for months we did not see that guard. There were also many times when he not only refused to intervene, but we were sure he encouraged the hostility in the first place.

Kim Il Sung had a favorite saying, which appeared frequently in the *Pyongyang Times:* "We must puncture the arrogance of the Yankee devils." This they did, humbling us daily. But they saved the worst humiliations for Bucher.

And the frustrating thing was, because of Bucher's mental attitude, there was almost nothing we, the other *Pueblo* officers, could do to help him.

In his verbal arguments, Super C liked to fence with the captain, trap him in a corner, watch him squirm. Often we could see what Super C was getting at and would jump to the conclusion, to get the skipper off the hook.

245

"You fucking bastards," he would scream at us later. "Stop thinking for me. I can do my own thinking!"

The next time we left him on his own, however, he would berate us for "deserting" him. "Why didn't you back me up?" he'd cry.

The problem was not that he had changed, but that he remained just as erratic and unpredictable as ever.

One such disagreement arose over the letters of apology the crew had been asked to write. Bucher didn't realize that our captors had suddenly changed their propaganda tack and were no longer holding the *Pueblo* crew personally responsible for the "crimes of intrusion."

Bucher kept insisting that he personally bore full responsibility for the *Pueblo* affair. Super C vehemently disagreed. Of course, Super C wasn't about to admit the party line was so changeable—he claimed that from the beginning the blame had rested with the U.S. government, not with us.

Bucher simply couldn't comprehend what was going on.

We were greatly concerned about him. For days he would sink into deep depressions. There were times we were not at all sure he would pull out. When he did, he often acted like a petulant child. He refused to play cards until the rest of us consented to gamble. To humor him, we finally gave in. But when someone beat him at bridge, he quit the game in anger and started playing solitaire. He couldn't stand to lose, whether at the card table, on the basketball court (where he seemed intent on setting a new record for fouls), or in life itself. And that was basic to his condition. Given his first command, he *had* lost, as badly as one could. And every day was a reminder of that fact.

"I'm not going to rot in this place much longer," he confided to me one day in the head. "If we're not out of here by May 15," he added ominously, "don't look for me to be around anymore."

More of Bucher's histrionics? I was afraid not. Checking with some of the other officers, I found he had made

similar remarks to them. We read them the same way—
an implied suicide threat.

We all did what we could to raise Bucher's spirits. Skip,
who was closest to the captain, worked especially hard at
this, but the mood persisted.

We were concerned for Bucher the man. Differences
aside, he was a human being, in deep trouble. But we had
another concern. We had to keep his pessimism from
infecting the crew. I tried not to think what the effect on
them would be, should Bucher make good his threat.

The letter-writing campaign had ended in March. Super
C never told us whether he considered it a failure or a
success. At least it hadn't accomplished its stated objective
—to bring the United States to its knees.

Everything considered, I suspected the letters were
probably of more value to the U.S. government than to
the North Koreans. They helped establish that the intrusion charges were bogus. They set down the repatriation
terms the D.P.R.K. was insisting upon. They gave hints
as to our personal situations. And, in the trick phrases,
the odd wording, they let our government, families, and
friends know that we were still hanging in there.

When the CIA charge had failed to fit the KORCOMs'
propaganda rationale, it was dropped. I had hoped that
once it became apparent that the United States would
never consent to apologize for crimes it hadn't committed,
this demand would be dropped as well.

But it wasn't happening that way. By now the Three A's
had become a catechism:

Admit to the intrusions.

Apologize for them.

Assure that same will not happen in future.

Bucher's depression was understandable. In all this we
could see little hope of release.

Gradually, from talking to Bucher over a period of
several weeks, I came to a startling conclusion.

He was not only worried about whether we would be released. He was also fearful of what would happen upon our return to the United States, if return we did.

There would be a Court of Inquiry—there always was, whenever a ship was lost. Then, almost inevitably, he felt, a court-martial. Several times he stated that he was sure he wouldn't get less than twenty years.

The interrogations continued, at irregular intervals. Yet the "hard" questions still went unasked.

If they were giving the captured documents close study, surely by now they would have some queries.

We had presumed that if North Korea lacked the technical knowledge to evaluate the classified materials properly, experts would be called in from Russia or Red China. Could it be that their code of juche kept them from asking for such help?

There was another possibility. Could they have given the documents to Russia in exchange for missiles and other military arms?

It was pure conjecture. All we knew for sure was that the right questions weren't being asked. Barring any positive proof to the contrary, we had to assume that all the classified documents seized aboard the *Pueblo* had been compromised.

Nor was that all. Great effort had been expended in destroying the machines in the research spaces. Steve Harris had been able to report one-hundred-percent success in this.

Now some of the CTs passed on a highly disturbing thought. Also aboard the *Pueblo* were schematics, detailed diagrams of all the machines, for use in their repair.

No one remembered seeing them in the materials that were burned or thrown overboard.

On April 22 Super C brought us together for an announcement. "Executive Officer Murphy is a new father. Red Cross telegram say daughter Victoria Rin born March

29. Mother and daughter doing fine."

Throughout our captivity, I had made a point of masking my true feelings from the KORCOMs, but there was no hiding my relief now. Before I left Japan, Carol and I had decided that if the child was a girl we would name her Victoria Lynn. I presumed that the name had gotten garbled in the translation.

There had been many such announcements during the three months since our capture. Excluding the apparently accidental disclosure of my mother's death, the personal news was always good. It was obvious the KORCOMs were censoring all incoming communications, eliminating any which might adversely affect our morale. I was sure that Super C must have an old Korean proverb in his vast collection to the effect that "Happy prisoners make no trouble."

Yet there were exceptions to this rule. We did hear bad news—if it furthered their propaganda mystique. Toward the end of April we were told that the Reverend Martin Luther King, Jr., had been assassinated and that rioting had broken out in most American cities. Later, in June, we would be similarly informed of the assassination of Senator Robert Kennedy. These two events proved, to the North Koreans, that American society was rapidly disintegrating. Both crimes, we were told, had been ordered by President Johnson's "ruling circle," Dr. King's slaying because he had opposed the slavery of the proletariat, Senator Kennedy's because he had spoken out against the Vietnam war. Similarly, the antiwar protests and the Poor People's March on Washington were described to us in vivid, and undoubtedly exaggerated, detail, because both illustrated, according to our captors, the struggle of the masses against the imperialist establishment.

There was no mistaking the evidence. The snow vanished. The wind turned warm. Weeds began sprouting on the playing field. Spring had arrived. For each of us it stirred dormant memories, and longings.

A chopped-up grass was added to our menu. Starved for greens, we ate it eagerly, for a while. Then someone noticed that the KORCOMs were bringing it into the compound in little Japanese-made trucks and dumping it behind our building, until ready to chop it up for use. In the interim, stray dogs, of which there were a large number around, frequently lifted their legs on it. Before long many of the men had worms.

Complaints to Super C about the inadequacy of our diet only resulted in our being told, again and again, that through the benevolence of Kim Il Sung we were eating as well as anyone in the D.P.R.K. True or not, the health of the men continued to deteriorate. Stomach poisoning was not at all uncommon. I had it twice. Forbidden to remove my shoes except when bathing or in bed, my foot trouble worsened until it was painful even to walk. Though a Christian Scientist, I probably made as many trips to the doctor—and nurse—as did anyone else. They provided a break in the routine, but little else, for the doctor had two standard remedies, whatever the condition: to paint the affected area with iodine, or to stick it with pins, the North Koreans still practicing Chinese acupuncture. Neither did anything to improve our major complaint, which was malnutrition.

When you are an officer, you tend to believe that all those in the enlisted ranks are dependent on you. The enlisted men, of course, know better, but the officers never seem to learn.

We worried about the effect the captain's pessimism might have on the crew. And in so doing we underrated them. Each day the grapevine brought new proof that they were doing all right on their own. The techniques of their resistance varied from outrageous tricks they played on the guards, such as marinating the apple, to numerous instances of individual heroism, as when one man would confess to an infraction to spare all the others in his room.

The enlisted men did as much for the officers' morale as the officers did for theirs.

The whole crew's lack of respect for the KORCOM officers, interpreters, and guards was reflected in the nicknames bestowed upon them. Some were named for fancied resemblances. "Oddjob" did look like the villainous beheader in the James Bond movie *Goldfinger*. Others were named for personal peculiarities. "Captain Queer" had a high, effeminate voice. And still others sort of named themselves. "Solutions" would barge into a room and demand, "You must give me solutions!" That puzzled us for a long while, until we realized he meant "salutations." Because of our isolation at the start of detention, there was a certain amount of duplication, as when several rooms gave the same guard a different name, but the following partial list gives an indication of the range of the crew's imagination: Super C, Fetch, Smiling Sam, Hatchet Face, Bush Around the Beat, Chipmunk, Square Head, King Kong, Imperialist, Colonel Scar, Artful Dodger, Colonel Specs, Twinkletoes, Possum, Sleezy, Robot, Major Mad, Silver Lips, Pockface, Flat Face, Major Rectum, Clean Floors, Wheezy, the Fly, Rosecheeks, Ensign Light Bulb, Tall Specs, Dumpy, Major Mouse, Deputy Dawg, Politician, Major X, Captain Joker, Feature Films, Max, Captain Nice, Captain Letters, Pistol Pete, Captain Rabbit, Bloke, Missile, Snake, Silent Sam, What Means, Smoothtalker, Fuzz, Bear, Jack Warner, Loverboy, and Snotnose.

It was perhaps best that not all of them understood English.

A general and his aide inspected us one day. While they were talking, I made a surprise discovery. I could understand almost every word they said.

I had begun picking up the Korean language almost unconsciously. From then on, I worked at learning it, but being especially careful not to betray, by either word or gesture, that I understood what they were saying. Steve Harris was doing much the same thing. There could be a

251

time, we knew, when such knowledge might prove useful.

One of their expressions had caused me some rough moments in the Barn. A number of times I had heard the guards talking just outside the door to my room. It sounded as if they were saying "hang young chong keyo." I had already learned that "chong keyo" meant "officer." I was afraid that my fate had already been decided, that they were going to hang the young officer.

Only after hearing the expression repeated several times did I realize that what they were actually saying was "hang jung chong keyo," and that "hang jung" meant "executive." I was "hang jung chong keyo," the "executive officer."

"Ishe-ee" was another word they used frequently. It was apparently the North Korean equivalent of "son of a bitch."

One day the cleaning woman brought in some strips of cheap paper. Wondering if it was stationery, I asked, "What's this for?" We were forbidden to speak to the serving women, and when we forgot and did so, it invariably produced a reaction. Exiting the room, she screamed "Ishe-ee bungho," words that made even the guard blush.

So they were learning, too.

May 15 came and passed, with Bucher still depressed, but, fortunately, making no move to carry out his threat. I was never sure why he had picked that date, unless he felt that we might be released on May 1, the international Communist holiday and the traditional day for amnesties. But the only difference between that day and any other was that we were allowed to visit each other's rooms.

We read the *Pyongyang Times* and searched the faces of every KORCOM we came in contact with for some indication, just the slightest hint, that repatriation was forthcoming, but there was none. It was not until June, when we received our first letters from home, that we heard more about the negotiations at Panmunjom. But the letters were so late arriving—most had been written in March—that the information they contained was far from up to date.

I received several letters from Carol, all written before the birth of Vicky. From them I learned that she and Eddie had returned to San Diego a month after receiving word of our capture, and that, as I had guessed, they were staying with Carol's parents. I was surprised how much information she managed to get into the letters, some of it with a skill that matched our best letter-writing deceptions. For example, she informed me that she had been able to dispose of our Japanese-made Toyopet automobile by saying she had sold the "pet." This had concerned me, because, in common with most of the other crewmen, I had never thought to give my wife power of attorney, and the car was in my name.

Her mention of the negotiations was encouraging: "We listen and read the news daily to keep abreast of talks leading to your release. We pray that the governments will reach an honorable solution. The Navy is certainly caring for all the dependents' needs. Everyone has gone out of their way to help. . . . Two weeks ago a girl in San Diego organized a public prayer meeting on the 100th day of the *Pueblo*'s capture. It was very nicely done and attended. It gave us all a great deal of comfort." So we weren't forgotten. Just knowing that others were also counting the days helped.

To our delight, one aspect of the letters gave our captors a hard time. Just as earlier they had been mystified by military abbreviations, so now were they perplexed by American slang. For example, Commissaryman Harry Lewis heard from his wife that she had left a "45" on the radiator of their Long Island apartment while she ran some errands. On returning she found the steam had been turned on and the 45 had melted.

The 45 was a pistol; our captors knew that. But what material was used in its composition that would melt so easily? Was this some secret new metal? And why did she need a gun in the first place? Did the government allow its citizens to have weapons?

When told the truth, that she had been talking about a

phonograph record, they refused to believe the explanation.

The confident way in which Carol wrote about our repatriation was encouraging. Yet there was a sad side to the letters, too. Reading them and finding no mention of my mother, I now knew for certain that she was dead.

Though the letters were most welcome, they had a mixed effect on morale. Some of the men received many; some received none at all. This was true of one of the officers, who through most of his imprisonment received no mail from his wife. In addition to Bucher, we now had another officer to cheer up.

The end of June marked the second change of season since our arrival in North Korea. With the coming of summer, the new lemon tree in my room burst into fragrant blossoms.

The attitude of the men toward the plants in their rooms varied. Because if you asked to go to the head too often you risked being cuffed by the guards, some used the soil of the plants as urinals. Of course, if you did this, as they soon discovered, you had to live with the smell. Bucher tried every trick he could to kill his plant, and finally succeeded. My attitude differed. In a way that isn't easy to explain, my plant provided companionship. It was a living thing, and I lavished a measure of the care on it that I would have given my new daughter, had I had the opportunity. I took such good care of the first rubber tree, in fact, that they took it away and brought me a sickly, untended one from the hall. When it flourished, I was awarded the lemon tree.

Yet I could also understand Bucher's attitude. The KOR-COMs showed far more concern for the health of the plants than for that of their prisoners. And killing the plant was a way of getting back at things Korean.

But by this time Bucher had less need to strike back at our captors. For he had found a substitute target.

21

"When we get back to the United States, I'm going to hang Steve Harris' ass. I'm going to make sure he gets tossed right out of the Navy!"

The skipper's vow, confided to me one day in the shower, indicated Bucher's new change of mood. Gradually he had surfaced from his depression. Now he was a man with an obsession—singular, intense, all-consuming. He was looking for a scapegoat.

The "dress rehearsal" for the Court of Inquiry had begun.

At the start, Steve Harris was Bucher's major target. Bucher tore into him whenever the *Pueblo*'s officers were together, at meals, over cards, while doing calisthenics.

Steve had lied to him, Bucher charged. He had stated that the destruction was proceeding satisfactorily, when it was not. Not only had he waited too long to begin the destruction in the first place, his CTs were so poorly organized they couldn't even carry out the simple task of tossing a laundry bag full of classified documents overboard. Steve stood indicted on that laundry bag alone. Why hadn't he thrown it over himself?

Because he never had the chance, Steve replied. Categorically he denied all of Bucher's charges. He was slow starting the destruction because Bucher was slow giving the order. Several times, Steve claimed, he had called the pilothouse requesting permission to commence destruction; he did not have the authority to proceed on his own.

255

Once permission was given, he was limited by the Navy regulation which forbade jettisoning in less than one hundred fathoms. Nor had he ever given Bucher the impression that all the classified materials would be destroyed. As for his failure to complete the burning and jettisoning, he was greatly hampered in this because Bucher had not called general quarters. At modified GQ—most of the crew remaining below decks—he lacked the proper personnel to do an efficient job.

Bucher's failure to call general quarters was a sore point, one of many, and he automatically fired back from the hip with a remarkable charge: Steve was derelict in his duty for not having started the destruction on his own, before any order was given.

It would have been funny, had not the charge been so serious. From the day Steve reported aboard the *Pueblo*, Bucher had fought him over the chain of command issue, arguing that he, not Steve, had ultimate and final authority over the research section. Now he was just as vehemently trying to pass the responsibility back.

Nor would he let up. Steve was at fault for the excessive amount of classified material aboard. Steve should have ignored the regulation about jettisoning. Steve had talked far too much in the interrogations. Finally, after days of constant badgering, Harris, in pure exasperation, gave in: *All right,* he was personally responsible for the whole damn mess; he admitted that; now, could we eat our meals in peace?

No, the skipper screamed. He, Bucher, the captain of the *Pueblo,* was responsible! Harris was only a department head!

Several of us moaned audibly.

Bucher wouldn't leave it at that. He sought out and questioned individual CTs, trying to find one who would back up his charges. Though he failed in this, he found something almost as good. One of the CTs said that sometime after the destruction had started he had heard someone—

he thought it was Lieutenant Harris, but he was not sure —order the burning stopped, because the North Koreans were firing at the smoke.

Steve flatly denied the charge. He had never ordered a cessation of the burning, not even temporarily. But, the vagueness of the identification notwithstanding, it became a part of Bucher's chronicle of events. He believed it; therefore, it was true.

Steve Harris did not remain Bucher's only target. One thing bothered Bucher even more than the loss of the documents: the death of Hodges.

As scapegoat for this, he picked a most unlikely target —Gene Lacy. Bucher claimed that in stopping the ship the second time Lacy had provoked the North Koreans into firing, inadvertently resulting in the death of Hodges and the wounding of Woelk, Chicca, and the others.

Gene politely, but quite firmly, reminded the skipper that he, Bucher, had stopped the ship the second time, just to see what would happen. Gene had stopped the ship only once, the first time, on Bucher's nodded concurrence.

The argument grew so heated, and confused, that it soon became impossible to keep track of exactly what Lacy was accused of having done. Bucher, at various times, accused him of starting the ship, stopping the ship, and increasing its speed—all on his own initiative.

Bucher then added a new charge, the implications of which were quite clear. It was Lacy who had taken it upon himself to follow the lead KORCOM ship. In so doing, he had in effect surrendered the *Pueblo*.

Again this drew a firm denial from Lacy. It also brought up an interesting question.

When had the actual surrender occurred? I had thought about this often in the months since our capture. The question was one I was sure would be asked at the Court of Inquiry if we were freed.

Had it been when Bucher waved his white hat? There was no doubt the gesture was intended as an emblem of surrender, though the KORCOMs had ignored it and continued firing. No, it had been before that. But exactly when? The first time the *Pueblo* stopped? When Bucher ordered the helmsman to follow in the lead ship's wake? Or earlier even than that—when Bucher decided that he wouldn't uncover and man the guns, wouldn't call general quarters, wouldn't defend the ship?

Technically, I supposed, the stopping of the ship constituted its actual surrender. Yet in the interlinking chain of events which had begun in Bremerton, Washington, and were played out to their ultimate conclusion in the Sea of Japan, it was difficult to draw clear, sharp distinctions, to say "This was the moment when it happened."

So much of what occurred seemed less the result of a single action than the accumulation of circumstances.

But for one man there was no such confusion. For Bucher had changed his tack still another time. He now began to maintain that he had never surrendered the ship, that it had been taken from him by force while he had been without the power to resist.

Article 0730 of the United States Naval Regulations reads: "The Commanding Officer shall not permit his command to be searched by any person representing a foreign state nor permit any of the personnel under his command to be removed from the command so long as he has the power to resist."

Bucher was building his defense.

Needless to say, as Bucher's witch hunt progressed, his executive officer did not escape censure. For me, Bucher had saved the charge of cowardice. As proof, he cited the time he came into the pilothouse to find everyone crouched down out of the line of fire. Only, he claimed we were not crouched, but lying prone, with no one manning the ship.

I was just as hot in my denial of this as were Steve Harris and Gene Lacy in rebutting the charges against them. We were crouched, not prone, I maintained, and Berens, the helmsman, had kept full control of the ship. As for my ordering the personnel to "hit the deck," I not only ad-

258

mitted having given the order, I had done so on at least two separate occasions when the pilothouse was under fire. And, in like circumstances, I would do it again. To remain unnecessarily exposed would be pure folly. If we were going to be convicted of ducking while being shot at, then Bucher would have to include himself among the accused, for he had done it numerous times on January 23.

Nor did I stop at that. If anyone behaved badly in the incident, it seemed to me it was Bucher himself, who several times completely lost his cool.

The suggestion that he might have done anything wrong on the twenty-third drove Bucher into a rage.

Schumacher also had his inning. Once, during calisthenics, Skip disputed Bucher's recollection of some phase of the surrender. Not wishing to be contradicted, Bucher ordered him to shut up.

"Why don't you let him talk?" I broke in. "You're beginning to sound just like Super C."

"Don't you ever compare me to him!" Bucher screamed.

Skip was off the griddle, I was back on.

Only Tim Harris escaped Bucher's wrath. As the lowest-ranking officer on the *Pueblo*, there was little for which Bucher could hold him irresponsible. Too, during these arguments, Tim rarely ventured any opinion, either in agreement or disagreement.

Even Bucher's wife, Rose, was not immune to his scapegoating. Happily Super C informed us that "Madame Rose" had been making speeches all over the United States, criticizing President Johnson for his handling of the *Pueblo* case. He handed Bucher a clipping on her activities.

Bucher's exact response on seeing the newspaper item is best not repeated verbatim. In essence, he complained that because of Rose's meddling he had probably lost any chance of ever getting a submarine command.

That he still felt he would be considered for one indicated how far separated he was from reality.

By now it was apparent that there were greatly differing recollections as to exactly what happened on January 23, 1968. This was not at all surprising, memory being what it is and the events themselves so emotion-charged. There was also the fact that, due to our varying duties, none of us was participant in every bit of the action. I remembered certain things one way, Skip another, Gene still another, and so on.

But Bucher wouldn't accept this. When the Court of Inquiry convened, there had to be a "single consistent account" of the events. Otherwise, Bucher claimed, the Navy would drop anchor on all of us. To get this story, he ordered all of the officers and the key enlisted men to write down their recollections, these then to be compared by him and melded into one account.

I opposed this, for several reasons. No matter how careful we were, if these pages fell into KORCOM hands our captors would certainly discover things they did not now know. In addition, the truth, as each of us saw it, would often contradict the "sincere" statements we had made. Also, under the threat of "severe punishment," we were forbidden to "make unauthorized writings." Several of the crewmen had already been caught exchanging messages or crossword puzzles and had been beaten for it. But the biggest argument against this, I felt, was that we would be usurping the functions of the Court of Inquiry. It was the Court's business, not ours, to listen to *all* the accounts, then judge their accuracy. In short, we would be prejudicing their findings.

I had still another reason for contesting Bucher's suggestion, but, for diplomacy's sake, kept it to myself. I strongly suspected that Bucher was not the least bit interested in learning what we thought, that his only concern was getting his own story accepted.

Unfortunately, I was right. Once Bucher had the different accounts, he set out to disprove any recollections which contradicted his own. "Don't you mean. . . ." "What you mean to say is. . . ." and "Isn't this the way it happened?"

became his favorite expressions. He had a whole bag full of tricks, and he used them all. He would give in on the small points, but hold fast on the large. If one officer refused to agree with him, he would try to get the support of another. When all the officers disagreed with his version, he would seek concurrence among the enlisted men. Often he found it, some of the men agreeing to statements they had no knowledge of, apparently simply because they were flattered that Bucher wanted them to settle a dispute among the officers. This didn't always happen. Many of the men, such as Law, had the integrity to make exceptions and hold fast to them, but when it did happen, Bucher would come back to us and say, "Five men disagree with you. Are you saying that you're right and all five of them are wrong?" Nor was he above reminding us that when we returned to the United States he was the man who would be writing our fitness reports.

In fact, he reminded us of this quite often.

Arguing with him did little good. It only made him more dogmatic. The KORCOMs, for example, had told us not to drink the water unless it was first boiled. But it was summer now, and hot, and like everyone else, Bucher wanted a cold drink. And there was a cold-water tap in the head. Cramps and diarrhea followed. But did he then stop drinking it? No, because we had made the mistake of arguing with him, telling him that he shouldn't. Within a month he looked like a skeleton. Much of the weight he lost while imprisoned was due solely to his own obstinacy.

When the evidence failed to fit Bucher's own version, he simply ignored it. While Bucher had been flailing at Steve Harris, blaming him for his failure to destroy all the classified documents, I ventured the opinion that had the TNT been picked up and brought aboard in Yokosuka, the whole story might have been different.

"What TNT?" Bucher asked.

I stared at him in disbelief. I might have doubted my sanity, had not Schumacher and Steve Harris, both of whom were present at the table in the Yokosuka Officers'

261

Club, looked equally nonplussed. Bucher had simply wiped the whole incident from his mind!

It was a mock trial, a Court of Inquiry, and a quest for absolution all in one. Bucher was obsessed with proving himself blameless. In the process, he simply wore us down. We had twenty minutes for each meal, about an hour and a half to two hours additional each day for exercises and recreation. These were the only times we had together, the only times we were not isolated in our individual cells. And Bucher was dominating every minute of them with his endless rehearsals. Occasionally we gave in on a point just in hopes that he would shut up.

There was also a psychological process at work. The more frequently we heard Bucher's version, the more familiar it became. After a while, we began to remember certain things not because we actually saw them but because someone else had described them so vividly and often. All this took its toll. The chronology of the twenty-third became terribly confused in the minds of everyone. It was only with a great effort that the individual could keep his own story straight. Inevitably, doubts began to creep in. Maybe I *am* the only one out of step, you found yourself thinking. Maybe I'm remembering it all wrong.

One by one, we caved in, not necessarily agreeing to Bucher's version, but no longer wanting to take the trouble, or weather the consequences, of contradicting him. It was difficult enough trying to resist the North Koreans, without having to fight the captain too.

Only on one point did Bucher remain indecisive.

Some days he would maintain that the KORCOMs had seized the ship by force, that no formal surrender had taken place, apparently forgetting he had ordered three men to help the boarding party up onto the deck.

Yet on other days he would admit that he had surrendered the ship. The reason, he now claimed, was the same one he had used to justify his confession: he did it to save the crew. His first duty, he embellished, was safe-

262

guarding the lives of the young men who had been placed in his charge.

It was apparent that he was trying out both accounts, to see which best fit.

He also began modifying each, touching them up a little here and there, polishing and refining. The one SO-1 subchaser became two SO-1 subchasers. Another P-4 appeared over the horizon, bringing the total of them to four. The jets, instead of just buzzing the *Pueblo*, dropped several torpedoes, all of which fortunately missed the ship. The number of shells fired at us increased tenfold. That none of us had seen these things bothered Bucher not a bit. Through repetition he was sure to pick up a few true believers who would support him. Hopelessly outgunned and outmaneuvered, the lives of the entire crew in jeopardy, he had no choice but to surrender the ship.

Thus a single account emerged, one which blended the best parts of both arguments. He tried it out on us as one would practice a speech in front of family, before delivering it in public. And as he rehearsed it, over and over, we could see that he had begun to believe it himself. Just as he undoubtedly believed Don Ho was one of his best friends. And he had master's degrees in a variety of subjects. And no TNT had ever been offered.

Although unaware of it at the time, we were watching the creation of still another chapter in the Bucher legend.

There was an irony here, to my mind a tragic one. In the North Korean movies we saw, one theme was constantly reiterated: There is no room for dissent in a Communist society. When it occurs, it has to be "corrected."

The actor who resembled Cantinflas and had starred in *The Tractor Driver* reappeared in a number of other films. Whether he was playing a factory worker, a bus driver, or a common laborer, he was always the Communist misfit, the person who was inclined to be lazier than everyone else, or to think differently.

The happy ending of each film was the same. The errant

individual is "reeducated" by the party worker to think and act like everyone else.

One thought, the state's; one version of history, the party's; no disagreement; no individual likes or dislikes; no dissent.

I could not help seeing parallels between the Communist tactic and the one Bucher had adopted for his mock court.

22

In mistaking Abelon, Aluague, and Garcia for South Koreans, the KORCOMs gave us a good idea for a possible escape plan. Properly dressed, the three Filipinos might stand a chance of getting through to the DMZ.

Knowing the language, even if only a few phrases of greeting, could be a big help. Chicca and Hammond, the two Marine interpreters, began teaching Korean to anyone willing to learn.

Many of the plans considered by the officers were heavily influenced by the movie *The Great Escape*. Though the idea of a mass break-out was tremendously appealing, we had to admit that even if it were possible, the result could be tragic, due to the poor health of most of the men. We decided that the plans that had the best chance of succeeding were those involving one to five men only. Tunneling was out: we were on the second and third floors of the building. This left two possibilities: overcoming the guards, seizing their weapons, and fighting our way out; or slipping out a few men, possibly in the back or under one of the vehicles, hoping that, for a time at least, they wouldn't be missed. The latter made the best sense, for North Korea was one large armed camp.

Tim Harris had noticed planes taking off and landing not too far from our compound. He proposed that we steal a plane; then, with luck, he could fly it to South Korea. Though the scheme had a certain derring-do fascination, we put it aside "for future consideration." Diplomatically, no one wanted to mention that Tim hadn't finished flight school.

One of the best and earliest plans was formulated by Chicca, Crandall, and Hammond. They told me about it while we were running together on the playing field one day, and asked if I wanted to come along. I did, very much, although, realistically, I had to admit that while my navigational training could prove helpful, the chances of my passing for a Korean were worse than nil. They just didn't make them that tall. In common with a number of the other plans, the men wanted to make their way to the sea, steal a boat, and row it to South Korea. What set their plan apart was the careful thought that went into it. And one key element. They proposed to wait until the monsoons started.

The monsoons could provide the cover we needed. They could also swamp the boat, if we were lucky enough to find one.

The KORCOMs actually handed me my escape plan, in a batch of their propaganda materials. In *Korea Today* I found a large, detailed map of the Democratic People's Republic of Korea. Studying it, I noticed something interesting. There was a river on the outskirts of Pyongyang. If you followed it south to its headwaters, you reached a mountain. On the other side of that mountain was another river, which went right through the DMZ.

My plan was to put together a small team of two or three men, follow the rivers to the border, then swim across at night.

I memorized the map until I could close my eyes and see every twist and turn of the streams, the exact number of tributaries on both sides and where they came in, every possible visual landmark: Then I computed the distance between each of the points, and figured out the sun angles in relation to nearby mountain peaks. When I was positive I had the route committed to memory, I passed the map along to Schumacher, who in turn gave it to Bucher for study.

As with all the other proposals, mine had obvious draw-backs. If we waited for the monsoons, the same bad weather which made possible our escape would also probably obscure all but the nearest landmarks. The place where the second river crossed the border could be mined or blocked by some obstruction such as barbed wire; undoubtedly it would be heavily guarded. And, no matter how skillful the remaining men were in covering our absence, long before we reached this point the KORCOMs would have missed us and sounded the alarm. With loudspeakers in every village, the word would travel fast. We had no illusions as to our fate, should the peasants capture us.

Bucher was very enthusiastic about the plan and later pronounced it the most realistic proposal submitted.

The monsoon season was due to start in August or September. Through the summer we waited impatiently for it to begin.

By the time August arrived, however, I had to face up to an unpleasant realization. My foot infection had worsened to the extent where I could hardly walk.

When the time came, if it did, I wouldn't be going along.

THE WHOLE WORLD ARE WITH US! proclaimed a headline in the *Pyongyang Times*. But obviously the whole world was not, for since midsummer Super C had been dropping none-too-subtle hints. He wanted us to suggest another press conference. Not wanting to participate in still another of the KORCOM farces, we took our time about making the "suggestion," and when we finally did, we added a kicker that made Super C squirm. How about bringing in reporters and photographers from *Life, Time, Newsweek,* and all the major American newspapers? They had a great influence on President Johnson, we said.

We didn't for a minute think Super C would buy the idea, but we delighted in watching him try to think up reasons why our suggestion was unacceptable.

Unknown to us, this time we had actually planted the seed of an idea, one which would soon bear strange fruit.

From a propaganda standpoint, the August press conference must have been a total disaster. Except for the inclusion of more crewmen—in addition to the six officers, civilian oceanographer Tuck and eighteen of the enlisted men participated—it might have been a replay of its predecessors. The same Korean journalists were present, to ask almost the same questions and receive nearly the same replies.

But Super C was not discouraged. On the contrary, almost immediately after the August playlet he started rehearsing us for another in September. That month marked the twentieth anniversary of the founding of the Democratic People's Republic of Korea, and journalists from all over the world would be arriving to cover the ceremonies. Thus he would be able to grant our request to invite foreign newsmen. We suspected the real reason was that the journalists had insisted on seeing us.

This time, however, Super C had learned his lesson. Something new was needed to set this press conference apart, something so sensational it would capture the attention of the whole world. We never learned whether the idea was Super C's or someone else's. Original it was not. To garner world headlines, it was decided that the crew of the *Pueblo* would confess that they had committed not six but seventeen intrusions!

Under the watchful, but ignorant, eyes of Deputy Dawg and the Imperialist, Law, Plucker, and I were ordered to authenticate the new charges. All eleven of the new "untrusions" were erroneous fixes the North Koreans had taken from the loran log. While Law and Plucker read them off to me, I plotted them on the chart.

Or, rather, pretended that the marks I made corresponded to the positions. For Deputy Dawg really outdid himself this time. He managed to accomplish something no U.S. Naval shipyard had been able to do. He made the *Pueblo* amphibious.

One set of coordinates placed the ship six miles inland

on the island of Kyushu. Another had her sailing right through downtown Wonsan. While still another had her climbing mountains, to reach a point thirty-two miles inland on the Korean mainland.

I could see the beginnings of a smile on Law's face, as he realized how badly they had goofed. I hadn't seen Law smile for some time. At the time of our capture Law had near-perfect eyesight. In early August he realized he was having trouble making out even close objects. By September he was nearly blind.

Doc Baldridge was sure it was a vitamin deficiency, as the same trouble was being reported by other crewmen, although, as yet, none were in as bad shape as Law. Although the KORCOM doctor gave him several shots in the eyeball, the condition worsened.

In one of my more pessimistic moments, I wondered if, by the time the United States got around to repatriating us, there would be anything left to repatriate.

Although we continued to receive mail at irregular intervals (in July I had for the first time seen a photograph of my daughter, in a *Christian Science Monitor* clipping sent to Steve Harris by his mother), the last letters we had been permitted to write had gone out in March. Now, in August, we were again encouraged to write home, stating that while we were still being treated with "humanitarian kindness," it was quite possible that we might be tried and executed if an apology from the United States was not immediately forthcoming.

Again the KORCOMs must have used their worst translators. I wrote five letters, managing to get something in each. In a letter to one of my sisters, Mary, and her husband, Jack Plankers, I said that I was yearning to return to the United States so that, like Jack, I could study engineering at Fuggleton University. I was sure my brother-in-law would get the point. Jack had never studied engineering, much less attended good old Fugg U.

"Not one of us want to stay in this alien land forever! Ain't that understandable?" I wrote my other sister, just before shoveling in some North Korean propaganda.

Some evenings, I wrote in my letter to Carol, we were permitted to go to the room of another *Pueblo* officer, whom I named, "to play cards, chess, or share our letters with him." I wanted Carol to know that he wasn't receiving mail from his wife. I was hopeful that she or one of the other wives could look into the situation and possibly correct it.

Super C also wanted each of us to write to a prominent government official. Giving the President and Secretary of State a rest, I told Super C that Cecil Jo Hindley, a friend of mine, was one of the most influential men in California. C. J. was manager of the Humboldt County Fair. In this letter I said, "If all the people of Humboldt County insist on our return, then our government will have to act promptly." In all of Humboldt County, located in the northwest corner of California, there were fewer than 115,000 people. It would be only a slight exaggeration to say that all were individualists. Although this occasion might be the rare exception, I couldn't see all of them agreeing on anything. But I thought C. J. might appreciate the image.

I also asked him to see if his influential sister Bofa would do anything in our behalf. If C. J. had a sister, I was fairly sure she wasn't named Bank of America.

I was so successful in hoaxing up this letter, I learned later, that C. J. was firmly convinced I hadn't written it.

Lacy one-upped me, with a letter to a friend on the Seattle Sewer Board.

As in March, we were photographed, individually and with other crewmen, prints of the pictures being enclosed with each family letter, to show that we were still alive.

Some of the photos showed something else. From Bucher we learned that a number of the crewmen, when it came their turn to be photographed, had given "the finger." Bucher had told them that if they thought they could get away with it, to do it whenever they got the chance.

That bothered me. And, unfortunately, I couldn't tell Bucher why.

I should have foreseen the possibility that this would happen. It was such an obvious trick. Now, with everyone doing it, there was a good chance it would come to the attention of the KORCOMs. If anyone told them the real meaning of the gesture, we were in trouble. One look at those early navigational photographs, and all hell would break loose. To cover ourselves, we passed the word that if the KORCOMs asked about the gesture, everyone was to say it was an old Hawaiian good-luck sign.

Just prior to the September 12 press conference, Super C informed us that an American journalist would be present, a reporter from the New York *Guardian*. None of the *Pueblo* officers had heard of the paper, but it was a fair assumption that it was somewhat left of center and that the correspondent's views were probably compatible with those of our captors. The possibility that he might be a U.S. intelligence agent, posing as a Communist, occurred to us too. Did we dare risk trying to pass him a message? Bucher wrote out one, which stated that the intrusion charges were false, then, just before we entered the room where the press conference was to be held, palmed it so it would be ready if the right moment presented itself.

More than eighty foreign journalists attended, among them representatives from the Soviet Union, North Vietnam, Cambodia, Poland, Hungary, Romania, Bulgaria, East Germany, Spain, Italy, India, Iraq, Indonesia, Guinea, Gambia, Finland, Norway, Algeria, the United Arab Republic, various African republics, Japan, Chile, Cuba, plus the American journalist.

He wore a houndstooth jacket, smoked a pipe, and looked very New England. See him anywhere in the world, and you would recognize him as an American. I could imagine the conflict within Bucher: Should I or shouldn't I?

Interestingly enough, though permitted to attend, the

271

Russians were not allowed to ask questions, while there wasn't a single representative from Red China. By now we had come to suspect that there was a schism between the two dictatorial warlords, Mao and Kim. Chinese participation in the Korean war, which had literally saved the life of the little Democratic People's Republic of Korea, had been almost eliminated from North Korean propaganda syllabuses.

This time the *Pueblo* officers, realizing that we were facing a much more sophisticated audience, decided to play it fairly straight. For example, I eliminated my repetitive references to the charts and records. I'd highlighted this before. To do so now might tip off some of the more astute reporters, the majority of whom we suspected to be Communists. Law, however, did get across one excellent point. He stated that all eleven newly confessed intrusions had been verified by loran, which was "a piece of very high-precision equipment"; therefore, the records were "both undeniable and unquestionable." Any navigator who had ever used loran knew the opposite was often the case.

This time it was the enlisted men who picked up the ball. Mack: "The most fervent wish I could make of President Johnson and also my most ardent desire is to be repatriated and rejoin my wife and family in the bosom of the fatherland."

CT Ralph McClintock followed with: "Oh, how I long to walk down the quiet shaded streets of my hometown, to swim again in the rolling surf of old Cape Cod Bay, and to indulge in the sumptuous feast of one of Mom's famous apple pies." With a far straighter face than the rest of us, he concluded: "I swear on my life that if I am ever allowed to return to my home and family, I will never again commit such a naughty crime as espionage against such a peace-loving nation as this."

Barnyard Barrett: "I don't think that I have to convince any of you that I am in perfect health. You can see this plainly for yourselves. However, in a more serious vein . . .

"The only thing lacking here are doctors and specialists

to mend broken hearts, and medicines to cure the grief and sadness that are prevalent among the crew because we are far apart from our families. . . ."

Law: "I myself have been planning for quite some time to have marriage in the month of November this year. I would like very much to return home to my beloved fiancée and exchange vows with her. I hope that you ladies and gentlemen of the press will understand these desires and my terrific longing to return home to become married, as you can imagine what my fiancée would think if I was late for our wedding. . . ."

The men of the *Pueblo* managed to suppress their smiles, but a few of the correspondents didn't. I noticed that there was no hint of a smile on the face of the *Guardian* man.

The press conference lasted five hours and was so propaganda-laden that one East German correspondent was heard to mutter, "Let's get this bullshit over with!" The foreign reporters were not as amicable as the North Koreans to sticking to the prepared script. Yet when they tried to ask their own questions, the moderator shouted them down.

The man from the *Guardian* rose to his feet. "I'd like to say that I'm convinced the *Pueblo* crew has been treated humanely here. . . . It is quite evident from the testimony of the officers and men that they were violating Korean territorial waters. I think the proof is irrefutable. And I would like to say that I agree with them that the U.S. government, our government, shirks moral responsibility for this. What I'd like to tell the members of the crew, as the only American correspondent here, is that I will do my best to convey their ideas, their aspirations to the people in the United States through our newspaper in New York."

I watched Bucher slip the note back in his pocket.

Following the press conference, the reporters watched us exercise, then toured our rooms. They were accompanied by a bevy of KORCOM interpreters, who listened to everything that was said. Yet, with all the activity, they couldn't keep track of everyone. I was left alone with a Spanish-speaking female. We conversed for a few minutes in Spanish. Nothing in her speech or manner encouraged me to confide in her. Which was fortunate, for less than ten minutes later one of the KORCOM officers burst into my room and demanded to know why I had never confessed to speaking Spanish.

Another correspondent, from a European Communist paper, spotted my pile of books and pamphlets and asked what I was reading. "Kim Il Sung," I replied. He groaned, "That's enough!" and exited with his hand on his forehead. Obviously he had had it up to there with Comrade Kim.

From the point of logic alone, the September press conference should have been self-defeating. In searching the *Pueblo,* the KORCOMs had found a CINCPACFLT order dated February, 1966, which authorized U.S. Naval vessels to approach to three miles from any landmass. The order was signed by a Vice Admiral. Subsequent to this, the U.S. government had decided that while it didn't agree to the twelve-mile claim, it would respect it, and our message orders, prepared by a Rear Admiral from COMNAVFOR-JAPAN in January, 1968, forbade us to go any closer than thirteen miles—the claimed twelve miles plus a one-mile buffer zone.

To shift the blame for the intrusions from the officers of the *Pueblo* to the U.S. government itself, the North Koreans now maintained that we had ignored the most current order and followed the earlier one, because CINC-PACFLT had higher authority than COMNAVFORJAPAN, and a Vice Admiral was senior to a Rear Admiral.

Thought through, the implications were ludicrous. If a man didn't want to obey an order from his commanding officer, who was, say, a Major, all he need do was dig up a contrary order from a General from the Revolutionary War and say it had precedence.

Yet, despite such inconsistencies, the North Koreans

apparently believed the international press conference a great success. A few mornings later I looked out my window and saw Super C emerging from his jeep. He had on a new uniform, including fancier shoulder boards and a new cap with a gold-braid chinstrap.

At lunch Commander Bucher announced: "Guess what? Super C is dead!" Which was Bucher's way of telling us that he had been promoted to General.

Obviously his old name was no longer appropriate. Borrowing from the long list of titles accorded his mentor, Kim Il Sung—who could afford to spare a few—we dubbed him "Genius General," or for short, "G.G."

The mock court continued. Bucher would try out an idea. If it encountered too much opposition, he'd drop it and move on to something else. But always returning to the key points: he didn't surrender the ship, Lacy did; he wasn't responsible for the failure to destroy all the classified materials, Steve Harris was; under pressure, his executive officer had turned coward and failed him; while the two remaining officers were too immature and inexperienced to provide any help.

One evening over cards he surprised us with a new story. He said that shortly after our arrival in the Barn, and following his severe beating, he had been taken by car to another building a short distance away, where he was shown a South Korean prisoner.

The man had been strung up by his fingers. His guts hung out, as did one eye. At first Bucher had thought him dead, but he saw that he was still alive, though barely. "This is what happens to spies," Bucher claimed Super C told him through an interpreter.

The vision of his young crewmen being treated similarly was the final straw that broke his resistance, Bucher said. Only after this had he agreed to sign a confession.

Gene, Steve, and I looked at each other curiously. I suspect the same thoughts were going through our minds. This story conflicted with Bucher's original account of why he broke. Too, Bucher was not one to let such a remarkable tale go so long untold, yet in the more than eight months since our capture, no mention of the South Korean had ever been made. Also, if the sight of the dying man broke Bucher, then why weren't any other members of the crew subjected to the same experience? And there was the presence of Super C, totally out of character. He was never present when the beatings or any other violence took place.

Since with each retelling the tale underwent modifications—the South Korean was hanging by his hands, not his fingers (someone had questioned whether that was possible); he had suffered so horribly that he had bitten through his lower lip, which hung down over his chin—I began to strongly suspect that Bucher had written himself some new dialogue for the Court of Inquiry.

Yet another story Bucher told us about the same time concerned us far more. This time, however, we had no doubts about its veracity.

One of Bucher's earlier assignments, while in subs, had been on the staff level. In this position he was brought into contact with some very hush-hush secrets. The story he told us—openly, one night over cards in the wardroom —was fascinating.

It was also, by its very nature, as highly classified as anything aboard the *Pueblo*. If learned by an enemy, it could have a tremendous effect on the security of the United States.

When he realized what Bucher was discussing, security-conscious Steve Harris looked appalled. Gene Lacy also looked at Bucher strangely. As he admitted to me later, he wasn't cleared for such information and couldn't understand why Bucher was talking about it in front of him. I wasn't worried about Gene, but I was worried about the North Koreans. We had no evidence that the wardroom was bugged, but because the freedom allowed us there was highly suspect, we had to presume it could be. When discussing something secret, such as escape plans, we either did so *sotto voce* or picked a spot, such as the playing field, where there was no chance we would be overheard.

Our startled reactions were not missed by Bucher, for shortly after this he approached me privately and explained that the only reason he had told us the story was because if he wasn't repatriated, and the rest of us were, we could tell U.S. Naval Intelligence that this information hadn't been compromised.

Only Bucher could have ventured such an explanation.

By October we had to face up to the obvious. The monsoons had missed North Korea this year. Inasmuch as the weather cover was an integral part of the escape plan, this realization should have had a depressing effect. But it didn't. Escape was now the farthest thing from our minds. For one evening early in October, G.G. had informed us: "You will be home not by Christmas, not by Thanksgiving, but by the end of this month!"

23

Genius General's remarks were not the first indication that the crew of the *Pueblo* was to be released in October.

In September both the quality and the quantity of the food improved, and increased attention was given to the men's medical needs. At first we thought the KORCOMs were merely trying to fatten us up for the international press conference, but when this event came and passed and the improved treatment continued, we knew something was up.

As if to assure that our final impressions of North Korean life would be pleasant, on three separate occasions during September the whole crew was bused into Pyongyang for various cultural activities.

Our first trip out of the compound was to attend the epic dramatic presentation of *Glorious Is Our Fatherland*, a musical production which depicted North Korea's struggle from "the beginning of time." Since all the dialogue and songs were in Korean, interpreters sitting among us offered a running commentary on the action. It was redundant, for, as the title indicated, this was nothing more than another form of propaganda, with the usual socialist happy ending—the first part stressing the horrors of Japanese oppression, the conclusion praising the "glorious freedom" of the reign of Kim Il Sung.

This event was held in the Grand Theater. The night we attended, there were no civilians in the audience, only North Korean Army personnel, who had probably seen the same epic once each year since their induction. But one contemporary scene had been added. We didn't need the interpreters to tell us the characters in the leather flight jackets were supposed to be the officers and leading petty officers of the *Pueblo*.

Our next outing was to the Acrobatic Theater, a European-type circus. We had presumed that this time we would be spared the propaganda, but no such luck. The clowns spent most of their time playing practical jokes on characters representing Japanese or Americans.

Our final visit was to the Morang Bang Above Ground Theater. The bill that night was the choir and ensemble of the Korean People's Army. Although the singers were well trained, and the dancing very professional, the lyrics were saturated with anti-American commentary.

Sitting there, I couldn't help thinking of a recent cultural disaster that had occurred in the compound. Steve Harris and Seaman Earl Phares at some point had admitted to the KORCOMs that they enjoyed singing. Immediately the two were presented with copies of the "Kim Il Sung Songbook" and ordered to practice the songs. Their debut, the two men singing offkey throughout, was bad even by North Korean standards. They were not asked to sing again.

On none of these three cultural junkets were the windows of the buses covered. We were able to pinpoint the exact location of our compound in relation to the city of Pyongyang. We were also able to see various exceptions to the KORCOM propaganda. The interpreters of our Friday-night movies had told us that North Korean men never carried huge loads of wood on their backs using the old fashioned A-frame packs; only in South Korea were the peasants still so oppressed. They were right about the North Korean men. We saw only women carrying the heavy loads.

As for *Juche,* in Pyongyang we added to our growing list of imported vehicles a couple more jeeps and a Volkswagen. My favorite contradiction, however, was a large statue of the legendary *chollima* horses in downtown Pyongyang. Our captors had spoken of this statue several times, with great pride. I noticed that the horse was facing north, as if running away from South Korea.

It was on the way back from one of these trips that I overheard a conversation between Silver Lips and the Bear, who were sitting directly in front of Bucher and me on the bus. I made out the Korean words for "Panmunjom . . . *Pueblo* crew . . . will be released on October eleventh."

The KORCOMs were not above planting a rumor—they informed one of the men of the bombing halt in Vietnam, then waited to see how long it took the news to reach the other rooms—but this time I was positive this was not the case. I had admitted to no one that I was learning the language.

I did so now, however, passing the information along to Bucher. When I told him how I had found out, he was sure the news was authentic. Something was going on; you could feel it.

But why October 11? Then I recalled reading that October 10 was the twentieth anniversary of the Workers' Party of Korea. What better time than in conjunction with a holiday, and a Korean one at that?

A number of the crewmen were betting we would be released just before Christmas, others guessed by Thanksgiving. Barnyard circulated the rumor that there was a clause in the armistice agreement which said prisoners could not be held longer than one year. He insisted that he had heard this at one of his duty stations. Even if this were true, there was a matter of semantics here. Did the clause say "prisoners of war"? If so, as the KORCOMs defined our status, that didn't mean us.

Early in October G.G. made it official. One evening, when the entire crew was together in the "clubhouse" on the third deck, he decided to end the speculation. With a smug smile, but no elaboration, G.G. told us, Major Spot interpreting: "You will be home not by Christmas, not by Thanksgiving, but by the end of this month!"

280

About this same time we were initiated into the mysteries of the "Gypsy Tea Room."

Over a period of about a week, individual crewmen were taken from their rooms, to be returned an hour or two later, smiling sheepishly and, in more than a few cases, quite tight. When questioned about what had happened, they seemed very reluctant to talk.

When my turn came, I was escorted out of our building to the upper deck of the range building, where the press conferences took place. Only the area had now been outfitted as a social lounge. Grouped around a coffee table were four cushioned chairs. Three were occupied by KORCOM officers, who politely asked me to sit down and make myself comfortable.

I recognized one of my hosts as a four-star captain who had served as interpreter during some of my early interrogations in the Barn; this was the first time I had seen him at the Country Club. The other two appeared to be "party" men—the KORCOM equivalent of American CIA agents. As they made small talk, two sweater-clad Korean girls brought in trays of apples, cookies, sausage, candy, and soft drinks. One of the girls was dressed in a green sweater and skirt; her companion wore an identical outfit, only in red. Later, comparing notes, we would nickname them "Merry" and "Christmas."

Though the other crewmen had been offered beer or wine, I wasn't. It was obvious they had my complete vita. They talked knowledgeably about my son and daughter, the schools I had attended, etc.

It was, I soon realized, a "sincerity test."

Would I like to return to North Korea someday? they asked. Of course, I answered, dripping sincerity. But I would like to spend a little time at home first, I added.

When returned to the United States, would I tell the truth about what life was like in North Korea? I promised that I would, really sincere this time.

If, on returning home, I should have a North Korean

281

visitor, would I make him welcome? I assured them that I would give him a welcome he would long remember.

Asked if I might enjoy visiting other parts of Asia, I avoided a direct answer, visualizing myself being taken on a solitary sightseeing tour while the rest of the crew returned home.

Later I learned that almost identical questions were asked of all the crewmen.

Before leaving, the officers asked me if I would sign a statement, verifying my signature with my thumbprint. I hesitated, until the statement was read to me. Then I did so gladly.

The statement read: "I promise not to keep this a secret from nobody."

Apparently the secrecy was intended as another test of our sincerity. When Squarehead, a senior duty officer, asked one of the enlisted men what had happened there, the crewman made the mistake of telling him. He was severely reprimanded.

But not beaten. The KORCOMs had substituted the carrot for the stick. Things had indeed changed.

Crandall and one or two other crewmen refused to answer the questions "sincerely." They weren't beaten either. But they were told that when the crew was repatriated, they would remain behind. After this, the *Pueblo*'s officers passed the word: "Drink their booze and say anything they want you to say. We'll have our chance to get back at them when we get home."

But one man decided that he couldn't wait that long. And because of his need to play the hero, eighty-one other men would lose two and a half months of their freedom.

Ridiculous as it seemed, the KORCOMs apparently felt that through the wiles of bad liquor and what passed in North Korea for "sexy broads," they would bring out the defectors in our midst. One suspected they had seen too many spy movies.

Our captors' attitude toward sex was curious, to say the least. In one of their films, a guerrilla leader married his sweetheart, then headed for the Manchurian backwoods to take on the Japanese. In his absence, he asked one of his comrades to take care of his new bride.

Hollywood's eternal triangle? Not in North Korea. For absolutely nothing happened. After many months the guerrilla leader returned home, headed straight for camp, found his comrade and embraced him fondly. Only later did he seek out his wife and tenderly take her hand.

The catcalls from the *Pueblo* crew drove Captain Nice and Captain Queer into a confused rage. "What's so funny?" they screamed. "Aren't you ever amorous?" one of the crewmen teased. "We are very advanced," Captain Nice shot back. "The Russians don't even sleep with their women!"

The feeling of repatriation was definitely in the air. And it was a heady brew.

Excepting only our arguments during Bucher's mock court, the skipper and I had gotten along fairly well through most of our captivity, much better actually than while still aboard the *Pueblo,* our common plight giving the *Pueblo*'s wardroom its first semblance of unity.

With the news of our forthcoming release, this came to an end.

The conflict was over what our conduct should be during the few remaining days of our detention.

Since this would be our last chance to get back at the KORCOMs, Bucher wanted to pull out all stops and "shove it to them" in any and every way we could. In encouraging the use of the finger gesture and other tricks, he had already started doing this.

I could sympathize with his attitude, because I knew exactly how he felt. For more than eight months the bastards had been stomping on us. I too wanted to give it back to them, preferably in kind, but, lacking that, in any

283

way possible. But, even more than that, I wanted to see the entire crew of the USS *Pueblo* freed. This, to my mind, was the most important thing. I was against doing anything that might jeopardize our release. This was not the time, I felt, to get cocky or overconfident.

The skipper vehemently disagreed. It was the familiar Bucher syndrome: he had to have the last word, come out on top, emerge the winner.

From then on, he openly flouted the KORCOM "Rules of Life." Often, with the duty officers or guards, he used double-talk or went into his lockjaw routine. The latter was nothing new. When trapped in a verbal situation he couldn't handle, Bucher often feigned lockjaw, claiming that he had been suffering from it off and on for years. It was a good trick, but it left the *Pueblo*'s other officers, who had no such out, on the spot.

As October 11 drew nearer, Bucher's antics increased. I finally suggested that he "cool it," at least until such time as our repatriation was assured. It was a mistake, telling Bucher what he should or shouldn't do; I knew that well by now, but this time too much was at stake for me to keep quiet.

Bucher reacted predictably. He flung a wild charge: Murphy was "collaborating" with the KORCOMs, because he wouldn't go along with his stunts! As always with Bucher, it was an either/or situation.

I was not so much surprised at the charge as amazed that he hadn't gone into his usual diatribe: that I was a "goodie-two-shoes," the religious nut who didn't smoke or drink and who opposed everyone else's fun.

I wasn't against Bucher's "fun" per se, but I was against having to stay in North Korea any longer than necessary just because it gave one man a little self-satisfaction and eased his guilty conscience.

There were other indications that our release was imminent. Each of us was ordered to rewrite his confession, making it as complete as possible. These documents, G.G. told us, would then be held as "insurance," to be released

284

only if upon our return to the United States we told "lies" about the humanitarian treatment we had received.

In addition, the whole crew was to write a final letter of apology to the North Korean government. Such earlier efforts had always been the work of a committee, but, possibly because several of the *Pueblo*'s officers felt this was not the time to rock the boat, Bucher decided to compose it himself.

It was a hilarious document. When Bucher read it to the crew, tears ran down the faces of many of the men, the effort of suppressing their laughter was so great.

"The rosy finger of dawn is now replacing the fickle finger of fate upon which we have been rotating for such a long time. . . .

"We had been fully authorized to penetrate their sovereign territorial waters whenever there was a prospect for adding goodies to our spy bag. . . .

"We knew, of course, that we were caught red-handed involved in spying and that this type of nastiness is punishable by death. . . .

"We, as conscientious human beings who were cast upon the rocks and shoals of immorality by the tidal waves of Washington's naughty policies, know that neither the frequency nor the distances of these transgressions into the territorial waters of their sovereign, peace-loving nation matter, because, in the final analysis, penetration, however slight, is sufficient to complete the act. . . ."

The phrase "penetration, however slight," was, as all servicemen know, the military definition of "rape."

"In conclusion, we eighty-two members of the *Pueblo* stand guilty before the fair world judgment, as superspies and the perpetrators of crimes so horrible they have seldom been exceeded in the history of the world."

The document was a tonic we sorely needed. It relieved a tremendous amount of accumulated tension and frustrated rage. It helped us lift our heads again. There was only one thing wrong with it. Unlike the individual confessions, G.G. made it perfectly clear at the start that this

285

apology *would* be published and released to the world press.

Bucher was apparently hoping that this would occur *after* we reached the other side of the DMZ.

He could have been right.

The document was read to the crew and signed by them on October 8. On the morning of October 10 we were each issued a small traveling bag and ordered to pack our tooth-brush, soap, and other personal items Three buses pulled into the compound and stopped below my window, their engines left idling as the drivers went inside the building.

We had been given haircuts and shaves the day before, and not long before this, issued new uniforms. Everything fell into place. The remarks of Silver Lips and G.G. The Gypsy Tea Room. The final confessions and apology. It was the summing-up, the last chapter. We were going home!

As additional confirmation, one of the KORCOM guards entered my room. He was one of the gentler souls among our captors, one of the few with whom we had had no trouble. Perhaps for this reason we had never gotten around to nicknaming him. He did not speak English, and I didn't let him know I understood his Korean, but he was trying to say good-bye. Reaching in his pocket, he brought out a small button. Examining it, I saw the figures of two acrobats. Remembering the troupe in Pyongyang, I nodded my recognition. Grinning, he slipped the button back in his pocket. Obviously it was one of his most treas-ured possessions, and in his fumbling, hesitant way, he wanted to share it with me. Here was at least one North Korean who still believed in personal property, one who also wanted me to remember him with something other than hatred.

When he left, I looked back out the window. The drivers had returned to the buses and were driving off! A sick feeling rose from the pit of my stomach. Had something happened to change the repatriation plans?

Much later that day several other buses arrived, and this time we were loaded onto them. We were told that our first stop would be the train station at Pyongyang, from which we would travel to Sinchon.

Although there was no mention of repatriation, many of us, Bucher and myself included, felt sure this would be the first leg of a journey that would take us to Panmunjom, and freedom.

The train was much newer and cleaner than the one that had brought us to our prison. We were even assigned individual berths. Since they were only 5½ feet long, the taller members of the crew spent a cramped night. But there were no complaints. We were on our way!

On getting off the train in Sinchon the following morning, we found three buses waiting, the same three we had seen in the compound the previous day.

The pride of Sinchon is its Atrocity Museum. Here is assembled all the "evidence" of atrocities allegedly committed by Americans during the Korean war. Accompanied by a camera crew, and guided by a young female KORCOM, we toured the exhibits.

There were huge photographic blowups of house flies and ants: used in germ warfare, we were told. A rusty nail: a "tool of torture." A large pile of shoes: found on the bank of a river where American troops had drowned hundreds of women and children, or so claimed our girl guide.

Other so-called "documentary" evidence in this chamber of horrors included Communist-party cards and last wills and testaments of Koreans allegedly beaten to death by Americans. The wills described the torture inflicted just before the Koreans succumbed. How the victims were able to write such long documents after such an ordeal, and why the Americans permitted them to do so, was never explained. Not too surprisingly, almost all the statements ended with words of devotion to the Democratic People's Republic of Korea and praise for its number-one, peerless

287

patriot, Kim Il Sung. Even dying, they managed to put down his long list of titles.

Later we were bused to still another building and shown two large gunpowder magazines, which we were told contained the ashes of mothers and children allegedly burned to death by villainous Americans.

The North Koreans attributed many of these atrocities to a single man, Lieutenant (J.G.) Harrison, sometimes also called Harris, the personification of the degenerate U.S. soldier. According to North Korean legend, he was captured during the war and confessed to hundreds of crimes.

This junior-grade U.S. Naval officer had also risen to fantastic military heights. He was in charge of the entire U.S. Army in Sinchon! They even had a photograph of him. Unfortunately, when it was taken, his back was turned.

There was, however, a large painting of U.S. military personnel around a conference table, allegedly plotting some dastardly deed against peace-loving North Korea, and Lieutenant Harrison was supposedly in this. I asked our guide to point him out. Without hesitation, she identified the man in the center. He wore corporal's stripes.

While at the museum, some of us asked to use the men's room. One of the KORCOM officers checked it, then motioned us inside. However, he didn't check it carefully enough, for I swung open a door to one of the toilets and exposed a squatting, enraged North Korean civilian.

It was, I whispered to the crewmen when we returned outside, the first time we had actually invaded a North Korean's sovereignty.

The slip-up bothered our guards—and we had an unusually large number of them accompanying us on our trip. The people of Sinchon particularly hated Americans, they told us. This was why the lower panes on the buses were covered, so they couldn't see and attack us. I suspected there was at least some truth in this. As unconvincing as the exhibits in the Atrocity Museum appeared to us, they must have had a strong effect upon local residents.

Our captors also told us that the extra guards were necessary, because South Korea had somehow received word that the Pueblo's crew was in Sinchon and was planning to stage a raid and assassinate us.

That afternoon, in what was the closest thing to a spontaneous press conference since our capture, a number of Korean reporters were allowed to question us. Asked what impressed me most in the museum, I told them it was a toss-up between the Bible in which Lieutenant Harrison transported state secrets, and that great number of shoes. "They were certainly the most damning evidence of the entire display."

Bucher used the occasion to wave his extended middle finger at the cameras and to go into what was, to the Pueblo's officers, a very familiar act.

He wished he could express his gratitude, it was so overwhelming, but he had this little lockjaw problem. Nothing serious, of course. It just came on him at the strangest times.

Few of the enlisted men had ever seen Bucher's routine, however, and as he continued mumbling through clenched teeth, most of them were on the edge of convulsions.

Now, suddenly, more than eight months after our capture, Bucher had stepped into the role of leader of the Pueblo's crew, a position he had been loath to adopt earlier, except to be first to abandon the Code of Conduct, first to confess, first to sign the petition to the President. Shove it to the bastards! You could almost hear the words, the feeling was so tangible. Encouraged by Bucher, others started cutting up, giving in to unwarranted cockiness.

Every word, every gesture, was recorded on tape and film.

We had presumed that once our attendance at the Atrocity Museum was duly exploited for all its propaganda value, the next stage would be a trip to Kaesong, then Panmunjom.

Instead, we were escorted back onto the buses, then onto the train, for a return trip to the Country Club.

October 11 passed without the release of the crew of the USS *Pueblo*. Later G.G. would inform us that our actions on this trip had proven that we were "not yet sincere."

On October 14 Bucher's "playful petition" was published in the *Pyongyang Times*.

On October 18 *Time* printed a photograph of the eight *Pueblo* crewmen in Room 13: Bland, Peppard, Layton, Goldman, Berens, Iredale, Scarborough, and Law. It was an unusual photograph, and it stretched across more than half the top of one page.

The caption read: "The North Koreans are having a hard time proving to the world that the captive crewmen of the USS *Pueblo* are a contrite and cooperative lot. Last week Pyongyang's flacks tried again—and lost to the U.S. Navy. In this class-reunion picture, three of the crewmen have managed to use the medium for a message, furtively getting off the U.S. hand signal of obscene derisiveness and contempt."

24

The crew of the USS *Pueblo* remained unaware of these developments. All we knew was that something unexpected had happened to the plans for repatriation.

Puzzlement replaced hope. Watery turnip soup again became the main staple in our diet. The new uniforms took on yet another meaning. They were winter issue. The prospect of spending yet another season in North Korea became as chillingly real as the cold winds that were already howling down from Siberia. The guards became rougher; minor infractions of the rules now brought severe punishments. Oddjob, the three-star colonel who was in charge of disciplining the crew, began strutting up and down the halls of the Country Club, smirking knowingly. Built more like a Sumo wrestler than a Korean, his presence cast an ominous shadow over our lives.

The routine remained the same, but beneath it was an undercurrent of fear.

We began talking escape again.

When considering the various escape plans, one thing had never been mentioned: what would happen to those left behind?

Perhaps it was never voiced because we already knew the answer. There would be reprisals, maybe even deaths; the KORCOMs would have no trouble justifying the latter; they could claim that they had occurred during the break.

Was it worth it to get one or two men to the other

side of the DMZ? This was the question the officers now had to consider.

Bucher remained indecisive. Finally someone asked what a token escape would accomplish. It would get word to the U.S. government that the *Pueblo* had never intruded, Bucher replied.

I was still not inclined to trust Bucher. Super C had planted his seeds well. Yet continued silence, at this stage, could be disastrous. Now, for the first time, I told Bucher about the erroneous intrusions I had charted, the repetitive phrases in the press conferences, the doctoring of the navigational records, the tricks I'd used in my letters. There was no doubt in my mind, I assured him, that the message *had* gotten through.

I was taking a calculated risk in telling him, I knew. If he asked, I also knew it wouldn't be easy explaining why I hadn't told him earlier. But he didn't ask. He was too relieved. At least that worry was not out of the way.

Though the officers still continued to talk of escape, and considered various new plans, no move was made to implement them. Even more important, at this point, was learning what was going on at Panmunjom. It would be tragic if we attempted to break out one or two men, only to learn later that the KORCOMs had been ready to release all of us.

Work on the radio was almost completed. One of the initial problems had been getting a nail that would hold a magnetic charge, the metal being too soft. But CT Angelo Strano had finally succeeded in manufacturing a crude battery, and with the discovery of an antenna just outside his window, still another problem vanished. The only thing lacking was some sort of earphone. Lee Roy Hayes was sure he could make one, if he could lift a few of the parts from the speaker of the projector used to show our Friday-night propaganda movies. The men were now awaiting a chance to steal them.

If we could pick up a South Korean or U.S. Armed

Forces radio station we were sure there would be some mention of the negotiations.

As we later learned, had we succeeded at this time we would have been bitterly disappointed. For during November there were no talks at Panmunjom.

In North Korea the *Pueblo* remained the big news. It was not so in the United States, and this greatly mystified our captors. They could not understand how a story could dominate the front page one day, and on the following slip to page thirty-two or disappear entirely.

The KORCOMs had avidly followed the U.S. presidential campaign from its start. Then, just at a time when interest seemed the greatest, the news broadcasts suddenly switched to news of the World Series and the upsetting of the heavily favored St. Louis Cardinals by the Detroit Tigers.

What kind of country was it where baseball was more important than politics? There was nothing in their propaganda syllabuses to explain this, and they concluded American elections must be farces.

I wondered if a single North Korean had ever stayed up late listening to election returns honestly unsure whether Kim Il Sung would be reelected.

Following the nominating conventions, we had been given capsule critiques of the Democratic and Republican candidates—both highly uncomplimentary. Vice-President Humphrey was a tool of the "infamous Johnson terriorists." But candidate Nixon, in the view of the North Koreans, was even worse. We were reminded he had been Vice-President during the Korean war.

Usually there was a gap between the time an event took place in the United States and when we were informed of it. This gave the KORCOMs a chance to play seer. The presidential election would be close, G.G. predicted, but Nixon would squeak through.

Since G.G. delivered his prognostication more than a week after the second Tuesday in November, we were inclined to accept it as fact.

293

What effect would this have on us? This was the topic in the wardroom. Would President Johnson make a major effort to have us released before he left office, or would he leave this as unfinished business for the President-elect? All the KORCOM propaganda had been directed against the "Johnson clique." It would be difficult for North Korea to transfer the blame for the *Pueblo* to the Nixon administration, but having witnessed some rather adroit shifts of the party line since our arrival, we suspected they could manage if called upon to do so.

We were equally indecisive as to why the repatriation plans had gone awry. Bucher refused to consider the possibility that his "fun-and-games" approach had anything to do with it. He maintained that G.G. had lied about our being released in October. I didn't think so; there had been too many other indications. G.G. did nothing to dissipate the mystery, except to tell Bucher that the United States had been "insincere," something he probably would have said in any case.

Through all this, I couldn't shake the feeling that something was building, and it wasn't release.

Bucher, however, was now making plans for our return. Sometime earlier he had come up with a "grand scheme." Once we were back in the United States, each member of the crew would put one hundred dollars of his back pay into a kitty. Then we would have a drawing, the lucky man winning eighty-two hundred dollars, which he could spend in one colossal binge.

At the time, Bucher had been in one of his depressed states, and though we weren't all that enthused with the idea, we had humored him along, because it kept his mind occupied.

At first I thought the "crew-book" idea was similar to the kitty idea, something that would quickly pass.

Movie producers and book and magazine publishers in the United States would be willing to pay a fortune for the "inside" story of the USS *Pueblo*, Bucher claimed.

We would be swamped with offers the moment we set foot back in the United States. The best way to capitalize on this, he said, would be to do a crew book: a single authorized account of the capture of the ship and our imprisonment.

We played around with the idea, trying it out on some of the enlisted men. Almost everyone was for it, myself included. Schumacher was particularly enthusiastic, and I think it was Skip who suggested dividing all the money into eighty-three equal shares, with Hodges' share going to his parents.

I liked the idea of everyone sharing equally, for we had certainly shared the horrors of our captivity. It occurred to me, for just a moment, that the book might be another of Bucher's tricks, a way to get his "single consistent account" for the Court of Inquiry. But I quickly dismissed the idea. I knew the crew. While a few might go along with anything Bucher said, the majority, I felt sure, would insist on "telling it like it was."

From our return from Sinchon in October through all of November, the main focus of the interrogations had been on statements in our letters and confessions. It was apparent that the KORCOMs were reviewing everything we had written. That wasn't good.

Nor was I made easy by something else that was occurring at the same time. Things that I had told Bucher privately, in confidence, began coming back to me, via not the other officers but G.G. Either Bucher was talking too much, or someone close to him was. Thus far none of the disclosures had been serious. But they were enough to keep me on edge, wondering what would come next; and more than enough to make me wonder if I had done the right thing in taking him into my confidence about the ways I'd undermined the intrusion charges.

I could not visualize Bucher intentionally telling G.G. anything. But I could visualize all too well Bucher entertaining him with his fund of interesting stories, while

G.G. played the rapt listener. Although it seemed ages ago, I couldn't help recalling Steve Harris agonizing over whether he should pull Bucher's clearance, because he talked too much.

I was also disturbed by the change in G.G.'s manner toward the rest of us, all too obvious since our return from Sinchon. When called before him, we found a cold, hard mask. There was little small talk now, no amenities. His questions were sharp, biting, incisive; his remarks etched with sarcasm. His face seemed frozen in one expression, but his eyes blazed anger. It was as if he were nursing a silent but highly explosive rage. I became convinced that he was methodically, piece by piece, accumulating evidence of our "transgressions," and that one day he would suddenly confront us with it. I confided my feelings to several of the other officers, hoping they'd persuade me that I was wrong. But they admitted they feared the same thing. We seemed to be sitting on the edge of a volcano, waiting for it to erupt.

It didn't happen all at once. There were warning signs.

Our old nemesis the Bear reappeared after a long absence. One day he pulled Iredale out of his room and smashed him against the wall. At the time, we thought he had mistaken Iredale for Ritter, as there was some resemblance, and the Bear had it in for Ritter.

Layton, Bland, and Goldman were taken out the following day, each to be worked over thoroughly before being returned to their room.

There was a pattern to the beatings, and we saw it, but we couldn't figure out the reasoning behind it. All the men were from the same room on the second deck, number 13.

Law, senior man in the room, caught Bucher alone in the head the next day. "They're asking about the finger gesture!" he whispered.

That evening G.G. summoned the *Pueblo*'s officers. We had been "insincere," he began. But something about G.G.'s manner indicated this was not to be the familiar lecture.

"You play us for the fool?" he quietly asked, at the same time pointing to the table in front of him.

Piled there was a stack of glossy photographs. Next to them was a single clipping.

"Come, look, read," the interpreter translated G.G.'s barked command.

The top photo was a group shot of the eight men in room 13. Even from a distance, I could make out the extended fingers. The same photo reappeared in the clipping, which I now recognized, from the thin rice paper, to be the Far Eastern edition of an American newsmagazine. In dead silence we read the caption: ". . . Pyongyang's flacks tried again and lost to the U.S. Navy . . . hand signal of obscene derisiveness and contempt."

Not a damn thing we might say was going to help us now. I stared at the stack of photographs as if mesmerized, wondering how often each of us was depicted there, wondering too how far back they had gone looking for their evidence.

But the finger gesture was only the beginning. G.G. assaulted us with charge after charge after charge.

A few were ridiculous: G.G. claimed the crossword puzzles the men exchanged were code; that we had handed back and forth "pages of secrets." Actually the latter was a "crotch" novel that Sterling, the *Pueblo*'s budding Hemingway, had written. It had been pronounced a literary masterpiece when after reading it several of the crewmen decided that the ancient serving women looked interesting.

But the rest of his accusations were all too accurate: lying during interrogations; writing insincere confessions, petitions, and letters; pretending sickness; pretending speech problems. With that he looked straight at the captain. Bucher flinched as if hit.

The Sinchon trip had proven, G.G. asserted, that we were not yet sincere. There was other proof. But there was no need to confront us with it, because we would soon write new confessions and confess it ourselves. Truthful confessions, he stressed, without lies. For these would be the very last confessions we would write. There would be no second chance.

Do you play us for the fool? That was the clue. We had made a fool of North Korea in the eyes of the rest of the world. I could visualize even Russia and Red China chuckling at their backward ally. The Democratic People's Republic of North Korea had lost face. And now we were going to pay for it.

Without waiting for a reply, G.G. dismissed all of us except Bucher. When we later questioned him about what had occurred, he replied, "The shit's hit the fan. We're heading into rough waters. Pass the word to jettison all contraband, and that includes the radio. Also tell the men that it's senseless to get knocked around unnecessarily. If you think they're going to find out about something, tell them." Then he added, as if in afterthought, "Tell everyone that the Hawaiian good-luck sign is no longer an adequate explanation for the finger gesture. If they ask about it, admit the truth."

Having to destroy the radio was a blow. Still lacking an earphone, it had never been assembled, the parts hidden under the floorboards and under drawers in Strano's room.

Each of us had some contraband. During most of our imprisonment we had been allowed to keep pencils. In recent weeks, however, they had been collected. I'd held out a few stubs. I ditched them now. When captured, I was wearing an electric watch. The battery had run out during the summer and Shephard had lent me his watch so I could time the rounds of the guards, etc. I still had the other watch, however, and by removing the battery had a place where I could keep small pieces of paper. I had also squeezed most of the toothpaste out of a tube and replaced it with a very thin piece of paper, with notes on the ship's actual course, the coordinates for the seventeen bogus intrusions, and reminders of some of the details of my last confession. If released, I hoped to carry this out with me, so I could expose their lies one by one. I had even

298

planned, if questioned, to tell the KORCOMs that their toothpaste was so good I wanted my friends in the United States to try it. Now I didn't dare take the chance. I destroyed these too.

When it came to the luminal, I hesitated. Steve Harris had been spotted by a guard while hiding some prayers in his lighter and had been roughed up for it, the first punishment he had received since our capture. The duty officers had threatened to beat the whole crew for his act. I didn't want that to happen because of something I did. Although this was probably the time I was most apt to need it, I finally dumped the luminal down the toilet.

It gave me an odd feeling doing so. With the powder, I always knew if things got too rough I had an out. I had that out no longer.

For me it began while walking down the hall to get a bucket of water from the head.

The way we walked was carefully prescribed. Heads down, hands rigid at sides, fingers clenched and fists facing downward, parallel to the floor. Apparently my left hand was off an inch or so, for, without warning, Swivel Head, one of the guards, delivered a judo kick to the knuckles that caused me to double over in agony. The hand would remain paralyzed for nearly a week; it occasionally troubles me even today.

Swivel Head was usually a very placid fellow. None of us had had any trouble with him before this.

The nightmare that we would call "Hell Week" had begun.

On December 10 the regular routine was abandoned. The officers were kept isolated in their individual rooms, the enlisted men packed in groups of a dozen or more to a room. That evening the guards brought around paper and pencils, and we were ordered to begin work on our "final" confessions.

When we weren't actually writing—while the KORCOM

officers were "reviewing" the pages we had written—we were forced to sit upright in the chairs, heads and torsos bent forward. We were not allowed to sleep. Doors to all the rooms were left open, and lights remained on.

My confession was "not acceptable," I was told. It was not "repentent enough." I was to start all over again, this time including all the things I had left out.

I racked my brain for "crimes" I had committed. Urinating on my plant. Showing disrespect to a guard. Telling someone about the Gypsy Tea Room. Laughing during the movies.

Then I heard the first sound, a groan. It was followed by a scream. Then what sounded like a body bouncing against a wall. As the hours passed, the sounds increased in number. It was January 29 all over again. I could feel the kicks and blows, the board between my legs.

As if memory weren't vivid enough, Major Spot and the Bear charged into my room, the major screaming that unless I was sincere my turn would come next. In almost loving detail, he recalled my torture.

I was afraid, and I'm not ashamed to admit it. Afraid that the night of January 29 would be repeated, afraid that this time they would go even further, but, most of all, afraid that if they did, eventually I would blurt out everything I had thus far successfully concealed, the classified information, the tricks I'd used to discredit their intrusion charges.

I began writing again. I confessed to small transgressions, a few at a time, to postpone what now seemed the inevitable. Sometime on the second day they brought in a bowl of watery slop. I was forbidden to eat it until I finished my confession. Yet even before I stopped writing they examined the pages and informed me that I had not confessed everything.

I had, I claimed.

No, you did not tell us about the dirty names you gave the guards.

While they waited, I wrote them down.

We know you insulted Kang Ban Sok, the revered mother of Kim Il Sung!

I wasn't too surprised that they had learned that. My nickname for her had gained wide currency among the crew. Dutifully I wrote down that I had disrespectfully called her "Gang Bang Suck."

You hid things under table with a nail!

I had admitted that to only a few people. Obviously it was at least one too many.

What you hide?

Sleeping powder.

What for?

To kill myself.

Think of more things, they demanded, stomping out.

More than forty-eight hours passed before they let me sleep, and then they reawakened me after what seemed only a couple of hours. Groggily I wrote on, not remembering now whether what I was writing had or hadn't already been confessed. I concocted elaborate lies, anything to keep the pencil moving. For the first time since the Barn, I tried the tactic of shaking with fright whenever certain guards entered the room. They paid no attention whatsoever.

They were on to many of our tricks. But by this time we had also figured out more than a few of theirs, such as the "friendly-unfriendly" routine.

Major Spot, a sadist if ever there was one, would insist that I confess certain things.

After he had left, Fetch, one of the "friendly" officers, would come in. Major Spot had wanted to beat me, Fetch said, but because he liked me, he had prevented this. He could not hold him off indefinitely, however. If I would just confide in him a few little things, he would see what he could do to restrain Major Spot.

I almost smiled openly at that, remembering a similar scene that had occurred in the Barn. One of the "friendly" officers had come in and shown me pictures of his son. He

301

knew I had a son too. We were alike in many ways, he said. He too did not smoke or drink.

The next day, passing one of the interrogation rooms, I saw him puffing away on a cigarette. I presumed that he was equally sincere about his abstention from alcoholic beverages and his male offspring.

But this time they did succeed in catching me off guard.

You did not tell us, Fetch continued, about the *Pueblo*'s escape plan.

That shook me. Who had talked about that? Mentally I started cataloging the names of the men who were privy to this information, then suddenly realized: He used the singular! He was presuming that there was only one escape plan, when there were easily eighty-two.

Pretending great reluctance, and waiting until he threatened to call back Major Spot, I wrote out the *Pueblo* escape plan:

Once we'd vaulted over the wall of the compound, we intended to head south and climb the Kumgan Mountains (the Kumgan, or Diamond, Mountains were the most rugged terrain in North Korea; I'd studied them on the map, seen them in the movies; they were the one area we were determined to avoid). During the day we intended to hide under the water in the rice paddies, breathing through bamboo shoots.

I went on like this for a dozen pages. Fetch appeared satisfied with my plan, for immediately he moved on to something else.

Now tell us about the radio the men were building, he asked.

Isolated as we were, there was no way we could learn what was going on in the other rooms. With a few exceptions. Steve Harris' room was opposite mine. When I felt sure no one was looking, I glanced across the hall. But it was a big risk. The same was true of looking into the rooms as I was escorted to the head or one of the interrogation rooms. I did it a few times, but my hand still throbbed from a lesser infraction than this.

The bruised faces I saw were enough to convince me that the sounds I'd heard were all too authentic.

After a time I realized there was nothing random about the beatings. The KORCOMs would go into a room, haul out or rough up someone there, then move on to the next room and do the same. But they also skipped rooms, so you never knew when or if your turn was coming.

Only later would we be able to put together a composite picture of Hell Week. Not everyone was beaten. Probably fewer than half the men were. But those chosen took a mauling that more than made up for the ones who had been missed.

Of the offenders in room 13, they had saved one man for special attention. Law, who began as the athletic co-ordinator, had developed into one of the crew's real leaders. The KORCOMs blamed him, as they did the *Pueblo*'s offi-cers, for every offense committed by the enlisted men.

They began hitting him with a two-by-two board.

When this broke, they beat him with one of the halves. When it broke, they did the same with the remaining half.

Nor did they quit then. They returned with a four-by-four post and hit him with that until it broke also.

Law's ordeal lasted thirty-nine hours. By the time they had finished with him, he had confessed to being the lone CIA man aboard the *Pueblo*, originating the finger gesture, and being the mastermind behind the escape plan. None of which were true. All of which spared others similar punishment.

Hammond committed a very foolish, and very brave, act. Aware that the last thing that our captors probably wanted was another dead man, the second night of Hell Week he took a broken piece of mirror and slashed his wrist.

On viewing his blood-soaked bed the next morning, the KORCOMs had panicked and kept asking "Why? Why? Why?"

Weak but sustained by a rage accumulated over ten

303

long months, Hammond told them. While his horrified cellmates looked on, the Marine cursed everyone in North Korea from Kim Il Sung on down.

For the rest of Hell Week they never touched him.

Two instances of many. Knowing that the others were holding up would have provided tremendous moral support. But, unfortunately, what we did learn was just the opposite. Repeatedly we were confronted with things others had confessed.

I was stunned by the mention of the radio. Since it had already been destroyed, there was absolutely no way they could know of it unless they had beaten the information out of someone.

Had they also extracted the knowledge that I knew about it? Probably.

Yes, I knew about the radio, I confessed.

Who made it? they asked. Where were the pieces kept?

I don't know, I told them. I never knew. No one had confided in me.

You lie.

No, I am telling the truth.

We can turn the guards loose on you. It will be just like other time.

Involuntarily I shuddered.

It was Strano, wasn't it? And McClarren? And Hayes? And Chicca? They all confessed. Others tell us too. No need you lie.

This put me in a difficult position. They appeared to know exactly which men were involved. But maybe they didn't. Maybe they had only one man's word. My confirmation could result in the punishment of the four men, maybe even their deaths.

Yet if the men *had* confessed, and I denied their participation, I could be placing them in jeopardy that way also. I could hear the KORCOMs saying: Executive officer say you lie. Name who really build radio.

Too, to deny that these four were responsible would be

304

to imply that others were involved, and that I knew who they were.

There was another option open to me. I took it. I continued to maintain ignorance of any of the details. I had heard talk that someone was building a radio, but that was all I knew.

Once, back in our Barn days, Super C had told each of the officers what he thought of him. On coming to me he shook his head, saying "You, Murphy, I do not understand."

I could have told him at the time, but didn't, that I was only following his advice, given in one of our first interviews, when he quoted an old Korean proverb to the effect: Never trust a man who talks too much.

I had played mum throughout our captivity; as much as possible, I continued to do so now. Yet even that had its dangers. Not knowing what the others were saying, even the most seemingly innocent answer could trigger a chain of terrifying repercussions.

They were zeroing in now, aiming at a single target. "Hamjung." The captain.

Oddjob was asking the questions, Silver Lips translating.

Hamjung tell you to use the finger sign, yes?

No, I thought of it myself.

Others tell us he do so. Why you lie?

I'm not lying.

Hamjung very bad man. He tell you to make up stories when questioned.

No. Each of us was on his own.

Hamjung not really sick. Pretend "jaws lock," eh?

It seemed useless to deny this, with all the film they had shot at Sinchon, but I did. They would not accept my answer, however, alternately questioning and threatening me until I admitted that, not being a doctor, I had no way of knowing whether Bucher was pretending illness or actually had these attacks.

But I wouldn't go beyond that.

Hamjung tell us he hate you, Executive Officer Murphy. He tell us everything bad you do.

That might be true, I thought, but I hadn't fallen for the ruse when Super C first tried it, and I didn't intend to do so now. What things did he tell you? I asked.

He tell us you write dirty things in your letters.

I already confessed to that.

He tell us you CIA man.

Then he lies, for there are no CIA men on the *Pueblo*.

He tell us you use finger gesture.

I'd admitted that too. But not when I first did so. Thus far they apparently hadn't discovered that I had used the sign in the navigational photos.

As they went on, I realized, frankly to my surprise, that Bucher hadn't talked. There was not a single mention of the things I had been most afraid he would say.

Again they were playing the old divide-and-conquer trick. I was sure they were subjecting Bucher to the same routine. I could only hope he too saw through it.

They were not after intelligence information this time. They were seeking retribution for having lost face. To accomplish this, they did everything in their power to humble us, bring us down, turn one man against another, all as punishment for our "insincerity." Our final confessions were intended to make us feel the lowest of the low. In this they were all too successful. One of the *Pueblo*'s junior officers fingered a number of enlisted men for offenses they had not committed, then, guilt-stricken, attempted suicide. He was unsuccessful. One of the men, whose cringing attitude toward the KORCOMs had worried his cellmates ever since our capture, contradicted the stories they told. For a time the men seriously considered murdering him. Apparently the North Koreans were not partial to squealers either, for as reward the Bear beat the man savagely. Crewmen were confronted with things their closest friends had confessed about them. Some of the psychic wounds inflicted during these days would remain unhealed long after the scars of the physical punishment disappeared.

Then, suddenly, on the morning of December 19, the interrogations stopped, and there were no more cries. The routine resumed almost as if never interrupted. The men were again allowed to eat together, the enlisted men in the mess hall, the officers in their wardroom.

We were a sorry-looking lot. Even those who hadn't been beaten were nervous wrecks. Everyone had lost more weight, weight none of us could afford to lose. Injuries ranged from black eyes to dislocated bones and broken jaws. Some of the men couldn't walk without assistance. Yet the KORCOMs even reinstated the exercise periods!

It took us awhile to believe it, but it was over. Though we would call it Hell Week, it had lasted nine days.

All at once the KORCOMs became solicitous. The meals improved: the soup thickened, there was even meat. Although our captors had not let "Doc" Baldridge care for the crewmen before, the North Korean doctor requested his help now. It was a patch job, hard-boiled eggs and paraffin packs to reduce the swelling and bring natural color back to purpled flesh.

But some bruises were immune to such treatment.

Bucher had been beaten more severely than the other officers, with some of the crewmen even being brought in and forced to watch. There were apparently two reasons for this. The KORCOMs felt he had instigated many of the offenses; and, at the last minute, Bucher had decided not to follow his own instructions. Rather than telling them what he was sure they knew or could find out, he had decided not to tell them anything. The rest of us remained unaware that Bucher had again changed the rules.

All the other officers had received their lumps. With one exception. Aside from my kicked hand, they hadn't touched me. Now I knew how Steve Harris had felt.

This alone made me suspect, at least to the captain. I

307

had betrayed him, he charged. I had told them everything he had done!

He hadn't seen through their tricks.

Although I should have taken into account Bucher's physical and mental condition, I bristled at the accusation. It had been his "fun-and-games" approach that had caused Hell Week. Because of his need to have the last word, Hayes now had a broken jaw, Law could barely walk, other men had smashed noses, floating kidneys, torn and battered flesh.

Characteristically, Bucher denied responsibility. He needed a patsy for Hell Week. I was it.

Perhaps it was best that I was still unaware that because of Bucher's immature hijinks, his inability to coolly assess the situation, his lack of responsible leadership, our repatriation may well have been delayed two and a half months.

Although I knew Bucher's charges were unjustified, I was not without guilt for my part in Hell Week. None of us was. There was no way of knowing whether in confirming or denying something we had unknowingly placed someone else on the spot. Over the next several days I made a point of seeking out everyone who had been mentioned in my confession even obliquely, apologizing for any harm that might have come of it. A number of the crewmen also approached me, individually, to do the same thing. Forgiveness did not enter into it. All of us realized that no one had confessed anything voluntarily.

This understanding, shared by almost all of the crew, was one of the positive results of Hell Week. There was at least one other. Despite all the mental and physical punishment the crew had undergone, *no* classified information was betrayed. The secrets we had been keeping throughout our captivity remained secret, including the information that the intrusion charges had been thoroughly discredited.

Immediately after supper on Sunday, December 22, I was ordered to the barber shop on the second deck. Steve Harris was already there, being outfitted in a crisp new khaki uniform. New togs were waiting for me also. Steve and I exchanged no words. Our eyes said it all. The uniforms were gray and lightweight, summer issue, totally inappropriate for the near-freezing December weather outside. These had to be our repatriation outfits. Yet I was almost afraid to admit the thought, our October disappointment being all too vivid.

We were also stripped and searched, the KORCOMs confiscating such personal possessions as pictures of our families, mementos that had come in letters or that we had carried with us from the ship. But this wasn't the time to protest.

That same evening G.G. assembled the entire crew in the clubhouse on the third floor. The United States had apologized, he announced through the interpreter. We were to be freed, before Christmas. He hoped, he added, that when we reached the United States we would tell the American people about the humane treatment we had received.

I'm not sure which shocked us most, G.G.'s announcement of our release, which, if he was telling the truth, was at most only days away, or the incredible gall it took to make the suggestion about our treatment only hours after all we had been through.

Our repatriation had been planned in great detail. Buses would take us to Pyongyang, where we would board a train to Kaesong. This would be an overnight trip, and on arriving in the morning we would be driven, again by bus, the few miles to the village of Panmunjom.

At Panmunjom, G.G. explained, the buses would approach the Bridge of No Return, the link between North and South Korea. Commander Bucher would be repatriated first, so he could identify the remains of Hodges. The *Pueblo*'s crew would then follow, one man at a time, starting with the lowest-ranking seaman and working up through the grades to the most senior officer.

I didn't miss the implications of this. As executive officer and second in command, I would be the last man to cross the bridge.

If anything went wrong, if there were any provocative acts, of any kind, by any member of the *Pueblo* crew, repatriation would be halted immediately, G.G. threatened.

I hoped and prayed that no one would be so stupid as to look back and give the KORCOMs the finger. At least not until all eighty-two of us were across.

The buses would leave this very evening, G.G. told us. If all went well, we would be free the following morning.

25

Before leaving the compound, we were subjected to a final press conference. Were we glad to be going home? the North Korean reporters asked. For the first time during one of these farces we could give a wholly sincere answer.

No one, fortunately, saw fit to play cute at this stage.

The whole crew was very subdued as we were loaded onto buses and driven to the train station in Pyongyang. The train was the same one on which we had traveled to Sinchon—and back. As it moved south, toward the end of our long nightmare, I tossed restlessly in the berth, trying to sleep but failing. Too many images were running through my mind.

Carol, Eddie, Vicky. The prospect of seeing and holding them in my arms made the remaining hours almost unbearable.

Christmas at home. In the United States.

To ease the disappointment, if disappointment it was to be, I tried to think of other things.

It occurred to me that the North Koreans, not the crewmen of the USS *Pueblo*, were the real prisoners. Despite all that had been done to us, we had retained the knowledge of what freedom was like. They had never known, and probably never would.

The whole country of North Korea was one vast prison, I realized. An entire nation in detention. Liberated from imperial Japanese rule, the people of North Korea had been taken over by a dictatorship no less oppressive. After

311

we were freed, we would resume our individual lives. They would continue to live in a cadenced society in which individualism had no part, marching to a common drum, even waking and exercising in unison.

Pity? No, I was still too close to the experience for that. Perhaps someday I would develop the virtue of forgiveness. But a long time would have to pass, I knew, before that occurred, if ever it did. In the interim, understanding would have to suffice.

The North Koreans had pirated our ship, stripped us of our possessions, robbed us of our self-respect, beaten us until we turned one against another and groveled at their feet, yet, in return, they had given us something important.

Before our capture few of us knew anything about our enemy. We knew him now. And all the brainwashing in the world couldn't eradicate that hard-earned knowledge.

It would be easy to dismiss Kim Il Sung as the Lord High Potentate of a Gilbert and Sullivan comic-opera kingdom, championing pure socialism while borrowing such capitalistic devices as the income tax, claiming self-sufficiency while running one of the world's biggest importing businesses, preaching the equality of all men while bestowing on himself title upon title.

We would no longer make that mistake.

Nor would we remain deceived by all the inconsistencies we had observed in his Democratic People's Republic of Korea. For in one thing Kim Il Sung was quite consistent; he had one goal, and he was pursuing it with the single-sightedness of the truly fanatic. This was the unification of all Korea under Communism.

There was no secret as to the means he was using in his attempt to achieve this end.

First was the psychological preparation for war, the constant whipping up of hatred against not only South Korea but also her allies the United States and Japan.

Second was the physical preparation for war, the retooling and extension of the five-year plans with almost total military emphasis.

Third and last was provoking the United States into striking a military blow against North Korea that would provide justification for the reinvasion of South Korea.

To effect this North Korea had embarked upon a campaign of hostile acts, each of which could be used to propaganda advantage.

The shooting down of a UN helicopter over the demilitarized zone in 1964, and the imprisonment of its two pilots, was one such incident. Another, less well known, was the sinking of an "aggressive spy ship"—actually a South Korean patrol craft, also in international waters, in the Sea of Japan—in January, 1967. And, a year later, the seizure of the *Pueblo*. Together with such episodes as the attempted raid on the Blue House and increased hostilities in the area of the DMZ, there was observable a pattern of harassments aimed toward this single end.

The North Koreans flatly stated that the "liberation" of South Korea and its assimilation under Communism will be accomplished within a generation.

From all I had seen, read, and heard, I become convinced that they will attempt it much, much sooner, perhaps within a decade.

Early in our detention, when I had balked at writing to the Secretary of State, Super C had referred to Bucher's letter to the President, adding, "There is an old Korean proverb: if a man is to enjoy the fruit of the tree, he must first plant and nurture the seed."

His meaning was clear. If I didn't help Bucher persuade the United States to apologize, then I would not share in the repatriation.

The meaning was less clear when practically applied. When the lemon tree in my room bore fruit, I was neither allowed to sample nor share it with the other crewmen. The KORCOM guards took and ate it all.

Yet now I could see still another, and far more sinister, meaning. In time, perhaps very soon, the seeds of hatred Kim Il Sung had so carefully planted and nurtured would bear fruit.

It would be exceedingly bitter. And I was quite sure the American people would not enjoy it.

Though the crew of the *Pueblo* might be leaving North Korea, I was convinced that in days to come we would be hearing more and more about that poisoned land.

Our release, we had been informed, would occur at nine A.M.

The train reached Kaesong shortly after dawn, then pulled onto a railroad siding, where it remained until after eight A.M., at which time we were escorted off and onto three of North Korea's antique buses.

There was a heavy overcast that made the day seem unusually dark and foreboding. It had snowed during the night, and the temperature hovered close to zero. Although I wore a short quilted topcoat over the lightweight uniform, plus two extra pairs of socks under the tennis shoes, I still shivered.

We had been assigned to the buses in order of repatriation. Bucher was on the first, which would follow the ambulance bearing Hodges' body. I was on the third and last, together with about twenty-five men, including all the other officers and the leading petty officers.

There was little conversation. It was as if we were in a dream, and to speak would be to risk waking.

We couldn't see out; sheets covered the windows. When the bus braked to a stop, we could only presume that we had reached Panmunjom. We waited. And waited. It was past nine now, nearly ten. Each passing minute increased the fear that something had happened. Yet even the delay, if that was all it was, wasn't enough to overcome the mounting excitement.

Bloke and Captain Queer had been assigned to our bus. They now passed out copies of the agreement that they said the United States had signed to obtain our release.

I scanned it once, quickly, then read it very carefully the second time, in near disbelief. It read like all the bogus confessions we had been forced to sign, complete even to

314

the three A's—admit, apologize, assure—and the clumsy wording. I couldn't conceive the United States government signing this. Yet there were the words before me:

The Government of the United States of America,

Acknowledging the validity of the confessions of the crew of the USS *Pueblo* and of the documents of evidence produced by the representative of the Government of the Democratic People's Republic of Korea to the effect that the ship, which was seized by the self-defense measures of the naval vessels of the Korean People's Army in the territorial waters of the Democratic People's Republic of Korea on January 23, 1968, had illegally intruded into the territorial waters of the Democratic People's Republic of Korea on many occasions and conducted espionage activities of spying out important military and state secrets of the Democratic People's Republic of Korea.

Shoulders full responsibility and solemnly apologizes for the grave acts of espionage committed by the U.S. ship against the Democratic People's Republic of Korea after having intruded into the territorial waters of the Democratic People's Republic of Korea.

And gives firm assurance that no U.S. ships will intrude again in the future into the territorial waters of the Democratic People's Republic of Korea.

Meanwhile, the Government of the United States of America earnestly requests the Government of the Democratic People's Republic of Korea to deal leniently with the former crew members of the USS *Pueblo* confiscated by the Democratic People's Republic of Korea side, taking into consideration the fact that these crew members have confessed honestly to their crimes and petitioned the Government of the Democratic People's Republic of Korea for leniency.

On behalf of the Government of the United States of America

Gilbert H. Woodward
Major General
United States Army
23 December 1968

Directly above General Woodward's signature, several lines had been blocked out. I wondered what they had said, feeling sure that if the North Koreans had gone to the trouble of eliminating them they had to be important.

There would be a delay, a long one, Captain Queer announced. While we waited and shivered—with the motor off, the bus had no heat, and it was soon as cold inside as out—he treated us to a political lecture. But quite unlike his mild effusions during the Friday-night movies, it was pure vitriol, and there could be no doubt we were hearing the party line. When we returned to the United States we would be forced to lie about the Democratic People's Republic of Korea, Captain Queer said. It was unfortunate that such things happened, but what could one expect from such an inferior country as the United States?

When he finally finished, Bloke had his turn. But his words were most welcome. "It is time."

I glanced at my watch. Eleven-thirty A.M.

Bloke then explained the procedure: as each crewman's name was called, he was to answer "Here" as loudly as possible, then quickly disembark from the bus.

The roll call began. It seemed to take forever, and as one familiar name after another was called, there seemed to be ever-longer pauses between them.

Then, in the background, I heard another voice. No mistaking it, Bucher's. He should have been the first repatriated. Had something gone wrong? Were they holding him behind?

Then I made out the words, and realized the KORCOMs couldn't resist one last chance to make the captain lose face. He was confessing. It was another recording.

"*Here!*" The first man on our bus had just been called. He scurried for the exit.

They *were* taking longer between the names. Several times I was afraid they had stopped.

Finally they called "Lacy." They had reached the officers. Gene, barely able to walk, made his way down the aisle and off the bus.

316

"Ensign Harris." Tim ran for the door.

"Schumacher." Skip was almost on his heels.

"Lieutenant Harris."

I was alone with Bloke. "What if your name isn't called?" he asked with a stupid grin.

I didn't trust myself to reply. The loudspeakers remained silent. Minutes passed. Did Bloke really know something? Was this another of their vicious hoaxes?

"Murphy."

"*Here!*" I yelled, pushing past Bloke and running down the stairs into a crowd of KORCOM officers, who funneled me toward the bridge.

The Bridge of No Return stretched for about 150 yards across a dry gulch. There were North Korean guards most of the way across; then, beautiful sight, men in American uniforms.

I spotted Bucher, shaking hands with Steve, who had just reached the other side.

I was the last man across the bridge. As the recording of Bucher's voice grew fainter, it was all I could do to keep from running.

Just as I reached the South Korean side, the sun broke through the overcast, bathing our end of the bridge in sunshine.

Some of the crewmen would later tell me that the sun didn't hit the North Korean side, which remained dark and grim. But I didn't see that, for the last thing in the world I wanted to do at that moment was look back.

Eleven months to the day after our capture, the crew of the USS *Pueblo* was free.

26

The faces were American, and they were grinning broadly. I guess that was the thing that hit me first, the smiles. It had been a long time since we had seen that.

The warmth of the greeting left us in shock. We were so unused to this open friendliness—handshakes, excited laughter, honest concern—that instinctively we retreated into our protective shells.

Almost immediately we were rushed onto buses—warm, comfortable, but, best of all, unmistakably American. It made all the difference. We still couldn't believe we were really free, but the awareness was beginning to get to us. Even the air of South Korea smelled cleaner.

A representative of the State Department sat next to me. It was a toss-up as to which of us had the most questions. His first threw me: at any time, either intentionally or accidentally, had the *Pueblo* gone past the twelve-mile limit? *Never,* I replied with as much vehemence as I could muster. Hadn't they gotten our messages? I asked, wondering if all our efforts had been in vain. They had, he reassured me; the paragraph trick in my letters, the inland wanderings of the *Pueblo,* its remarkable bursts of speed—they had caught all of it. But he needed verbal confirmation.

I admitted that I was stunned by the apology the KOR-COMs had shown us. I couldn't conceive the U.S. government admitting to such lies. They hadn't, he told me. Those lines that the North Koreans had marked out read: "Simultaneously with the signing of this document, the undersigned acknowledges receipt of 82 former crew members of the Pueblo and one corpse." What Woodward had signed was simply a receipt for the crew. Even before signing it, he had announced that the rest of the document was a fraud.

This "overwrite" proposal was nothing new, he told me. A similar statement had been signed to effect the release of the two helicopter pilots in 1964.

Very briefly he reviewed the history of the *Pueblo* negotiations. They had begun in late January, but North Korean insistence that their terms—admit, apologize, assure —were nonnegotiable had made quick agreement impossible. In mid-February the bogus navigational records had been introduced, as KORCOM "proof" of the intrusion charges. When Navy experts examined them, they quickly spotted the discrepancies. They said nothing about this to the North Koreans, however, fearful of placing the crew in jeopardy. Instead, in March and April, the U.S. negotiator introduced several proposals, including an offer to have a third party investigate the alleged intrusions with a promise of apology, if one were warranted. The North Koreans quickly vetoed this. They were not about to let an impartial observer snoop behind the Juche Curtain. On May 8 the North Koreans handed a document to our negotiator at Panmunjom almost identical to the one he eventually signed. However, at that time the State Department considered the terms too preposterous to discuss.

In late September the North Koreans finally agreed that when a mutually acceptable document was signed, the crew would be repatriated.

There were three meetings in October, during which the "overwrite" suggestion was discussed.

The plan had obvious propaganda advantages for both sides. Washington could claim they never signed the document, they only wrote across it; Pyongyang could insist that the American government had capitulated.

North Korean interest in the plan was so apparent that the United States began making arrangements for our repatriation in October, sure it would be only a matter of

319

days. Then suddenly, with no real explanation except that the United States had been "insincere," the KORCOMs had broken off the talks. They had not resumed again until December.

"Did something happen in October which could have caused them to postpone your release?" he asked.

Remembering all too well, I nodded my head. But I didn't explain. This seemed neither the time nor the place. Switching to a safer and far more pleasant subject, I asked when our families would be notified of our release.

Chances were they already knew, he said. The moment I reached the South Korean side of the bridge, word had been flashed to the United States that all eighty-two men were free. The families had been notified a day earlier that there had been a breakthrough in the talks and that release appeared imminent.

The awareness that Carol now knew, and was waiting just as impatiently as I, helped erase the bitterness I first felt on discovering that Bucher's antics may have cost us over two months of freedom.

Only upon reaching the United Nations building, which served as advance camp, did the full realization hit me, and it came when I spotted the Christmas decorations. They were simple—a tree and a few ornaments and lights —but to us, long deprived of such sentiment, tremendously moving. More than a few had to brush the tears from their eyes as we were escorted into the mess hall and given our first American food in eleven months.

The cooks had prepared steak, hamburgers, chicken, mashed potatoes, and apple pie. But after the medics took one look at us, we got chicken-noodle soup, bologna sandwiches, and fresh milk. Even that seemed a feast, although, our stomachs having shrunk, we could eat only a little of what they gave us.

I guess we were a pretty sorry sight. I had lost 45 pounds, Bucher 40, Law 45, Woelk 55, Commissaryman Ralph Reed 68, and Engineman Joe Higgins a record 70.

Rear Admiral Edwin M. Rosenberg, representative of Pacific Fleet Commander, Admiral John J. Hyland, had been one of the men who greeted us at the end of the bridge. He had been assigned as Navy "chaperon" for the crew until it reached the United States. After I had finished eating, Rosenberg took me aside.

"There isn't any easy way to say this, Lieutenant Murphy. Are you aware that your mother passed away?"

I told him that I had suspected that this was true, asking when it happened. "Three days after your capture," he replied.

As exec, I still had responsibility for the crew. Had any other family members died during our imprisonment? Just one, the Admiral answered. The same week the parents of CT Angelo Strano learned that he had been captured, they had received word that another son, James, had been killed in Vietnam.

I told the Admiral that Strano had learned this while still imprisoned. He seemed relieved that he wouldn't have to tell him.

Angelo and his brother had been very close. Why the KORCOMs passed on this information, yet withheld other bad news, was a mystery. We suspected, however, that it gave them a sadistic pleasure to announce the death of an American soldier in Vietnam.

While still at the advance camp, many of the men learned that they had been promoted. Among the officers, Tim Harris had been upped to Lieutenant JG. Duane Hodges had been promoted posthumously to Third Class Petty Officer.

Our public-affairs liaison, Captain Vincent Thomas, had scheduled a press conference for Commander Bucher. After praising the conduct of the whole crew, and telling how glad everyone was to be free, Bucher said, "I know that some of the things that you're most interested in are the reasons for our capture and this sort of thing. Well, to begin with, I would like to set the record straight for what actually happened the day of the capture and during

321

the entire operation that we conducted in the Sea of Japan."

Bucher stressed that at no time had we intruded, and that he had done nothing contrary to his written and verbal orders. Then he came to the capture. And it was as if the long and frequent rehearsals had never happened.

"We—I—surrendered the ship because it was nothing but a slaughter out there, and I couldn't see allowing any more people to be slaughtered, or killing the entire crew for no reason.

"And I just couldn't, I couldn't fathom what was happening at the time, and to this day I'm not sure of everything that happened. . . ."

Question: "Could you tell us if you got rid of some or part of the secret equipment?"

Bucher: "We made an attempt to destroy everything. Well, there, truthfully we did not complete it."

Asked how he had been treated by the North Koreans, Bucher replied: "I was beaten less than anyone else. But I don't know, sir, that I was beaten all that much. I was mostly terrified of possible beating, and I was kept in solitary confinement during the entire eleven months. . . ."

That last statement would soon give me one big headache.

Bucher's extreme nervousness was apparent. He was in rough shape, both physically and emotionally, and the admiral, realizing this, allowed only a few more questions before bringing the press conference to a close.

The last question was: "Commander Bucher, one of the news conferences that was filmed by the North Koreans showed the crew with their fingers in a very unusual position, as if they were trying to tell us something."

Bucher: "They were trying to tell that we'd been had. They were trying to tell you that we'd been had. We continued that campaign throughout the time we were there whenever we had the opportunity to do so. We realized that if we were discovered it was going to be 'Katie bar the door,' but we felt that it was important that if we could in some

322

way get that information out so that there would be absolutely no room for doubt in your minds, the American people's minds, that we'd been had."

Bucher's pride in the accomplishment was obvious. It was as if Hell Week had never happened.

We were flown by helicopters to the 121st Army Evacuation Hospital near Seoul. We touched down on the helo pad to a brass band welcome.

We were assigned to a hospital ward. Hot showers and a change into American uniforms were the first order of business. Then someone managed to "liberate" some egg nog and the crew's release, Tim Harris' promotion, and the holiday season were all duly celebrated, even Executive Officer Murphy joining in the toasts, to Commander Bucher's amazement.

But that night, our first night of freedom, there was little boisterousness, not even much talk. Each of us was pretty much alone with his thoughts.

There was some question as to whether we would remain in the hospital just overnight or longer, until we were all in shape to travel. On learning this, each crewman minimized his medical complaints.

Early the next morning Admiral Rosenberg informed the press that we would leave the same day for the United States. Deeply moved by his contact with the men of the *Pueblo*, the admiral went on to say, "I have the utmost admiration for Captain Bucher and his crew. . . . As far as the U.S. government and the Navy are concerned, these men at all times acted in an extremely honorable fashion. . . ." Bucher was, he concluded, "a hero among heroes."

That same afternoon, following a memorial service for Petty Officer Duane Hodges, we were loaded onto two Air Force C-141's for the trip home. It was Tuesday, December 24, in Korea. But because we would gain a day crossing the international date line, we would still arrive in the United States in time to spend Christmas Eve with our families.

Bucher's strange remark, "How do you know we'll ever

323

return to Yokosuka?" had proven to be prophecy after all. The crew of the *Pueblo* wouldn't be returning to Japan. Except for a single refueling stop at Midway, we would be flying directly to the United States.

Once on the plane, I wanted to relax and dream about my reunion with Carol and the kids. Eddie had been just two when I last saw him. Would he even remember who I was? And Vicky—what would my first introduction to my nine-month-old daughter be like? How, in time to come, could I explain to those two children why their father had been absent for so long? Could I tell them the truth in a way that would plant the seeds of understanding rather than fear?

There were many such questions, the answers to most of which would have to wait. But the Navy had foreseen at least one. Most of the year 1968 had been stolen from us. What had happened in the rest of the world while we had ben imprisoned behind the Juche Curtain?

To provide at least some of the answers, the Navy had prepared a Public Affairs Kit for each member of the crew, containing a summary of 1968 world news, sports, and entertainment; a military round-up; and a sampling of press coverage of the "*Pueblo* incident."

From it we learned that Jackie Kennedy had married aging Greek shipping magnate Aristotle Onassis; London Bridge was to be torn down and transported to Arizona; former President Eisenhower was recuperating from his latest heart attack; the crew of Apollo was at this very moment orbiting the moon; Bobby Unser had won the 1968 Memorial Day 500 Race at Indianapolis driving a turbo-charged Offenhauser; Pope Paul VI had banned the pill; miniskirts were still popular, while "hairy-chested sailors in this man's Navy are now allowed to display their masculinity by throwing away their old regular elliptical-neck skivvie shirts and letting it all hang out"; and Congress had approved a bill giving the *Pueblo* crewmen sixty-five dollars a month hostile-fire pay for their period of captivity by the North Koreans.

Obviously, explaining some of the world events to eighty-two uninformed men presented problems to the writers of the press package. For example, the latest cultural phenomenon was described as follows:

> The newest pop hero to surface in America is a strange-looking man who looks like a woman. His name is Tiny Tim, and he is without a doubt the most bizarre entertainer this side of a Barnum and Bailey sideshow. Tiny Tim's specialty is pop songs from the early decades of this century. He sings in a high falsetto voice and accompanies himself on a ukulele. He is a success and he is getting rich.

Although Bucher was riding on a separate aircraft—he was in charge of one, I the other—one item captured his attention, for later he would comment on it. It was brief:

HALL OF HEROES

> President Johnson dedicated the nation's new Hall of Heroes at the Pentagon during May, in ceremonies during which the Medal of Honor was awarded to four servicemen—including a Navy PBR boat captain.
>
> The Hall contains exhibits of the medals and name-plates for each of the 3,210 men who have been awarded the Medal of Honor.

This, together with Admiral Rosenberg's spontaneous remarks about "a hero among heroes," would provide the genesis of Bucher's "heroes' lists." Despite published accounts to the contrary, the plural is used advisedly, for there would be not one but two lists, the second with some interesting revisions.

About fifty loose pages in the press package consisted of reprints of clippings about the *Pueblo,* from the time of its seizure in January to the events leading to our December release. I wanted to go through them but had to put this off until a later time, as there was work to do.

Although we were now without a ship—the USS *Pueblo* remaining behind as prized booty of the KORCOM pirates —we were still officially its crew. As exec it was my responsibility to brief my crewmates on what the procedure would be upon our arrival in the United States, acquaint them with their legal rights, and prepare them for the press. Three Navy captains, including Thomas, had been assigned to help me in this, and had started briefing me even before we left Seoul.

As second in command I was back in the all-too-familiar position of delivering tidings both good and bad.

The good. Our families would be awaiting us when we landed at Miramar Naval Air Station in San Diego. Through the generosity of the people of San Diego, hotel rooms would be provided for them at no cost.

The bad. Until such time as the medical examinations were completed we would have to stay in the Naval Hospital at Balboa.

The moaning and bitching, once this announcement was made, drowned out the noise of the engines.

However, I added, Christmas Eve and Christmas Day would be spent with families, in the hospital, and overnight passes would be issued once the medical exams had been concluded.

Regarding press interviews, Captain Thomas informed me that the Navy had no intention of "muzzling" the crew. They did insist, however, that no press interviews be given until after we had been debriefed by intelligence experts. Classified material would, of course, remain just that, and as such couldn't be discussed. No one would be required to talk to the press. If a man chose to do so, however, the interview would have to be arranged through the Command Information Bureau to coincide with Defense Department policy that information should be provided to the media on an equal basis.

It was easy to foresee one of the problems that was sure

to arise. The press would be avid for inside information on our experiences. Failing to get it from the crewmen themselves, they would immediately seek out the next best source, their families. For this reason, until after the intelligence debriefings, the crew would have to tell their relatives and friends as few details as possible.

For some, I suspected, the temptation to share their "war stories" would be quite irresistible. The inevitable result would be the publication of secondhand information, ripe with errors and distortions. But when I discussed this with Thomas, he could see no other workable procedure.

The situation in regard to our legal rights was much more complex. Basically we were protected by the Fifth Amendment. We did not have to say anything which might tend to incriminate us. However, it was essential that the intelligence debriefers be given any and all information which might help them in their twofold task: (1) determining exactly what classified information had been compromised; and (2) learning from the nature of the KORCOM questioning, and other observations we had made, the specific interests and background knowledge of the North Korean interrogators. In short, if the intelligence debriefings were to be effective, we would have to be free to tell everything.

To facilitate this, and at the same time to protect our own interests, Navy legal counsel had drawn up a guarantee, which would be signed by a representative of the United States government and given to each of us prior to our debriefings. It read:

> You are assured that the intelligence debriefing is an informal fact-finding venture and that all information obtained from you directly or indirectly during the debriefing process will be carefully safeguarded and held exclusively as privileged information and will not, in any way, directly or indirectly, be used against you in any judicial, nonjudicial, administrative, or any other disciplinary proceedings.
>
> You are also assured that no information received

during the intelligence debriefing will be used in any way by the Court of Inquiry, or the members connected therewith. You are also assured in this connection that the information will not be used against your best interests.

This stipulation or agreement is made to encourage you to freely divulge all the information you know concerning the *Pueblo* and all matters relating thereto.

What I couldn't foresee, in reading this to the crew, was that the guarantee was not quite as foolproof as it appeared. And that I was to be its first victim.

After I had finished briefing the crewmen on our plane, several approached me privately with a "problem."

What about the enlisted man who had gone overboard trying to please his captors? Did the Fifth Amendment protect *them* from having to testify against *him*?

It was interesting how attitudes had changed. While we were still in prison, some of the same men had seriously considered killing the man. Now that we were free, and he no longer represented a danger to the others, they had become almost protective. There were a couple of reasons for the switch. They knew what he had gone through, that "there but for the grace of God go I." Too, he was a *Pueblo* crewman. It was one thing to be judged by his own, something else to be judged by outsiders.

This attitude was to manifest itself in a variety of ways in the days ahead.

Although I was fairly sure I knew the answer, I consulted with the captain in charge of advising us on legal matters. No, the Fifth Amendment protected only the individual, he told me. I then suggested he talk to the man himself, and advise him of his rights.

He had no trouble getting him alone. He had been ostracized by the rest of the crew since our release. I didn't know what punishment lay ahead—if any did—but I did know that he was already paying a part of the price.

At Midway, Bucher and I switched planes, so I could brief the rest of the crew. During our brief stop on that lonely island, Bucher was again interviewed by the press. His nervousness had increased, and much of what he said was rambling and disconnected.

Admiral John H. Hyland, Commander in Chief of the Pacific Fleet, had met us on our arrival. The look on his face as Bucher was talking indicated he was not pleased with Bucher's speech.

A few of the questions were quite pointed, indicating that Admiral Rosenberg's remarks at Seoul had been personal rather than official. Rosenberg now qualified them somewhat, saying, "This is not the time and place to judge the crew. This is not the place to hold court. That will be done in a moderate way under better conditions at San Diego."

The shadow of the Court of Inquiry already loomed over us.

As the hours passed, the tension and excitement increased. It was already late afternoon of Tuesday, December 24.

Finally someone yelled, "Land to starboard!" We strained against the seat belts to look out.

The United States! I still couldn't believe it.

Minutes later we rolled down the landing strip at Miramar.

The other plane had landed first, and the crew was getting off. The crowd must have numbered in the thousands. Far too many to make out individual faces. But as our plane came to a stop, I tried.

"The Lonely Bull." The USS *Pueblo*'s theme song. I could hear it even before the plane's doors swung open.

As we deplaned, an Army band graciously played "Anchors Aweigh." Then, as we moved across the concrete strip toward the waiting crowd, the band switched to "The Navy Hymn." The all-too-familiar words came to mind, but now joyful, triumphant, an answered prayer:

> Eternal Father, strong to save,
> Whose hand doth bind the restless wave,

Oh hear us as we call to thee
For those in peril on the sea. . . .

I looked for Carol but couldn't find her. Then I spotted
her parents, Gay and Allen Danks. Eddie was with them.
And right next to them was a stroller, occupied by the
prettiest little girl I had ever seen.

They had brought the children with them in their family
car, Allen told me, so Carol could ride to the hospital with
me on the bus. Apparently in the confusion she was waiting
at the wrong place.

I grabbed up Eddie and held him. No, I wasn't a stranger,
for his smile was a miniature version of mine. Then Vicky's
and my eyes met, and locked. It was love at first sight.

And then I saw Carol, and she was in my arms, and all
we could say was, "I love you," over and over, but that was
all there was to say. That said it all. I was home.

27

Military and political dignitaries from all over the United States had flown into San Diego to welcome the crew of the *Pueblo*, but I found it difficult paying attention to anyone other than my family.

However, even here ship's business intruded. After the official welcomes had been extended, Vice Admiral Allen M. Shinn, Commander Naval Air Force Pacific Fleet and the man responsible for the crew from the time of our arrival to the end of the Court of Inquiry, sent word that he wanted to speak to me privately. Shinn told me that because of Commander Bucher's obviously distraught emotional state, the Navy had decided that he should have no further contact with the press or public. Until such time as his health was better, he was to be placed in isolation and I would be the crew's acting CO.

After the Dankses left with Vicky and Eddie, Carol and I got on one of the buses being used to transport the crew to Balboa Naval Hospital. It was a short ride, much too short to catch up on the happenings of almost a whole year, but we had to make do, aware that these few minutes might be the only time we would have for the next several days.

"Good news!" For Carol those two words, heard over the telephone shortly after midnight on Sunday, December 22, had meant the end of the long nightmare. The call had come from Lieutenant Bill Gnass, a casualty assistance calls officer assigned to the families of the *Pueblo* crew. As Carol sleepily tried to convince herself that this wasn't a dream, he gave her the details of the planned repatriation.

For Carol, I now learned, the nightmare had begun even before the capture of the *Pueblo.*

On the Saturday before the seizure of the ship, Carol took Mary Ellen Lacy, Gene's wife, on a tour of our house at Ishi Hyama. Discovering there was no hot water, and suspecting the pilot light had gone out, she decided to try to relight it, and struck a match. The explosion knocked both women into the next room.

Looking at Mary Ellen, Carol exclaimed, "Your hair is singed!" "Thank heavens you can *see!*" was Mary Ellen's reply. Carol's face, hands, and arms were covered with painful second- and third-degree burns.

"Should I have the Navy notify Ed?" Carol asked Judy Fryburger, wife of a senior officer and a good friend. Stating it would only cause me to worry, Judy said, "We Navy wives can make do." As evidence of this, Mary Ellen insisted that Carol and Eddie move in with her while Carol was recuperating.

About six A.M. on Wednesday, January 24, 1968, the telephone rang in the Lacy home. Mary Ellen didn't hear it, so Carol went downstairs to answer. The caller was another of the *Pueblo* wives, but so hysterical that all Carol could understand was that something had happened to the *Pueblo* and the news was on the radio. Waking Mary Ellen, she turned to the Armed Forces station to hear the broadcaster say the USS *Pueblo* had been boarded and captured by the North Koreans.

Mary Ellen's immediate reaction had been: *"Oh, God, what has Pete done now?"*

The news had been on since midnight, but permission to notify the families did not arrive from Washington until the next morning. Even then, official notification did not come until that afternoon, via a mimeographed form letter, much of which was devoted to telling the families of the crew what they could and could not say to the press. Long before this, however, Carol, as senior wife to the eleven dependent families in Japan, had arranged for the wives to be briefed by naval officials. The Navy had first suggested that she serve as intermediary, as Rose Bucher was doing in the United States, but she was sure the women would want the news straight, not secondhand.

The Navy would make no predictions as to when the men might be released. However, Commander Clark, skipper of the *Banner,* assured the wives that they would be free in a few days; or a couple of weeks at most. What were they to do in the interim? the wives asked. Should they remain in Japan? They would have to, the briefing officer replied. Due to Navy regulations, travel expenses couldn't be authorized until after the men had been prisoners for thirty days.

At this time there was little information available on the capture itself, and no definite word on the fate of the crew, beyond the North Korean claim that they were prisoners.

On Thursday morning, January 25, less than forty-eight hours after the *Pueblo*'s capture, Tokyo radio picked up a news broadcast from the Korean Central News Agency (KCNA) that quoted Commander Bucher's alleged confession that the *Pueblo* was a spy ship and that she had been seized while intruding deep into North Korea's territorial waters. A tape of this confession, this time reputedly in Bucher's own voice, was played later the same day and monitored in Japan.

For many of the wives this was the first indication that the *Pueblo* was an intelligence ship.

The following day the KORCOMs announced that one *Pueblo* crewman had been killed and several others seriously injured while resisting capture. Cruelly, no names were supplied. There was little Carol could do to ease the tension, except to try to share her own inner strength. "At this point we just have to pray," she told the other wives. "We have to know that there is a God and that he is watching over our men as well as us."

I couldn't help marveling at her faith. The North Koreans had just released their first picture of the captured officers, the one from which I was missing because I was helping to carry the wounded Woelk off the train.

Thinking that it might help if the wives could talk to their families in the United States, the Navy let them call home. It was in a call to her own parents, made that Sunday, that Carol learned my mother had died three days after the capture of the ship.

My sisters had kept the news from Mom. But there had been a television set in her room, and it was possible that she had heard it this way. No one would ever know.

Carol arranged to fly home to attend the funeral. While in the United States she talked to Rose Bucher and various Navy officials, but actual news was scarce. It was not until February 7 that the dead crewman was identified as Duane Hodges.

The "few days" the Navy felt we would be held by the North Koreans became several weeks. And the crew remained no closer to freedom than at the time of their capture.

The State Department now decided that when the crew was released they would be flown directly to the United States, bypassing Japan entirely, so as not to embarrass the Japanese government by their presence there. The families would return Stateside after all. Carol was eight months pregnant. If she waited until after the baby was born, she would have to remain in Japan six more weeks before she would be permitted to travel. Foreseeing the possibility that I might be released and returned to the United States, while she remained stranded in Japan, she flew back with Eddie on February 17.

She told me also of the months that followed: the waiting, the false hopes, the temptation to despair. During my absence, she had compiled a dozen scrapbooks of press mentions of the *Pueblo*. She had written a long chronology of personal and family events that had happened while we were apart. She had made tape recordings, so I wouldn't miss Vicky's first sounds and Eddie's expanding vocabulary.

Yet even with all this, I knew that in a very real sense we would never be able to bridge entirely the gap created by those eleven lost months. After our initial isolation by the North Koreans, we could see our fellow crewmen daily, and knew they were all right. The families had no such reassurances. Every statement made by the North Koreans was suspect. Even when letters finally did arrive, they were months old, and weren't even proof that we were still alive.

Faith was all they had. And the help of others who cared too. From Carol I now learned how great the debt of gratitude was that I owed: to military and government personnel who put their careers on the line to pass on classified information about the status of the negotiations; to Marcee Rethwish, an El Cajon teen-ager who, saving the money she had earned baby-sitting, conducted a mammoth prayer vigil in San Diego on the one hundredth day of our imprisonment; to the San Diego *Union,* which ran in a box on its front page a daily reminder of the number of days the *Pueblo*'s crew had been held captive. There was no way I could repay any of these people. The woman who helped Carol pack. The lieutenant commander who rushed Eddie and Carol to the plane, via the almost incomprehensibly confusing Japanese railway system. The soldiers who entertained Eddie on the plane trip back, while his mother worried about giving birth amidst a planeload of servicemen. People seen once, never again, yet always remembered.

From her I learned also of the "Remember the Pueblo" groups, a few of whose leaders had used the families and our plight to further their own political, personal, or monetary goals, but the vast majority of whose members were simply people who cared, cared enough to take the time to write a letter to the President or to put a bumper strip on their car.

Talking to a reporter shortly after our return, Carol said, "I feel when this is all over, when we can finally relax, I'll find somebody I've never met before."

Carol had changed too. While our common ordeal could just as easily have embittered her, she had matured. As had our love.

To house the *Pueblo* crew the Navy had especially renovated a four-story medical corpsman building known as the "Pink Palace." Bucher and I shared a suite, while all the other crewmen, both officers and enlisted, had double rooms, fitted with such luxuries as carpeting, writing desks, and *long* beds. The adjacent RX Club, previously used for the hospital staff, had been turned over to the crew for its exclusive use, as a place where we could visit families, watch TV, or snack—sandwiches, milk, coffee, and soft drinks being available.

As if this weren't dreamlike enough, there was the attitude of the people with whom we came in contact. Entering the RX Club, I noticed the bemused look on a young sailor's face, He explained, "An *admiral* just fetched me a cup of coffee!"

I had little time to inspect our new surroundings. Shortly after our arrival at Balboa, Admiral Rosenberg informed me that he had scheduled a press briefing.

Some two hundred reporters, from newspapers, wire services, radio, and television, were impatiently waiting in the hospital auditorium when I walked in. Rosenberg took the microphone to explain that since Commander Bucher was ill, the *Pueblo*'s executive officer would fill in for him until further notice. Rosenberg also placed very strict limitations on what could or could not be discussed. If a question in any way touched on security, I wouldn't be permitted to answer it. Also, until after the intelligence debriefings were concluded, several days from now, I would not be allowed to discuss either the capture itself or the activities of the crew while in detention. Although Rosenberg did relent slightly on the last point, allowing me to run through our daily schedule while imprisoned, the "muzzling" angered the reporters.

I couldn't blame them. They wanted meat, and all I was

336

able to give them was, literally, watery soup—the food we had been given was one of the few things I could discuss.

As the questions grew sharper, I finally stopped and said, "Look, fellows, we're on the same side!" After that, the tension eased.

Even with the restrictions, I couldn't help contrasting this with the rehearsed KORCOM "press conferences," where even the questions came from a prepared script.

Had we intruded? No, never, at no point, at no time. Had we been brainwashed? Not in the ordinary sense; if anything, it was brainwashing in reverse, our talk about life in America obviously coming as a revelation to the KORCOM guards. Who was in charge of the crew if Bucher remained in "solitary" for the entire eleven months?

This was the first indication I'd had that Bucher's statement, made both at the advance camp and at Midway, had been misinterpreted. I explained that what the skipper really meant was that the officers had individual rooms. There were many occasions when the whole crew was brought together, although, of course, not as often as we would have liked.

Despite the limitations on what I could say, I felt that the press briefing went well, as did Captain Thomas and Admiral Rosenberg.

Bucher felt otherwise. Cornering me later, he yelled, "How dare you contradict me about my being in solitary confinement!"

Only then did I realize that he had intended to have the reporters make the conclusion they had. This struck me as incredible, since there were eighty-one others who, if queried, knew full well that Bucher hadn't spent the entire eleven months in isolation.

Now I could see why the Navy didn't want Bucher to meet the press.

Christmas Eve, Mrs. Roxie McDonald, a seamstress from the hospital, worked all night altering dress uniforms so the crew could wear them the next day. The personnel who

337

ran the hospital exchange gave up Christmas morning with their families so we could shop for presents for ours.

The people of San Diego had inundated the children of the crew with toys and Carol and I had already decided to exchange presents later. My first purchase was a new watchband for CT James Shephard, to replace the one I'd worn out while in captivity. Shephard's loan of his watch, when the batteries in mine had run out, had helped me preserve my sanity. The watch was not only a companion, it was a link with the outside world. I now learned that while I was figuring out what time it was in San Diego, and trying to imagine what Carol and the kids were doing, she had been doing the same thing in reverse.

As we walked up and down the aisles of the exchange, marveling at the variety of merchandise on display, I tried to visualize what would happen if Deputy Dawg, Wheezy, Clean Floors, Fly, Robot, and the sad little guard whose greatest possession was a little button, were to have the same experience. Their political officer would have one hell of a time explaining this away.

He'd probably give up when it came to the food.

At noon the crew, their families, and guests were served turkey with all the trimmings. That evening we had steak and hamburgers, in one meal receiving as much meat as we had during most of our time in North Korea.

I couldn't believe how flavorsome the foods were, even a plain piece of bread.

The two meals were just about the only time I had with Carol and the kids. "The *Pueblo* is still listed on the books as a commissioned U.S. naval ship and will remain so," announced a Navy spokesman. Although we were the crew of a ghost ship, the ship's organization remained in force, and there was still ship's business to be transacted.

With the exception of Abelon and Aluague, who didn't want their families to make the long trip from the Philippines, each of the crewmen had been met by some member or members of his family. Since many could stay in San Diego only a few days, medical exams, uniform fittings, debriefing sessions, etc., had to be coordinated to give each man as much time as possible with his relatives.

Each had individual problems—ranging from pressing bills to finding a hotel room for an unexpected uncle and aunt. Some wanted permission to marry. Quartermaster Law, who had entertained us during a KORCOM press conference with his earnest desire to "make marriage," decided to do just that. This good news almost, but not quite, balanced the bad tidings. Initial examinations by Navy doctors indicated Law's vision problems were uncorrectable.

For many the return home meant the end of agonizing fears. The officer who hadn't heard from his wife during most of our imprisonment now learned why. Someone, apparently well-meaning but misinformed, had advised her against writing, claiming the North Koreans would use the letters for propaganda. Not until the other wives learned of the situation from my letter were they able to set her straight, and by that time it was too late for more than a few letters to reach him. As it was, Carol told me, letter writing was always difficult for the wives. In addition to their fear of worrying the men, there was also the possibility that the most innocent remark might be misinterpreted by the Communists, resulting in punishment for the crewman.

Other problems were not so easily resolved or explained. Two of the men returned home to find their wives pregnant. One of these marriages would eventually end in divorce, as would several others.

For most, however, the most pressing concern was getting overnight liberty. Many of the excuses offered were of Academy Award caliber. Unfortunately, the admiral in charge of the hospital had forbidden any passes until the medical exams were completed. I did succeed, however, in arranging for half the crew to be granted liberty New Year's Eve, the other half New Year's night.

The enlistments of more than twenty of the crewmen had expired while we were in detention. Perhaps understandably, considering what they had gone through, only a small number wanted to reenlist. For them there was less than happy news: the Navy decided to extend their enlistments until after the completion of the Court of Inquiry.

Each day the shadow of the forthcoming proceedings loomed larger. In an attempt to lessen apprehension, Captain Gale Krouse, Judge Advocate for Commander Naval Air, Pacific Fleet, conducted a special briefing on the crew's legal rights.

Krouse stressed that legal assistance was available to anyone who requested it. Military counsel would be available without charge; civilian counsel would also be permitted, but at the individual's own expense. Commander Bucher, on his return, had found that his wife, Rose, had already employed a well-known civilian attorney, E. Miles Harvey, to represent both herself and him. As well as being a member of a prestigious San Diego firm, Harvey had served in Naval Intelligence, so he was already a member of the "club." In addition, Bucher also obtained a military counsel, Captain James Keys.

Tim Harris and Skip Schumacher were using the same attorney. Steve Harris was inclined to do the same, or dispense with legal counsel entirely. Recalling Bucher's vow to "get" Steve, I strongly advised him to employ his own attorney, which he eventually did.

Like many another man, when it came to advice, I was quite free to give it but in no hurry to take it. Thus far I still lacked an attorney myself.

A second press briefing was held the day after Christmas. Again I filled in for Bucher, who Captain Thomas explained was "in a complete state of nervous exhaustion." Thomas also announced that ten crewmen would receive Purple Hearts for wounds sustained at the time of capture, and named those of us who would receive them, including Petty Officer Duane Hodges, whose award would be made posthumously.

The major part of the briefing, however, was a rebuttal of the North Korean intrusion charges. The reporters, hun-

340

gry for "meat," got it now. For the first time, with the aid of enlargements of the fraudulent KORCOM navigational records and charts, and with the quite able assistance of Captain Thomas, I was able to conclusively disprove the false accusations.

One by one we noted the inconsistencies, discrepancies, and contradictions in the North Korean evidence, including the three times the statistics placed the *Pueblo* aground, and fourteen instances of the ship traveling faster than its 12.2-knot top speed (these ranging from 17.3 to 2,500 knots).

For the American press this was the first positive proof of the falsity of the intrusion charges, as well as the first indication that, through the errors and other tricks, we had managed to get word back to the U.S. government that the charges were without foundation.

The presentation was so damning to North Korean claims that several weeks later Quartermaster Law and I were flown back to Washington, D.C., to help make a special motion picture of the evidence, which was subsequently shown around the world to counteract the North Korean propaganda.

Although at no point did I take credit for getting the message through, purposely underplaying my role in this, Bucher was again unhappy, telling one of the other officers he was damn sick and tired of Murphy trying to hog the spotlight.

Rest, lots of vitamins, and plenty of nourishing food were our prescription.

But Bucher had other needs. Ignoring the Navy's quarantine, one night at midnight he summoned all of the *Pueblo*'s officers to his room and kept us there until three A.M., going over a "heroes' list" he had compiled.

Both Admiral Rosenberg and Admiral Hyland had publicly referred to the crew of the USS *Pueblo* as "heroes." Their remarks had drawn fire from some quarters. Senator Richard B. Russell, chairman of the Senate Armed Services committee, had vowed to investigate the seizure. "These

341

men are being hailed as heroes," Russell observed. "They are heroes in the sense that they survived the imprisonment. But they did sign a great many statements that did not reflect any great heroism in my mind. I'll have to investigate further to see just what hero-type things they performed."

Both Rosenberg and Hyland had later qualified their statements, probably because, though their observations were heartfelt and personal, they sounded official, and appeared to be usurping the function of the forthcoming court.

The majority of the crew felt no medals were warranted. A questionnaire was distributed to all eighty-two crewmen, asking if they felt medals should be given, and if so, who they felt most deserving of them. Well over half voted against any awards, their reasons ranging from "No one did any more than was expected of him" to "To single out a few would slight the others." Of the twenty-five or so who did feel individuals deserved special recognition, most named Quartermaster Law.

But Bucher wanted a heroes' list, and right now. Admiral Rosenberg would be returning to Hawaii shortly, and he wanted him to carry the list back to Admiral Hyland, so action could be started immediately.

There was no question that some members of the crew had performed bravely, while under fire and/or during detention. There was also the possibility that Bucher had a secondary motive for wanting the crew commended. If the men were awarded medals, it would help shape public opinion and put pressure on the forthcoming Court of Inquiry. Also a third motive occurred to me. The heroes' list, in common with the fitness and evaluation reports which Commander Bucher still had to write for each of the crewmen, could help assure that his "one consistent account" was accepted.

However legitimate its initial purpose, the heroes' list was also bait. Lacy, who in the pretrial rehearsals in North Korea had been cast in the villain's role, the man who

Bucher claimed had actually surrendered the ship, was, on this original list prepared by the captain, commended for both the Bronze Star and the Navy Marine Corps Medal for Heroism; while Steve Harris and I, neither of whom ranked very high in Bucher's esteem, one allegedly bearing full responsibility for the capture of the classified documents, the other reputedly a coward under fire and a betrayer under the threat of torture, were also both listed for the Navy and Marine Corps Medal.

It was as if Bucher was saying: If you'll go along with me, I'll let bygones be bygones.

That Bucher did not actually say the words did not make the implications any less obvious.

This, however, was not my major concern.

Bucher had recommended a total of forty-six men be given awards. Of these, twelve had been picked to get the Silver Star. When it comes to awards, the U.S. Navy holds far stricter to the requirements than any other branch of the service. The Silver Star is given for one reason, and one only: "gallantry in action." With only two or three exceptions, the dozen men Bucher named did not meet this definition. All had done their jobs, and well, but that was it. Ordinarily this would have caused no problem, since the recommendations would simply have been rejected at the next level of command. However, at a very emotional meeting at Miramar, Bucher had assured the parents of Duane Hodges that their son would receive the award posthumously. And there was no way he could make good his promise. In the weeks ahead, I went up and down the chain of command, using every argument I could muster, even literally begging for the award. The answer was invariably the same: while Hodges had been killed while carrying out his duty, and for this reason qualified for other awards, including the Purple Heart, his actions did not fit the Navy's rigid requirements for the Silver Star; as a CO Bucher should have known this; he had no business making a promise he knew he couldn't keep.

Bucher refused to face up to the problem he had created.

He could have explained the situation to the Hodgeses. Coming from their son's skipper, they would have understood. Instead, he took his usual way out.

Acting on Bucher's assurances, the Hodgeses had ordered a replica of the medal embossed on their son's tombstone. This had to remain covered until after the award was made. When, understandably concerned, they called and wrote, asking when the ceremony would take place—Bucher had also promised them that he would fly to Cresswell, Oregon, to personally make the presentation—Bucher's comment to me was an exasperated, "Get those goddamn people off my back!"

If anything, Bucher had understated the case when he said we would be deluged with book, magazine, and motion-picture offers on our return. The letters, telegrams, and long-distance calls came not only to Balboa, but also inundated our families, the schools we had attended, even friends.

Bucher placed Skip in charge of the arrangements for the crew's book. At Bucher's suggestion, Schumacher consulted with an attorney in E. Miles Harvey's office, who helped him draft a Joint Venture Agreement covering the book project. Each member of the crew was to sign it. In the interim, while the agreement was being drawn up, Schumacher brought the crew together for several talk sessions, which were recorded as background material for whoever wrote the book.

This was Skip's "baby"; he had nursed it from its original conception, and I admittedly paid little attention to it. At the time, I was far more interested in some of the other messages received. Both President Johnson and President-elect Nixon wired their congratulations on our safe return, as did governors, senators, congressmen, and the crew of Apollo 8 on their landing after orbiting the moon. And there were memories from the past: the three fishermen Lee Elliott and I had rescued from the crab boat sent their warmest Christmas wishes, as did the couple whose little runabout, the *Kittyhawk,* the *Pueblo* had towed back to Puget Sound. Classmates I hadn't heard from in years wrote or called. Many, I now learned, had done so throughout our captivity, offering Carol any assistance they could.

The intelligence debriefings were thorough. Four to six interrogators took turns questioning each crewman. As soon as one had finished, another came in and approached the subject from a different direction. The last man to interview me was a captain who asked: "Can you think of any other classified material that might *conceivably* have been compromised during detention? We want to know anything and everything that will enable us to determine the extent of compromise."

I recalled a number of small things, clues to KORCOM knowledge of which had been indicated in the questions they asked. I mentioned these. Then I remembered the ultrasecret story Bucher had told us in the recreation room in the Country Club. Prefacing my remarks with the statement that I wasn't sure the information had been compromised, because we weren't sure whether the room was or was not bugged, I related the story.

He jerked back in his chair. "How in hell did you ever hear about that?"

I told him.

"Pete must have been out of his mind to mention that!" was his shocked comment.

The use of Bucher's nickname should have alerted me, but I didn't think of that until later.

Though Bucher was still isolated from the crew, only his wife, attorneys, and doctors being allowed access to him on a regular basis, the whole crew still had mess together. The next morning as I sat down to breakfast with the other officers, Bucher jumped up, screaming, *"You've been trying to fry my ass ever since we got back, Murphy! You're trying to get my command!"*

The crew listened in amazement to the long angry diatribe that followed, thoroughly mystified as to what had

345

prompted it. But I was able to piece together a picture of what had happened. At the conclusion of my debriefing, the captain, who had served with Bucher in submarines, had called him, asking "Just what happened to you over there that you talked so damn much, Pete?"

I was just as angry as Bucher, though for different reasons. We had been assured, both verbally and in writing, that the intelligence debriefings would be privileged. And already that promise had been broken. I went to Captain Krouse, telling him what had happened. Stunned, he took me directly to Admiral Shinn. I told the admiral that if we couldn't speak freely, I refused to continue with the debriefings; moreover, I couldn't encourage the rest of the crew to participate. Admiral Shinn was equally disturbed. He kept saying, "We set this up so carefully, with every possible safeguard. How could something like this happen?"

The admiral ordered an immediate investigation. It developed that the captain was not a regular debriefer. He had been asked to sit in, for any assistance he might be able to give, and had not been made aware of the privileged nature of the questioning.

That afternoon Miles Harvey got me aside and apologized for his client. I had done the right thing in bringing up the incident, he told me. Bucher had been in the wrong talking about such matters. He could only explain his blowup at breakfast as due to his nervous condition. Bucher was a sick man, and he hoped I understood that. I assured him I did.

The following evening Bucher called me to his quarters. He asked me how the crew was doing, and I discussed the arrangements for the New Year's passes.

Bucher then personally apologized for his outburst. Though he said the words, I was sure his attorney had prompted them. Bucher went on to tell me that he had intended to tell the debriefers about the incident himself. What had made him angry was not that I had told them but that the captain had heard it. The captain had a lot of influence. He could keep him from getting a sub-marine command.

Throwing his arm around me and grasping one of my hands and holding it tightly, he said, the words this time unquestionably not Harvey's but Bucher's very own, "Ed, they're out to get us, all of us. The whole Navy, all the military, and all the politicians are trying to hang us. The only chance we have is if we stick together, back up each other's stories. You let me down when you contradicted me about being in solitary. And now this.

"Don't you understand," he added, his voice now almost a whisper, "that there's a conspiracy to scuttle us?"

Belatedly, I asked Captain Krouse if he could recommend a good attorney. Still very disturbed about the breaching of the debriefing agreement, Krouse recommended a close friend, a Captain Richard Stacer, "one of the best defense attorneys in the Eleventh Naval District."

Captain Krouse brought Captain Stacer to my room, then, having introduced us, left us alone to talk. I liked Stacer immediately. He was serious, yet had a quiet sense of humor that would prove one of our most valuable assets in the weeks ahead. If he had preconceptions about the *Pueblo* incident, he didn't voice them, not during this first meeting. He simply listened, nodded from time to time, made notes, and asked few but always meaningful questions.

I was hampered somewhat by the fact that, unlike Harvey, Stacer had not yet been cleared to hear the intelligence material. That would have to wait until his "ticket" came through. But I was able to tell him the basic story, noting my differences with Bucher, both before and after the capture, and giving him at least a partial picture of what it had been like to serve aboard the USS *Pueblo*.

I talked for nearly three hours.

When I finally finished, Stacer leaned back in his chair, whistled softly, and with a look of pure amazement asked, "What kind of a crowd did you have on that ship?"

347

28

"Avoid Bucher. Both inside and outside the Court of Inquiry, stay clear of him."

This was Captain Stacer's advice, offered after he had spent days interrogating me extensively on every point in my account.

The saga of the USS *Pueblo* both amazed and appalled Stacer. But it didn't blind him to the dangers inherent in the current situation. All this should be made public, he told me, if only to help make sure that similar situations did not occur in the future. But the Court of Inquiry was neither the time nor the place.

Patiently Stacer explained the composition and function of the court to me, in the process demolishing more than a few of my innocent presumptions.

The court would be composed of five admirals. They would decide which questions to ask, what topics were germane to the proceedings. Their interests would be specific, selective, perhaps even narrow. They would not be interested in airing the dirty linen of the USS *Pueblo*, the wardroom squabbles, the personal differences between her officers. Nor would they want to hear a junior officer criticizing his superior, no matter how relevant he personally might feel his testimony to be. If there was criticism, they would make it. When it came my turn to take the stand, I was to answer truthfully and concisely. I was not to volunteer information. Nor, unless specifically asked to do so, was I to say what I "thought." They would want the facts

348

and the facts alone; drawing conclusions would be their job.

Thus, from the start, by the very nature of the proceedings, the *Pueblo* probe would be limited in scope.

Earlier Captain Stacer had told the press that the primary purpose of the Court of Inquiry would be to establish the truth or falsity of the intrusion charges. It was Captain Stacer's guess that my second press conference had disposed of the intrusion issue, to the satisfaction of almost everyone concerned. The major interest of the court, Stacer believed, would be whether Commander Bucher had a viable alternative to surrendering his ship. This, as far as Stacer could tell, was the paramount concern. Bucher was the first American naval commander to surrender his ship in peacetime since the USS *Chesapeake* had been boarded by the crew of the HMS *Leopold,* off Cape Henry, Virginia, in 1807. Had Bucher any other choice?

The second biggest question would undoubtedly be: Was negligence a factor in the loss of the classified documents? If so, who was to blame?

Other topics would be discussed, Stacer was sure, including the Code of Conduct and the behavior of the crew while in detention, but the first two questions would be the big ones. They were the questions that were also being asked in every ship's wardroom, every officers' club, every Navy bar in the country and outside.

And from the testimony the court would have to produce answers.

It would be the court's job to sift the facts, decide whether any military codes or regulations had been broken, and, if warranted, make appropriate recommendations to Commander in Chief, U.S. Pacific Fleet, for criminal or administrative action.

The court could recommend medals. It could also recommend courts-martial.

The court itself had no punitive powers. It was officially only a fact-finding commission. Yet I shouldn't let this definition fool me, Captain Stacer said. The court's findings, whether honored by the convening authority or not, could "make" or "break" naval careers.

Commander Lloyd M. "Pete" Bucher's career was on the line. With his affinity for producing scapegoats, his habit of passing any and all blame, it was especially important that I avoid conflicts with him. Stacer was sure that the attorneys for the other *Pueblo* officers were similarly advising their clients, because he had talked to most of them.

"I can't praise Bucher," I told Stacer. "Nor can I get up there and lie for him."

"That's the last thing in the world I'd want you to do. Tell the truth. Answer their questions forthrightly and with candor. But don't go out of your way to pick a fight."

"And if he starts it first?"

"We'll deal with that when it happens. It may not. Harvey knows you can scuttle Bucher. He'll be doing everything in his power to keep him in check. His apology for Bucher's outburst is proof of that. He—and the court, and every one of the attorneys—want to keep this thing low-key, to avoid making waves. You've never seen a Court of Inquiry get out of hand. I have. The innocent can get cut up just as badly as the guilty.

"Thus far Bucher is the only person who has been named 'party' to the proceedings," Stacer added. "We want to keep it that way."

"Maybe it's naïve," I replied, "but I guess I anticipated the whole truth coming out."

"That may have to wait for your memoirs," Stacer said.

There were still other factors at work that mitigated against the full story coming out during the Court of Inquiry.

One was the fitness reports.

Miles Harvey informed Captain Stacer that Bucher was considering giving me an unfavorable fitness report.

The news came as no surprise. Bucher had told me in North Korea that he intended to give me an unfavorable

350

report. At the time, I had replied, "If that's the case, then I suppose I'll have to live with it." That wasn't, I felt sure, the answer he wanted, for he brought up the subject several more times toward the end of our detention.

A derogatory fitness report was by no means fatal, Bucher assured me. Any good officer worth his salt had one or two. "And you know, Ed," Bucher had added, "there are *degrees* to even a bad report."

The implication was clear. I chose not to recognize it, at least not at that time. I asked Bucher his basis for a negative report. This was during the period when the skipper was holding his mock court and busily hunting scapegoats. At one time or another he had accused me—and Steve Harris and Gene Lacy—of about every crime in the book.

My cowardice on January 23 was an established fact, he replied. And there was no way I could deny that, he added.

I not only could deny it, but did, and would continue to do so. I told Bucher that if he accused me of that, I'd rebut the charge with affidavits from every man who had been in the pilothouse that day.

This wasn't his only charge, Bucher went on, as if he hadn't heard my reply. From the moment I'd reported aboard the *Pueblo,* my performance as executive officer had been unsatisfactory.

I could rebut that also, I told him, but didn't tell him how. Apparently Bucher had forgotten that he had already written one fitness report on me, after my first two months aboard ship. Although covering a brief period, it was an important one insofar as the preparation of the *Pueblo* for her mission was concerned. In this report, which covered the period ending June 30, 1967, Bucher had called me "a very fine officer, of great value to the service" and recommended, as a possible future assignment, "CO of a small auxiliary" such as the *Pueblo.* Bucher had further found that "Lt. Murphy, although recently reported aboard the *Pueblo,* has demonstrated a solid background fitting him nicely for his assignment. Lt. Murphy is cheerful and enthusiastic. He quickly assesses problem areas and devotes

351

his talents toward proper solution. Lt. Murphy has further shown himself to possess keen tact when dealing with sensitive situations. The myriad of administrative details associated with commissioning a ship have been handled effectively and thoroughly by Lt. Murphy. He is recommended for promotion when due."

Although this earlier report would help counterbalance any later charges Bucher might make, I didn't count too heavily on it. Bucher could always say that when the chips were down, when confronted with a crisis situation, I had buckled.

Too, although Bucher was correct in saying that almost every officer is given a bad fitness report at some time or another—if you stay in the service long enough, there are bound to be personality clashes—it's equally true that a bad report can haunt a man all the way through his service career. It not only can keep him from receiving promotions, it also can affect his future assignments.

I decided then, while we were still in North Korea, that if and when we returned, and Bucher did carry through on his threat, I would use every legal avenue available to me to fight it.

I told Stacer about all this when he informed me of Harvey's remark.

Maybe we wouldn't have to go to all that trouble, Stacer observed. He was sure there were Navy regulations covering such situations. After some checking, he found what he was looking for in *BUPER's Directive*.

A commanding officer is required to issue periodic fitness reports on every officer, and evaluation reports on every enlisted man, under his immediate command. This is a duty; it is also a power, and the Navy recognizes it as such. It is conceivable that a situation might arise where a commanding officer, charged with a military offense, might use this power to blackmail his subordinates into giving false testimony. To forestall this possibility, Navy Regulations provided that if a CO is under suspicion of having violated a Navy article, his power of writing such reports can be suspended. The reports are then written by the officer immediately senior to him in the chain of command.

Bucher had already been named a party to the Court of Inquiry. There was also good reason to believe that during his testimony he would be informed that he was suspected of having violated Article 0730 of *Navy Regulations*, the article that prohibits allowing a foreign power to board or seize a ship and/or its crew.

This being the case, Stacer felt we had sufficient grounds to ask Admiral Shinn to suspend Bucher's power to write fitness reports on the officers and evaluation reports on the enlisted crewmen of the *Pueblo*.

Stacer and I took the request to Captain Krouse and Commander Ray Crater, the latter legal aide to Admiral Shinn. Commander Crater appeared quite sympathetic to our request, and indicated the problem would be taken under advisement.

However, for reason or reasons unknown to us, Admiral Shinn decided to allow the reports to be submitted. During the entire time of the Court of Inquiry, Commander Bucher retained the power to write fitness or evaluation reports on each and every member of the crew.

(There was only one partial exception. Because Steve Harris was a "detachment" rather than a "department" head, his primary fitness report would be written by his actual commanding officer, Captain Everett Gladding, in Hawaii, and not by Bucher, a circumstance which couldn't help but gall him.)

While we could only guess at why Admiral Shinn did not carry through on our request, the most obvious possibility was that Shinn, or someone above him in the chain of command, had felt that if Bucher's authority in this area was lifted, and the public learned of it, it would appear that the verdict of the Court of Inquiry was foreordained, that Bucher had already been judged and found guilty. This remains only a guess, for no explanation was ever given us.

If the heroes' list was bait, the power of writing fitness

353

and evaluation reports was a club, one which was to hang over every member of the crew during the entire time of the Court of Inquiry.

There was still another force at work, and, in its own way, it was even more effective than those already mentioned.

The spirit of Christmas had not lasted much beyond the holiday season. By early January the emotional reunion of the crewmen with their families was past history. Now the press was beginning to ask some hard questions.

"What were the considerations which caused the *Pueblo* to be sent upon its mission?" James L. Kilpatrick asked in the January 2 issue of the Los Angeles *Times.* "Why was no air cover kept available? Why were no supporting vessels stationed within convenient reach? . . .

"We are entitled to ask—especially in light of the attack on the *Liberty*—why procedures were not perfected for destruction of vital encoding machines in moments of manifest peril? In the case of the *Pueblo,* nearly three hours elapsed between the North Korean interception and the actual seizure. What precisely did Bucher do in those three hours? It seems a long time. What messages did he send? What orders did he receive? Whose decision was it to delay destruction of the machines and other secret devices?"

Kilpatrick concluded: "It seems a far cry, somehow, from Stephen Decatur and John Paul Jones."

Time, in its January 16 issue, wondered why "Bucher was given as his first command so highly sensitive an assignment?" Though the article was generally favorable to the skipper (placing most of the blame on "higher-echelon complacency and shortsightedness"), it did speak of Bucher's "slow realization that the North Koreans meant business."

An "old Navy hand" was quoted in a later issue of the same magazine as saying of Bucher, "This guy is going to finish his career counting blankets in the Aleutians."

354

Denied access to the crew itself, the reporters began digging elsewhere. Some went right to paydirt.

George Ashworth, correspondent for the *Christian Science Monitor:* "Defense intelligence sources generally familiar with rules governing such ships as the *Pueblo* say privately that they were very much surprised when the crew and ship were taken. Normally, these sources say, the ship would have been expected to move away from the scene of confrontation, if at all possible. And every possible effort should have been made to avoid boarding."

Yet even such indirect criticism of Bucher was rare. When censure occurred, it was generally along the lines of damning Bucher for breaking tradition, and, without firing a shot, giving up his ship.

Yet except for such isolated comments, plus a couple of wild charges from organs of the radical right, who saw the *Pueblo*'s CO as a betrayer of his country, there was surprisingly little open condemnation of Commander Bucher's actions. Combined with nervousness over the result of the forthcoming proceedings, it was enough, however, to add a vague substance to Bucher's privately expressed claim that there was a conspiracy afoot to hang him.

It is impossible to pinpoint the origin of a rumor, or to follow it through its many manifestations, or to stop one once it gets started. Whatever the source, word passed among the crew that the upcoming Court of Inquiry was going to be a "witch hunt," that "they"—usually identified as "Navy brass"—were out to "get the skipper."

The reaction was instinctive. It was exactly the same as when the KORCOMs attacked Bucher in North Korea. Almost automatically the crew closed ranks about their commander.

Even those of us who had major differences with Bucher were not entirely immune to this phenomenon. I might personally feel that Bucher's blunders had contributed greatly to our capture by the North Koreans, but even I bristled when hearing this charge made by an "outsider," someone who hadn't been aboard the *Pueblo* on January

23, 1968; who hadn't shared our eleven-month-long imprisonment; who hadn't been beaten and tortured by the Communists.

Again under fire, the crew of the USS *Pueblo* drew together. An attack on one became an attack on all. Though personal differences were not forgotten, they were muted, put aside, held in abeyance until this new ordeal was through.

This, too, would have its effect on the hearing to follow.

The first several weeks in January 1969 were mostly spent completing medical examinations and preparing for the Court of Inquiry, now scheduled to start on the twentieth. Since Bucher was still isolated from the crew most of the time, I was able, to a certain extent, to heed Stacer's advice, though crew's business did bring us together occasionally. During this period the crew collected fifteen hundred dollars, which was donated to the Creswell, Oregon, High School library to buy books in memory of our shipmate Duane Hodges. Seaman Stuart Russell beat Quartermaster Charlie Law to the altar by several weeks, in a ceremony in the hospital chapel, where Bucher made one of his rare public appearances. He also turned up at a dinner put on for the crew by one of the "Remember the *Pueblo*" committees, and got a chance to meet his all-time hero, John Wayne.

Bucher spoke to me only when it was absolutely necessary. I did the same. It was a truce of sorts. Neither of us had any illusions as to how long it would last.

Bucher spoke to Steve Harris even less often. It now appeared that Bucher had finally made his choice, picking Steve, rather than Gene Lacy or me, as his primary villain.

Or so it seemed when the Court of Inquiry into the capture of the USS *Pueblo* finally began.

29

Outside, torrential rains belted southern California with gale force.

Inside the low-slung auditorium at the Naval Amphibious Base on Coronado, a few minutes before 0900 hours (9:00 A.M.) on January 20, 1969, Vice Admiral Harold Bowen, Jr., called the *Pueblo* Court of Inquiry to order. The appointing order was read; the court—consisting of four rear admirals and Vice Admiral Bowen—was sworn; and Commander Bucher was advised of his rights.

Bucher was also asked if he felt sufficiently well, mentally and physically, for the proceedings to begin. He replied that he did, observing he had regained eighteen pounds since his return.

Bucher was the first witness. He would remain on the stand five days, narrating his version of the *Pueblo* story.

I was not present at these sessions, nor were any other members of the crew. By regulation, witnesses expected to testify in the probe could not attend, except when called to the stand. As a party to the inquiry, Bucher was allowed to be present at all the sessions, with his attorneys; in addition, his two counsels were permitted to cross-examine witnesses.

The general public could attend, however, and in addition to the newspaper, radio, and TV accounts, plus the twice-daily summaries of testimony issued by the Command Information Bureau (CIB), I had access to two

357

excellent "spies." One was far prettier than the other. In the days ahead, however, I was to see much more of the second than the first. Carol sat in whenever time permitted; Captain Stacer rarely missed a session. Late each afternoon Stacer and I would get together and go over the day's testimony. Often these discussions lasted late into the night.

During his first morning on the stand, as he cataloged the problems we had encountered outfitting the ship, Bucher told it fairly straight. This was not true of that afternoon, when he reached the Japan phase. In some detail Bucher reviewed his efforts to obtain adequate destruct devices for the ship. Thermit was suggested, but he turned it down, both because the Navy opposed its use and because he feared some mentally disturbed crewman might deliberately trigger it. What he really wanted, he told the court, were some fifty-pound cans of TNT, but his efforts to obtain them "were unsuccessful, because they were not available."

"He's pretending the incident in the Yokosuka officers' club never happened!" Stacer said, truly shaken by Bucher's audacity.

The temptation to say "I told you so" was near irresistible, but I managed to overcome it, instead inquiring, "And now what do *I* do if the court asks me about it?"

"You tell the truth," he replied, the wonder still on his face. "But if they don't ask"—the attorney in Stacer had again taken over—"don't volunteer it."

Bucher's taking the stand first put all of us in a curious position. His story would become *the Pueblo* story. And we had either to go along with what he said, or, in effect, call him a liar.

I wasn't alone in my confusion. Law, Lacy, and I discussed the mounting number of discrepancies in Bucher's account. Bucher, for example, had told the court that the closest the *Pueblo* had ever come to the North Korean landmass was "13.0 or 13.1" nautical miles. Law knew better, having been present on the bridge on the one occasion when Bucher brought the ship in to 12.8 miles. Law wasn't about to let this fiction stand; he intended to correct the skipper when his turn came.

Since only officers had been present during Bucher's mock court, Law was unfamiliar with how Bucher had reconstructed events. "Where in the hell," Law asked, "did that extra SO-1, that fourth P-4, and those 'thousands' of shells come from?"

"From the same place as the four airborne torpedoes, I imagine," Lacy replied dryly.

As Bucher was relating the events of January 23, 1968, it became apparent that he was shuffling the chronology to fit the image that he wished to project, that of an alert skipper, quickly assessing each situation and acting with prudent caution, but at the same time with dispatch.

For example, Bucher, seeing the P-4 rigged for boarding and realizing that this was no ordinary harassment, decided to depart the area in "as dignified a way as I possibly could," by "easing out." Actually he had rung up full speed, but then had been forced to stop and proceed at one-third when it was discovered that the Nansen bottles were still in the water.

There was no indication that it had taken Bucher one and a half hours to reach the conclusion that the KORCOMs meant business.

When it came to the destruction efforts, he now stated that he had passed the word to "prepare to destroy" the classified materials before even a shot was fired. When the first shells hit the ship, wounding Bucher and the others on the signal bridge, he was up off the deck within five seconds to yell down the voice tube, "Commence destruction." In reality, the order to "prepare to destroy" followed the first shot. Even then it was another ten or fifteen minutes, after at least one frantic phone call from the sod hut, which I took and relayed to Bucher, before he finally gave permission to "Commence destruction."

And there were the by now familiar explanations, old hat to us but new to the court. He had elected not to sound general quarters prior to the firing because it would be viewed as a provocative action. He had not ordered the guns manned because: (1) Admiral Johnson had instructed him not to uncover them until all else failed; (2) he did not want to appear hostile; (3) the exposed placement of the gun mounts would have resulted in anyone he sent there being shot; and, besides, (4) the canvas covers were frozen over. When the KORCOMs had tried to take them off, it had taken over thirty minutes.

Stacer had watched the five admirals carefully throughout this, and he doubted seriously whether they were buying it.

Bucher concluded his second day of testimony with the statement that while he was in captivity a North Korean general had told him that if he hadn't stopped the ship it would have been torpedoed.

The Court of Inquiry was not to be wholly repetitious. There would be numerous surprises. The above story, which I now heard for the first time, was one of them.

Another new one was that Bucher became so enraged at the North Korean ships that, in frustration, he had thrown his coffeecup at them.

By a curious coincidence, Commander William Clemons, associate counsel to the court, had been so enraged at the Japanese attack on Pearl Harbor that, standing on the deck of the battleship *Nevada,* he had picked up the only thing immediately at hand, potatoes, and tossed them at the attacking planes.

The morning of Bucher's third day on the stand brought a radical departure from the well-rehearsed script we had heard so often in North Korea.

Bucher stated that when Lacy had asked if he should stop the ship, "I nodded my head."

Bucher also admitted that he had stopped the ship the second time himself, in order to inspect the status of the

360

destruction. (Just why it was necessary to stop the ship to do this, he did not make clear.)

Gene Lacy appeared to be off the hook.

Also it appeared that Bucher had finally decided exactly when he made the decision to surrender the *Pueblo*. It had occurred when he ordered the ship stopped the first time. Bucher stated that he felt at this point that he would "surrender the ship, that the crew would be slaughtered if he continued, that resistance would be useless."

The admirals began asking questions now, pointed ones.

Admiral Bergner: "For clarification, what significant event occurred just prior to your making the decision to stop? What prompted you to make this decision?"

Commander Bucher: "No particular action took place. My feeling was, we would be hopelessly riddled and perhaps sustain an inordinate number of casualties, which would interfere with the destruction of the classified matter. . . ."

Admiral Pratt: "Had you ever rehearsed the modified GQ?"

Commander Bucher: "No, sir, I had not."

Admiral Bowen: "Your ringing up stop, this was to do what?"

Commander Bucher: "To comply with his orders to heave to, and to hope that the firing would stop."

We were dead still in the water when the "heave-to" flags had been hoisted. This was why the message had puzzled us so.

That afternoon Bucher had just finished describing the boarding and the blindfolding of the *Pueblo* crew when the court ordered a five-minute recess. At its conclusion, Captain William Newsome, chief counsel for the court, slowly rose and said: "Commander Bucher, it is my duty to apprise you . . . that facts revealed in this Court of Inquiry render you to be suspect of a violation of U.S. Navy Regulation Article 0730." Newsome then read the regulation: "The commanding officer shall not permit his command to be searched by any person representing a

361

foreign state, nor permit any of the personnel under his command to be removed from the command by such persons, so long as he has the power to resist." Newsome then informed Bucher that he had the right to remain silent, that anything he said could be used as evidence against him in a subsequent trial.

Bucher had known this would probably happen. He had discussed it as early as our detention in North Korea.

Miles Harvey admitted, in his statement which followed, in which Bucher waived the right of silence, that they had "obviously anticipated" this. Harvey's whole defense tactic was predicated on it, as he now made clear by asking Bucher a single question, "Commander Bucher, at the time the North Koreans set foot on your ship, did you any longer have the power to resist?" to which Bucher replied, "No, I did not."

Only the general public was unprepared for the announcement.

Bucher resumed his testimony, describing the boarding and what followed. In the course of his narrative, he stated that when the KORCOMs asked him what the ship was doing, he told them that the *Pueblo* was engaged in oceanographic research and electromagnetic study involving sunspots.

At this point apparently none of the admirals picked up on the fact that Bucher had just admitted to abandoning the Code of Conduct.

The letters and telegrams arrived by the hundreds, then the thousands. They went to the White House, the Pentagon, Coronado, and probably every naval base in the United States.

As liaison between Captain Thomas and the *Pueblo* crew, I saw batches of them. "How can you crucify that man, when all he did was try to save the lives of his crew?" "It's an obvious frame-up." "Just give us the word, Commander Bucher, and we'll storm the place and free you." "Bucher deserves a medal, not a trial." "Hang the higher-ups, not Bucher."

Literally overnight, Commander Bucher became a national martyr, an antiestablishment figure, a modern naval hero who dared challenge the antiquated traditions of the military-industrial complex.

And the Navy suddenly awoke to find itself facing one of the worst public-relations crises in its history. Explanations were tendered: "This isn't a trial; it's only a fact-finding commission," Navy spokesmen kept repeating over and over, but their protests did little or no good.

Harvey then pulled a brilliant ploy. He called a press conference to announce that Bucher felt he was receiving "eminently fair treatment" by the court.

"They made him say it!" was the consensus. The public thronged to him in even greater numbers.

A group of doctors accused the Navy of subjecting Bucher to "physical and mental torture." Political pundit Max Lerner wrote of "Bucher's Gethsemane," saying if he were sitting on the court, he would vote "not censure, but compassion." During one of the intermissions, Tim Harris slipped into the courtroom and handed Bucher a note. It read: "We've made it this far together, and we'll finish it together," and was signed "Bucher's Bastards." Released to the press, the phrase caught on.

The Bucher legend had become public property.

Meanwhile the Court of Inquiry continued. Bucher's fourth day on the stand was January 23, 1969—one year to the day after the capture of the USS *Pueblo*. The press did not have to emphasize the drama inherent in this. More than enough was occurring in the courtroom.

Bucher described the crew's arrival at the Barn, and the interrogations and beatings that followed. He told how, when the KORCOMs forced him to kneel and held a pistol against his head, he . . .

At this point Bucher began sobbing.

Captain Newsome asked him if he wished a recess.

363

No, Bucher said, he wanted to get this over with. In a voice choked with emotion, he related how, to keep his mind off the gun, he repeated, over and over, "I love you, Rose."

After a long pause, Bucher was able to resume his narrative. After he had called their bluff, and discovered the gun was not loaded, the KORCOMs had kicked and beaten him until he lost consciousness. Then: "At ten o'clock that night, Chipmunk and Super C came with drawn pistols and told me they would show me what happens to spies. . . . I was led up half a flight of stairs, and then down again into a semibasement.

"A South Korean was there with a strap around his chest, strapped to the wall. They explained to me that he was a South Korean spy. He was alive but had been through a terrible ordeal. He had a compound fracture of the upper right arm. The bone was sticking out. He was stripped to the waist. He had completely bitten through . . ."

Again Bucher sobbed, interrupting his narrative. After wiping his glasses, he began again: "He had completely bitten through his lower lip, and his lower lip was hanging down from the side of his mouth. His right eye had been put out. His head was hanging down. There was a lot of . . . black matter which had run out of his eye and down his right cheek. . . ."

As the audience listened in shocked silence, Bucher said he blacked out, to awaken in the Barn. He was then told that unless he signed a confession, each member of his crew would be shot, starting with the youngest.

From the CIB summary: "Cdr. Bucher said he was convinced that these people, whom he termed 'animals,' would carry out this threat and said he was not prepared for this type of mental torture, particularly after not having eaten or slept for about a day and a half. He therefore signed the confession."

Later, after being returned to his room, Bucher had tried unsuccessfully to kill himself by sticking his head in his water bucket.

If the spy story was already familiar, except for the added embellishments, Bucher's testimony during the afternoon session came as a decided surprise.

On returning to the stand, Bucher explained that although his first confession was dated January 24, he had not actually signed it until the early-morning hours of January 25. In this initial confession, he said, there was no mention of intruding. Not until later that same day had he signed an amended confession which included the admission that the ship had been seized while in the territorial waters of the Democratic People's Republic of Korea.

He had done so, he stated, after learning from Super C that Lieutenant Edward R. Murphy, Jr., the ship's navigator, had already signed a confession admitting the intrusion. From the CIB summary: "Cdr. Bucher said he heard later that Lt. Murphy had been severely beaten and kicked in the head and that a confession had been extracted from Murphy."

"The implication from this is that I broke and confessed first!" I told Captain Stacer. "He's got me confessing at least five days before I actually did so—even before I heard the tape of his confession!"

"But notice how careful he is," Stacer observed. "He doesn't actually say that. He says Super C told him this. He doesn't say he believed him, although he certainly leaves that impression."

"There must be some way I can disprove this," I told Stacer.

There was. But months would pass, with the Court of Inquiry long over, before I would discover it.

Photographer's Mate Mack had a problem, not dissimilar to mine. While on the stand Bucher had told how Mack had stopped him in the hall in the Barn one day, saying, "They're asking me about carriers, Captain. What should I do?"

The problem: it was me Mack stopped, not Bucher. Hav-

365

ing heard the story from one or the other of us, Bucher had adopted it as his own. With an embellishment: he and Mack had been caught talking, and both had been badly beaten as a result.

"I don't want to contradict the skipper," Mack said. "But that just isn't true. What happens if they ask me about it?"

"I don't think they will," I told him. "But if they do, tell the truth. That's the rule of thumb the rest of us are going by. Above all, don't perjure yourself."

"But why would he say that?" Mack persisted.

"Probably he's just confused," I told him. "He's under a hell of a lot of pressure. And he's not entirely well. Commander Bucher is still a very sick man."

I was beginning to feel as if I had an acute case of schizophrenia myself, the contrast between my activities as exec, and the talk sessions with Captain Stacer, when I could really level, was so extreme.

A reporter caught me one day. "Hey, Murph, is it true that Bucher cried at the ship's commissioning, and that he choked up when—"

"Whoa," I stopped him. "You know I can't talk to you until this whole thing is over. But I can give you a word of advice. Until you've been through what that man's been through, don't start throwing stones."

The story never appeared.

In the weeks to come, many of us would come close to breaking down on the stand, some would. Though our physical wounds had healed, there were others, psychic ones, which went even deeper, over which the scar tissue was newly formed. The Court of Inquiry would rip these open again.

There were nights when some of us would awaken, bathed in perspiration, convinced that we were still in North Korea. Even after the soothing words, the assurances that it had been only a dream, that we were really home again, sleep never came easily. For a residue of fear, and guilt, would remain. This would be true all the way through

366

the Court of Inquiry. And for a long time after. For some of us it remains true even today.

When Bucher finished his fifth day of testimony he was told that he would be called back at a later date for further questioning. Before leaving the witness chair, the commander related how it had appeared that the crew would be released in October, but after the KORCOMs discovered the "internationally recognized gesture," the mood changed, Hell Week being one result.

This was the closest Bucher would ever come to admitting that his fun-and-games approach had backfired.

January 25: Admiral Thomas Moorer, Chief of Naval Operations, addressing the American Bar Association in Chicago: "A court of inquiry . . . is a fact-finding body— that and nothing more. . . . I am deeply troubled—the Navy is deeply troubled—that what was a routine and totally correct legal procedure has been widely misinterpreted . . . the Navy is looking for facts—not scapegoats. . . ."

January 29: California's Governor, Ronald Reagan, declared that Bucher was being made a "scapegoat" to cover up the shortcomings of the Johnson administration. At the time of the seizure of the *Pueblo*, Reagan was quoted as wanting to give the North Koreans a twenty-four-hour ultimatum. If it was ignored, the United States was to go in and get the ship out by force, using nuclear weapons if necessary.

January 30: Commander Bucher said, through a spokesman, that he appreciated "the thousands of telegrams and letters he has received from across the country in his support. He would like to answer each personally, but at this point he doesn't have time to open all of them."

The admirals seemed especially attentive when Commander Clark took the stand to describe the harassment experiences of the *Banner*.

Clark made no mention of his concern over Bucher's failure to utilize the information gleaned from the *Banner*'s prior missions. He described the *Pueblo*'s CO as having been a friend since 1955, and an officer considered professionally well qualified by senior officers. To a large extent, Clark's testimony supported Bucher's. Although always anticipating harassment, and ever fearing a collision situation, he had never expected one of the AGERs would be seized while on the open seas.

Clark differed with Bucher on only two points, but they were telling. He said he believed a commanding officer should fight back just as long as he could in the case of a boarding attempt, and "do anything he could" to avoid capture.

My turn came on February 4. Stacer had me well prepared. I had the navigational information down pat. It helped that four of the five admirals had served off Wonsan, Vice Admiral Bowen having been awarded the Legion of Honor for his actions there during the Korean war, as I didn't have to simplify my explanations.

Yet on one question Stacer didn't try to advise me. I'd have to settle this with my own conscience.

"I'm sure they're going to ask you the big one, Ed: Given identical circumstances, would your decision have been the same as Commander Bucher's?"

Which decision? I wondered. Placing the gun mounts in positions where they couldn't be reached in an emergency? Apparently deciding that continuing a good party was more important than getting up early to haul TNT aboard? Not getting out of a potentially explosive situation while the getting was good? Trying to save face with insulting signal hoists while the situation became more and more untenable? Delaying issuing vital commands, such as calling general quarters and starting the destruction, which could have greatly reduced the amount of classified information seized?

No, I wouldn't be asked any of these things. The end result was all that mattered to the court.

I anticipated the question would come from Harvey, but instead, toward the end of my testimony, Rear Admiral Grimm put the query to me. He did so in such a way that answering posed no problem. He asked me what I would have done had Commander Bucher been killed in the attack on the ship and I had succeeded to command.

"My decision would have been essentially the same," I told him. "However, I did not have all of the facts and input that the captain had." It was a guarded but honest answer. By this time the die had been cast, because when the KORCOMs began firing, the *Pueblo* was hopelessly trapped.

Harvey did ask me whether "at the time the North Koreans boarded the ship" Commander Bucher had any longer the power to resist?

To this I replied, no, not at that time.

PUEBLO EXEC SUPPORTS DECISION TO SURRENDER, one headline read.

MURPHY BACKS BUCHER, read another. WOULD HAVE DONE EXACTLY THE SAME THING.

That was not what I'd said, but I was in no position to clarify my response.

Another question gave me far more trouble. Prior to the hearing I'd wondered what I'd answer if I were asked if there were any one thing which tipped the scales and made surrender inevitable. I'd thought about this often in North Korea, wishing there was some way I could turn back the clock and do it all over again, differently this time. Yet even then I couldn't pinpoint a single action—after the initial failure to disengage. Rather, it was an accumulation of circumstances.

After I'd given this answer, I could tell it wasn't the

369

explanation the admirals wanted. They wanted something firm they could grab on to: at exactly such and such a moment in time this occurred, after which everything else became inevitable. But it hadn't happened that way.

Many other questions I'd anticipated, and sweated over, were never asked. For just a moment, though, I felt sure the TNT story was to be made public. I was asked if any TNT had ever been brought aboard the ship. After I replied no, the questioning moved to something else. But it left me wondering how much the court really knew.

When I'd completed my testimony, Bucher stood and perfunctorily shook my hand. I was sure Harvey had put him up to it.

That afternoon Steve Harris testified, describing the destruction efforts on the twenty-third as "optimum, feverish, and frustrating." In the course of his narrative he contradicted Bucher several times. He firmly stated that he and the commanding officer had exactly the same clearance, and that the CO could enter any spaces on the ship he so chose. He added that although Bucher was not conversant with all the details of some of his projects, he needed only ask and he would have briefed him. There was also more than an undercurrent of criticism in his statement that the destruction efforts in the sod hut had been hampered by the failure to call a full GQ, since the people who were in the sod hut at the time were not those who had been assigned to the destruction task.

Steve admitted, however, when questioned by the court, that at no time had he suggested to the commanding officer that he go to general quarters.

Earlier Bucher had described how, sometime after the destruct order was given, he had gone to the sod hut and found a tremendous amount of classified cargo still there. He had ordered Steve Harris to "get rid of this material right now." Bucher claimed that when Steve later called the pilothouse, asking permission to inform Japan that he had been unable to destroy all his classified publications,

370

he presumed Steve meant there were only a few scraps of paper left. He was appalled, when later taken to the sod hut by the KORCOMs, to find two mattress covers, filled with documents, still there.

(There remains considerable confusion as to how many containers of these documents there were originally, how many left undestroyed, even whether the documents were in mattress covers or laundry bags or weighted sacks. Langenberg, who threw one overboard, said there were two originally and that they were laundry bags. Some of the CTs couldn't remember having seen any.)

Now queried about this, Steve admitted that, due to the fire from the KORCOM ships, there had been no opportunity to throw these materials overboard.

Steve too said nothing about the TNT. Nor did he mention Bucher's lax attitude toward security, and his own agonizing over whether to pull Bucher's clearance.

When Steve finished his testimony, Bucher did not bother to shake his hand.

It was inevitable that one of the reporters would discover the schism between Steve Harris and Bucher. *Newsweek's* highly capable Karl Fleming, after inviting Skip and Tim to his surfside home for the weekend, returned with the story. He first wrote about it in *Newsweek,* then later, in expanded form, in an article entitled "The C.O. and the Super Spy" in the Los Angeles *Times.*

The irony was that by the time Fleming's second piece appeared, the schism no longer existed, thanks to his first article.

"We were able to survive and come out fairly well, I think, and I want to say this was due to the fine leadership of the commanding officer. I observed a man who bore the burden of all eighty-one other crewmen. He inspired all of us to respect and follow him, which I'm sure all of us would like to do in the future."

Timmy Harris?

Skip Schumacher?

No, *Steve Harris.*

Indications of a turn-about in the relationship of Bucher and Steve Harris became obvious shortly after Fleming's first piece appeared. Rose Bucher and Esther Harris suddenly began working together on various *Pueblo* projects. In one week, *Time* observed, the two couples went to one nightclub and two concerts together.

There was no rift between himself and Commander Bucher, Steve Harris told the *Time* reporter. He had nothing but praise for his commanding officer, whom he viewed as one of the most honest, responsible officers he had ever come across.

I couldn't blame Steve. In our attempts to save ourselves, we'd all compromised to a certain degree. It was the realistic thing to do.

That didn't make it any easier to live with it.

Steve needed all the help he could get. As one after another of his CTs took the stand, they presented a devastating case against their detachment head.

CT David Ritter remembered seeing Lieutenant Harris in the research spaces on the afternoon of the twenty-third but added that no one was "really supervising" destruction.

CT Michael Barrett said that, at about the time the SO-1 had hoisted its "heave to or I will fire" flags, he, not the lieutenant, had told the personnel in the sod hut to prepare to destroy the classified material.

CT James Layton was on watch in the research section when the incident started. He recalled Lieutenant Harris walking in shortly after the firing started, but he couldn't remember him giving any orders, and he did not see the lieutenant participate in the destruction of materials. Layton himself told the others to start with the most highly classified materials and work down.

Most of the CTs never saw the destruct bill for the sod hut; none had ever gone through a destruct drill.

The most damning testimony, however, came from Steve's senior enlisted man, Chief James Kell.

Kell stated that at no time on the twenty-third had he heard Lieutenant Harris give an order. He said that after the firing had started Harris had called the bridge and asked for permission to begin destruction, but that Harris informed him it had been denied. Kell admitted that, on his own, he had ordered it started anyway, actual permission not being received until about two minutes later.

In response to a query from the court, Kell described Lieutenant Harris as "an average officer—nothing outstanding and nothing bad."

Later, recalled to the stand, he would retract this statement, saying that since he had reported aboard the *Pueblo* only some twenty days before the incident, he didn't feel qualified to give an opinion on what kind of officer Lieutenant Harris was.

But the rest of his testimony remained. And it was as damaging to Bucher as to Steve Harris, for Bucher was still maintaining that he had ordered destruction started within seconds after the first shot, and Kell's testimony clearly contradicted this.

Chief James Kell would not appear on the second heroes' list.

As serious as the Court of Inquiry was, it was not without its lighter moments.

Some occurred in the courtroom: Commissaryman Ralph Reed perfectly described the food the North Koreans served us by saying it "wasn't anything you'd have second helpings of." During detention Fireman John Mitchell had been assigned clean-up duties in Commander Bucher's room. He testified that he talked to the skipper every day. One member of the court asked what they talked about. Mitchell seemed amazed at the question, the answer being so obvious. "The basics of life," he replied, "generally meaning food, cars, and girls."

Others took place behind the scenes and were never publicized: There was the letter to the editor of a newsweekly, a most eloquent defense of Steve Harris, who

373

emerged the shining knight of the *Pueblo* affair. Sheepishly, Steve admitted that the letter had been written by one of his relatives.

A photo provided some merriment. On our return to the United States we discovered that the most widely publicized photograph of the USS *Pueblo* (which appears on the jacket of this book), was one which, upon close inspection, showed the ship going backward. When I was in Washington making the intrusion film, I informed the Navy PR people of this. They quickly, and with red faces, yanked the picture out of circulation. The photo remains, in its own way, all too symbolic of the whole *Pueblo* fiasco.

Some other photos also proved entertaining. In one week both *Newsweek* and *Life* had cover stories on Commander Bucher. An alert CT, glancing through them, noticed something interesting, and quickly spread the word to his fellows.

One of the *Life* photos showed Bucher as a lieutenant commander. He was wearing eight medals.

In the *Newsweek* cover photo, however, taken after Commander Bucher's return to the United States, he had only seven, including the recently awarded Purple Heart.

Apparently after his rise to prominence Bucher had decided to shed a couple of self-bestowed awards.

It was the consensus that, however the heroes' list came out, Bucher was surely the only one who would end up *losing* medals. Ironically, one of the vanishing awards was the Korean Conflict Medal.

30

While division seemed to be the order of the day, there were at least a few occasions during the Court of Inquiry when the crew was one hundred percent united.

One occurred when Captain John H. D. Williams took the stand. Williams was a security "expert" from the Pentagon. A fascinating portion of his testimony dealt with the changes that had been made in the AGER and related programs since the capture of the *Pueblo*. Classified documents intended for *Pueblo*-type ships were now first sent to the fleet commander for screening, then, if deemed necessary, to the ships, reproduced on water-soluble paper. Moreover, the prohibition against carrying incendiaries such as Thermit had been permanently rescinded.

It was good to know some lessons had been learned from our experience. Williams did not stop there, however.

He further testified that, in his considered opinion, the destruct devices aboard the *Pueblo* had been quite adequate, and that the crew should have been able to destroy *all* the classified cargo, even under enemy fire, *in about one hour!*

Miles Harvey tried to shake this incredible testimony, but Williams only became more dogmatic. Harvey did succeed in getting Williams to admit that though he stood by his one-hour estimate, he couldn't approximate the total man-hours involved.

Those of us who risked our lives that afternoon in a vain attempt to destroy all the security materials the *Pueblo* carried in the few hours we had, did not take too kindly to a Washington expert telling us we just didn't work hard or fast enough.

Each and every crewman had his personal response to Williams' testimony. The comments remain, in this era of permissible publishing, unprintable.

In addition to Governor Reagan, a great many other Americans had been concerned when the United States had failed either to rescue the ship and crew or to retaliate for their seizure. The court spent several days delving into the "on-call" support arrangements the *Pueblo* had been assured existed.

For those of us who had been aboard the ship waiting, it was an eye-opener. Even the court reacted. Admiral Bowen, questioning Admiral Frank L. Johnson, finally declared, with ill-concealed disgust: "You have referred frequently to this on-call concept, which I believe is somewhat misleading, since nothing was on call."

Fifth Air Force had jets in South Korea. Had they been on strip alert, they would have reached the USS *Pueblo* about one half-hour after being given orders to do so. But they were not on strip alert, and furthermore, they were armed with nuclear weapons, which would have had to be replaced with conventional payloads. Estimates vary as to the time this—plus briefings, fueling, etc.—would have taken, but most agreed that, though they were actually closest to the *Pueblo*, these planes couldn't have made it before dark. And after dark would have been too late.

Fifth Air Force also had jets on Okinawa. Although they weren't on strip alert either, they were armed with conventional weapons. Moreover, the Commanding General of Fifth Air Force—on his own initiative—ordered the planes to the air as soon as he received word from the Navy that the USS *Pueblo* was in trouble. They almost made it, landing in South Korea for refueling before dark, but just minutes too late to reach the scene in time.

Seventh Fleet did not have any destroyers in the immediate vicinity. One was dispatched, but the quickest it could have arrived would have been the following afternoon. The aircraft carrier *Enterprise* was just five hundred miles away, however. Her planes *were* ready, and could have arrived one hour after being given the order to take off. But there was the rub. No such order was given. For there was no preexisting plan covering such a contingency, and no one, in either Washington or the Far East, was willing to take responsibility for a decision that could conceivably have caused World War III. Thus, while messages ran up and down the chain of command, time ran out for the USS *Pueblo*.

Why were we so totally unprepared? Though the wording differed, witness after witness gave a similar answer. Nothing like this had happened in more than a hundred and fifty years. Countries just did not attack the ships of other countries on the open seas in peacetime. Those were the rules.

Apparently no one had ever considered the possibility that some country might choose not to play by them.

There were, of course, other justifications. One, seemingly quite valid, was that U.S. support forces were spread so thinly, due to the Vietnam war, that they could not provide for every possible emergency. It was also argued that, even had the planes been sent, they couldn't have reached the ship before she was boarded. This was true. From the *Pueblo*'s first unmistakable distress call—the first message indicating that something other than ordinary harassment was involved—to the time of boarding was one hour and five minutes. But four hours and thirty-five minutes transpired between the first call and dark. The question was then raised as to what the jets could have done to change the situation, since the KORCOMs already held the ship.

Unfortunately, the Court of Inquiry never asked any of the crewmen of the *Pueblo* this question, for they had the answer. The planes could have attacked the P-4s and SO-1, getting them off our backs. With this visible support, I sincerely believe we could have overcome the small number of boarders. I think every man on that ship was just waiting the opportunity.

There were other questions. Why—with the Blue House raid, the threats over Radio Pyongyang, the increased hostilities in the DMZ—were we not warned that the *Pueblo* was venturing into a touchy situation?

Bucher would later state that had he received such a warning he would have operated farther out to sea. While there is no assurance the KORCOMs wouldn't have attacked us there, we at least would have been ready for something more than ordinary harassment.

There was an answer to this question, a most shocking one. It transpired that someone at the National Security Agency *had* sent such a message, questioning the "minimal" risk evaluation of this particular mission, but it had become lost somewhere in the chain of command. At least, no one ever admitted having received it.

The most mind-boggling testimony came, however, when Rear Admiral George Cassell took the stand. Cassell, who had been a captain at CINCPACFLT when the *Pueblo* stopped in Hawaii, was asked why no strip alert had been called. Cassell observed that in his opinion, had a strip alert been called, it probably would have been necessary to reassess the risk evaluation, changing it to something more than "minimal," and anything higher than that would have meant aborting the mission.

Thus, if Cassell was correct, the *Pueblo* actually rated on-call support only if she couldn't make the trip.

There is an expression probably as old as the U.S. Navy. In its attempt to fix responsibility, the Court of Inquiry ran into it time after time. Though always more evasively phrased, the answer seemed invariably to be: "It didn't happen on my watch."

Although it is a harsh charge, the record supports it: the *Pueblo* Court of Inquiry made no real attempt to discover exactly which persons in the chain of command above the USS *Pueblo* had "goofed," and so badly. After a very few days of such testimony as the above, the court, with an almost audible sigh of relief, turned its attention back to the crew of the ill-fated ship. They, at least, were present, and could be held accountable.

Though only a few discoveries emerged from the limited questioning, those rankled. Most of the crew, including all of her officers, chose to suppress their personal reactions, at least for the duration of the hearing.

But one crewman disavowed silence, and when he spoke, it was as if the voice were not his alone, but also that of eighty-one others. Questioned on the stand about his treatment at the hands of the KORCOMs, CT Don E. Bailey remarked: "All the beatings that I and the rest of the crew took didn't hurt half as much as the fact that when we were pleading for help, we got none from the largest Navy in the world."

31

No, his differences with his executive officer didn't amount to a "personality clash." That was a "little bit too harsh," Commander Bucher told the Court of Inquiry. It was just that they had different ways of doing things, Lieutenant Murphy being "surface-oriented" and having "a limited amount of at-sea experience."

"Apparently he's still convinced the *Pueblo* wasn't a surface ship," I told Captain Stacer when we met to discuss Commander Bucher's latest appearance on the stand. "I've a notion to—"

"No, you don't," Stacer said. "We've made it this far by not making waves. Just because Bucher is getting panicky doesn't mean you have to follow suit. The court has both your service record and Bucher's. They're quite well aware that, prior to reporting aboard the *Pueblo*, Bucher hadn't served on a surface ship in thirteen years. And they know that during your time in, you can match and probably better him when it comes to sea duty. He's lashing out at anything and everything because he's beginning to feel trapped. They've got him now, and he knows it."

"The trouble is, he's got us trapped, too."

Stacer nodded, aware that I was referring to the fitness reports. "But I've got an idea," Stacer admitted. "It may not work, but at least we've got nothing to lose."

At this point I didn't know what Stacer had in mind, but I certainly agreed that we had nothing to lose. Since our return to the United States, Bucher had been making wild charges against me, not publicly, but in private conversations, yet in a way that invariably they got back to me.

For example, he told one of the attorneys that, being a Christian Scientist, I had refused to perform my duties as ship's medical officer; specifically, I would not give the crew shots.

On hearing this, I went straight to "Doc" Baldridge, who volunteered to make a tape-recorded statement to the effect that shots were given to each and every member of the crew when they were due. Baldridge further noted that I was always among the first to take the shots, as an example to the others; it was the skipper who did everything he could to avoid them. The only way we had been able to get him to take flu shots, Baldridge recalled, was to tell him that they were vitamins.

Again Bucher was looking in the mirror and casting stones. The problem with such charges was that they took time to disprove, time that could have been used for more important things. Stacer was convinced Harvey would never let Bucher air them on the stand, yet, knowing how erratic he was, we couldn't be sure that one day he wouldn't simply get up and start flinging accusations.

This made us doubly apprehensive about the fitness report, for Bucher would not have to document any of the statements he made there. A straight fitness report in which Bucher cited actual differences was one thing; this promised to be quite another.

It was a messy business. If it had a positive side, it was that a number of crewmen, having heard the rumors, approached me individually and said they would be willing to testify on the stand, or to sign affidavits to the effect, that I had performed my job ably and competently.

I turned down the offers, but I was very moved by them. Because I knew the chance they were taking. I wouldn't be writing their evaluation reports; Bucher would.

The discrepancies between Bucher's story and what others remembered continued to pile up.

381

Gunner's Mate Wadley testified that when he examined them on the morning of January 23, the canvas covers over the machine-gun mounts were not frozen. He estimated that it would have taken at the most five to ten minutes to prepare the guns for firing. Bucher had already stated it had taken the KORCOMs thirty minutes just to get the covers off. Although he tried, Miles Harvey was unable to get the gunner's mate to qualify his testimony. Wadley further stated that he was not satisfied with the placement of the mounts, adding that he desired a placement that would have afforded an arc of 180 degrees. Wadley did admit, under Harvey's questioning, that one gun did have nearly an 180-degree arc.

Friar Tuck testified that when he went to the forward winch, which was used in making Nansen casts, there were some ice crystals on the cover, but he was able to get it off by himself. Harvey brought out, in questioning Tuck, that the location of the guns would probably result in a greater amount of icing than was true in the case of the winch.

Signalman Leach testified he could not recall hoisting flags reading "I am in international waters." "Leach is mistaken," Bucher snapped; "I am positive."

Leach too would not be on the second heroes' list.

Lacy estimated that at most thirty 57mm shells had been fired at the ship. He declined to estimate the number of machine-gun rounds fired. Lacy stated that the first time he knew the ship was to be surrendered was when Bucher ordered assistance for the boarding party.

The focus of the Court of Inquiry now turned to the detention period. On February 17 I returned to the stand to describe the torture I had undergone prior to my confession.

I stuck to the agreement not to make waves. I could have said that in my opinion the voice I heard in the recording was Bucher's. I didn't; I said I was unsure, as I had been, at first. I could have brought up Bucher's departure from the Code, and how the individual crewmen one after another privately stated that it was the CO's failure to abide by it, first on the train, then in the Barn, that had caused them to break. I bypassed the opportunity, just as most of the crew would when called to the stand.

I simply told what had happened to me from my first interrogation on January 25 to my final collapse on the morning of the thirtieth.

When I finished, I wondered if those five men would ever understand. As Skip, Tim, Gene, and the senior petty officers followed me to the stand, some to break down and sob, the admirals were, according to those present, at first solicitous, then embarrassed, then impatient, and finally bored. No, it wasn't getting through. And there was no way it ever could, not completely.

In an effort to compensate for the bad publicity, the Navy overreacted. Suddenly a spokesman for the court announced that each and every *Pueblo* crewman would be called to the stand to testify.

Rather than digging to the core of the material already collected, the court set up an endurance contest.

The logic behind the decision was obvious. No one could say this was another Warren Commission. Each man would have his day in court, whether he wanted it or not. A great many didn't. My primary duty for a time was trying to soothe bad cases of stage fright.

Nearly all of the questions now were about the Code of Conduct. Each man was asked why he had abandoned it: why he had given more than name, rank, and serial number; why he had signed false statements; why he had broken.

". . . fear . . . no choice . . . fear and the uselessness of it . . . I didn't feel the Code applied to our situation . . . fear of torture . . . we just gave out . . . our situation was unique and different . . . fear of death . . . couldn't endure the pain any longer . . . the mental pressure . . . to exist . . . because I knew they would beat me until they got what they wanted . . ."

There were variations. Skip said he broke because he

felt it was unrealistic to try to physically resist them, as they had overwhelming power; accepting this, he decided to preserve himself physically and mentally and resist them intellectually.

Gene Lacy, after matter-of-factly describing to the court how he had been beaten, then forced to sit on a hot radiator, cited as one reason for his decision to sign a confession his belief that the North Koreans would "leave other, more sensitive areas alone." A number of crewmen testified to this point. They had confessed to what the North Koreans had wanted to hear, but they had betrayed no classified information. CT Francis Ginther stated that he deviated from the Code "in order to safeguard classified information I did have."

The history of the Code was cited. It had been adopted by President Eisenhower in 1955 as a guide for prisoners of war. The North Koreans refused to consider us such, several crewmen noted. We were, in their estimation, war criminals. "It just didn't seem to apply to our situation." CT Elton Wood said he was familiar with the Code mainly through recollections of a film narrated by Jack Webb that was shown during basic training. He believed that none of the situations depicted applied to the *Pueblo*'s circumstances. Quartermaster Law made an interesting point. The Code, he felt, had been written for the foot soldier, who rarely carried more than his weapons and his dog tags. We had been captured with all our personnel records, plus incontrovertible evidence of our mission. Under these circumstances, Law felt it ridiculous to deny what our captors already knew.

When asked why he had departed from the Code, CT Wayne Anderson said, "I don't feel I did." CT John Grant stated that he did not feel he had disgraced either his country or himself. Storekeeper Third Class E. S. Russell, a University of Southern California graduate, said that although he had gone against its provisions, he didn't feel he had violated the "spirit" of the Code.

Asked if they felt the Code really applicable to our times,

one after another hesitated, then said the Code was "good, but . . ." Seaman Stephen Ellis said the Code was "an instrument to live up to, but difficult under certain circumstances; at times it was almost inhumanly impossible to uphold."

My own feelings, as expressed on the stand, were along these lines. I felt that the Code of Conduct should be retained, but that conditions had changed so radically since it came into being that its provisions might have to be revised in order to permit individuals to cope with situations that exist today.

After additional thought, I've come to the conclusion that perhaps revision isn't even necessary, if we accept the Code for what it was originally intended, and remains: neither a law nor a prohibition, but a series of guidelines, to be followed if at all possible, to indicate the directions of one's resistance if not.

These discussions of the Code of Conduct touched on deeper issues. The Court of Inquiry chose not to examine them.

Though it must have been in the minds of many, no one mentioned that the United States government itself had departed from the letter of the Code in signing a confession admitting to the intrusion charges.

Other issues went even deeper. Faced with an enemy who doesn't play by our rules, do we stick to our principles or abandon our standards and adopt his tactics? Are our national principles fixed, or do they need reevaluation from time to time? Confronted with a greatly changing world, one in which our very values are challenged, will the procedures of the past suffice?

I don't pretend to have easy answers to any of these questions. Yet until we as a nation come up with some, "incidents" will continue, both here in the United States and abroad.

The Court of Inquiry could have performed a valuable service had it even posed these questions. It did not choose to do so. Perhaps it was felt they were not relevant.

Tim Harris started the ball rolling, Schumacher following. After that, before leaving the stand most of the crewmen made a point of praising Commander Bucher. ". . .
an outstanding leader . . . I would follow him anywhere
. . . the finest officer I know . . . a real great skipper
. . . one of the greatest men I have ever known . . . it would
be a privilege and an honor to serve under him again . . ."

"It's going to backfire on him, Ed," Captain Stacer told
me. "If I were Miles Harvey, I'd do everything in my power
to stop it right now. The public will eat it up. But those five
admirals up there are going to wonder: If you've been
doing your duty, why are you so damned popular?"

Yet the appearance was not necessarily the reality. As
day after day crewmen took the stand to praise the CO,
behind the scenes a process of disenchantment was setting in.

For some it had begun shortly after our return. San
Diego radio station KDEO had gathered $3,171 from lis-
teners on behalf of the crew. Its disposition was left up to
us.

Bucher, never having given up entirely on his lottery
scheme, suggested that it be used for one grand, never-to-
be-forgotten party for the whole crew.

Most of the crew opposed this. Many wanted it divided
equally; they needed the money. Others felt it should be
used to buy a *Pueblo* ring for each crewman. Sergeant
Chicca had designed a handsome ring, and a jeweler had
already agreed to make it for us.

"All right," Bucher declared petulantly. "You're always
objecting to how I handle your money. This time I bow
out. You can do whatever you damn please with it."

A committee was appointed, which decided the money
should be divided into eighty-two equal shares.

About this same time, one of the REMEMBER THE
PUEBLO committees suggested a party for the crew. This
was the one that John Wayne, Pat Boone, and other ce-
lebrities had promised to attend. Bucher accepted for the

386

whole crew, although we were still under hospital quarantine. Very disturbed upon learning of this, Rose Bucher stepped in, insisting that there be no drinking. This would be the first time the *Pueblo*'s crew would appear together socially since our return to the United States, and she wanted to forestall any incidents.

Commander Bucher agreed to her condition, and the admiral in charge of the hospital, faced with a fait accompli, reluctantly granted us permission to leave the hospital for the evening.

Midway through the party, which was held in the Le Baron Motel in Mission Valley, stewards came in bearing cases of champagne. "This is my gift to my wonderful crew," Bucher declared, as Rose broke into tears.

There were no incidents. But later, when the committee checked the fund raised by the radio station—which Bucher was keeping in a private rather than a Navy bank account—it was discovered that the crew itself had actually paid for the champagne, Bucher simply taking some eight hundred dollars out of the fund to pay for it.

Law and some of the other enlisted men were furious about this. There had already been considerable criticism of Bucher's habit of giving *Pueblo* cigarette lighters and shoulder patches to newsmen and almost everyone he met. Commanding officers often pass out mementos, but traditionally they pay for such gifts. These had been purchased by the crew.

There were other incidents. The disenchantment reached even such stalwarts as Skip.

"Bucher won't sign it," Schumacher told me, an angry look on his face.

"Sign what?" I asked, having not the slightest idea what he was talking about.

"The crew's book agreement. It seems that while I've been working my tail off getting this thing set up, Bucher has known, from the time we got back to the United States, that there isn't going to be a crew book."

I now learned from Skip that while Commander Bucher

387

was still a prisoner in North Korea, Rose Bucher had hired Miles Harvey to represent both her and her husband, agreeing that if Commander Bucher was released, he would write his personal account of the *Pueblo* experience. Harvey's legal fee would be a percentage of the advance on the book.

What most irritated Skip, besides the fact that Bucher had failed to inform him of all this, was that one of the attorneys in Harvey's office had helped draft the Joint Venture Agreement. If the attorney knew of Bucher's personal deal, he never mentioned it, though he must have been aware that, without the CO, there couldn't be an official crew book.

The word that the book deal was off did not reach most of the crew until late February, after an announcement in Neil Morgan's column in the San Diego *Evening Tribune* that Rose Bucher had sold her story to *McCall's* for $50,000 and that Commander Bucher was considering book offers in "six figures." The news was not well received.

Final arrangements for the sale of Bucher's book were not made until after the end of the Court of Inquiry, at which time Doubleday and Company, Inc., won the competitive bidding with an offer of $375,000.

Prior to our capture, I had decided to leave the Navy. I'd made the decision even though I'd been informed that my next shore assignment would be the U.S. Naval Postgraduate School at Monterey, California, a choice billet that would mean a promotion to lieutenant commander and would have brought me a step closer to a command at sea. Since then, I had added more than a year to my time in the Navy (though admittedly through no choice of my own), giving me nearly nine years toward retirement. I'd also had second thoughts about my decision to resign, realizing that at the time I made it I'd lost perspective, let Bucher's conduct embitter me toward the Navy itself. I was now strongly inclined toward continuing my career in the Navy, both because I felt it had something to offer

388

me and more than ever convinced I had something to offer in return. But one thing now stood in the way.

No matter what the outcome of the Court of Inquiry, Bucher held the power to finish my career with a little piece of paper. Unfortunately, he was quite well aware of it.

I could, of course, appeal the report, once it was made, but that would take time, and there was no assurance the Navy would grant a hearing. Captain Stacer suggested trying one last alternative. It could fail—it probably would, in fact—but at least we'd lose nothing by trying.

It was Captain Stacer's suggestion that he approach Bucher to see if he could persuade him to voluntarily relinquish the writing of my fitness report. The report would then be written either by Bucher's immediate superior or by Admiral Shinn, as CINCPACFLT representative.

I told Stacer the mission was doomed to failure from the start, but agreed it was at least worth a try.

The following version of the meeting appears in *Bucher: My Story*, Doubleday & Company, Inc., 1970 (which will be discussed in some detail in the Epilogue):

Not long before the end of the Court of Inquiry, Bucher experienced something which upset him greatly. An officer senior to him in rank, who was providing counsel for one of the other *Pueblo* officers (who remains unnamed, except for four dashes), came up to him and threatened that if he, Bucher, gave ___ ___ ___ ___ a bad fitness report, they would tell all they knew about Bucher and his antics. According to Bucher, Miles Harvey was with him when this dialogue occurred. Bucher gave this Naval officer a devastating reply. ___ ___ ___ ___'s performance had been totally unacceptable, he said. And he intended to tell it as it was. Moreover, the suggestion of moderating a fitness report was not only improper, it made him sick to his stomach.

Assuming that Edward R. Murphy, Jr., was the unidentified officer and that Captain Richard Stacer was the senior officer referred to, Bucher's account bears only a passing relation to what actually happened.

Stacer did approach Bucher during one of the recesses of the Court of Inquiry. There was a small room in which the witnesses could rest, and at the time, not only Harvey and Bucher but also Captain Keys, Skip Schumacher, Steve Harris, and Steve's attorney, George Powell, were present. If Stacer was suggesting such a serious breach of ethics, he certainly picked a public place to do it.

One thing in Bucher's account of the meeting *is* correct. Once Stacer made the proposal that Bucher relinquish the right to submit the report, Bucher got mad, absolutely livid, according to Captain Stacer, not only refusing to consider the suggestion but also hurling one charge after another, among them: *"Murphy tried to kill me twice in Korea!"*

If he was referring to Hell Week, Captain Stacer replied, it was his impression that he, Bucher, not Murphy, was the one who saw fit to feign lockjaw, mimic the North Koreans, and engage in the other little amusements that resulted in severe beatings for many of the crewmen.

At this point, Stacer said, Bucher literally turned purple. Not entirely calm himself, Stacer turned and left the room, as Bucher was screaming, *"Murphy collaborated with the enemy!"*

Even after this, Stacer wasn't willing to give up. He knew how much was at stake, and how damaging a hatchet job could be to my career. Since it was now obvious that there was no possibility of discussing the proposal rationally with Bucher, Captain Stacer wanted to try talking to his attorneys, Harvey and Keys, to see if they could influence him. A second meeting occurred either the next evening or the one following, and was attended by Miles Harvey, Captain Keys, Captain Stacer, and myself, but not Bucher.

Stacer made it very clear in this meeting that we had nothing against Bucher writing a report "on the merits," but that if he was going to use the fitness report as a weapon to get back at Murphy, this was something else entirely.

390

This was the longest of the two meetings, and lasted several hours, during which, at Harvey's request, I aired in some detail my differences with Commander Bucher, Harvey in turn admitting that Bucher was far from reasonable when it came to the subject of his executive officer, that, "Frankly, he hates your guts, Lieutenant." Harvey, quite realistically, was not at all hopeful that Bucher would even be willing to discuss the matter again, but he agreed to approach him himself when Bucher was in a calmer mood. Since Harvey never brought up the subject again, we presumed his efforts had been unsuccessful.

In his account Bucher implies that the senior officer and __ __ __ __ were attempting to blackmail him. It was Bucher, however, who held the club, certainly not us.

The best refutation of Bucher's allegation is the time frame. Not having attended the first meeting, I did not think to note the date, but Captain Stacer is sure it wasn't more than a day or two before the second meeting, which I did note, and which took place on February 26.

By this time there was no longer any question of my blowing the whistle on Bucher and his capers, as he put it, even had I been inclined to do so.

My last appearance before the Court of Inquiry had occurred at least a week or more earlier, on February 17.

"Now, how do I disprove a charge of collaboration?" I asked Captain Stacer, just as sick to my stomach as Bucher claimed to be.

"You don't," Stacer replied. "Even Bucher isn't foolish enough to make such an irresponsible accusation."

I was not at all sure Stacer was right.

Before its start, the Associated Press had predicted that the *Pueblo* Court of Inquiry would be probably "the most exhaustive investigation ever conducted into the loss of a Navy ship."

Though its comprehensiveness was open to question, exhaustive it certainly had been. Originally expected to take a few weeks, it had lasted almost two months. The court was tired of it. The public was tired of it. And the witnesses were very, very tired of it.

It was now drawing to its close, however.

On March 10 Commander Bucher asked the court's permission to read a short statement. He then named forty-nine *Pueblo* crewmen who he felt had behaved with heroism during the detention period.

This was Bucher's second heroes' list. His first list had been divided into two sections: incident to capture, and detention. To this second category, he now added the names of a number of enlisted men and one officer, Tim Harris, who, on the original list, had been cited for his work during the incident (keeping the running narrative) but not for the detention period. And Bucher had deleted the name of one officer previously cited for his conduct during the detention period.

Bernard Weinraub described the scene in *The New York Times:*

> Bucher himself leaped from mood to mood, sullen one day, almost giddy the next. He chose in the closing days of his testimony to perform as a punishing father. He asked—and received—permission from the court to read a list of officers and enlisted men who he felt had behaved exceptionally in North Korea, who had shown leadership or resistance.
>
> He read perhaps half the names of the crew—with only one officer conspicuously omitted. The officer, Lieutenant Edward R. Murphy, Jr., and Bucher had an uneasy relationship before the capture: "Mr. Murphy had a limited amount of at-sea experience. . . . I expected perhaps too much of Mr. Murphy." Yet Mr. Murphy was also one of the most savagely beaten crewmen in prison—he was kicked in the head and beaten into unconsciousness and his ear was split open. There was some feeling that the reading of such a list by Commander Bucher—who was beaten less than most members of the crew—was more than a little gratuitous.

Inconsistent to the end, Bucher, in the testimony which followed, stated that of all the escape plans submitted to him while in detention, that of his executive officer was the best thought out and had the most chance of success.

The court was not quite finished with Commander Bucher. On March 11 he was asked a number of pointed questions.

Responding, he admitted that while in Sasebo he had made no attempt to obtain TNT charges; that the machine-gun covers could have been cut off, in two or three minutes; and, questioned again as to exactly who was responsible for stopping the ship the first time, he stated he "ordered the *Pueblo* to stop and, although he did not personally ring up the order, it was done with his tacit approval."

Bucher then attempted to strengthen some of the weak points in his testimony.

He said he still felt the guns had been installed at the best places on the *Pueblo*, that he had ruled out placing them on the bridge or above the research spaces because of the noise factor and the effect on the sensitive equipment.

He said that at the time of boarding he suspected that the North Koreans may have believed the *Pueblo* to be a South Korean ship, bent on sabotage, and that once they saw this wasn't true, that the boarding party might leave.

This was an entirely new justification for permitting the boarding, and one which did not take into account that huge American flag we had hoisted.

But Bucher then remembered the flag in another context. He now claimed, reiterating this several times, that he did not feel he had surrendered the ship, because at no time had he "struck colors."

Miles Harvey introduced into evidence a number of documents attesting to the high regard in which several of his fellow officers, including one former commanding officer, held Bucher.

It was almost over now.

On March 13 Bucher read his final statement to the court. It was brief. In it he said, "As commanding officer, I am solely responsible for the results of our attempt to destroy classified material. I am therefore totally accountable for anything that may have happened. . . . I hereby state unequivocally that at the time of the seizure we did not have the power to resist. . . . The overall conduct of the officers, enlisted men, and civilians assigned to the *Pueblo* was outstanding, and I commend each and every one of them."

After Bucher had finished, Miles Harvey delivered a concluding statement: "A Court of Inquiry such as this is, by its very nature, a cruel business, because it cannot bring back Duane Hodges, cause the return of the USS *Pueblo*, completely heal the scars that many of the crew will carry for the rest of their lives, or eliminate the nightmare that will continue for most of the crew due to the brutal and inhumane treatment they received at the hands of the North Korean barbarians.

"Probing into disasters at sea may seem merciless because almost everywhere else we, as a nation, have abandoned the requirement of accountability.

"However, on the sea there is a tradition older even than the traditions of our nation, and wiser in its trust than our new morality. It is the tradition that with authority goes responsibility and with both goes accountability. During these last eight weeks, Commander Bucher and his crew have rendered their account. The story has been fully and sometimes painfully told—the record is now complete. . . ."

Harvey didn't avoid the discrepancies in the testimony. He faced the problem head on: "There have been many conflicts in the testimony: weighted bags are missing, the state of the sea has been variously described, time frames have varied, and other differences in the statements of witnesses exist. It must be remembered that these men have testified to events occurring fourteen months and longer ago. Such discrepancies are normal and to be expected. . . ."

Harvey also noted that Bucher had been criticized in his fitness report by the shipyard commander at Bremerton for "attempting to obtain those things which are now minimum standards on an AGER. . . .

"Commander Bucher now appears as either a prophet or a man ahead of his time," Harvey said. "He knew what was needed on an AGER. Destruct gear now installed has been described by the experts with great pride—Commander Bucher would have settled for three cans of TNT. We have seen a demonstration of water-soluble paper. Commander Bucher would have settled for reduced publication allowances. Detachments are now departments. Commander Bucher was promised this almost two years ago. The fifty-caliber guns have been removed. Commander Bucher thought they were inappropriate when put aboard. . . ."

Harvey then ventured onto less secure ground, stating that though Bucher did permit the North Koreans to come on board the ship, "He did *not* surrender his ship. He never struck his colors, nor did he give any manifest indication to the North Koreans that he was delivering either the ship or the crew to them."

Harvey's tack was obvious. With the claim that Bucher had "never struck colors" he had provided the Navy with a face-saving out, if it wanted to use it.

Bucher did not have the power to resist, Harvey continued. Not one shred of evidence that he *could* have resisted was presented to the court.

He then described Bucher as "a man of whom we should all be proud," noting that his feat of bringing back to the United States eighty-one American fighting men "is one of the most outstanding performances of leadership in recent times."

Those who attended the session studied the faces of the five admirals to see how this speech had affected them. They were totally expressionless, offering no clues to their reactions.

Vice Admiral Bowen brought the proceedings to a close.

One hundred and four witnesses had been heard, and approximately thirty-four hundred pages of court transcript accumulated, containing more than a million words.

The *Pueblo* Court of Inquiry was over. Except for the verdict.

The crew had reached the end of the road also. Nearly all of the men had finished their medical reevaluations, and most already had their orders. On March 17, St. Patrick's Day, a final crew party was held. The jokes were loud, the backslapping frequent, but the underlying mood was one of loss. We'd been through a lot together. That most of it had been bad, rather than good, did not make the parting any easier.

"Don't forget," Bucher told everyone, "we've got a reunion every five years, come hell or high water!"

32

The court had promised to release its findings in two weeks. Nearly two months passed with no word on the "verdict."

While waiting, I went on leave, spending as much time as possible with my family, convincing Vicky and Eddie that they really did have a father, teaching Carol that she no longer had to open doors for herself, slip into coats unassisted, wash the car, make household repairs.

I saw Captain Stacer infrequently during this period. He did report that the heavy betting was that the court would fence-straddle: no medals, no courts-martial. And we did discuss one possible reaction to the findings. No matter what the court decided, it was likely the probe would be labeled a "whitewash." If the public was expecting "higher-ups" in military and government to be cited for negligence and poor planning, they were going to be disappointed. Although few reporters had made this clear in their accounts, there were definite limitations on "how high" the court could go. By regulation, the five admirals could not make findings against anyone senior to them in rank.

Any hope the crew had of forgetting the *Pueblo*, even temporarily, was destroyed when, in April, the KORCOMs again decided to recapture the headlines.

As a birthday present for Kim Il Sung, North Korean MIGs shot down a U.S. Navy EC-121 airplane.

The EC-121 incident differed from that of the *Pueblo* in one important particular: her entire crew of thirty-one perished in the Sea of Japan. But the other parallels were all too familiar.

The EC-121 was an electronic intelligence plane, doing much the same work the *Pueblo* had done. Although much slower than the jet fighters, it had neither air nor sea support. The plane was shot down over international waters. U.S. Air Force observers in Japan witnessed the encounter on radar, so, as in the case of the *Pueblo*, the U.S. military knew of the incident almost the moment it happened. However, it took a full hour for news of the tragedy to be relayed to Washington. And once the word was received there, it was decided there would be no military response.

The New York Times, comparing President Nixon's reaction to that of his predecessor, described him as "a model of restraint, confining himself to diplomatic protest that was very much in the Johnson-*Pueblo* style." Kim Il Sung obviously wanted war. The United States had no intention of acceding to his wishes. We would still play by our rules, though it hurt, and badly.

"They want you to be in Admiral Shinn's office at 0715 tomorrow morning, Ed," Captain Stacer told me on the phone the evening of May 5. "I think the verdict is in."

Rear Admiral Donald Chapman, Deputy Judge Advocate General, had flown to San Diego from Washington. He had asked Captain Stacer to dinner that night, but throughout the meal had declined to discuss the reason for the early-morning meeting.

Arriving at the admiral's office shortly after seven, I went into the men's room to check my dress blue uniform. Bucher was there, wearing work khakis. I couldn't help recalling our first meeting, exactly two years and one day ago.

"What's happening, Ed? What have they told you?"

We exchanged the little bits of information we had. Miles Harvey had been invited to breakfast with the admiral, but, as with Stacer the night before, Chapman would say nothing about the meeting. Apparently he was under strict orders to remain silent until the appropriate time.

Bucher was peeved. If the findings of the court were to

be made public, then he had been betrayed. He had been promised that he would learn the news twenty-four hours before anyone else, so he could prepare a press statement.

Admiral Chapman was very nervous. His hands shook as he removed the papers from his briefcase and began reading from them.

The verdict was in. The meeting had been timed so release of the news could be made simultaneously in the East by Secretary of the Navy John Chafee. At the same time this was occurring, Steve Harris, on leave in Massachusetts, was also being informed of the findings over the telephone.

The Court of Inquiry had recommended that Commander Bucher stand before a general court-martial for five alleged offenses: "permitting his ship to be searched while he had the power to resist; failing to take immediate and aggressive protective measures when his ship was attacked by the North Korean forces; complying with the orders of the North Korean forces to follow them into port; negligently failing to complete destruction of classified material aboard USS *Pueblo* and permitting such material to fall into the hands of the North Koreans; and negligently failing to ensure, before departure for sea, that his officers and crew were properly organized, stationed, and trained in preparation for emergency destruction of classified material."

Bucher turned a deathly gray. It was then I realized that he hadn't foreseen this, that he had probably been expecting not censure but the Congressional Medal of Honor.

Chapman continued. Trial by general court-martial had also been recommended by the Court of Inquiry for Lieutenant Stephen Harris. As officer in charge of the *Pueblo*'s research detachment, Harris was alleged to be derelict in his duties "in that he failed to inform the commanding officer of *Pueblo* of a certain deficiency in the classified support capabilities of the research detachment; failed to train and drill the research detachment properly in emergency destruction procedures; and failed to take effective

399

action to complete emergency destruction after having been ordered by the commanding officer to dispose of all remaining classified materials."

For Lieutenant Edward R. Murphy, Jr., Admiral Chapman continued, the court had recommended nonjudicial punishment, in the form of a letter of admonition, for "alleged dereliction in the performance of his duties as executive officer, in that he negligently failed to organize the crew on the day of seizure, especially in the ship's major internal task of emergency destruction of classified material."

That a letter of admonition was the slightest disciplinary action that could be recommended, little more than a slap on the wrist when compared to a general court-martial, did not make the accusation any easier to take. I felt the charge totally unwarranted. I glanced again at Captain Bucher. He looked as shocked as I felt.

Chapman was still reading. Much more serious letters of reprimand had been recommended for Rear Admiral Frank L. Johnson and Captain Everett B. Gladding. The court charged that Admiral Johnson, Commander of Naval Forces, Japan at the time of our seizure, "was derelict in the performance of duty in negligently failing to plan properly for effective emergency support forces for contingencies such as occurred during the execution of the *Pueblo*'s mission, and negligently failing to verify effectively the feasibility of rapid emergency destruction of classified equipment and documents carried by the *Pueblo* research detachment."

Remembering how Admiral Johnson couldn't do enough for his little fleet, even agreeing to Bucher's plexiglass windshield, I felt the accusations against him unfair. Higher command than Johnson had ruled against the carrying of destruct devices and the use of strip alerts for AGER missions. Johnson apparently was simply the highest link in the chain that the court could reach.

Not being familiar with the exact specifications of the charge against Captain Gladding, I wasn't sure whether he had been cited just as unfairly. Gladding, who during our outfitting was director of Naval Security Group, Pacific, and Steve Harris' boss, was alleged to be "derelict in the performance of duty in negligently failing to develop procedure to ensure the readiness of *Pueblo*'s research detachment for the mission assigned, and to coordinate other services and agencies to provide intelligence support to *Pueblo* during the mission."

However, there would be no courts-martial, Admiral Chapman informed us. Admiral Hyland, Commander in Chief of the U.S. Pacific Fleet, had recommended diminishing the court's recommendations for courts-martial for Commander Bucher and Lieutenant Harris to letters of reprimand. Hyland sustained the reprimand for Admiral Johnson and the lesser admonishment for me, and completely exonerated Captain Gladding. The Chief of Naval Operations, who had final military authority in this matter, concurred with Admiral Hyland's recommendations.

At the same time we were being informed of this, Secretary of the Navy Chafee was announcing that all charges had been dropped, because "they have suffered enough, and further punishment would not be justified."

With the secretary's granting of "executive clemency," the Navy obviously intended to close the book on the *Pueblo* affair. It was over and done with and now best forgotten.

I couldn't agree. Five naval officers, including a rear admiral, were left under a cloud. All had been charged with serious offenses. None had been given the opportunity to clear himself. We had been pardoned, not exonerated. Though the public would applaud the decision as humane, for all intents and purposes five Navy careers had been washed up.

"My God, you were crawling around picking up classified documents off the deck while the KORCOMs were firing at you. You organized the men on the mess decks when they'd stopped work after Hodges was shot. You—"

401

"The man in the middle," I interrupted Captain Stacer. "Again."

I had gone directly to Stacer's office after learning of the findings. After calling Carol and giving her the news, we sat there, in a state of shock, trying to comprehend exactly what had happened. No evidence of the charges against me had been presented to the court, Captain Stacer observed. Had there been, had I been named a party to the proceedings, we would have introduced a defense. As it was, we had no idea what basis, if any, existed for the accusations.

And might well never know. For during the meeting with Admiral Chapman we also learned that although the findings of the court have been made public, the deliberations, which led to those findings, would remain classified.

Captain Stacer placed a call to one of the counsels to the court. Not for attribution, exactly what evidence had been introduced against Murphy? he asked. There wasn't any, the officer said; the findings had surprised him just as much as us. As far as he could figure, having decided to cite both the commanding officer and the officer in charge of the research detachment, the admirals had simply sandwiched me in, since I was second in command.

It wasn't a very satisfactory answer. But to this day we haven't received a better one. The court report remains classified. As the *Denver Post* commented, "The citizen did not stand in the chain of command. He could hear much of the testimony but not all of the verdict. The Navy sailed on, answerable to its own helm."

Privately, Bucher and I had exactly the same reaction to the verdict. We both wanted to demand a court-martial. Miles Harvey apparently told Commander Bucher that if he did, this was "sayonara, where I get off." In my case, the court not having recommended a trial, there was no way I could demand one.

Publicly, Harvey told the press that Bucher was "definitely satisfied with the outcome. . . . As far as we are concerned, Commander Bucher has been cleared." Steve Harris told reporters he was "very, very happy" over the decision.

"I guess I'm fated to remain the *Pueblo*'s dissenter," I told Captain Stacer. I promised to make a statement at a later date, declining at this time to say anything more than that I was deeply disappointed in the verdict. I was not about to say: Thank you, Mr. Secretary, for pardoning me for a crime I didn't commit.

Nor was this the only bad news that came that morning. Following the reading of the verdict, Admiral Chapman had read the assignments for all of the *Pueblo* officers except Commander Bucher. Instead of being sent to the Naval Postgraduate School at Monterey, I had been given an administrative job on the staff of the Fleet Anti-Submarine Warfare School in San Diego.

There was more than a touch of irony in this, but at the time I failed to appreciate it, for it was obvious that with this assignment the Navy was putting me on the shelf.

Chapman then asked Bucher his preference. Bucher replied that he had been promised he would be sent to the Armed Service Staff College in Norfolk, Virginia.

"Schools are not being considered," the admiral flatly stated.

Within twenty-four hours this decision would be reversed, in Commander Bucher's case, Bucher receiving my choice, the Postgraduate School at Monterey. The reason for the sudden switch has never been made public. There were rumors of a behind-the-scenes deal—Bucher agreeing to moderate his criticism of the Navy in return for the Monterey assignment—but they remain just that, rumors. In his book Bucher would later profess his own surprise at the change. In my case, the assignment remained the same.

"What do you intend to do now, Ed?" Captain Stacer asked me.

"I can't see that I have any choice," I answered.

403

Captain Stacer nodded and said nothing, aware that with this blot on my record, and no way to expunge it, my career in the U.S. Navy was finished.

Carol and I had planned to fly East as soon as the verdict was in, to revisit our alma mater, Principia, and to see my sister, Anne. We left that same afternoon. When we arrived in St. Louis, there was an urgent message waiting for me. I was to call a number in Washington, D.C., and ask for a certain extension. I did, more than a little surprised when the operator answered, "The White House."

The extension belonged to a former Principia classmate and Navy buddy, presently a legal aide to President Nixon.

How soon could I fly to Washington? he asked me.

I told him I could be there the next day, if it was important.

It was, he assured me, suggesting we stay with him and his wife.

The morning after our arrival in the capital, I was driven to the White House, where I had breakfast with a number of the President's top civilian aides. Afterward we went to an office in the upper level of the west wing.

The President was not satisfied that the whole truth had come out during the Court of Inquiry, I was informed. He wanted to know if there was another version of the *Pueblo* story, besides Bucher's. I told them there was. I spent the entire day relating the story much as I have told it here, and answering literally hundreds of questions.

From the questions alone it was apparent that far more was known about the behind-the-scenes activities aboard the *Pueblo* than I had ever suspected. This knowledge extended even to our period of detention. Aerial photographs —taken by an SR-71—had been made of the USS *Pueblo* the day after her capture, while she was still in Wonsan harbor. Within days after this, U.S. Intelligence had located our first detention site, the Barn. Our second site, the Country Club, had been photographed a number of times

404

by satellite, some of the photos actually showing the crewmen outside exercising.

I observed that I wished we could have known this, for although it wouldn't have changed our situation, it would have done wonders for morale.

Although for obvious reasons the sources must remain undisclosed, I also learned that the U.S. government was far from unaware of what was transpiring in the prison compounds.

During a break in the questioning, one of the men approached me privately and told me that if I chose to remain in the Navy, I needn't worry that my career would be adversely affected by the findings of the court.

If ever an officer had a chance to write his own orders, this was it. But I also knew that an officer who gets his assignments and promotions through "PI"—political influence—is a marked man, as far as his fellows are concerned. Too, though it may be old-fashioned, if I get somewhere I'd like to make it on my own.

What I really wanted was something I couldn't have. I hoped that there might be some way for the case to be reopened, and the charges examined on their merits. But I knew this was unlikely, as the President had already stated, through his press secretary, that he had personally reviewed the findings, and concurred in the Secretary of the Navy's decision. Officially, as far as the United States government was concerned, the *Pueblo* case was closed.

I was glad the President would now know the full story. But I was beginning to wonder whether the public ever would.

Returning to St. Louis, I spent the next several days working on one of the most difficult letters I'd ever written.

"It is with deep regret and serious misgivings that I must now tender my resignation as an officer of the United States Navy," I wrote. "The results of the Court of Inquiry into the USS *Pueblo* matter and subsequent actions of the Navy in regard to my career seem to leave no alternative."

405

I then reviewed the allegations of the court, noting that "I had no hint of these charges during the investigation, and within my own conscience I cannot agree with them."

I mailed the letter on May 13, and the following day held a press conference to make public my resignation.

As soon as the news broke, a number of friends wrote, wired, or called, urging me to reconsider my decision. I was pleased that among them were many fellow shipmates, including a number of crewmen from the *Pueblo*. Elmer Haskins, administrative assistant to Congressman Don Clausen, who represented my home district in northern California, asked me to hold my resignation in abeyance until the congressman could investigate the matter. He also asked if I would reconsider remaining in the Navy if reassigned to the Postgraduate School. However, I told him what I had told the others: the decision was final.

Though I was hopeful my release would be granted before I was to report to San Diego in mid-June, it was not. Later I would learn that my letter had been misrouted somewhere in the chain of command.

I wasn't too surprised.

There was still another factor behind my decision to resign, a most important one.

Shortly before our repatriation, Carol had received a letter from DeWitt John, editor of the *Christian Science Monitor*, who suggested that his paper would be interested in an exclusive series of articles based on my experiences.

I respected the *Monitor*, and knew it had an excellent journalistic reputation. After talking to DeWitt John and several other editors, I agreed to do the articles just as soon as the crew was released from the publicity ban imposed during the Court of Inquiry.

This was not the only publicity ban, however. Since I was still in the Navy, the articles had first to be "cleared" with Naval Intelligence. And with the first batch sent, the Navy made its position quite clear. It balked at even the insinuation of a schism between Commander Bucher and myself. It excised a reference to the State Department's role in the outfitting of the ship. And it stated that as a naval officer it was improper for me to comment on the pros and cons of U.S. diplomatic relations with Communist nations.

As far as I was concerned, these matters had nothing to do with national security. The Navy was simply using this as an excuse to censor that which they did not wish made public. Again I was on the spot, for about this same time I was informed, unofficially, that resignations had been known to take as long as a year to go through. While I doubted seriously the Navy would keep me in any longer than necessary, we decided to go along with the cuts rather than postpone the series indefinitely. Although the *Monitor* had no desire to antagonize the Pentagon, they backed me completely in resisting one other change. The Navy wanted any and all mention of the Yokosuka TNT incident deleted. We felt this too had nothing whatever to do with national defense or present security, and so argued. The Navy reluctantly capitulated, but with a stipulation: the article in question must state that Commander Bucher was offered Thermit in Sasebo but had decided not to take it.

This was the first I'd heard of this, and I was most reluctant to include it without firsthand knowledge of its accuracy. However, in order to get the stories cleared, I finally agreed to mention it, but clearly specifying that this was the "official" Navy version, not mine.

(The Thermit story intrigued me. On the surface it appeared to explain Bucher's failure to bring aboard the TNT in Yokosuka. If Bucher was aware we would be picking up Thermit when we reached our next port, there would be no need for the TNT. Left unexplained, however, were Bucher's excitement at learning that TNT had been found, and Schumacher's guilty admission that he hadn't gotten around to picking up the cans. *If* the Sasebo Thermit story is true, it doesn't clear Bucher of the charge, but compounds it, for it means he was *twice* offered explosives that could have been used to destroy the classified materials and/or scuttle the ship, and *twice* failed to avail himself of the opportunity.)

After the findings of the Court of Inquiry were released, *Washington Post* staff writer George C. Wilson called the verdict "a skillful political compromise." Wilson went on to say, "While nobody wins under this compromise, nobody loses all the way either—except for the public, still waiting for a full accounting on the whos and whys of this foul-up which cost the nation so much."

I'd thought often of Wilson's remarks, agreeing that the American people *were* owed a full accounting, and that thus far they hadn't gotten it. Twice—during the Court of Inquiry and in the *Monitor* articles—official restrictions had kept me from telling my side of the story, a disclosure necessary, I felt, if the whole *Pueblo* incident were to be put in perspective. I now realized that probably the only way I could do this, in full, was in a book. I also realized that as long as I remained in the Navy, I'd have to do all my typing with both hands tied, and that once the book was finished, it could be censored to death, all in the name of national security.

This was my other reason for leaving the Navy. I wanted the truth to be told.

In mid-June I reported to San Diego, and found my last assignment just as unchallenging as I had expected. My predecessor in the job had been transferred a couple months before. As far as I could tell, no one seemed aware that he had gone.

Meantime, I was trying to discover what had happened to my letter of resignation. It was finally located and duly processed, and on June 23 I received a letter granting my request.

In it I was informed that my assignment to the Fleet Anti-Submarine Warfare School "was a result of the detailing process and did not involve political considerations."

The last two paragraphs of the letter were especially interesting: "With regard to your comments on the *Pueblo* incident, it would be inappropriate, in view of the fact that the entire matter was the subject of a very thorough Court of Inquiry, to make further comments on the matter at this time.

"The Chief of Naval Personnel wishes you every good fortune in your transition to civilian life and in all your future endeavors. It is hoped that you will continue an active interest in the affairs of the Navy."

My discharge from the United States Navy took place on June 30, 1969. Coincidentally, Admiral E. E. Grimm, one of the five admirals on the *Pueblo* Court of Inquiry, was retiring from the service at the same time. As I left the base, I passed the parade grounds where the ceremony was taking place. The Navy band was playing "San Diego Sun," a song the admiral had written. My exit occurred with much less fanfare.

While prisoners in North Korea, Gene Lacy and I had often discussed a subject that fascinated us both: the whole recreational vehicle phenomenon, campers, mobile and motor homes. On my return to the United States, Carol and I had purchased a motor home, one of the new Condors. When, shortly after my release from the Navy, I was offered a job managing one of the divisions of Hale Enterprises Coach 'N Camper Center in El Cajon, a suburb of San Diego, I took it.

Although I made a quick adjustment to civilian life, the *Pueblo* incident was never far from mind. There was work on the book. And there was the still unresolved matter of the fitness reports.

A few days before my release from the Navy, I received the last two fitness reports Commander Bucher had written on me.

Captain Stacer and I had anticipated that they would be gross. Commander Bucher lived up to our expectations.

In the first one, which covered the period May 4, 1967, to January 22, 1968, Commander Bucher wrote: "Lt.

Murphy was not professionally prepared to assume the responsibility of executive officer of a small, independently operated ship. He rarely completed any assigned tasks in a timely or satisfactory manner. Mr. Murphy is however soberly disposed. Procrastination and disorganization together with very weak leadership qualities contribute to his inability to get the job done. He was unable to provide any constructive assistance to this command in preparation of the ship's organization. . . ." Bucher concluded this report with, "Mr. Murphy is most competent when making excuses for his procrastinations and other shortcomings."

Bucher saved his Sunday punch for the second report, which covered the period from the day of the seizure, January 23, 1968, to the day of our release, December 21 of that same year. By now I thought I'd heard all of Bucher's wild, irresponsible charges, but in this report he surpassed his best previous efforts.

"On the afternoon of 23 January, during the period that the USS *Pueblo* was under harassment and attack by North Korean Naval and Air Forces, Lt. Murphy in his capacity as Executive Officer received minor wounds resulting from enemy fire but was not incapacitated. He did not perform the functions of reporting the organization assigned and expected of him during this encounter. He appeared partially paralyzed by fear. It was necessary for the Commanding Officer to demand that Mr. Murphy get up from a prone position on two occasions. He did not make normal reports regarding progress of destruction of classified matter nor did he prove of any real assistance to the command in carrying out explicit orders given to him by the Commanding Officer. His inaction and failure to demand reports on progress of destruction was, in the opinion of the Commanding Officer, largely responsible for the loss of any classified documents."

So Bucher had finally settled on his scapegoat. I was the one who was now responsible for the loss of our classified cargo.

410

Bucher continued, "Following the illegal seizure of the ship by the North Koreans and while in detention, Lt. Murphy did show occasional bravery and loyalty to the command. However, he resisted the Commanding Officer's attempts to organize an escape committee and only reluctantly joined passively in attempts to thwart and discredit the North Koreans. His lack of positive leadership prompted the Commanding Officer to bypass him and work through the ship's junior officers and responsible petty officers in putting various plans and actions to disconcert our captors into effect. Mr. Murphy did disclose to the Commanding Officer one well-thought-out escape maneuver and did on occasion give thoughtful advice but those occasions were infrequent."

All the officers had served on the escape committee. At no time had I opposed its organization. I had, however, criticized a couple of Bucher's own escape plans, which I'd felt impractical, judgments in which the other officers concurred. Apparently he was still smarting from that.

Bucher had saved his biggest blast for the conclusion. Captain Stacer had been wrong. Commander Bucher was quite capable of accusing me of collaboration, just so long as he could do it in private and wouldn't have to back up his accusation.

"During the latter part of the crew's captivity, Mr. Murphy told the North Koreans all the many discreditations of our captors which had been perpetrated by the Commanding Officer and of the chain of communication that we had developed within the crew. He has never clearly justified these deeds, nor can the Commanding Officer offer reasonable explanation of his apparent abandonment of his shipmates. It is the frank opinion of the Commanding Officer that this act of Mr. Murphy's would have led to the ultimate death of himself and other officers and crew members by torture within a short period, had the release of the crew not been arranged within a week of his act. He was not mistreated or beaten by the North Koreans before he gave them all the details alluded to

411

herein. I cannot attest to Mr. Murphy's state of mind or sanity at the time of this incident."

In accordance with Navy regulations, I protested these fitness reports in a statement to the Chief of Navy Personnel, a copy of the following also being sent to Commander Bucher:

1. I hereby protest the subject Reports of Fitness as follows:

a. The subjective assumptions contained in the subject reports are basically untrue. For example, references to my alleged cooperation with the North Koreans during the latter part of detention are nothing more than unfounded suspicions on the part of Commander Bucher.

b. The subject reports were filed not at the conclusion of the reporting periods, but during the height of the Court of Inquiry during which the Commander was under extreme stress. He himself was "suspect" of having broken Naval regulations and he was extremely chagrined that I was not vigorously coming to his defense.

[Although I did not receive them until June, the two fitness reports were dated February 28, 1969, two days after Captain Stacer and I met with Miles Harvey and Captain Keys.]

c. In the first report, he alludes to my lack of seasoning on a surface ship. The fact is that the USS *Pueblo* (AGER-2) was my fourth assignment to duty on a surface ship. Commander Bucher had served on only one surface ship (as an Ensign) before commanding *Pueblo*.

d. Commander Bucher frankly admits in his latter report that he bypassed the chain of command in working with the junior officers and not through the Executive Officer.

e. This was the case not only in captivity, but from the early days of precommissioning at Puget Sound Naval Shipyard, Bremerton, Washington. His lack of respect for standard organization caused early dissension and morale problems among the officers and crew.

f. Commander Bucher took the lead in breaking the military Code of Conduct soon after our illegal seizure. He placed the rest of the officers and crew in the difficult position of having to back up the information—both factual and unfactual—which he freely gave to the North Koreans.

g. Many of the crew—including myself—were seriously concerned about Commander Bucher's mental condition all through captivity. Several times during detention he indicated quite strongly to me that he was considering taking his own life.

h. In my opinion, the childish pranks played by Commander Bucher on the North Koreans, in the latter part of detention, served absolutely no purpose but to delay our repatriation and endanger the well-being of the entire crew. When I respectfully let my point of view be known to Commander Bucher, he emotionally accused me of disloyalty.

i. The rash of brutality just prior to our release (referred to as Hell Week) resulted from Commander Bucher's lack of finesse and sophistication in trying to outsmart our captors.

Contrary to his statement, I was mistreated during Hell Week. I did not betray Commander Bucher at this time—or at any other time. But I do have some evidence that he betrayed me to the North Koreans.

j. These two reports, again, were written at a time when the Commander was under heavy stress and would find it extremely difficult to be objective in his evaluation of my service as Executive Officer under him. And they are in conflict with the previous report which he filed—a report which shows no great concern about my training or ability to serve as *Pueblo*'s Executive Officer.

This was the fitness report in which Bucher suggested as a possible future assignment for me, the command of a small auxiliary such as the *Pueblo*.

No matter what the provocation, criticizing a senior

officer is a serious business in the military. I inserted the next paragraph to make clear that this was an unusual situation that necessitated an unusual response:

2. I have refrained from indicting Commander Bucher. This reply is not intended as a violation of Article 1701, U.S. Navy Regulations, but it is felt in view of the language used in the subject reports, that license was given to amplify the factual base upon which I have been condemned. I do not take issue with the Commanding Officer's responsibility to evaluate personnel performance.

3. I respectfully request that these reports of fitness be set aside since they lack fact, objectivity, and are only indicative of the personal vindictiveness and animosity which Commander Bucher has harbored toward me since the illegal seizure of the *Pueblo* in the Sea of Japan.

The Navy denied my request to set aside the two reports of fitness. Captain Stacer and I then requested an open hearing to determine: (1) whether Commander Bucher's retention of the power to write fitness and evaluation reports while suspect of violation of a Navy article was illegal; and (2) whether the allegations in the reports were true or false.

To date, this request has been denied us, repeatedly, at various levels of the chain of command. We intend to continue to pursue it, taking our case into the federal courts if necessary. I want Commander Bucher to take the stand to make these charges openly. And I want to have the opportunity to refute them, not just through my own testimony but also that of other witnesses who can attest to their falsity.

Until this happens, I, for one, will never consider the case of the USS *Pueblo* closed.

414

= Epilogue: Bucher's Book =

In June of 1970 *Newsweek* sought out Commander Lloyd M. Bucher at the Naval Postgraduate School at Monterey, to interview him for its "Where Are They Now?" column.

The commander had been forced to drop out of his class because of recurrrent headaches, *Newsweek* reported. Bucher had other complaints. He was unable to obtain even a confidential clearance. He was convinced that, for both medical and political reasons, the Navy would never promote him. And he had not had a fitness report in more than two and a half years.

Although sorely tempted to write and tell him I had two fitness reports which I'd be glad to give him, I resisted the impulse.

Two months later Bucher's fitness report was made public. Co-authored with Mark Rascovich, author of *The Bedford Incident*, it was published by Doubleday & Company, Inc., under the title *Bucher: My Story*.

Reporters, covering the early days of our return, when Bucher himself was quarantined and therefore not available to them, sought out his friends and former shipmates to get their impressions of Bucher the man. They then depicted him as a maverick, a hard-drinking, rough-riding, surfaced submariner, given to doing things his own way, and damn the consequences.

Apparently the image bothered Bucher, for the central character in his personal saga is not like that at all. In his book, Bucher is an officer who respects the chain of com-

415

mand; always looks for his answers in Navy Regulations; and obeys, never questions, orders, even if they are wrong. Moreover, nearly all his waking moments are spent agonizing over the problems of his ship. When, in those rare instances he is away from it, all his thoughts are on what he can do to improve the *Pueblo*.

Given his dedication, it is amazing that by the time the *Pueblo* sailed she still had serious problems.

There were, of course, good and valid reasons for many of her inadequacies, and Bucher cites them. Budget cuts. The frustrations of trying to adapt an old ship to a new role. Confusion over exactly what that role was, due to the need for security. Yet, even after these legitimate justifications are noted, important work on the USS *Pueblo* remained undone, needed modifications that could have been made were not, projects vital to the *Pueblo*'s mission were never carried through. Why? Bucher admits that he finally reached the point where he had to give up. His quest for perfection was irritating Navy brass. Fearful of losing his first command, "I had to be satisfied or otherwise clinch my dismissal as Commanding Officer (and ruin any subsequent Naval career). My stubbornness in making *Pueblo* the most efficient intelligence gathering ship in the Navy had evidently reached its limits and the time had come to roll with the punches."

A similar explanation is provided for his failure to persist in his quest for adequate destruct and scuttling devices. After searching Yokosuka for TNT, and learning that even Clark of the *Banner* didn't carry it, "I decided it was time for me to give up. All I could accomplish by pressing it further was to upset Admiral Johnson and his staff by giving them the impression they had a skipper on their hands who seemed obsessed with the capability to blow up his own ship. I didn't want to cross the boundary between chronic worry-wart and outright nut!"

In Bucher's book there is no indication that TNT *was* found in Yokosuka, and that he neglected to have it brought aboard.

Nor, interestingly enough, is there any mention of the "official" Navy version, that he was told he could pick up Thermit in Sasebo.

His silence on both points is perhaps understandable. If he uses the Navy story to justify Yokosuka, he still has to explain Sasebo.

There is still another reason why the *Pueblo* was less than the most efficient intelligence-gathering ship in the U.S. Navy. Her executive officer was incapable of carrying out even the simplest assigned tasks. In addition to being "quite rusty in the sailor's arts," Murphy was "often absent in both work and recreation." But, inefficient though he was, Bucher does not replace him, the decision to do so coming only when it's too late and the *Pueblo* is already in the Sea of Japan. Eight months and one excellent fitness report after Murphy comes aboard.

Bucher alternately objects to Murphy being on deck bright and early at 0600 hours and never being around when he needs him. But then what can you expect of a Christian Scientist who doesn't smoke, will drink only *Cokes* when he's out with the boys, and *keeps animal crackers in his desk!* (It was perhaps fortunate that during his inspection Bucher overlooked the Play Clay that was there too. Both, incidentally, were kept on hand to occupy the children when the *Pueblo* families visited the ship.)

Unmentioned are Bucher's own all-too-frequent absences from the ship, as well as the numerous occasions when he was aboard but incapacitated. In his book, drinking is not one of Bucher's problems, though the not drinking of his executive officer is. Thus, when the incident with the San Diego shore patrol occurs, Bucher hears of it not when coming aboard ship with Tim Harris after an evening of partying, but rather is rousted from bed; this, of course, makes the shore-patrol officer's official complaint, that Bucher was drunk and abusive, appear ridiculous.

Unmentioned too are the real issues that divided us: his habit of playing hopscotch with the chain of command;

whether the *Pueblo* should be run as a surface ship or a sub; where the guns should be positioned; what training the crew should receive; from which position the ship should be conned in a general-quarters situation.

As for the other members of the wardroom cast, I suspect it must have startled Steve Harris, after his many arguments with the skipper, to read: "Our relationship was cordial in spite of our being totally divergent personalities, and it was supported by a respect and understanding of each other's problems."

Bucher, however, is unable to maintain this fiction. He needs Steve too badly as one of his scapegoats. By the time the *Pueblo* is off station, Bucher's bitterness on being overruled in the detachment-department controversy surfaces. "A ship can have only one captain, but I had frequently to remind Steve of this fact, often in language heavily interspersed with invectives." Though Bucher speaks of the sod hut as being the *Pueblo*'s one reason for existence, it is obvious this galls him. There are even indications that his distrust of Steve at times approaches paranoia, that he thinks Steve may be spying on him: "Steve was writing up his own technical message which would go to different addresses than mine. His message was written in a language all its own, which could only be clearly understood by another intelligence specialist. It annoyed me that he was reporting to a different commander and that he had the authority to release messages that might wittingly or unwittingly reflect adversely on the *Pueblo*."

Bucher does not repeat his earlier charge that there were times when he was not allowed access to the sod hut, but he does state that when on one occasion he attempted to inspect Steve's office, Steve told him there was information in the files that he was not cleared to see.

Thus the groundwork is laid. Even he, the commanding officer, did not really know how much classified information the ship was carrying.

By contrast, his other officers can do no wrong. For

example, entire blame for the near collision of the *Pueblo* on the reefs en route to Sasebo is laid on his exec's poor navigation, with nary a mention that the green officer he made OOD, Tim Harris, failed to make the necessary course corrections.

They can do no wrong, that is, until we come to January 23, 1968.

When *Bucher: My Story* appeared, several reviewers commented on the commander's powers of near-total recall. He not only could remember every single event that happened, he could time each precisely, in minutes, even seconds. After "three minutes" this occurred, while "ten seconds later" that took place. In Bucher's narrative of that fateful January afternoon it would appear that every moment has been accounted for, that Bucher has forgotten nothing.

Only when you compare Bucher's account with a time-table of the actual events that took place that afternoon—realizing that from the sighting of the SO-1 to the moment of boarding, approximately two hours and thirty minutes transpired—does it become obvious that, though exact when it comes to minutes and seconds, Bucher does less well with quarter, half, and whole hours, and that his powers of recall are in fact highly selective.

This criticism is not minor, for the result of this synopsizing of events (in some cases combining several incidents into one, in others shifting their sequence or omitting them entirely) is to give the impression that the Commanding Officer of the USS *Pueblo* was a man who never hesitated, never faltered, but met each new challenge with a swift and appropriate countermeasure, until, time finally running out, he and his ship are trapped in the inexorable rush of events totally beyond his control.

It makes for a dramatic story. As history, however, it leaves something to be desired. To help refresh the commander's near-perfect memory, we'll look a little more closely at Bucher's account, putting back in those omissions and examining some new and quite startling additions.

In Bucher's book, the SO-1 is first spotted, approaches, the *Pueblo*'s nationality is questioned, the American ensign is raised, the P-4s are sighted, the *Pueblo*'s position is repeatedly checked, the KORCOMs hoist the HEAVE TO OR I WILL FIRE message, its meaning is puzzled over, the *Pueblo* replies I AM IN INTERNATIONAL WATERS, the first Pinnacle is drafted and sent, the P-4s arrive, break formation, and surround the *Pueblo*, and Bucher writes: "It had only been a little over twenty minutes since the SO-1 was first sighted."

(Bailey was on the teletype to Japan. The exact time of each of his messages was recorded there. Bailey noted the sighting of the SO-1 by tapping COMPANY OUTSIDE at exactly noon, 1200 hours. He sent the first Pinnacle message at 1254 [12:54 P.M.] fifty-four minutes later. Bucher has already managed to misplace more than a half-hour.

(But there is an even more important discrepancy hidden here. Bailey announced the sighting of the P-4s at 1244 [12:44 P.M.] with GOT COMPANY OUTSIDE AND MORE COMING. Say it took five minutes for Bailey to learn what was happening outside. This still means Bucher had nearly forty minutes to leave the scene before the P-4s were even sighted. In his book they have arrived and surrounded the *Pueblo* in a little over twenty.)

Bucher queries Lacy on how long it would take to scuttle the ship; Lacy replies two hours. Bucher has Leach hoist INTEND TO REMAIN IN THE AREA (Bucher's book omits UNTIL TOMORROW). Two MIGs buzz the ship, a fourth P-4 appears (appropriately "out of nowhere"), plus a second SO-1 (which again only Bucher sees), Lacy asks Bucher if he should go to general quarters, Bucher replies negatively, Skip begins work on the second Pinnacle, the SO-1 and one of the P-4s close to form a boarding party, the P-4, fenders rigged for boarding, approaches the *Pueblo*, and Bucher decides the moment has come to leave the area.

(Bucher doesn't mention the time. But at 1318 [1:18

420

P.M.] Bailey started transmitting Pinnacle 2, which refers to Bucher's intention to depart the area, so the actual starting of the ship must have occurred about this time or shortly before. Thus, give or take a few minutes either way, it was approximately one and a quarter hours after the sighting of the SO-1 before Bucher decided it might be best if he followed orders and disengaged.)

In Bucher's book, as the P-4 approaches the *Pueblo*, intent upon boarding, he quickly responds by calling down the voice tube, "All ahead one-third. . . . Build up speed to two-thirds, then full. We are making a dignified withdrawal, not a run for it." Then, noticing the Nansen bottles are still in the water, he orders them hauled aboard as the *Pueblo* steams on.

(As I recall the episode, Bucher first ordered, "All ahead full," then was forced to slow to one-third when Tuck reminded him of the Nansen cast, several minutes passing before Bucher was again able to increase the speed. Others, including Schumacher, support Bucher's story, noting that Bucher includes in his second Pinnacle that he intended to do this. This point was one of many disputed during Bucher's "mock court," Bucher being so insistent upon his version that most eventually gave in.)

Bucher then gives the order to "prepare to destroy" all classified material, and tells Leach to signal THANK YOU FOR YOUR CONSIDERATION—AM DEPARTING THE AREA. He was not being cocky in hoisting this message, Bucher explains, rather he "had a long signal hoisted which I hoped would cause a stall while they broke it down. . . ."

(The insulting flag hoist was ordered before Bucher gave the "All-ahead-full" order, not after; while the "prepare-to-destroy" command was not given until much later, after the shelling had started.)

Lieutenant Murphy's voice "rattled out of the tube with a less than confident tone," asking if he should try to raise Kamiseya on the Hi Comm circuit to let them know what was transpiring.

Bucher: "The emergency had reached the point where

421

the use of the Hi Comm voice communication with Japan was justified. 'Affirmative—go ahead and get them on the line,' I agreed."

(My decision to try to reach Japan on the Hi Comm was made on my own initiative, without consulting Bucher. Missing from his account is that he later read me out for this, screaming, "Do you think I want the whole world to know what's happening?")

With the explosion of the first shells from the SO-1, Bucher yells down the voice tube, "Commence emergency destruction. . . ."

(At this time Bucher ordered "prepare to destroy." The "commence-destruction" order did not come until later, after Bucher's return to the pilothouse and as a result of a frantic call from Steve. Omitted also is any mention that even then Bucher first denied permission, then changed his mind.)

Bucher recounts how he felt when the firing started: "My own feelings were of an almost overwhelming need to retaliate by shooting back, to bring my ship to General Quarters and Battle Stations. The command was on the tip of my tongue, but I choked it down. There were in fact no Battle Stations on *Pueblo* and General Quarters really meant nothing more than manning Damage Control."

Bucher then calls down the voice tube to set a "modified general quarters."

(To the best of my recollection, this order was not given until after the order to commence emergency destruction, but I may be in error on this. I do know that it occurred after Bucher moved the conn to the pilot house, and was delivered in person, rather than over the voice tube. And it was hardly the decisive act Bucher recalls, since he first told me to order general quarters over the 1MC, which I did, then, almost immediately changed his mind and had me make that a modified GQ.)

Finally realizing that the signal bridge is less than the safest place from which to conn the ship when under at-

422

tack, Bucher scampers down the ladder to the pilot house. (In his account, he follows Law, Leach, and Robin; in theirs they almost land on top of him.) Bucher enters the pilot house, to find his officers and men cowering on the deck. He angrily orders them to their feet, all but Murphy obeying. Murphy remains prone on the deck, whining, "But sir . . . they are still shooting at us!" Bucher helps Murphy up with a well-placed kick to his backside.

(As noted earlier, this wasn't the way it happened; it also wasn't "when" it happened. This incident didn't occur until much later—after the ship had been twice stopped, Hodges and the others seriously injured, and Bucher had waved his white stocking cap as an emblem of surrender. The cap-waving incident is never mentioned in Bucher's book; instead, he throws a coffeecup at them. Nor, though Bucher himself testified to it during the Court of Inquiry, does Bucher in his book at any point tell Lacy or anyone else that he is considering surrendering the ship. The reasons for these significant omissions will soon become apparent.)

During this period Bucher is firing off orders almost as fast as the P-4s are spewing bullets.

(My recollection of Bucher's activity during this period, which coincides with the recollections of others present, is that Bucher wandered back and forth across the pilot house, muttering curses at the North Koreans but doing little else.)

At this point the real villain of Bucher's book appears.

Throughout our detention and during the Court of Inquiry, Bucher had vainly sought to avoid one inescapable fact: given his first command, he had surrendered the ship. There was something very pathetic in his search for an alternative to this unpleasant truth, a quest that had taken him from the explanation that the ship had been seized by superior force to the justification that the *Pueblo* obviously hadn't surrendered because she had never lowered her flag.

Now, finally, Bucher finds his answer, and his chief scapegoat.

In a sudden turnabout, Bucher admits that the USS *Pueblo* was indeed surrendered.

But he, Commander Lloyd M. Bucher, didn't surrender her.

The guilty party was Chief Warrant Officer Gene Lacy!

As another burst of shells from the SO-1 crashes through the pilothouse, everyone, Bucher included, hits the deck.

"I was stunned by Gene Lacy's wild-eyed look as he dragged himself back to his feet and suddenly yelled at me:

" 'Are you going to stop this son-of-a-bitch or not?'

"There was only a fraction of hesitation before he [Lacy] reached out himself and yanked the handles of the annunciator to All Stop. The blindly alert engineers isolated three decks down instantly rang the answering bells. . . . I kept staring at Gene in utter disbelief for another fifteen seconds. Fifteen seconds that brought the stark realization that my most experienced officer, my most trusted friend aboard this ill-starred little ship, had robbed me of the last vestige of support in my efforts to save the mission, leaving me alone with an Executive Officer who had proven to be unreliable and two very young and inexperienced junior officers [Schumacher and Tim Harris] on my bridge. Suddenly the complete uselessness of further resistance flooded my brain. It would only result in our being shot to pieces and a lot of good men being killed to no avail, because the North Koreans would in the end get most of our secret documents. Instead of lunging for the annunciator and racking it back to All Ahead Full, I turned my back on it and Gene, walked out on the starboard wing of the bridge."

(Questioned during the Court of Inquiry as to who stopped the ship the first time, Bucher stated, according to the CIB summary, that "he ordered the *Pueblo* to stop and, although he did not personally ring up the order, it was done with his tacit approval." Earlier he told the court that when Lacy asked if he should stop the ship he "nodded" his concurrence.)

424

Bucher then stands on the starboard wing, "for perhaps ten seconds," musing on the fact that "Four of my officers were on the bridge with me, but none of them came forward with a single word of advice. . . . None of them came forward to advise even the simplest alternatives: to go down fighting or to strike our flag then and there. None of them said a word to me. There was, during those critical ten seconds, no communication between us whatsoever. It was all up to me, and me alone."

Inexplicably, Bucher then turns around, reenters the pilothouse, and announcing that he intends to stall as long as necessary to complete the destruction, orders the undependable Lacy, the man who in his wild-eyed panic had just surrendered the ship, *to take the deck!*

With Lacy in command of the ship, Bucher goes below to see how the destruction is progressing. Although reconciled to the likelihood the *Pueblo* will be boarded by the KORCOMs, he is convinced that this will be nothing more than a search operation, that they won't dare seize the ship while in international waters. Entering the sod hut, he finds Steve Harris "had wedged himself behind the protection of a rack of radio receivers," while his CTs are all lying on the floor. Ordering Steve out and the men to work, Bucher says of Harris: "His actions were dazed and uncoordinated, like those of a man on the brink of panic, and it forcibly struck me that here in the sod hut, as well as on the bridge, leadership was failing me in the emergency."

His fifth and last officer having betrayed him, Bucher then returns to the bridge, where, spotting the SO-1's signal, he personally orders the *Pueblo* to follow at one-third.

(Why Bucher doesn't blame Lacy for this too is a puzzle. He did at one point during detention.)

Bucher then goes below to see if all the classified material has been removed from his stateroom, then gives his pistols to one of the sailors to throw overboard. On his return to the bridge he discovers, to his astonishment, that Lacy has rung up the speed from one-third to two-thirds.

Lacy feebly explains that the KORCOMs ordered it. Bucher bellows that he is giving the orders, not the North Koreans, and has the annunciator handles yanked back to one-third.

Although Lacy has just added to his growing list of irresponsible actions the disobeying of a direct order, Bucher leaves him with the conn!

(It should be noted that although in his book Bucher has me standing transfixed and slack-jawed behind the helmsman, I was actually below at the time of the alleged incident, checking the progress of the destruction, ordering those men not already working to do so, and inspecting my own stateroom to see if any classified material remained. Each of the officers in turn did this. Therefore, not being present, I have no personal knowledge of whether Lacy did or did not increase the speed. During detention, Lacy would deny having done so.

(I had returned to the pilot house, however, by the time the following event took place.)

We come now to the second stopping of the ship, a critical decision, for it brought about a resumption of the shelling and resulted in the death of Hodges. During the early phases of Bucher's "mock court," he had accused Lacy of this also, then later backed down and admitted he had done it himself. At various times he had offered differing explanations for his act: (1) he wanted to see what would happen; (2) he wanted to inspect the status of the destruction; and (3) he wanted to stall for more time. In his book, Bucher reiterates the third explanation, but with one new and most significant addition: he wants to "take back whatever time the Koreans had just gained" because of Lacy's increasing the speed to two-thirds.

Thus at least a portion of the burden of guilt for Hodges' death is shifted onto Gene Lacy.

The KORCOMs react almost instantly, with a renewal of the shelling. Realizing his mistake, Bucher orders the ship started again, but the firing continues. Learning there have

426

been casualties and extensive damage, Bucher gives the unreliable Lacy both the deck and the conn and goes below. Seeing the seriousness of Hodges' condition, he calls the bridge and orders me to lay below and break out the morphine. On his return topside, he finds me absent from the bridge, and "presumed" I was following his orders about the narcotics. The implication, which is never corrected, is that possibly I was not. From this point on, Bucher has me absent from the bridge. Much later, just before the actual boarding starts, he returns to his stateroom, to find me "sort of listlessly fumbling about over nothing in particular, then looking surprised at seeing me. . . ." Bucher then observes: "I thought it had been a long time since he [Murphy] left the bridge without especially being missed."

(Here again Bucher has made a number of changes. The call for morphine came moments after the report from damage control, and although I can't recall whether it was from Law or Baldridge, it certainly wasn't from Bucher, as he was standing next to me in the pilot house and I had to ask his permission to leave the bridge. I then immediately went below, broke out the morphine, sent a man for oxygen when Baldridge called for it, and realizing the burning had stopped, got the men organized and working again. I remained with Hodges some time, until after he lost consciousness. It was only then that Bucher came down, at which time I started back to the bridge, stopping on the O-1 level to pick up and throw overboard the classified documents that I saw there. In the interim, Bucher had returned topside, for when I ran across the deck he was standing on the port wing, frantically waving his white stocking cap and yelling, "Stop firing, you bastards!" Just as I entered the pilot house, the SO-1 let loose another barrage, and I yelled for everyone to hit the deck. This was when Bucher, upon entering, called us all cowards.

(Curiously, Bucher's book reveals he was not totally immune to the impulse to seek shelter when being fired upon: ". . . I threw myself down on the deck to dodge the lethal

427

hail. . . . All four of us flattened ourselves on the deck. . . . Everybody on the bridge flattened down before this hail of fire . . . we hit the deck . . . listening for the following pizzicato of machine gun bursts to let up before returning upright. . . .")

Steve Harris calls and asks permission to notify Japan that he can't destroy all the classified material. Bucher asks Steve what remains. In Bucher's book, Steve replies: "'Mostly technical pubs and such. We simply can't get to them all, sir, but . . .' his voice faded into an agitated whimper '. . . but I think we've gotten rid of everything else.'" Bucher grants permission to send the message, "if that's the situation as you see it," but urges him to continue the destruction anyway.

(I was in the pilothouse when Steve called, but, of course, heard only Bucher's side of the conversation. I've tried to remember the words he used, but can't. All I can recall is a lot of swearing.)

Reassured by Steve that most of the classified material has been destroyed, that only technical pubs and such remain—only later, to his horror, will he learn that this was not the case, the unstated implication being that had he known this, his next act might have been different—Bucher now decides to obey the new KORCOM signal to stop the ship. With all the North Korean guns still pointed at the *Pueblo*, "I had no alternative but to order Gene to ring up All Stop and to stand by to receive boarders."

(With Bucher's permission, I had left the bridge and was on my way below while this was occurring. I didn't see the SO-1's signal hoist, but I did spot the P-4 approaching, fenders rigged for boarding, and I did feel the change in the engines and heard Bucher order over the 1MC for a crew to help the KORCOMs board.)

In Bucher's book, it is Lacy who gets on the 1MC and orders the deck watch to help the North Koreans.

Lacy asks Bucher if he should make an announcement about the Code of Conduct. "This pertinent suggestion calmly spoken took me somewhat by surprise after the way he had been acting during the past hour. It was in its way reassuring that he was yet able to function rationally."

Giving Lacy the deck and the conn, Bucher lays below to change uniforms. The KORCOMs then board, capturing the USS *Pueblo* and all her crew. Their intentions, Bucher finally realizes, go beyond just searching the ship.

Bucher strongly protests the seizure, but is knocked down and kicked for his efforts. When one of the KORCOM officers, who can apparently read and write a little English but not speak it, writes "many mans" on a piece of paper, Bucher consults with the ship's yeoman and writes down "83."

This was something the KORCOMs could quickly ascertain, by simply counting the men, but it also marks Bucher's first departure from the Code of Conduct. It is, from the evidence of his own book, not the last. With the subsequent boarding of an interpreter, there begins a "dialogue of accusations and denials" that continues until the ship reaches Wonsan, through the time on the bus, and then all night on the train. Bucher repeatedly denies he is CIA, reiterates the peaceful oceanographic-research story, gives a variety of witty answers to other queries—the mission of the ship was to measure sunspots, the fires aboard were to make ice cream—but never once again thinks of the Code. He does note that throughout the night he was taken from one car into another, to be reinterrogated, the same questions being asked, the same replies given. "These repeated sessions lasted anywhere from ten to twenty minutes before I was taken back to my seat in the other car. Then again a half hour later, and regularly through the rest of this journey through darkness."

It never occurs to Bucher that possibly the KORCOMs are using his willingness to talk to persuade the crew that it is useless to remain silent, since their captain obviously isn't doing so. The thought never crosses his mind.

We arrived at the Barn in the early-morning hours of

January 24. Later that morning, the *Pueblo*'s officers were removed from their rooms and taken down the hall for their "trial," at the conclusion of which we were told we would be shot before sundown.

This was when Commander Bucher performed what I then felt, and still feel, was an incredibly brave act, telling the KORCOMs, "If you will release the ship and crew, I will remain in North Korea in their place."

In Bucher's book this becomes, "Shoot me! But let my officers and crew return to our ship and take it home."

Bucher then describes his own interrogations and beatings, the sight of the dying South Korean spy, and the threat which finally caused him to break and sign his first confession: that if he didn't sign, each member of the crew would be shot, starting with the youngest.

Although the confession was dated January 24, according to Bucher the signing occurred sometime in the early-morning hours of the twenty-fifth. In his book, as in the Court of Inquiry, Bucher states that this initial confession contained no reference to intrusion, that some hours passed before Super C brought him back to the interrogation room and demanded that he include the intrusion charge. Bucher refused. Super C informed him that his executive officer and navigator had already admitted to this.

Bucher's book: "So they had worked over Ed too! My heart sank. Poor Ed, I thought. . . . For all the troubles there had been between us during the past months, I was sure that he would only cooperate with these people under extreme duress—as I myself had done." When Super C then asks Bucher if he would like to see his executive officer's confession, Bucher refuses the offer. After all, it is only a piece of paper. They had extracted something similar from him. So what?

Again threatened with the execution of his crew, Bucher reluctantly adds the intrusion admission to his confession.

When, during the Court of Inquiry, Bucher first implied that I had confessed first, at least five days before I actually did so, I didn't know how to disprove the allegation. But then, following the completion of the court, I thought of a possible way, and began going through the scrapbooks of clippings on the *Pueblo* incident that Carol had kept. From the first shattering headlines that announced our capture to the much happier ones that told of our release eleven months later, Carol had faithfully clipped and pasted, filling more than a dozen huge volumes. Page by page, I began looking for a clipping that would indicate exactly when my confession was first released. It seemed to me that, coming from the ship's navigator, the North Koreans would waste no time in making the confession public, because of its importance to their case.

I'd signed the confession on the morning of January 30. Therefore, I reasoned, it should have been released that day or at most a day or two later. If I could find a clipping supporting this, it seemed to me it would be strong circumstantial evidence of the falsity of Bucher's allegation.

I found when Bucher's confession was made public. On the morning of January 25 Tokyo radio had monitored a news broadcast from the Korean Central News Agency that released portions of what it alleged to be a confession of Commander Bucher made during a press conference. Later that same day, a tape of this confession, reputedly in the Commander's own voice, was also monitored in Japan. Both included the intrusion admission.

I also found that the North Koreans had released the confessions of three of the other *Pueblo* officers (Steve Harris, Tim Harris, and Schumacher) by February 3, but mine, I discovered, had not been released until February 5.

I'd found what I was looking for, but, I now realized, it proved nothing. Though I might argue that my confession hadn't been released until long after Bucher's, Bucher could argue just as convincingly that if the KORCOMs had waited six days to release my confession, they could just as easily have waited eleven or twelve days.

Only then did it occur to me that my logic had been faulty. The North Koreans could have any number of good

431

reasons for delaying its release. For example, they might have kept it in reserve to use as a surprise rebuttal to any charges made at the UN or during the negotiations at Pyongyang.

Not until reading the clippings did I discover the most likely reason. What they had released was not my first confession, which admitted to a single intrusion, but the revised version, in which the number of intrusions had been increased. As far as I could determine, my first confession, to a solitary intrusion, had never been made public. Apparently I'd broken and confessed too late for the document to be of much use to them, for just after this they decided to up the ante.

All this left me exactly where I had been when I started. I had some circumstantial evidence that I'd confessed after Bucher, but no real proof.

It was not until reading Bucher's book that I found it. Perhaps fittingly, it was Bucher's mania for exact times that provided the evidence I needed.

On arriving at the Barn, I was placed in a room with Ginther, Rosales, and Spear. I was taken out once that first day, late in the morning, when all the *Pueblo* officers were brought together and told they would be shot before sundown. After that, we were marched back to our rooms. I would remain in mine the rest of that day and all that night, with my three cellmates. With the exception of brief trips down the hall to the head, usually accompanied by one or more of the others, I was not again taken from the room until approximately eleven A.M. on January 25, at which time I had my first solitary interrogation.

Three men—Ginther, Spear, and Rosales—can attest to this. Two of them—Ginther and Rosales—can also affirm that I was gone about one hour, since when I returned the noon meal had been served and they had just started eating. During my absence, Spear had been taken out, to return much later, after having been savagely beaten.

In his book, Bucher does not say precisely when he signed

the amended confession, admitting to the intrusion, except that it was sometime on the morning of January 25. But he does say that after he did so, he was returned to his room and served breakfast, he made a trip to the head and "within a half hour" after this he was taken back to the interrogation room, where Super C began rehearsing him for a press conference, which would take place "exactly thirty minutes from now." So, by Bucher's own reckoning, he had to have signed the confession at least one hour before he faced the KORCOM press.

This press conference was solo, with Bucher the only *Pueblo* officer present. During it, according to the *Pyongyang Times*, this exchange occurred:

Journalist: "Were you captured while carrying out espionage activities after intruding deep into the territorial waters of the Democratic People's Republic of Korea?"

Bucher: "I was captured while carrying out espionage activities after intruding deep into the territorial waters of the Democratic People's Republic of Korea."

In his book, Bucher does not specify exactly what time the press conference took place. Nor, returning to the newspaper clippings, could I find any reference to the time, except that it had occurred that morning. I was just about to give up, sure I was pursuing another blind lead, when I decided to scan my file of CIB summaries from the Court of Inquiry.

There I found it, in Bucher's own testimony, as he gave it on the afternoon of January 23, 1969: "He noted that on the morning of the twenty-fifth he was told that a press conference would be held at about ten A.M. and was provided with the questions to be asked and the answers he was to read."

By Bucher's own estimates, he had signed the amended confession, admitting to the intrusion, at least an hour before this, which would make the time no later than nine A.M. I was not taken out of my room for questioning until eleven A.M.

Just when, Commander Bucher, did I have the chance to confess first?

433

At this time Bucher, of course, was isolated from the rest of the crew, and had no firsthand knowledge of what we had or hadn't admitted. It is quite possible that Super C, in his attempts to extract the amended confession, did tell Bucher that I had already confessed to the intrusion. As already noted, Super C was a master at the technique of divide and conquer. The real point, however, is that Bucher apparently believed him, that even this early he was falling for Super C's tricks.

Questioned during the Court of Inquiry about his sessions with Super C, Bucher bragged how, using his native ingenuity, he outfoxed him time and again. From the start, Bucher said, he had "a distinct impression I was winning these psychological battles."

In reading the section of Bucher's book dealing with our time in the Country Club, I was surprised to find an admission by Bucher that he had attempted to hammer out one consistent account of the capture of the ship. The section contains a number of startling revelations.

"I had tried to review the events of those fateful few hours, principally to discover whether I had blacked out sometime between being fired upon and wounded, and the boarding of the *Pueblo*," Bucher writes, a statement as amazing as it is sudden, for it comes without prologue. Up to this point, Bucher has not once indicated the slightest doubt about his recollections of those events. "No hour of January 23, 1968, escaped my examination. . . . To try and clear my mind, I asked during our mealtime gatherings that all officers give me their individual recollections of the action, scribbling them down on smuggled notes, or passing them on to me verbally when they could. Everybody eagerly complied including Gene Lacy, but I was struck by him omitting any mention of his having rung up All Stop without my orders, then disobeyed them completely when I was checking things in the sod hut by speeding up the ship in compliance to KORCOM signals as they escorted us toward Wonsan. When I questioned him about this, he flatly de-

434

nied having done any such thing. He had a look of chagrined horror on his face. I knew Gene well enough that I
knew that he was not deliberately lying. Whose memory
had blacked out, his or mine? I had to know."

Managing to speak to Quartermaster Law alone in the
head, Bucher questions him about the incident. According
to Bucher, Law confirms his version, as do "some of my
other officers." With the aid of these eyewitnesses, Bucher
is able to "make Gene realize that he must have done something terribly wrong at a time of which he had no recollection. He became so crushed and despondent that I
began regretting ever having brought up the matter. . . ."

One portion of the above story is correct. Lacy's look of
horror, which followed Bucher's accusation, was real. I was
there, and I saw it. Like the rest of us, Gene was stunned
by the lengths to which Bucher would go to find a scapegoat for his own actions. But contrary to Bucher's assertion
that Lacy finally admitted his guilt, he firmly and emphati-
cally continued to deny, until Bucher finally dropped the
subject, this and all the other charges Bucher made.

Bucher continues: "It took several weeks to snap Gene
Lacy out of his private misery and rejoin us in our com-
munal one."

Bucher then notes that each of the officers had to live
with his own guilts: Gene "a particular hell trying to penetrate the blank spot of his mind that hid actions which he
only knew from the account of others"; Steve Harris
"agonized over his inability to completely destroy the classified material in his sod hut"; Ed Murphy "worried over an
accumulation of failures." The list goes on, with one exception, Bucher himself. Having personally done nothing
wrong, he magnanimously says, "I suffered for all of them."

There are a few times in his book when Bucher comes
close to admitting possible error. There is the sudden
change in the KORCOM attitude in October: "Had I led
them [the crew] too far in our 'resistance' capers and compromised their chances of release? There were ominous

435

signs that this was so." But the feeling soon gives way to another. On being shown the magazine photograph of the finger gesture by Super C, Bucher observes: "As he ranted and raved about it, I could not help a feeling of triumph that we had actually got through to the United States with one of our efforts to expose KORCOM lies about the *Pueblo*. . . ."

A second volume could be written consisting of just the omissions from Bucher's book.

The lengthy Court of Inquiry—which lasted from January 20 to March 13, 1969—rates only eight pages in Bucher's book and contains few direct quotes from the testimony, although Bucher, unlike the *Pueblo*'s other officers, as a party to the proceedings had access to the transcript. This section may have been shortened in the interests of brevity. One cannot help noting, however, that this condensation enables Bucher to say of the court's findings against him: "I cannot recall there was a single word of testimony to support the charges, except for the loss of the classified materials to which I had already admitted in court." To aid in his recollections, the court found Bucher should be tried for five alleged offenses. In addition to the loss of the classified documents, one—"permitting his ship to be searched while he had the power to resist"—he disputed. This leaves three: (1) "failing to take immediate and aggressive protective measures when his ship was attacked by the North Korean forces"—Bucher himself admitted in court that he decided against manning the guns; (2) "complying with the orders of the North Korean forces to follow them into port"—Bucher himself admitted in court that he gave the order to do this; and (3) "negligently failing to ensure, before departure for sea, that his officers and crew were properly organized, stationed, and trained in preparation for emergency destruction of classified material"—and this Bucher himself also admitted in court, stating that no destruct drills were ever held aboard the *Pueblo*.

Bucher's brevity also eliminates any need to explain the many discrepancies between the version which appears in his book and the story Bucher and the other witnesses told in court. With one unavoidable exception. Why, when he appeared before the Court of Inquiry, did Bucher make no mention of Lacy's irresponsible actions? Especially when in his book he states of the forthcoming proceedings, "I knew I had to tell the full story of *Pueblo* even if some of it hurt. I owed this, and much more, to my country and the Navy." He did tell the intelligence debriefers, Bucher explains, but when it came to the court, "I decided to testify . . . only on those aspects of *Pueblo* operations that applied to my own conduct, omitting any references to poor or unsatisfactory conduct on the part of any of my crew of officers." Like Steve Harris?

I wasn't too surprised, in reading Bucher's book, to find still another omission. There was no mention of the charge that I had betrayed both him and the crew to the North Koreans. Bucher was well aware that these accusations could not stand the light of exposure.

There are also, as has already been amply indicated, numerous statements in Bucher's book that are contrary to fact. Because of their implications, and the importance Bucher himself accords them, two more deserve mention.

Discovering the lack of proficiency in the Korean language of our two Marine interpreters only after we are at sea, Bucher states, italics his, *"If I had known their interpretative inability, I would have refused to undertake the operation until they had been replaced by personnel who could handle that assignment."*

Bucher did know. Chicca and Hammond had told Steve Harris, upon reporting aboard in Yokosuka, that it had been three years since they had studied Korean in school and that neither had used it since. This was one of the reasons they gave for wanting to get out of the assignment, neither man wishing to make the trip, since both had pregnant wives, Chicca's expecting her baby in just a month. Steve Harris had immediately gone to Bucher

437

with this information, and though Bucher had cursed out Steve for this, as if he personally were at fault, to my knowledge he never suggested postponing the trip. While agreeing totally with Bucher that we should have rated competent interpreters, and that if we had we might well have avoided the encounter by monitoring the ship-to-shore messages of the SO-1, Bucher's charge carries the implication that either Chicca and Hammond hid their shortcomings from Steve Harris and then lied when questioned about it during the Court of Inquiry, or Steve himself, for reasons of his own, never bothered to pass on this information. Neither is true.

In emphasizing this, Bucher obviously intends to give the impression that had not the true facts been concealed from him, the trip would have been postponed and the whole incident might well have never happened.

Also contrary to fact—and common sense—is Bucher's explanation for the seizure of the *Pueblo* in the first place. In his book, Bucher firmly states his conviction that the North Koreans mistook the *Pueblo* for a South Korean ship, carrying saboteurs intent upon landing and assassinating Premier Kim Il Sung, in retaliation for the attempt on the life of South Korean President Park.

To support this contention, which he puts forward as almost a certainty, he cites the following evidence: the mistaking of our three Filipino crewmen for South Koreans while we were in detention; South Korean ships are painted exactly like U.S. ships and are often of American construction; plus he refers to certain information which has come into his possession since his return to the United States, information which, one presumes for security reasons, he declines to discuss.

It's a good yarn, if one is willing to ignore considerable evidence to the contrary. The day prior to our seizure we were photographed by the two KORCOM trawlers. If we were close enough to make out the faces of the men on their decks, as we were, they were certainly close enough to see ours, and to realize that with only a few exceptions

438

(who may well not have been above deck at the time, due to the nature of their duties), we were awfully white-skinned to be South Koreans. The SO-1 and P-4s also came close. And, like the trawlers, they must have realized that the letters "GER 2" and "*Pueblo*" weren't Korean ideographs. Too, Bucher apparently forgets we did identify our nationality, immediately after being asked to do so, by raising a big American flag. But there exists even more conclusive evidence than this that the North Koreans knew exactly who we were, and even suspected what we were up to.

Although we were unaware of it until after our return to the United States, American intelligence monitored the ship-to-shore communications of the SO-1 while the incident was taking place. Exactly how this was done has never been declassified. It is known, however, that the AGERs were only one part of the American intelligence network, that the United States also has spy satellites, EC-121s, and powerful land-based monitoring stations, the latter at various points in the Far East, presumably including South Korea. Whatever was responsible for the intercept, at 1210 hours, ten minutes after noon, on January 23, 1968, as the SO-1 first approached the *Pueblo,* she sent a message to shore which was translated as: "The name of the target is GER 2. I judge it to be a reconnaissance ship. It is American guys. It does not appear that there are weapons and it is a hydrographic mapping ship."

Although the Pentagon was against making this information public, arguing that to do so would compromise some of its secrets, President Johnson gave Ambassador Goldberg permission to include it in his speech to the UN because of the importance of another part of the same message, in which the SO-1 gave its position as 16.8 miles from shore, clearly placing it, and the *Pueblo,* well outside territorial waters. Thus, apparently not long after the incident took place, the United States had at least one piece of evidence indicating the *Pueblo* had been in international waters at the time she was attacked.

439

(While it is unlikely the intercept could have been translated, then relayed to the *Pueblo* in time to be of any benefit to the ship, one does wonder: did the North Korean equivalent of the word "target" mean the KORCOMs had already decided to attack the ship, which seems unlikely, or was it simply the way they designated an object of surveillance; if the latter is true, at exactly what point in the rest of the intercepted messages, some of which have never been made public, was the decision reached to fire on us, and was that decision made on the SO-1 or by higher command ashore; exactly how long after the message was monitored by the United States did it take for someone to realize its implications, and what, if anything, was then done; and how much duplication is there in our intelligence-gathering activities —in short, other than for training purposes, was this trip really necessary? National security being what it is, it's unlikely we'll ever know the answers to these questions, though they would help dispel a great many puzzles.)

Though the intercept raises far more questions than it answers, it does demolish the myth that the North Koreans did not know we were an American ship.

One question remains. Why, in his book, does Bucher advance an explanation so contrary to the evidence?

Maybe it's a matter of saving face, both that of himself and the United States. Given the enmity between North and South Korea, which knows no boundaries, international or otherwise, place a strange ship on the scene and add a threat to the life of beloved Kim Il Sung (one would like to know where Bucher got this), and it follows that, no matter what he did or did not do, Bucher was powerless to save his ship. Under the circumstances, the *Pueblo* incident was therefore unavoidable, the seizure a case of mistaken identity, an accident.

I don't pretend to know why North Korea decided to attack and pirate an American ship while she was in international waters. But one thing is clear from the foregoing evidence. Whatever their motivations, the North Koreans knew damn well what they were doing. The attack on the

USS *Pueblo* was no accident. It was a deliberately hostile act. If we fail to realize this, contenting ourselves with the comfortable assurance that mistakes sometimes happen, we'll have learned absolutely nothing from this costly tragedy.

Following his return to the United States, many proclaimed Commander Lloyd M. Bucher a modern hero, a man who, given the choice between following a hoary old naval tradition, that the captain must never give up his ship, and saving the lives of the more than eighty men aboard, stood resolutely on the bridge of the USS *Pueblo* and—though knowing that to do so would probably mean the end of his naval career—made the latter choice, placing human lives before outmoded honor.

There is evidence that Bucher was not unwilling to bask in the glory of this particular image.

However, in claiming that he never surrendered the ship, that Gene Lacy did, it would appear that Bucher would have to forfeit this distinction.

But, consistently inconsistent to the last, Bucher tries to have his cake and eat it too. In the concluding pages of his book, Bucher states that, as far as he is concerned, the court's recommendation of a trial by general court-martial "boils down to my being charged for refusing to order my men to commit suicide." Of this Bucher says: "I do not regret that decision and in fact would make the same decision in similar circumstances every time." He then notes that General Wainwright, faced with wholesale slaughter of his entire army by the Japanese if he continued to defend Corregidor, chose to surrender, though he still had guns and ammunition. The situation he faced aboard the USS *Pueblo* was not dissimilar, with one exception. Wainwright "was awarded high honors for his common sense."

Thus, in his book Bucher manages both to shed the guilt and to take the glory.

441

Yet for this accomplishment he would pay a high price, losing the one thing he seemed most to need and desire —the respect of his crew.

The critical reception to Bucher's book was generally good. There were a number of laudatory reviews. Even those reviewers who found fault with it were, on the whole, temperate in their judgments, obviously not wanting to criticize a man who had already gone through so much. Yet there were some voices of dissent, albeit reluctant ones. William A. McWhirter noted in *Life:* "As someone who was frankly sympathetic to Bucher's ordeal during the *Pueblo* hearings, I was dismayed to find my own impressions of the man reduced considerably by his own book."

Others felt this even more keenly, though they wrote no reviews. For many of the crewmen of the USS *Pueblo* this was the first glimpse of Commander Bucher as others of us had known him, a man who would go to any lengths to disavow responsibility for his own shortcomings, with almost a chronic compulsion to transfer his failings onto others.

Yet if it was difficult for them to reconcile this image with their own impressions, it was impossible for them to visualize Gene Lacy as the irresponsible, wild-eyed hysteric Bucher depicted. In most cases they knew Lacy even better than they did their commanding officer, and they simply couldn't believe this sudden Jekyll-Hyde transformation. Their impressions of Lacy were consistent. He was level-headed, solidly dependable, probably the least flappable officer on the ship. He knew his job, did it well, and expected others to do likewise. When he leveled criticism, it was merited, and the recipient knew it. He was well-liked, not because he courted the crew's favor, but because in all their dealings with him he treated them fairly. I think it would be safe to say that to a man they respected him.

Those whose duties brought them to the bridge at various times that afternoon knew something else. Although everyone there, including Gene Lacy, was shaken by what was happening, they saw no evidence of panic in any of his actions.

Several, and I number myself among them, felt the description in Bucher's book far more accurately fit Bucher himself than Lacy.

Bucher's charge that the *Pueblo*'s engineering officer, not her commander, was responsible for the stopping of the ship made instant headlines. Perhaps Bucher did not anticipate all the attention it would receive, for it was, as he must have realized, a charge that could not stand close examination.

Armed with an advance copy of the book, Wallace Turner of *The New York Times* set out to contact the men who had been on the bridge when Bucher said Lacy, on his own initiative, stopped and, in effect, gave up the ship.

Ronald Berens, helmsman when the incident occurred, reached by telephone at a Navy school in Florida, refused comment. I could guess what he was going through.

Tim Harris was at sea, on an LST, therefore unavailable. However, with fourteen other *Pueblo* crewmen, Harris had collaborated on a book, *The Last Voyage of the USS Pueblo,* which had appeared in 1969. In this account, when the shelling restarted, "Everyone hit the deck again. As Gene Lacy got to his feet, he yelled, 'Let's stop this goddamn ship before we all get killed!' Bucher said, 'Okay,' and ordered all stop. Lacy rang up the emergency stop himself."

Contacted in Seattle, at the Navy dock where he was assigned, Gene Lacy vehemently denied the charge, saying, "I don't know whether he's grasping at straws or what the hell the deal is on it." Lacy then described Bucher's appearance at the time the incident took place. "He was kind of wild-eyed, which was normal under the situation. He walked back and forth across the bridge, didn't say anything to anybody, and I asked him if he was going to stop the ship." Bucher then "nodded assent to me, and I did bring the annunciator back."

In his book Bucher specifically singles out Quartermaster

Law as being a witness to the incident. Not only did he see what happened, Bucher claimed, Law also, during detention, along with "some of my other officers," helped persuade Lacy that he was suffering a lapse of memory regarding his act.

Turner located Law at Whidbey Island Naval Base in Puget Sound. Law flatly denied both accusations. Lacy's version, not Bucher's, was the correct one, he said.

"We came in and they had stopped firing, and they started again," Law recalled. "We took some more hits, and he [Bucher] cursed at them. Then finally Gene Lacy said, 'Let's stop this goddamn thing.' The skipper looked around a little bit and then he gave the order to All Stop. Gene Lacy was on the indoor [engine-order] telegraph, and he's the one that rang it up."

Contacted by Paul Houston and Harold Keen of the Los Angeles *Times*, I confirmed Gene Lacy's version, adding a point I felt needed stressing. "If Bucher didn't want the ship stopped, all he'd have to do was walk over to the annunciator and signal Ahead."

Skip Schumacher later published his own account of the *Pueblo* story, *Bridge of No Return*, written in collaboration with *Washington Post* staffer George C. Wilson. In his description of what happend, Schumacher, the last of the five officers on the bridge to be heard from, chose to quote Commander Bucher—but not from his book, rather from his testimony before the Court of Inquiry: "I nodded to Mr. Lacy and Mr. Lacy rang up All Stop."

Though recollections differ as to whether Commander Bucher verbally issued the order, or simply nodded his assent, all are unanimous on one point: Commander Bucher gave the order to stop the ship.

To date, not a single person has come forward to support Bucher's allegation.

Yet one participant in the incident still maintains this is what happened. For him the fictions have become realities.

This is one part of the tragedy of the USS *Pueblo*.

444

There are others, not the least of which has been the effect of Bucher's book on his former crew.

"How could he do that to Gene Lacy, Mr. Murphy?" an anguished crewman called and asked me. He had just finished reading Bucher's book, and had to ask someone, anyone, even if it meant awakening him in the middle of the night.

He was not alone in his anguish. Nor was Berens alone in not wishing to talk to the press. Even among themselves, members of the crew try to avoid the subject. Mention of it, more often than not, brings a puzzled, pained look to their faces.

Following the dispersal of the crew after the Court of Inquiry, Stu Russell started a newsletter, with which he hoped to keep the crewmen informed of the activities of their fellows. Though Russell's newsletter was discontinued after Bob Chicca took over as unofficial secretary of the *Pueblo* Alumni Association, having been replaced by Chicca's own informative bulletins, the first issue, sent out long before the appearance of *Bucher: My Story,* ended with a poignant P.S.

Russell wrote: "Help us to recapture the unity we had in Korea and lost in San Diego."

To some of the former crewmen of the *Pueblo,* Commander Bucher will remain the ideal commanding officer, a man who could, and did, do no wrong. I have no illusions that this book will convince the true believers. Myths are durable creatures, and often they outlive the facts, especially if the need to believe is strong enough. Knowing from personal experience what they've gone through, and how one after another of our certainties was destroyed, I would not deny them that. But the public record is something else. Bucher's several versions of the *Pueblo* story have gone too long uncontested. *Second in Command* is my contribution to setting the record straight.

Closely examined, the Bucher myth that was born in the glare of publicity during the Court of Inquiry was not one

445

myth but many. Whether seen as an existential hero, a solitary figure standing up against the establishment, a humanist broken by the military-industrial complex, a victim of the pawns of power, or modern man trapped in the complex confusions of his times, the myth was less a picture of what actually existed than a reflection of the needs of the society that spawned it. Behind the legend was simply a man, not big enough to measure up to the task assigned him. As such he is a not untragic figure, with a difficult cross to bear. For the rest of his life he will have to attempt to live up to a legend that, deep within, he knows isn't true.

To me the real tragedy of the Bucher myth is that we are so lacking in real heroes that we must fashion one of such unlikely clay.

Bucher: My Story ends: "This book has been written in the hope that the telling of my story will be of some benefit to others. This has been my story. As of this moment, it is complete."

Although, like Commander Bucher, a great many of us would like to write finis to the saga of the USS *Pueblo*, unanswered questions remain. Observed the *Denver Post*, "Long after the little freighter was gone, they circled in her wake like an albatross."

What of the Code of Conduct? Is it outdated, or does it still retain some validity, even in our highly relative times? Were we guilty of abandoning it, or, never betraying any classified information the KORCOMs did not already have, were we faithful to its spirit? After hearing weeks of testimony, the Court of Inquiry declined to answer these questions. Nor another, equally important, which was one of the primary reasons for holding the court in the first place. At what point does a commanding officer no longer possess the power to resist? Commanders of other U.S. Navy ships seeking guidance on this life-or-death question won't find it in the proceedings of the *Pueblo* Court of Inquiry.

The question of who should be held accountable was also

446

never really answered. The court chose to cite five men. Higher command declined to censure one, while the Secretary of the Navy dropped charges against the remaining four, not because they were believed innocent—in making his announcement, Secretary Chafee stated he was making no determination of their guilt or innocence—but because they had "suffered enough." The result is a less than satisfactory answer. Congressman Otis G. Pike noted of the *Pueblo* affair, "There's blame enough for everybody here." Maybe it will have to be left at that. Maybe in a government as large as ours, where decisions are often made not by single men but by committees, it is impossible to localize responsibility. Still, one would like to know, just to satisfy curiosity if nothing else: Who received and failed to follow through on the warning that the *Pueblo*'s mission evaluation might no longer be "minimal risk"; who decided against sending planes to the aid of the ship, while there was still time to do so; and who chose Bucher for such a sensitive assignment in the first place? James Reston, writing of the Court of Inquiry's findings against Commander Bucher in *The New York Times*, observed, "Maybe he was unfit for command. . . . But other men chose him for command and pushed him into a situation beyond his capabilities— and they are invisible, unidentified, and uncharged." And apparently will always remain so.

One also wonders what facts might have emerged from the Court of Inquiry had not the interests of the court been so narrow, had public opinion not been so strongly behind Commander Bucher, had Bucher not been the first to take the stand so that all who followed had to go along with his story or openly contradict him, and had he not retained the power to write fitness and evaluation reports on most of the witnesses? And what information might have come out had the senior member of the court not been a vice admiral, who lacked the authority to make findings against anyone above him in the chain of command, but rather the Chief of Naval Operations?

Such questions, of course, carry us well into the realm

447

of "what might have been," and bring us, like a magnet, back to the events of the afternoon of January 23, 1968.

What would have happened if, with the arrival of the SO-1 on the scene, we had lit off our engines, and following the practice of the *Banner* and our own operational order, disengaged, making for the open sea? The SO-1 could have followed, but would it have? Or would the "incident" have ended then and there?

I think it would have. But it is only an opinion, for I was neither then nor am I now able to read the minds of the North Koreans. For whatever that opinion is worth, I believe that if at any time during those nearly forty minutes when the SO-1 was our only adversary, if even in the ten or fifteen minutes after that, after the sighting of the P-4s but before they took up positions surrounding us, we had swallowed our pride and hightailed it out of there, it could have made all the difference.

After that, there are fewer certainties.

What would have happened if, on seeing the SO-1 was at general quarters, we had gone to general quarters also, to show them we were prepared to defend ourselves?

Had the guns been positioned so we could use them, had the TNT been brought aboard, had the commanding officer's relationship with his officers been such that they could have felt free to advise him, had he made quick, rather than fumbling, hesitant decisions, had we never made the insulting flag hoists, what then?

What would have happened if, with the first shots from the SO-1, we had headed the ship for the open sea, lashed down the helm, sent everybody below, and then broken out the small arms, poking them out the portholes to hold off the boarding party?

The answer, of course, is that, never having tried any of these things, we'll never know. General quarters wasn't called, the guns weren't positioned where we could get to them with relative safety, the TNT wasn't aboard, the skipper wasn't one to encourage possibly contrary opinions, quick decisions weren't made, and none of us even thought of that last scheme until, after returning to the United States, it was suggested by some armchair strategists. Nor did various other ideas, such as disabling the engines so the ship would have had to be towed into Wonsan, maybe giving us enough additional time for help to arrive, occur to anyone until much too late to be more than wishful thinking.

I would be lying or claiming some sort of divine omnipotence if I said that, had we returned their fire with our own; had I, or anyone else, been in command rather than Bucher that day—the ship would not have been seized. However, I do feel, and strongly, that more than any other person, more than the Navy itself, Commander Lloyd M. Bucher must bear the major portion of responsibility for the series of oversights, blunders, and just plain confused thinking which, beginning in Bremerton, Washington, and ending in the Sea of Japan, closed off one after another of the alternatives that should have been available to us, until we were finally, hopelessly trapped.

It did happen, and nothing will change that, but it needn't have happened.

There remains the ultimate question: Did we really learn anything from the *Pueblo* incident?

Only time will answer that.

Of the eighty-two men released from the prisons of North Korea, one has since died. In what was seemingly a freak accident, former engineman Bill Scarborough was asphyxiated while repairing his car.

Of the remaining enlisted men, less than half chose to stay in the Navy. One, "Doc" Baldridge, proved that Bucher's prophecy wasn't correct, at least as far as he was concerned; he returned to Sasebo. Of those now outside the service, a better than average number are in college. By contrast, former radioman Lee Roy Hayes now travels the country as a lecturer for the John Birch Society, giving

449

talks on the *Pueblo* and campus violence. But then we always were a diverse crew.

Of the six officers, I am the only one, to date, to resign his commission and leave the Navy entirely—though we remain in touch, and will continue to do so until that matter of the fitness reports is cleared up. (For the record, the manuscript of this book has not been submitted to Naval Intelligence, the Pentagon, or anyone else for clearance; with all due respect to that branch of the service to which I gave nearly nine years—and that respect is considerable—my experience with the *Christian Science Monitor* articles convinced me that I could not tell in full my own story, which this is, if I did so.) Skip Schumacher has left the regular Navy, but remains in the reserves. He did not, as he once intended, go into the ministry, but sells insurance for his family's company in St. Louis. Tim Harris and Gene Lacy remain on active duty, as does Steve Harris, who, at last account, was still in the more secret echelons of the Navy. Together with CT Francis Ginther, Steve collaborated with author Don Crawford on a paperback book, *Pueblo Intrigue.* Subtitled "A Journey of Faith," it dealt with the religious story behind the detention experience. On the more controversial aspects of the *Pueblo* incident, including Bucher's book, Steve has continued to decline comment. Shortly after our return to the United States, Steve Harris was promoted to lieutenant commander. Although Bucher attended his wetting-down party, less publicly he succeeded in making sure during the Court of Inquiry that Steve was not given a medal for activities prior to his *Pueblo* assignment. With the exception of the Purple Heart (first awarded to those of us who had been wounded on January 23, 1968, and finally given to all members of the crew for maltreatment during detention), there have been no other medals. The general sentiment of the crew was, to quote a common Navy phrase: "None required, none desired."

Commander Lloyd M. Bucher has announced that he

intends to request retirement from the Navy in the fall of 1971, upon completion of twenty years' service. He believes that what the Navy really needed in the *Pueblo* Court of Inquiry was "a goat to be sacrificed" to take the heat "off a great many people who would otherwise be called to account for their part in this affair," and that he was it. His health is not good. Although he has gained more than eighty pounds since his return, like many others he has never completely recovered from the effects of detention, and he is still plagued by some of his earlier problems. A promotional tour in behalf of his book had to be canceled because of illness. There was some talk that *Bucher: My Story* might be filmed, with the lead role, that of the heroic skipper of the USS *Pueblo*, being played by John Wayne but to date nothing has come of it. Unable to complete his postgraduate schooling at Monterey, Bucher has been reassigned to limited duty in San Diego until his retirement. Although we both live in the same general area, thus far our paths have not crossed since the morning we heard the verdict of the Court of Inquiry, and I suspect we'd both prefer to leave it that way. I no longer feel any bitterness toward him, only pity, and a kind of sadness that everything turned out the way it did, for him as well as for the rest of us. Recently he told a reporter: "What I'd like best is to work for the National Geographic Society, to sail a boat into distant ports, to photograph and gather information. I think I'm qualified for that sort of job."

When Commander Clark took the stand during the Court of Inquiry and testified that since the seizure of the *Pueblo* the *Banner* had been operating seventy miles from the shores of foreign countries, the implications, though unstated, were clear. Limited in both the quantity and quality of intelligence collected, the AGER program was dead. The official announcement came in 1970, a year that also saw the decommissioning of the *Banner* and the *Palm Beach* (the latter, because of our experience, got no closer to its operating area than Norfolk, Virginia). Thus the program was aborted before it really got started, only the *Banner* getting a chance to really prove the concept, which is unfortunate, for many of us felt it a good one.

Only one AGER remains. The central character of this story.

American intelligence apparently knows the exact location of the USS *Pueblo,* but isn't telling. There have been rumors, however. One has her traveling back and forth between various North Korean ports. Another says she is berthed at the port of Najin, close enough to the Soviet border so the United States would think twice before attempting to bomb or recapture her. There was a time when veterans' groups passed resolutions vowing to go and get her back, but you don't see many REMEMBER THE PUEBLO bumperstrips anymore. Eventually one suspects she will be turned into an atrocity museum, complete, no doubt, with photographic blowups of her sinister crew; their confessions (newly revised to fit Comrade Kim's latest propaganda line); plus simulated atomic bombs and other diabolical weapons allegedly carried in her cramped spaces.

Whatever her fate, she remains the last of the AGERs. True to tradition, the United States Navy has never given up the ship. To this day the USS *Pueblo* remains listed on official rosters as a commissioned ship of the United States Navy, assigned to the Seventh Fleet.